D0327114

"This book is an outstanding and important look at the most important requirements for directing a company toward the goal of maximizing opportunities with
today's customers. Its focus on agility, speed, and fragmentation through differ-
entiation is critical to success. Each element is covered in a direct and well-organ-
ized manner and can be used to help identify positive change. It will help you
rethink the strategic direction of your company."

—*Marc I. Balmuth*
President
Caldor, Inc.

"*Agile Competitors and Virtual Organizations: Strategies for Enriching the Customer*
fulfills a pressing need for an easy-to-read, comprehensive introduction to the
fields of agile competition and virtual organizations, tactics already deployed in
several important industries. An impressive range of subject matter is treated with
simplicity and elegance. Just what you need to know for success in global
competition today."

—*Zion Bar-El*
Vice President
Ideation International, Inc.

"*Agile Competitors and Virtual Organizations* advances these rapidly emerging
business and manufacturing paradigms to a new level of maturity. The automotive
industry has been at the forefront in aggressively restructuring itself around the
principles of lean production and is now looking beyond lean to agile. During the
past several years, agility has become one of the most discussed business concepts
around the world. Confusion is rampant, particularly related to conversion of agile
thinking to practice. Clearly, the concept of agility is the embodiment of form
following function in everything. This is a particularly difficult challenge for
Americans because of our preoccupation with form and the desire to preserve it
at any cost. The authors have presented a practical, yet scholarly, analysis that
brings our thinking to a new level of insight and understanding, and provides a
road map to put agility into action."

—*David E. Cole*
Director, Office for the Study of Automotive Transportation
University of Michigan Transportation Research Institute

"I certainly hope that my competitors don't read this book! Goldman, Nagel and Preiss describe the late-20th century industrial revolution—a fundamental restructuring of business: demanded by sophisticated customers around the globe; propelled by the increasing value-add of intellectual capital; and facilitated by international information infrastructure. The book contains myriad provocative examples of avant garde business endeavors, enough for many sleepless nights."

> —*Dr. Craig Fields*
> Former President and CEO
> MCC

"In today's fiercely competitive world, you have to develop the capacity and courage it sometimes takes to change. *Agile Competitors and Virtual Organizations* is a road map to change.

Agile Competitors is a very valuable tool for anyone involved in today's competitive race. It is essential reading for anyone involved in today's competitive world."

> —*Doug Fraser*
> Past President of the UAW (Retired)

"This book is right on target! It clearly and concisely depicts the dramatic changes that are taking place in the marketplace. I recommend this book to every company that wants to remain competitive in an agile world."

> —*Jerry Junkins*
> Chairman, President, and CEO
> Texas Instruments

"As a smaller organization, we are continually seeking ways to make money in a turbulent and intensely competitive business environment with limited resources. In *Agile Competitors and Virtual Organizations,* Goldman, Nagel and Preiss present the concept of agility as a comprehensive on-going process, which, if successfully internalized, can create a difficult to duplicate enabling ability in any organization."

> —*Robert J. McKenna*
> President and CEO
> Acme Electric Corporation
> East Aurora, NY

"This magnificent work will inspire a new generation of business leaders to anticipate customer requirements, create new markets and balance the people, process, and technology resources of the enterprise to delight customers and enrich not only customers but also all members of the agile virtual enterprise."

—Aris Melissaratos
Vice President, Science Technology and Quality
Westinghouse Electric Corporation

". . . Answers the need articulated by industrial leaders for a definitive book on the agile concepts and how to take advantage of them in their own organization. . . . These specific actions and examples are what industrial leaders are looking for."

—Rusty Patterson
Chairman, Board of Directors, AMEF;
Metal Fabrication Operations Manager
Texas Instruments

"For managers plunging into the wilds of manufacturing to seek the source of future competitiveness, this is an indispensable handbook. Don't expect to find ordinance surveys that will take you straight to the Fountain of Agility, though. It's too soon for that kind of detail—but too late to wait around for it. What's here is a treasure map. All the main landmarks are pointed out, leaving plenty of elbow room for exercising your imagination and creativity."

—Otis Port

"America was very late in identifying the current lean production paradigm, and this fact has created great anxiety throughout the country. We cannot afford, as a nation, to miss the next production paradigm . . . AGILITY.

This book provides insightful perspectives on the important elements of this emerging production paradigm. It's a must read."

—Donald L. Runkle
Vice President and General Manager, Saginaw Division
General Motors

"Brazilian entrepreneurs and executives are considered to be fast/flexible/creative; in a word, agile. And yet the authors' new book teaches us a great deal about agile competition and a conceptual framework for speed and agility as a tool of competitiveness."

—César Souza
Vice President
Odebrecht Contractors of Florida, Inc.

"Goldman, Nagel and Preiss present a compelling vision of the kind of productive enterprise that America requires. Their vision invigorates a wealth of ideas—such as employee empowerment, customization, team production, flat organizational structures, concern for societal values, strategic alliances—which have gained significant credence during this time of turbulent change, by integrating them with powerful concepts of technologically enabled agility and of creative partnering with both customers and competitors in innovative alliances in the pursuit of value. It is a critically important book for everyone who is concerned with how we succeed in the face of changes, challenges and opportunities presented by the global economy."

>—*Lynn R. Williams*
>Past President
>United Steelworkers of America (Retired)

"This highly readable and thought-provoking book makes a very convincing argument for agile strategies—strategies that enable mastering change and uncertainty, the lynch pins of commercial leadership in the next generation. The most insightful manufacturing book since *The Machine That Changed the World.* Essential reading."

>—*Michael J. Wozny*
>Director, Manufacturing-Engineering Laboratory
>NIST

AGILE
COMPETITORS
and
VIRTUAL
ORGANIZATIONS

STRATEGIES FOR ENRICHING
THE CUSTOMER

AGILE
COMPETITORS
and
VIRTUAL
ORGANIZATIONS

STRATEGIES FOR ENRICHING
THE CUSTOMER

Steven L. Goldman
Roger N. Nagel
Kenneth Preiss

VAN NOSTRAND REINHOLD
I⊤P™ A Division of International Thomson Publishing Inc.

New York • Albany • Bonn • Boston • Detroit • London • Madrid • Melbourne
Mexico City • Paris • San Francisco • Singapore • Tokyo • Toronto

Jacket design: Jon Herder

Copyright © 1995 by Van Nostrand Reinhold
IⓉP™ A division of International Thomson Publishing Inc.
    The ITP logo is a trademark under license

Printed in the United States of America
For more information, contact:

Van Nostrand Reinhold
115 Fifth Avenue
New York, NY 10003

International Thomson Publishing GmbH
Königswinterer Strasse 418
53227 Bonn
Germany

International Thomson Publishing Europe
Berkshire House 168–173
High Holborn
London WCIV 7AA
England

International Thomson Publishing Asia
221 Henderson Road #05-10
Henderson Building
Singapore 0315

Thomas Nelson Australia
102 Dodds Street
South Melbourne, 3205
Victoria, Australia

International Thomson Publishing Japan
Hirakawacho Kyowa Building, 3F
2-2-1 Hirakawacho
Chiyoda-ku, 102 Tokyo
Japan

Nelson Canada
1120 Birchmount Road
Scarborough, Ontario
Canada M1K 5G4

International Thomson Editores
Campos Eliseos 385, Piso 7
Col. Polanco
11560 Mexico D.F. Mexico

All rights reserved. No part of this work covered by the copyright hereon may be reproduced or used in any form or by any means—graphic, electronic, or mechanical, including photocopying, recording, taping, or information storage and retrieval systems—without the written permission of the publisher.

1 2 3 4 5 6 7 8 9 10 RRDHB 01 00 99 98 97 96 95 94

Library of Congress Cataloging-in-Publication Data

Goldman, Steven L., 1941–
    Agile competitors and virtual organizations : strategies for
  enriching the customer / Steven L. Goldman, Roger N. Nagel, Kenneth
  Preiss.
      p. cm.
    Includes bibliographical references and index.
    ISBN 0-442-01903-3
    1. Competition.   2. Organizational change.   3. Customer service.
  I. Nagel, Roger N.   II. Preiss, Kenneth.   III. Title.
  HD41.G65   1994
  658.8′12—dc20   94-35220
                                                           CIP

To my wife, Risa
    S.L.G.

Dedicated to my family—my wife, Arlene; my son, Bruce; and my daughter, Deborah. For their understanding, encouragement and faith in me, I will always be grateful.
    R.N.N.

To my late grandparents and parents, who set the context; to my wife and partner on life's journey, Miriam; and to my daughters, Michal and Yonat.
    K.P.

CONTENTS

FOREWORD

Ever since the Iacocca Institute at Lehigh University issued its report on agility, people have been asking me what agility is and how it will help them be better competitors. Now I can tell them—read the book!

Agile Competitors and Virtual Organizations answers the question, What is agility and why do we need it? It shows why agility is an inevitable part of the new industrial order and illustrates how companies are using agility as a strategic framework for mastering change and uncertainty.

Beyond mastering change, the book develops the role of virtual organizations and introduces the use of agility as a means of enriching the customer, strategies we all need to think about.

By documenting more than one hundred examples of agility emerging in industry, *Agile Competitors and Virtual Organizations* makes a convincing argument to consider agile strategies very seriously.

The second half of the book is organized around using agility in your own organization. I wish these guys had written this book a few years earlier—I would have appreciated it more back then.

I'm proud of our guys—they've done a great job in writing an important book. This is the kind of book you will enjoy reading, and you will want to keep handy while you are putting your own agile strategies in place.

Good luck!

Lee Iacocca
August 1994

PREFACE

This book is about a new form of commercial competition that is spreading rapidly in the technologically most advanced societies. It has been named *agile competition,* and it possesses decisive advantages in what are today the most profitable markets for goods and services.

Broader product ranges, shorter model lifetimes, and the ability to process orders in arbitrary lot sizes are becoming the norm in these markets. The information-processing capability to treat masses of customers as individuals is permitting more and more companies to offer individualized products while maintaining high volumes of production. The convergence of computer networking and telecommunications technologies is making it possible for groups of companies to coordinate geographically and institutionally distributed capabilities into a single *virtual company* and to achieve powerful competitive advantages in the process.

These market characteristics have triggered structural changes in how companies are organized to create, produce, and distribute goods and services. At the same time, the economics of doing business have shifted. The robustness of the mass-production system—its ability to function well in *less* developed societies—makes it increasingly difficult to realize profits large enough to justify locating such a facility in the *most* developed societies. Operations that produce market-segmenting, knowledge-based, service-oriented products customized to the requirements of individual customers, however, can still be profitable in those societies.

Agility-based competition keyed to these kinds of products is thus destined to displace mass-production-based competition as the norm for global commerce.

The convergence of goods and services emerged in the 1980s as a distinctive feature of highly profitable products. It is forcing a reconceptualization of what we mean by the terms *production* and *product* as well as of how, where, and by whom the various activities required by the total production process should be performed. By contrast with mass-production-based competition, the bottleneck limiting an agile company's ability to exploit profitable new customer opportunities shifts from manufacturing to design. Design becomes a continuing aspect of a holistic production process optimized for lowest total product development, or lowest "concept to cash flow," time. The attraction of virtual companies lies in their promise of minimizing development time, costs, and risk while creating mutually valuable interactive relationships among the participating companies.

Furthermore, *what* is designed and produced by agile competitors is determined by the choices of individual customers. The boundaries between producers and customers, between suppliers and vendors, are becoming increasingly blurred. What commercial and consumer customers alike buy in the agile marketplace are not discrete products, but variable combinations of physical products, services, and information—combinations that are expected to evolve and that are designed to be capable of evolving, as customer requirements change.

Agility is an umbrella term. It extends over a spectrum of correlated developments that together define a comprehensive change in the prevailing system of competition:

- At the level of marketing, agile competition is characterized by customer-enriching, individualized combinations of products and services.
- At the level of production, agile competition is characterized by the ability to manufacture goods and to produce services to customer order in arbitrary lot sizes.
- At the level of design, agile competition is characterized by a holistic methodology that integrates supplier relations, production processes, business processes, customer relations, and the product's use and eventual disposal.
- At the level of the organization, agile competition is characterized by the ability to synthesize new, productive capabilities out of the

necessary resources—the expertise of people and the physical facilities—regardless of their physical location within a company or among groups of cooperating companies.

- At the level of management, agile competition is characterized by a shift from the command and control philosophy of the modern industrial corporation to one of leadership, motivation, support, and trust.
- At the level of people, agile competition is characterized by the emergence of a knowledgeable, skilled, and innovative *total* work force as the ultimate differentiator of successful companies from unsuccessful ones.

This book focuses on the marketing, organization, management, and human resource levels of agile competition. It identifies emerging patterns of competition and their implications for how companies and people need to change in order be able to prosper in the new environment. As with almost all innovations, implementation precedes understanding. The aircraft industry, to cite one example, was decades old before a theoretical basis for designing aircraft began to develop, and decades more passed before theoretical models were mature enough to allow new designs to be deduced from them. No one is waiting for a theory of agility before responding to competitive pressures. Agility is happening. This book is an attempt to understand what is happening and to capture that understanding in a first-generation model.

Agile competition is not someone's "great idea" of how businesses *ought* to be run; it is how more and more businesses, of all sizes and across all industries, *are being run* today in order to stay in business. Businesses, however, are present-oriented. Each business responds to its own marketplace challenges and typically does so on a piecemeal basis, changing now one facet of its operations in order to achieve a particular goal, and now another.

We offer a forward-looking, strategic view of a competitive environment that more and more companies are encountering. Such a system-level view reveals how the particular changes that companies have been making relate to one another. It explains why these changes work and why they sometimes do not. In the process, it provides a framework for planning coordinated, companywide change in advance of market-induced crises.

The individual elements organized within this strategic framework may seem familiar to companies that have been fighting to improve profitability. But what is familiar in one context—mass-production-based competition—takes on new and very different meanings when the context changes. Furthermore, a system-level view reveals unanticipated synergies that can be created by exploiting interrelationships among its elements that exist in the new system, but did not exist in the old.

Our account of agile competition is *not* a cure-all for everyone's business problems. It is not a formula for a magic pill that guarantees corporate profitability forever after. To the contrary, the agile competitive environment precludes such a formula because the agile business environment is intrinsically dynamic.

To succeed in such an environment, companies must learn to *thrive* on change and uncertainty, not merely to cope with them. Senior management must reinvent the company repeatedly, the better to focus its core competencies on meeting the changing needs of its customers. The company must be routinely repositioned in the competitive "spaces" that it occupies, adjusting its organizational structure, product and service lines, business processes, managerial practices, personnel and technology utilization policies, and marketing strategies to multiple, *changing* customer opportunities.

Intel CEO Andrew Grove is reported to have said that only the paranoid survive in technology-driven markets. The observation is only partly correct. It is true of successful competitors in *all* markets subject to the terms of agile competition, that is, in all markets subject to rapid and uncertain change. In spite of its negative associations, the term *paranoid* expresses the urgency and the intensity of focus of successful agile competitors. Only companies that are paranoid about losing their customers, about being overtaken by competitors, about increasing the customer-perceived value of the goods and services they sell will thrive in these markets.

Agile competition is being pulled into place by marketplace developments in industry after industry, across economic sectors, in the

United States, in Japan, in western Europe, and in southeast Asia. Companies are responding to these developments by implementing changes in their product development, production, and marketing operations that are undermining the foundations of the mass-production-based system of competition. These changes, in turn, are undermining the conventional wisdom of how companies should organize and manage the human and the physical resources required to create and distribute goods and services. As a consequence, executives are exploring new forms of intraenterprise and interenterprise organizations, installing new technologies, and introducing new approaches to motivating personnel to become a more entrepreneurial production resource.

With these changes, we have crossed the threshold into a new industrial order, one in which the terms of economic competition are defined by the characteristics of agile markets and organizations. As agile competition becomes the primary source of wealth creation in the developed economies, its displacement of mass-production-based competition will cause sweeping personal, social, and political—not to mention economic—changes. Agility will have as profound an effect on life in the twenty-first century as mass production has had on life in the twentieth century.

This book is an attempt to explain the nature of agile competition and to help prepare for the sweeping changes that will accompany its implementation. We believe that it can provide companies with a guide to forging competitive success in an agile business world, that is, to finding a stable basis for profitable operation in an intrinsically unstable competitive environment.

Part 1, Confronting Change and Uncertainty, describes what many companies are experiencing in the marketplace and what they are doing about it. It provides an overview of agile competition, answering the most obvious questions, such as what *agility* means, what the distinctive characteristics of agile competition are, and what companies need to be able to do in order to acquire agile competitive capabilities. The opening chapter identifies the market forces that are eroding the value of mass-production-based competition and pulling companies toward acquiring agile business capabilities. Chapter 2 addresses the question of why *agile* competition specifically is the successor to the mass-production system. Chapter 3 presents a model that incorporates in a comprehensive way the many piecemeal efforts that companies have made in an effort to respond to their changing competitive environments.

The model is of a four-dimensional agile competitive "space" within which companies can position themselves to create and exploit profitable customer opportunities. The dimensions of this space are:

Enriching customers
Cooperating to enhance competitiveness
Organizing to master change and uncertainty
Leveraging the impact of people and information

How can companies use this model to evaluate their products, processes, business practices, organization, and management? How does the model define a strategic framework for responding to the kinds of competitive challenges outlined in the first three chapters? Chapter 4 summarizes the major implications of agile business capabilities from the perspective of implementing them in real companies. Included in the chapter are more than 100 instances of agile business behavior, identifying the elements of agility they exemplify. Many of these examples appear elsewhere in the text.

Part 2, Thriving on Change and Uncertainty, begins the open-ended process of creating agile competitors, taking a more methodical approach to agility than Part 1 does. Chapter 5 addresses the leadership requirements of agile companies. Chapter 6 describes six types of virtual organizations and the different circumstances under which a decision might be made to form one. Chapters 7 and 8 provide strategies for identifying, developing, and marketing customer-enriching products. Chapter 9 examines barriers to implementing agility that management must overcome, and Chapter 10 describes the enabling systems and supporting infrastructure that must be put in place if a company is to become an agile competitor. In Chapter 11, a first set of management tools is offered for assessing the agility of a company.

THE ROOTS OF THE AGILE VISION

A broad-brush description of agile competition—highlighting virtual companies as a powerful cooperative strategy for achieving agility—was first presented in a report published by Lehigh University's Iacocca Institute in the fall of 1991: *21st Century Manufacturing Enterprise Strategy: An Industry-Led View.* Since then, more than 25,000 copies of the report have been ordered, and scores of presentations, seminars, and workshops on its vision of agile competition and virtual enterprises have been held for thousands of personnel from hundreds of companies. By the winter of 1992, an industry-led organization, the Agile Manufacturing Enterprise Forum (AMEF), had been created within the Iacocca Institute and charged with developing the original vision further and disseminating it widely in U.S. industry.

This book is one expression of the AMEF's continuing growth and activity.

Operating as the Agility Forum, the AMEF in 1994 became the central information resource for industry-funded, as well as government-funded, projects aimed at accelerating the acquisition of agile competitive capabilities by U.S. companies. By mid-1994, Agile Manufacturing Research Institutes for the machine tool, aerospace, and electronics industries were in operation at the University of Illinois, the University of Texas, and Rensselaer Polytechnic Institute, respectively. A pilot real-time agile apparel production facility is in operation at [TC]², a North Carolina–based clothing industry consortium. Information networks supporting the electronic commerce requirements of virtual companies are in pilot-phase operation, among them, EINet, developed by the Microelectronics and Computer Consortium (Austin, Texas) and CommerceNet, developed by Enterprise Integration Technologies (Palo Alto, California). Others, such as AgileWeb in northeastern Pennsylvania and ECNet serving the Southwest, are linking small businesses into interactive production networks.

The *21st Century Manufacturing Enterprise Strategy* report was prepared in response to a congressional request to identify the requirements for U.S. industry to return to global manufacturing competitiveness.

Manufacturing executives from 13 companies, together with an independent consultant (Rick Dove, Paradigm Shift, International) and the authors of this book, spent the spring, summer, and fall of 1991 studying this issue. Their unanimous conclusion, validated by reviews of their work by executives from almost 200 companies, government agencies, and public organizations, was that incremental improvement of the mass-production system of manufacturing could not regain competitiveness for U.S. companies.

The study argued that rapidly maturing, computer-based production, information, and communication technologies were being synthesized into an altogether new system of competition. In this system, novel approaches to interconnecting human, physical, and intellectual resources—distributed within companies and among groups of companies that were simultaneously competing *and* cooperating—were leading to a fundamental redefinition of industrial production. The traditional sharp distinction between manufacturing industries and service industries was rapidly disappearing. As it disappeared, so did the traditional perception of the physical processes of manufacturing as the center of the value added by industry to its products.

The new *agile* competitive environment, as the report dubbed it, was being driven by the customer-perceived value of information and services embedded in physical products and delivered over a period of time through continuing relationships between vendor and customer. Furthermore, the cost of these physical products was only a small fraction of the cost of supporting the customer in that relationship. As a result, improving the unit cost efficiency of mass-production manufacturing amounted to fighting a war that was already over.

Future competitive battles, the report concluded, would require that companies be able to develop short-lifetime, easily customizable, information-rich products and services targeted at niche markets, and to do so much more quickly and much less expensively than was possible under the mass-production-based system.

The authors of this book were the Iacocca Institute facilitators of the study that originally envisioned agile competition. They were also the editors of the *21st Century Manufacturing Enterprise Strategy* report. What we learned in the course of preparing that report was the beginning of a continuing involvement with the agility movement, including participation in many of the activities of the Iacocca Institute and the Agility Forum, in whose formation and growth we have played active roles. Our goal in writing this book is to share with a wider audience our evolving understanding of agile competition and virtual organizations.

Van Nostrand Reinhold and the authors have adopted the agile paradigm in their approach to publishing this work. Van Nostrand Reinhold is able to provide corporate customers with the opportunity to purchase non-returnable, customized editions of *Agile Competitors and Virtual Organizations* based on their specific needs. For information, please contact the Special Sales Department at Van Nostrand Reinhold, 115 Fifth Avenue, New York, NY 10003 or call 212-254-3232.

For information on executive training courses scheduled by the authors, please send a fax to 610-398-1220.

ACKNOWLEDGMENTS

We are especially indebted to:

Chuck Kimzey of the Office of the Secretary of Defense, for his foresight in challenging us, in the Spring of 1991, to create a vision of a post–mass-production manufacturing system, and for his consistent support of the process we implemented to produce that vision.

Lee Iacocca, for lending his name and the resources of the Iacocca Institute in support—first, to the process that resulted in the report *21st Century Manufacturing Enterprise Strategy: An Industry-Led View;* then to the dissemination of the report among U.S. industrial leaders; and finally, to the creation of the Agility Forum, as well as for his trust in us to succeed in these efforts.

The members of the "Inner Core" of the Iacocca Institute-facilitated study that formulated the initial conceptualization of agile competition, a group of executives whose extraordinary commitment to the challenge of envisioning a system of production that would restore global U.S. industrial competitiveness, laid the foundations on which this book rests:

Len Allgaier, General Motors
Rick Dove, Paradigm Shift International
Richard Engwall, Westinghouse
Jack Ferrell, TRW

Gino Giocondi, Chrysler
John Hilaman, Boeing
Robert Morris, General Electric
Ted Nickell, IBM
Bill O'Brien, FMC
James O'Neil, Kingsbury Corporation
Rusty Patterson, Texas Instruments
Frank Plonka, Chrysler
Leo Plonski, Department of Defense
Wyckham Seelig, AT&T
Robert Senn, Air Products
Susan Wood, Westinghouse
Ted Woods, Motorola

We acknowledge the extraordinary personal and institutional support of the leadership of Lehigh University: Peter Likins, President; Al Pense, Provost; the late Sunder Advani; Mike Bolton; Jim Gunton; Alastair McAulay; Jim Schmotter; and Harvey Stenger. We acknowledge as well the support of the leadership of Ben Gurion University of the Negev: Avishay Braverman, President; Dov Bahat, past Rector; and Nahum Finger, Rector.

Our colleagues at the Agility Forum have been a continuing inspiration: Rusty Patterson of Texas Instruments, First Industry President and Chairman of the Forum's Board of Directors; Aris Melissaratos of Westinghouse, Industry President; Terry Schmoyer, Executive Director; Ron Miller; Orapong Thien-Ngern; Jim Tolley; Joyce Barker; Dawn Bold; Kathy Dillon; Elizabeth Ensmenger; Tom Falteich; Bob Gilbert; Pat Heimbach; Jane Hontz; Peggy James; Marcia Martin; Nicole Matson; Judy Mattei; Barbara Parry; Ray Patterson; Sallie Smith; Dan Stahlnecker; Phil Staas; Ferdinand Surita; Kelli Wait; and Beverly Ward; and the loaned executives past and present comprising Tom Biltz and Mark Gardner, Deloitte & Touche; Scott Gray and Gary Laughlin, Sandia National Laboratories; Al Hall, General Motors; Jim Ridings, Westinghouse; Rick Sutphin, Acme Electric; and Scott Wade, Texas Instruments.

We are particularly pleased to acknowledge the role that a farsighted group of government officials have played in promoting agility as being in the national interest, independent of their narrower constituencies: Senators Bingaman, Inouye, Mikulski, Nunn, Specter, Wofford; Congressmen McDade, McHale, Murtha; also William Andahazy, Chris Aldridge, Joseph Bordogna, Lee Buchanan, Richard Collins, John Gerhart, Mary Good, Kevin Kelly, David Kilian, and Steven Linder.

We appreciate the feedback we received from the editorial advisory board who read early drafts of our manuscript: Dexter Baker (ret.), Air Products; Robert Bell, Loughborough University of Technology; Walter Braithwaite, Boeing; Charles Carter, Jr., the Association for Manufacturing Technology; Margaret Eastwood, Motorola; Nigel Hey, Sandia National Laboratories; Craig Kaplan, the IQ Company; Jeff Kenner, Kenner & Company; Cal Kirby, Hughes Aircraft Company; Frederick Kovac, Goodyear Tire & Rubber Company; Randall Miller, Deloitte & Touche; Al Narath, Sandia National Laboratories; Lazlo Nemes, the Australian CRISCO; Peter Nowak, Suffolk University; Bill O'Brien, FMC Corporation; Takayoshi Ohmi, AIST, MITI; Rusty Patterson, Texas Instruments; Jack Purchase, Ainsworth Technologies Ltd; Jack Russell, the Modernization Forum; Heinz Schmitt, Sandia National Laboratories; Stephanie Schoumacher, the Council on Competitiveness; Hans-Jurgen Warnecke, the Fraunhofer Society; and Gerfried Zeichen, the Technical University of Vienna.

Many colleagues with whom we interacted in the Agility Forum's Supplier Support and the Performance Metrics Focus Groups contributed ideas that influenced our evolving understanding of agility. These include Len Allgaier of General Motors; Mike Austin, FEMA; Joe Danowsky; Ruth David, Sandia National Laboratories; Mike Gnam, NCMS; Robert Hall, Target AME; Nancy Humphries, Metropolitan Development Foundation and Emerging Technology Consultants; John Leary, AT&T; Ron Meier, Iowa State University; John Meilner, Deloitte and Touche; William Miller, Alcatel Network Systems; William Moore, IBM Corporation; Michael Resner, Naval Sea Systems Command; Bill Shaflucas, AT&T; Thomas Smolenski, Chrysler Corporation; Gary Thompson, Rockwell International; Bill Wadsworth; and Phil Weinzimer, Unisys. Keith Krenz and Dinesh Khaladikar of Technology Systems Corporation in Bethlehem, PA, contributed information on financial and other barriers to agility.

In addition to these, a number of other people reviewed our manuscript, and offered valuable comments and other assistance. They include Joel Amir, Scitex; Mark Balmuth, Caldor; Zion Bar-El, Ideation; Lothar Behlau, the Fraunhofer Society Headquarters; Karyn Blumenfeld; Robert Brown, Deneb Robotics; John Caspari; David Cole, University of Michigan; Stephen Cutcliffe, Lehigh University; John Decaire, NCMS; Michael Dettmers, Dettmers Industries; J. Elghovl, U.S. Army TACOM; Ken Fiduk, MCC; Craig Fields, MCC; Douglas Fraser; John Fyfe; Rudy Gedeon; John Gleason, Acme Electric Corporation; Mikell Groover, Lehigh University; Hank Hayes, TI; Laurence Hecht; Carl Heyel; H. Humpal, Humpal-Pearson; Hans Jung, Fraunhofer Headquarters; Dwayne Hansen, the NET Ben Franklin Technology Center; Rick Jackson, NIST; Jerry Junkins, TI; Harold Kerzner; Jan Kosturiak; Frank Krause, the IPK Frauenhofer Institute, Berlin; Mark Lang, the NET Ben Franklin Technology Center; Larry Leson of the Leigh Bureau; David Lando, AT&T; Vernon Lovejoy, Textron Inc.; Patricia MacConaill, the General Industry Unit, European Commission; Thomas Malone, Milliken; John Marano, Jr., Aeroquip Corporation; Kenneth McGuire, the Manufacturing Excellence Action Coalition; Robert McKenna, Acme Electric; Jack McNichols, Jr., of Aeroquip Corporation; Kira Mendez, Lucas McPhee and Company; Ed Miller, NCMS; Gayle Morse, NIST; Benzion Naveh; Takayoshi Ozaki; Daniel Petrozzo, Taylor Petrozzo Associates; Otis Port; Dennis Powers, Symmetrix; John Rannenberg, the Joint Staff; Christiane Riefler; Edith Ritter, the Pennsylvania Manufacturing Extension Program; Don Runkle, General Motors; Paulo Mozart Gama Silva of IBM, Brazil; Jack Simon, General Motors; Cesar Souza, Odebrecht; Leslie Spero, Strategic Management Group; Tony St. John; Guy Stanley; Odo Struger, Allen Bradley; J. Marty Tenenbaum, Enterprise Integration Technologies; Stephen Yencho; Lynn Williams (ret.), International Steel Workers of America; Mike Wozny, NIST; Emory Zimmers, Lehigh University; and Paul Zirkel of IFR Systems.

We are very appreciative of the foresight of Van Nostrand Reinhold in undertaking this publishing project; for the continued personal encouragement that we have received from Marianne Russell, Bob Esposito, and Jeanne Glasser; and for the highly professional support provided by Richard Blander, Jon Herder, Louise Kurtz, Olive H. Collen; and by Linda Kallman and Teri Medd of Kallman Associates.

We have, separately and together, given presentations, seminars, workshops, and courses during the past three years on the subject of this book. We have interacted with thousands of people who have helped us by offering examples drawn from their experience, explanations, ideas, and above all, challenging questions. The intense interest displayed by so many people in the concepts of agile competition and virtual organizations encouraged us to pursue the issues raised in the book. We hope that the presentation in this book does them justice.

Any errors and omissions in the book are the authors' responsibility, and not attributable in any way to any of the above-mentioned people.

Steven L. Goldman

Roger N. Nagel

Kenneth Preiss

August 1994
Bethlehem, PA

The ideas presented in this book are generic and strategic. Their specific application to a particular company must be the responsibility of the management of that company, based on management's understanding of their company's procedures, culture, resources, and competitive situation.

Confronting Change and Uncertainty

1

What Is Agility and Why Do We Need It?

Rapid, relentless, and uncertain change is the most unsettling marketplace reality that companies and people must cope with today. New products, even whole markets, appear, mutate, and disappear within shorter and shorter periods of time. The pace of innovation continues to quicken, and the direction of innovation is often unpredictable. Product variety has proliferated to a bewildering degree (Seiko markets 3000 different watches; Philips sells more than 800 color TV models), and imitative competition is swift and profit-destroying. Agility is a comprehensive response to the challenges posed by a business environment dominated by change and uncertainty.

For a company, to be agile is to be capable of operating profitably in a competitive environment of continually, and unpredictably, changing customer opportunities.

For an individual, to be agile is to be capable of contributing to the bottom line of a company that is constantly reorganizing its human and technological resources in response to unpredictably changing customer opportunities.

But marketplace change is only one dimension of the competitive pressures that companies and people are experiencing today. At a deeper level, we are changing from a competitive environment in which mass-market products and services were standardized, long-lived, information-poor and exchanged in one-time transactions to an environment in which companies compete globally with niche market products and services that are individualized, short-lived, information-rich, and exchanged on an ongoing basis with customers.

Only companies that respond to the deeper structural changes taking place in the underlying system of commercial competition will be able to make sense of—and profit from—the superficially chaotic changes occurring at the level of the marketplace. A more complete definition of *agility,* then, is that it is a comprehensive response to the business challenges of profiting from rapidly changing, continually fragmenting, global markets for high-quality, high-performance, customer-configured goods and services. (A working definition is developed beginning on p. 41 and in Chapter 3.)

Agility is, in the end, about making money *in and from* a turbulent, intensely competitive business environment.

TACTICAL VERSUS STRATEGIC REFORM

Reforms introduced by companies since the early 1980s to improve their competitiveness—just-in-time logistics, the quality movement, "lean" manufacturing—have been tactical responses to marketplace pressures. These reforms aim to improve how companies are doing what they are already doing. Although these efforts are appropriate and valuable, they reflect an acceptance of the status quo, rather than a recognition of the need to confront a *new* competitive reality, one that challenges what companies *ought* to be doing, not just how they can do a better job of what they are already doing.

This new reality is defined by the structural changes taking place in the underlying competitive environment; current marketplace pressures are symptoms of these changes. In addition, if tactical reforms are to have an enduring impact on a company's competitiveness, they must be coordinated with one another. They must also be incorporated into strategic goals matched to the new competitive realities. If they are not, they will be assimilated into the prevailing system paradigms, however revolutionary the changes their implementation may seem to require.

As a matter of fact, most companies have adopted a succession of tactical initiatives without anchoring the rationale for their implementation in new ends that mandate fundamental changes, true paradigm shifts, in how those companies operate. The result is that, in company after company, disillusionment with the "alphabet soup" of managerial reforms has invariably set in. The disillusionment is not truly a reflection of the failure of the reforms to deliver on their promises, however. Innovative tactics will always be short-lived unless they are embedded in comprehensive organizational change that is in turn anchored in new strategic goals.

Agility challenges the prevailing paradigms of organization, management, production, and competitiveness. It is explicitly strategic rather than tactical, taking no established practices for granted. *Agile competition demands that the processes that support the creation, production, and distribution of goods and services be centered on the customer-perceived value of products. This is very different from building a customer-centered company.* Enhancing the satisfaction that a customer experiences in dealing with a company adds value and can improve focus and even efficiency. But customer-centered operations are fully consistent with the mass-production paradigm. Centering a company on product lines that enrich customers—products whose prices are determined by the value that customers perceive those products to have for them—moves beyond the traditional mass-production system, however efficient it may be.

Successful agile companies, therefore, know a great deal about individual customers and interact with them routinely and intensively. Neither knowledge of individual customers nor interaction on this level was relevant to mass-production-era competitors. As purveyors of standardized, uniform goods and services, mass-production-era competitors relied on market surveys that created an abstraction: the "average" or "typical" customer. Individuality that was more than skin deep could not be accommodated in a mass-production competitive environment.

By contrast, offering individualized products—not a bewildering list of options and models but a choice of ordering a product configured by the vendor to the particular requirements of individual customers—is the hallmark of agile competition. Success entails formulating customer-value-based business strategies for competing in the highest-value-added markets, that is, in what are today the most profitable, and the most competitive, markets.

Beyond the Customer-Centered Company

The production operations of a successful agile company, its organizational structure, management philosophy, personnel requirements, and technology investments, are all "pulled" by these customer-opportunity-centered business strategies (see pp. 13–14). In an agile competitive environment, there is no one right way to organize and operate a company. Management can adopt the mix of multiple, concurrent strategies that will be most profitable for that company, given the variety of customers it serves and the various *changing* markets in which it competes. No one strategy, no one mode of organization or operation, will be successful for long. Nor will any strategy be optimal for all customers or all markets. The life expectancy of decisions that work for a company at any particular time will depend on the rate of change in the markets in which that company competes, but it will always be far shorter than companies are used to nowadays.

In order to succeed in such an environment, a company must be able to routinely and profitably exploit both short- and long-term market opportunities for knowledge-based, customer-configured goods and services. To do this, a company must have the right core competencies with which to create new customer opportunities and to respond to customer opportunities that present themselves—often unpredictably. A company must be able to move from "concept to cash flow" in a small fraction of the time that it takes to do so now. It must be able to develop, and to sell at a profit, products in a wide range of models with short *model* lifetimes while simultaneously cultivating long-term customer relationships that will sustain long-lived product *families.*

What is required to accomplish this goes beyond flexible manufacturing, operational efficiency, or rapid response time. To succeed, an agile company must operate in a way that allows it to synthesize new productive capabilities very quickly. These capabilities may be synthesized from the human and physical resources that are internal to the company but are distributed among its various departments or divisions and at a number of locations. It is increasingly advantageous, however, to develop new products and services cooperatively with other companies, including with direct competitors.

For reasons of cost, speed, and access to expertise, facilities, or markets, new business capabilities may best be synthesized by forming alliances with other companies that already possess the resources required. In addition to participating in traditional alliances such as partnerships and joint ventures, companies are exploiting a dynamic type of alliance called a *virtual company.* In such a company, complementary resources existing in a number of cooperating companies are left in place, but are integrated to support a particular product effort for as long as it is economically justifiable to do so.

The virtual company alliance minimizes investment in personnel and facilities dedicated to the new project. It minimizes, as well, the disruptive impact of new projects on existing operations. Resources are selectively allocated to the virtual company if they are underutilized, or if they can be more profitably utilized there than in the "home" company.

A Next Generation Paradigm

Agility redefines the terms of industrial competition and thus requires a new mind-set for the organization and operation of commercial enterprises. It also requires the invention of new metrics appropriate for assessing the performance of companies operating in an agile mode. Efficiency, cost of production, direct and indirect costs, return on capital, assets and investments all remain relevant measures of company operations, but they must be redefined to fit the new mode of operation, or they will obstruct it. In addition, the cost to companies of implementing the changes necessitated by becoming agile must be weighed against the cost of being unable to compete in lucrative markets that are accessible *only* to agile competitors.

At the outset, we defined *agility* as the ability to thrive in a competitive environment of continually and unpredictably changing market opportunities. The need for companies and people to acquire this ability is not this month's good idea for how to gain a competitive edge. Like the evolution of lean manufacturing out of the competitive necessities that confronted Japanese industry in the 1960s, the evolution of agile competition is rooted in what is increasingly acknowledged as a new marketplace reality, one that promises to determine the conditions under which companies and people will have to function for a long time to come. That reality is the emergence of what Hans-Jürgen Warnecke, president of Germany's Fraunhofer Organization (the umbrella for 47 Fraunhofer Institutes) and author of *The Fractal Company,* calls a "post-mass production paradigm."

© 1991 Iacocca Institute • Lehigh University • Illustrator: Gene Mater

WHY DO WE NEED AGILITY?

If agility is the solution, what was the problem?

Without consciously intending to render the mass-production system obsolete, producers and consumers have fundamentally altered the processes by means of which goods and services are currently being defined, created, distributed, and consumed. The terms used to describe markets, products, business processes, and operating metrics are the ones we have always used, but what these terms refer to is no longer the same. As the context of commercial competition changes dramatically, the conduct of business changes correspondingly. Either new terms must be invented to describe that conduct, or, at the risk of confusion, the old terms can be used; but we must recognize that they have acquired new meanings in the altered context. Signs of this alteration abound, in the form of marketplace forces that are "pulling" responses from growing numbers of companies threatened by these forces:

1. Market fragmentation
2. Production to order in arbitrary lot sizes
3. Information capacity to treat masses of customers as individuals
4. Shrinking product lifetimes
5. Convergence of physical products and services
6. Global production networks
7. Simultaneous intercompany cooperation and competition
8. Distribution infrastructures for mass customization
9. Corporate reorganization frenzy
10. Pressure to internalize prevailing social values

Market Fragmentation

Markets of all kinds are fragmenting at what seems like an accelerating pace. Magazines, beer, soft drinks, and snack foods; radio stations and cable TV channels; audio and video equipment; cameras, fax machines and copiers, printers, and scanners; appliances, clothing, and financial, shopping, and business services all come in a bewildering array of choices aimed at constantly proliferating market niches. Personal computers are available in a very wide range of desktop varieties, but there are also portable computers ranging from luggable workstations to laptops, notebooks, subnotebooks, and palmtops, which themselves come in a number of distinct varieties.

Personal communication devices have evolved from simple beepers to increasingly sophisticated pagers, from bulky portable telephones to shirt-pocket-size cellular telephones to wireless digital beepers, pagers, telephones, and handheld computers offering various combinations of capabilities. The "general-purpose" restaurant has been overwhelmed by rivals that specialized first in national cuisines, then in regional cuisines, and then in "fusion" cuisines (Tex-Mex, Thai-French, etc.). The only constant is that new models and more variety are sure to appear.

In effect, the dynamics of the fashion, advertising, and entertainment industries—this season's "look," today's prize-winning ad campaign, the superstar of the hour, the Andy Warhol "15 minutes of fame" syndrome—have established new competitive norms for industry in general. Even prosaic manufacturing and service sectors of the economy from washing machines (with or without "Fuzzy Logic" controls) to banking and investment instruments have been affected.

Three market fragmentation strategies, none of them new in and of itself, are being extended by companies to more and more markets for more and more kinds of goods and services. The common denominator of all three strategies is the creation of products whose price is a function of the degree to which customers believe that they, personally, have benefited from—have been enriched by—the purchase.

1. Companies are segmenting customer groups and pricing the same goods or services differently depending on the circumstances of the transaction. With virtually unlimited packaging possibilities, the same weight of the same candies, for example, can be priced very differently. Mars exploits this strategy particularly effectively with over 70 different packaging formats for M&M candies.

Passengers on the same airplane flight pay very different fares for the same class of ticket, depending on such factors as age (rates for children and senior citizens), time of purchase, length of stay, connections to other flights, applicability of government or corporate rates, and qualification for promotional fares (buy one–get one free, frequent flier, etc.).

The same banking, credit, and investment services may be priced differently depending on age, credit history, number of accounts, level of account activity, or size of balance.

2. Companies are "sneakerizing" their products, transforming them from relatively low-priced commodities to relatively high-priced specialty items. Sneakers used to be general-purpose, inexpensive mass-market commodities. But sneakers are, as they say, history— and thus candidates for resurrection as higher-priced, nostalgia products in a niche market! Sneakers have been replaced by "sport shoes"—special-purpose, expensive, occupying niche markets and yet produced in large volume.

Specialized for tennis, basketball, baseball, track, field, walking, hiking, jogging, running, aerobics, bicycling, and cross-training and, within each of these categories offered for various levels of user ability and commitment, sport shoes employ technologies and command prices beyond the wildest dreams of sneaker manufacturers. Indeed, within some of their niches, further segmentation has taken place: There are specialized versions of bicycling shoes, for example, targeted at road, criterium, track, and off-road racers and wanna-bes, keyed to different pedal-shoe "systems," and commanding higher prices than the more "general-purpose" bicycling shoes.

The market for nonprescription sunglasses, on which Americans spent more than $2 billion in 1993, is following the path blazed by sneakers. Until recently, nonprescription sunglasses were a drugstore commodity item, often kept near the checkout counter in order to maximize impulse buying. They were low-priced, general-purpose, low-technology, and mass-produced for a mass market. Ray-Ban, a subsidiary of Bausch and Lomb, was the driving force behind "fashion" sunglasses, retailing for $15 and up. Ray-Ban segmented the market and triggered a period of explosive, high-profit growth.

Today, "premium" sunglasses have further segmented the market. Revo, also a Bausch and Lomb company, offers models in 80 different frame styles and four different lenses, with a top retail price of over $200. Newcomer Nikon has entered this market with a high-style line of nonprescription sunglasses that come in only about 30 frame *styles* but in five lens *types* keyed to the distinctive requirements of five different kinds of outdoor activities: skiing, hiking, flying, shooting, and water sports.

Supported by aggressive and bold advertising appealing to the emotions, what had been an inexpensive, practical, low-margin commodity has been transformed into a specialty product, associated with "image" and produced in large volume for numerous niche markets, the selling price determined by the extent to which the individual customer feels enriched by the purchase.

Because manufacturing and information technologies are making it possible to diversify both products and services at little additional cost over mass production, the profitability of customer-enrichment pricing strategies can be very high—for a while. At the same time, however, and for the same reasons, imitation of highly successful products and services is inevitable, in large measure because the technologies for designing, producing, and delivering goods and services are almost universally available. And with the imitation comes great downward pressure on prices and profits precisely *because* of the wide gap between production costs and selling price. The innovator bears the costs associated with creativity, but the imitator has lots of room to lower prices and still make a profit.

Thus imitation is the cause of the "paradox of sneakerization": Almost as fast as someone thinks up a way of converting a low-margin commodity into a high-profit specialty product, it is on its way to being a commodity again! As the phenomenon is all too familiar to businesspeople and all too painful, one illustration should suffice. When Motorola's MicroTac cellular telephone was introduced in 1989, it carried a retail price of $2500. In mid-1994 it was readily available for little more than $100, and cellular telephone companies frequently offered it free to new subscribers, reflecting a shift in value from physical products to services (see p. 21).

The lesson is clear. In the emerging agile competitive environment, *sustained success* goes to companies that are capable of continually adding new value to existing products and services, as well as creating a steady stream of new ones.

3. Companies are segmenting markets according to function, exploiting economies of scope made possible primarily by the generalizability of microelectronics technologies. In a sense, the extraordinary range of computer chip–based consumer, commercial, and industrial products is an expression of the packagability of this technology.

Increasingly, workstations, desktop computers, portables, laptops, and notebook and subnotebook computers utilize not only the same underlying technology but the very same processing chips, for example, the Intel 386, 486 and Pentium CPUs, and the PowerPC chip created jointly by IBM, Motorola, and Apple. Handheld computers are on the threshold of acquiring this kind of power, as second-generation versions of the Apple Newton and its clones, and variants such as the Motorola Envoy move into production. Pagers and beepers have evolved into a broad range of lightweight, wireless personal communication devices with constantly expanding computing and information exchange and display capabilities, ranging from sending and receiving faxes to uploading and downloading data remotely to and from on-line data services that literally span the globe.

Production to Order in Arbitrary Lot Sizes

It is already possible for each of the many products made on a high-volume production line to be made differently from each of the others with little or no increase in production costs. This capability, which resulted from the collapse of traditional information costs, has revolutionary marketing consequences. Individualized production increases competition in existing markets, opens new markets, and creates competitive advantages by offering to mass-market customers individualized goods and services at as close to mass-production prices as a company chooses to price them.

In addition, more and more companies are discovering that they can produce customer-configured products to order instead of to forecast. Doing so generates benefits far beyond savings from the elimination of inventories. The knowledge, as every product is made, that it has already been sold to, and thus is being made for, a particular customer can have a dramatic impact on company operations. It certainly transforms the nature of sales, from pushing inventory to pulling production.

Finally, production equipment innovations continue to provide greater and greater functionality at smaller scales and at significantly lower costs. For large and medium-size businesses, this development makes it easier and more cost-effective to target niche markets, producing goods and services efficiently for smaller clusters of customers. At the same time, it is also causing a "democratization" of production opportunities by making entry into niche markets for low-volume, individualized products accessible to businesses of *all* sizes. Just a few illustrations of this democratization are desktop publishing hardware and software; digital video, audio, and audio-video studio-quality production equipment; print copying, graphics, and digital image reproduction and manipulation services; information searching and packaging services; electronic music playing and recording with increasingly sophisticated synthesizers; ovens that make minibakery and minirestaurant operations practical as both stand-alone businesses and within larger enterprises, for example, department stores and supermarkets.

Atlanta's Bank South Corporation has located 30 percent of its 143 branches inside Kroger supermarket branches. Each minibank typically costs $250,000 to open, compared to $1.5 to $2 million for a traditional branch. The minibanks become profitable in their first year of operation rather than after four or five years for a traditional branch.

Hamilton Bancshares of Columbus, Ohio, the state's second-largest bank, is replacing 40 percent of its existing branches with small, full-function, but remotely staffed banks. Hamilton discovered that the bulk of its profits come from young and middle-aged customers who are frequent users of ATMs. It is therefore establishing workerless banks that provide 24-hour interactive video access to remotely located personnel for transactions that require it (e.g., loans); most transactions are handled using enhanced ATM-style machines.

Traditionally, economic order quantity (EOQ) calculations determined the smallest lot size that could be profitably produced. These calculations involve a mix of technology-dependent variables and accounting and financial metrics in which assignment of labor, materials, and setup costs plays a major role. In a competitive environment characterized by pricing based on customer enrichment, and driven by a demand for customizable products that increasing numbers of companies are already capable of satisfying, the concept of EOQ needs to be reexamined.

With the spread of individualizable production equipment, the EOQ should be whatever the customer wants. The important figure becomes the ratio of production lead time to customer tolerance time. If the ratio is less than 1, a company can produce to order; if it is greater than 1, a company can only build to forecast while reducing its production lead time to below its customers' tolerance time . . . if it wants to keep its customers!

The ability to produce to order in arbitrary lot sizes may or may not be a function of the use of advanced technologies. At its St. Louis aircraft manufacturing facility, McDonnell-Douglas reduced its EOQ by linking what had been 100 individual computer numerical control (CNC) machine tool cells to a single production-scheduling computer in order to achieve direct numerical control (DNC) of machining operations.

Motorola's Boynton Beach, Florida, plant serves as an evolving test-bed (recently converted to a second generation of production technologies) for manufacturing customer-configured products to order. Cellular pagers are assembled, tested, packaged, and shipped, all by computer-controlled machinery, within hours of the receipt of remotely entered orders. More recently, Motorola has converted its two-way radio manufacturing plant in Plantation, Florida, to a build-to-order capability. The plant produces 500 different models of two-way radios. In 1994 the radios are being made to individual order in two hours, as compared to ten days as recently as 1990.

At its newly constructed Kyushu assembly plant, Nissan has invested in very flexible, high-technology production equipment in its pursuit of the corporate goal of manufacturing any model of any of its automobiles, in any configuration, in any sequence, on any of its (new) production lines. The objective is very rapid assembly to customer order; profitability is achieved at 10,000 units of any given model. Similarly, Matsushita's Shah Alam, Malaysia, TV plant has been designed so that any of 60 different color television models can be assembled simultaneously.

At the other extreme, with very little new technology, Toshiba assembles all its portable computer models—more than 20, with many different customer-selected options for each—on a single production line in batches of 20 per model and can afford to do it in batches of 10. At each work point, a notebook computer provides instructions for assembling the next model, the configuration of options for each unit, and the number to be assembled. In the words of Toshiba President Fumio Sato, "Every time I go to a plant, I tell the people 'smaller lots!'" Sato is committed to enabling Toshiba to make money on shorter and shorter production runs of any product while producing many different products.

Toshiba's production scheduling is organized around small batches on a single line. IBM's PCDirect and Ambra telemarketing divisions, on the other hand, echoing Motorola's pager capability, manufacture each of the PCs they sell to customer order only, as the orders are entered into their system.

Universal Instruments of Binghamton, New York, a manufacturer of capital goods for the electronics industry, discovered that building to order rather than to forecast was for it more a matter of mind-set than of technology. Setting aside the old practices and analyzing its operations without tradition-bound prejudices, it discovered that its production lead times and costs would be very nearly the same if it built to order and that inventory costs and customer lead time would go down. Once the transition to this new system was made, the company discovered that product development time became much shorter as a result of the active customer involvement that building to order encouraged. Interacting more intensively with customers, in turn, revealed new, cost-free ways of adding value for the customer. For example, installation and changeover time for new equipment was significantly reduced through an improved understanding by both parties of the requirements for installation upon delivery.

At its Moline, Illinois, plant, John Deere currently manufactures seeders—which can be configured in more than 2 million varieties built on 81 different chassis—to customer order only, one at a time, in any sequence, on a single production line. What is most impressive about Deere's transformation in 1993 of an older plant, is that it involved almost no new technology at all—no robot assembly machines, no next-century computer network, no artificially intelligent process controllers. Plant management rethought the production process, the flow of work, and the utilization of the work force, giving operational personnel more information, more responsibility, and a direct stake in meeting production goals. These changes have eliminated inventory and improved product quality.

Information Capacity to Treat Masses of Customers as Individuals

Agile competition goes beyond the Japanese marketing strategies known as *lean manufacturing* by permitting the customer, jointly with the vendor or provider, to determine what the product will be. The Japanese utilized the efficiency and flexibility created by their production process innovations to expand model variety. The proliferation of types of motorcycles, cameras, audio equipment, watches, color TVs, and VCRs reached avalanche proportions. Initially, this astonishing variety attracted many new customers, created new markets, and won major shares in existing markets—all to the benefit of Japanese manufacturers. Eventually, however, as the variety and options increased, a burden was placed on customers, who typically lack the expertise, the time, or the motivation to study the cascading numbers of choices suddenly made available to them.

The problem lay in choice being driven by producers, who declared: "Thou shalt have these choices. Now go and choose!" With agility, choice is driven by consumers. Choice moves from being the customer's responsibility to being the producer's responsibility. The producer initiates the interactive relationship through which the product to be produced is jointly defined. Of course, there are constraints, but the center of gravity of the transaction process shifts. It becomes the producer's job to help customers articulate their needs and their requirements. This includes "growing" customers—knowing enough about what customers do, what they want to do, and what they should want to do, to be able to show them how they can benefit from a product customized to their needs. Agility means knowing enough about customers to be able to show them that they ought to want some capability that they do not now want, because it would create some advantage that would benefit them.

Focusing on the individual customer has evolved from the unilateral producer-centered customer-responsive companies inspired by the lean manufacturing refinement of mass production to interactive producer-customer relationships under the terms of agile competition. The evolution of Ross Operating Valves is a case in point. This company is an old-line manufacturer of hydraulic valves, with headquarters in Madison Heights, Michigan, and plants in Lavonia (Georgia), Frankfurt, and Tokyo. Although the Madison Heights plant continues to manufacture standard, "catalog" valves, at Lavonia, Ross management created an agile facility called *Ross/Flex*.

All valves produced by the Ross/Flex system are custom-designed jointly by customers and Ross "integrators"—engineers and veteran machinists—using proprietary CAD software and Ross's valve design library. The integrators are responsible for transferring prototype design data to CNC machine tools for fabrication, for testing the prototype valve, and for shipping the prototype to the customer. The customer can request modification of the prototype, which goes into production only after the customer approves it for production. By integrating the design, sales, and production processes, Ross has reduced both the cost and the time needed to develop prototype valves to one day and $3000, instead of ten days and $30,000.

Ross management has chosen not to charge extra for this customization and interactivity. Instead, Ross/Flex is the foundation of its marketing strategy; it is the core of the value added for their customers. Since Ross/Flex was implemented, in 1992, business has increased dramatically and the Lavonia plant has become the model for renovating the Frankfurt and Tokyo plants. Ross management's next step is to offer its customers remote access, on a fee basis, to its design software. If customers have the capability, they can design the valves they want and then have Ross integrators validate the design and initiate production.

Shrinking Product Lifetimes

The decreasing lifetimes of products, increasing proliferation of models, and accelerating pace of the introduction of new or improved models are among the most brutal facts of contemporary competition. Sony's Walkman line seems to change models daily. On a recent visit to one store in Tokyo's Akihabara electronics district, more than 400 Walkman-size products, offering some combination of AM, FM, cassette tape playback and/or recording capabilities, were *on display.*

Hard on the heels of its Six Sigma program triumph, in which reliability defined quality, Motorola initiated its Ten X program, designed to improve all its processes, especially product cycle, or concept to cash, time by a factor of ten every five years! Having achieved a great global success head-to-head with the best Japanese manufacturers in the cellular telephone market, where it enjoys a dominant 45 percent market share, Motorola is aggressively pursuing a competing wireless digital communication technology, called *Motorola Integrated Radio Service,* which combines voice and data in a compact two-way radio device.

Today, Panasonic's consumer electronics product cycle time is three months. That is, the lifetime of any given model of CD player, TV, VCR, cassette deck, or stereo receiver is just 90 days. During that time, its successor is being designed, tested, and put into production. The design, development, production, distribution, and marketing processes are continuous and overlapping.

Intel works on three generations of chips at a time: one in volume production and facing declining unit profits, one in beta testing being readied for limited production, and one being designed. Since the autumn of 1981, when the IBM PC was introduced, Intel has moved from the 8086 to the 8088 to the mostly ignored 80186 to the 80286 (which launched the IBM AT class of PCs), the 80386, the current desktop standard 80486, and the state-of-the-Intel-art Pentium/

80586, with the next generation 80686 (P-6) being hurried into preproduction testing. Eight generations in 13 years, and the ninth waiting to be born! Motorola's 68000 processing chip has been through four generations during the ten years that the Macintosh has been on the market, and now a new family of Macs is beginning its evolution, powered by the Motorola-manufactured PowerPC 601 chip.

Perhaps even more astonishing, the lifetime of mainframe computers has recently been halved, with significantly higher-performance models being introduced every two years rather than every four. In 1994 the rapidity of mainframe innovation and IBM's technology advantage led Hitachi, a major mainframe competitor, to sign an agreement under which it would cease competing and buy its mainframe technology from IBM, including whole systems that it would resell with the Hitachi logo.

Automobile model changes used to take place every five or six years, with only styling changes and subsystem improvements occurring in between. Today, the leading Japanese manufacturers can introduce a new model in three years, and Toyota, at least, aims to be able to do this in under 30 months by 1995. Chrysler's award-winning new large sedans (the Concorde, Vision, Intrepid line) and Neon subcompact were each developed in approximately 40 months, and Ford's redesign of the Mustang (not a completely new vehicle but much more than a styling change) was accomplished in three years, whereas four years had been the norm for such projects at Ford.

During the summer of 1991 the AT&T Safari was a leading-edge notebook-size computer at approximately 8 pounds with a 20-MHz Intel 386, a 40-Mbyte hard disk, bright screen, and quality construction. It had been created by AT&T's marketing and engineering personnel working innovatively with the Marubeni Trading Company, a Matsushita-led network of suppliers, and the industrial design firm Henry Dreyfuss Associates. Brought to market in eight months, it was obsolete in less than a year, and within two years notebook computers were under attack by subnotebook-size machines less than half the weight and with equal or greater computing power.

By integrating business functions, creating interactive relationships with customers and suppliers, and rethinking company operations and processes, companies can often reduce their product cycle time dramatically. The barriers to shortening the concept to cash time are, in the main, structural, a reflection of the mind-set of mass-production competition. With a change of mind-set, what had never been attempted before suddenly becomes very doable and, indeed, a necessity for being competitive.

Convergence of Physical Products and Services

The traditional distinction between goods and services—reflected, for example, in the different rates at which the revenues generated by their creation and consumption are taxed—and between the kinds of companies and personnel that produce them is vanishing. This distinction is being replaced by markets for "fusion products," physical products the value of which lies overwhelmingly, if not exclusively, in the information and/or services to which the physical product provides access. A direct result of this convergence is that hardware companies are acquiring the capability to create both information and services or they are working increasingly closely with information and service companies in order to create fusion products.

Sega and Nintendo game machines, for example, are sold at cost—at best. The machines are merely platforms for selling games, which have generated all the profits these companies have earned. The machines are therefore developed in collaboration with game developers, the technology driven by the requirements of games that will excite buyers. Sega management has chosen to rely primarily on external developers, from whom it may buy games or to whom it may pay royalties. Nintendo attempts to collect a larger portion of software profits by employing its own programmers and developing new games in house.

Similarly, however high their technology, CD and CD ROM players, cameras, and personal computers, like so many other modern consumer products, become low-margin commodities soon after they redefine the state of the art. (See the earlier discussion of the paradox of sneakerization.) The real value of these items lies in the sales of CDs, film, developing and printing services, and software, respectively. CDs, software, and so forth typically have retail prices that are one to two orders of magnitude greater than their physical production costs, whereas the CD players and computers generate smaller and smaller unit profits.

Apple contracted with Sharp to manufacture its revolutionary Newton Personal Digital Assistant, knowing full well that Sharp would almost immediately release its clone, the Sharp Expert Pad, in competition with the Newton. On the one hand, there was no way that Apple could manufacture Newtons profitably on its own, given the inevitable Japanese competition. On the other hand, the primary revenue flow from the Newton will lie in software applications, royalties, and licensing fees. Apple's strategy must be to create as broad a user base as possible in order to stimulate third-party software and hardware developers to produce products for the Newton. The strategy is one that kept the original Apple II alive and very profitable for Apple for a decade, in spite of the extraordinary rate of innovation in the PC industry. Literally thousands of companies created products for the Apple II, and as *they* strove to be profitable, Apple shared in their successes and bore none of their failures. The goal is to achieve the same kind of win-win community of support for the Newton, a community reinforced by Apple, which will share system design information and Newton product development strategies, but made up of independent risk-taking entrepreneurs.

There are three important consequences of this convergence of physical products, information, and services:

1. The dynamics of competition shifts from advantages deriving from manufacturing techniques, technologies, and processes to advantages deriving from people—from their knowledge, initiative, and creativity. During the mass-production era, the knowledge it took to create and produce products was invisible. It was buried in management, marketing, and production processes, and there was no sign of it in the product.

In the era of agile competition, the fulcrum of value-adding commercial activity shifts from manufacturing to innovative, knowledge-based information and service applications of manufactured products. The success of more and more products is a direct function of the customer-perceived value of the knowledge, information (including entertainment), and services "captured" in, and delivered to them by, those products. This is just as true for commercial products as it is for consumer products, entertainment aside.

Manufacturing companies must therefore take the initiative in making their contributions to the total end-user product as valuable as possible. The unique value added to CD players and VCRs by the manufacturers of the tapes, motors, switches, laser devices, and playback/recording heads is invisible to the customer. The rewards for these manufacturers are determined by the extent to which they (the manufacturers) maximize the value of their contributions to those who will benefit the most from the performance of the end product.

Today, applications purveyors retroactively determine the value of manufacturing activities as some fraction of the value that the customer places on the applications. Manufacturing excellence is taken for granted, a situation created by modern production technologies that are so capable and so robust that very sophisticated physical products, such as magnetic recording tape, videocassettes and audiocassettes, compact discs, lasers, hard discs and CPUs, can be manufactured in high volume at low cost almost anywhere in the world.

At the same time, this shift in the dynamics of competition threatens the foundation of the Japanese postwar economic "miracle." The Japanese have prospered primarily as a result of the excellence of their manufacturing operations. Over and over again during the past 15 years we have been told of the Japanese skill in taking foreign innovations and commercializing them, of the superior yield of Japanese semiconductor manufacturing, of the superior efficiency of their automotive assembly operations. We have been told the stories of the origin of the portable transistor radio, the consumer VCR, and the Sony Walkman. But as the dominant value added to the highest-profit products shifts from manufacturing to information and services, the Japanese find themselves in a very unfamiliar competitive position, one requiring techniques very different from lean manufacturing.

2. Instead of a discrete sale at a single point in time, the sale of knowledge-based products holds the potential for a continuing relationship over time between producers and consumers. What the customer is really buying is information and services. If producers enhance these commodities over time in step with changing customer interests or requirements, customers will continue to be customers, buying new information and service products. They will also buy hardware enhancements that provide different, or more convenient, access to information and services.

Agile-era products are thus open-ended. If designed appropriately, they can evolve indefinitely. Consider the families of releases of computer programs such as word processors or spreadsheets, together with coordinated utility programs, or computer hardware that is user-upgradable and reconfigurable. Indeed, a symbiotic relationship has existed for more than a decade between computer hardware and software at all levels, from PCs to mainframes. The original PC, the first release of MS-DOS, and the Intel 8088 CPU have *co*-evolved into vastly more powerful Intel Pentium-based machines, running MS-DOS 6.3 with OS/2 2.1 or Windows 4.0.

In effect, in an agile environment the bottleneck for optimally profitable operation shifts from manufacturing operations to design operations. It is the efficiency with which design is integrated into production, and how design and production are merged with marketing and sales, that determines the ultimate profitability of a company in an agile competitive environment. This remains the case whether the product is a physical product serving as a platform for information and services or a "pure" information or service product that has no physical platform.

3. **Information has emerged as a product in its own right.** With such vast quantities of data being collected and stored, companies are being built on a foundation of managing other companies' information or selling information products created by packaging data. Sometimes the data are freely available in the public domain, collected for some other purpose, or the data may have been specifically collected to be repackaged in a particular way.

EDS runs a multi-billion-dollar network of information management services for its clients that rivals the national rail system in complexity.

American Airlines' profits on the fees it charges for access to its SABRE reservation system have, at various times during the past decade, exceeded its profits from its flight operations. Financially troubled Federated Department Stores created a highly profitable subsidiary, its Sabre Group, that sells software for integrating front- and back-office operations and for managing inventory to other retailers. Ryder Truck Rental has established a Dedicated Logistics division. Its product, Integrated Logistics, is a system-level logistics management system, that is, an information product keyed to a logistics methodology that, Ryder claims, will reduce inventory investment, lower transportation and order cycle costs, and improve customer satisfaction.

Under CEO James Unruh, Unisys is shifting the foundation of its business from selling computer hardware to selling computer-based information, information management, and management information services. Hewlett-Packard and IBM management are being reorganized to exploit the same market. IBM has abandoned its geography-based organization in favor of one based on the industry being served, the better to provide comprehensive information-based solutions to customer problems instead of the hardware and software elements of such solutions. As even the most sophisticated hardware becomes a commodity through price pressure from imitators, the opportunities to add value for customers increasingly lie in the application of hardware to solving customer problems.

Companies are repackaging census, telephone, and ZIP code data and offering them for sale as advertising, marketing, canvassing, and market research products. The discount coupons that appear on the back of supermarket receipt tapes are an example. By matching digitized atlas and Yellow Pages data, companies can target businesses near individual supermarkets and, for a fee, offer them an opportunity to reach customers by means of this type of advertising. One such company has signed up 3000 supermarkets nationwide that serve as hubs for this kind of advertising, in exchange for free, preprinted register tapes.

By analyzing purchasing patterns, credit card companies decide which merchandise advertising inserts to enclose with which members' monthly statements. This "matching" increases the likelihood of purchases and thus of commissions to the credit card company for the sales.

A number of companies are selling professional sports team data to fans. Fingertip for STATS offers Apple Newton owners the opportunity to download updated statistics into Newton baseball game software for about a dollar a day. With a cellular modem in the PCMCIA slot, Newton users can do their updating even while sitting at the ballpark! Microsoft's "Complete Baseball" program includes an on-line daily baseball "newspaper," with one "photo," for $1.25 a day.

Whole new industries are springing up based on repackaged information products. Molecular Designs and Schnyder Consulting, both Swiss-based, sell information to chemical and drug manufacturers that has been repackaged by proprietary software operating on chemical manufacturing databases that Molecular Designs and Schnyder collect. Molecular Designs helps manufacturers find optimal synthesis pathways; improve process designs; find customers for intermediaries, excess production, and by-products; and comply with waste treatment, safety, and environmental requirements in different national markets. Schnyder specializes in accident analysis and safety improvement.

The mind-numbing rate of growth of data accessible via the Internet has resulted in the development of several generations of increasingly sophisticated programs for automating data-search and data-collection operations: Gopher, Archie, WAIS, WorldWideWeb, Mosaic. These will become the prototypes for commercial data-packaging programs that will be the tools for "mining" data in much the same way that mineral ores are mined.

Canada's Journey's End motel chain is an example of a company that is mining its own, heretofore ignored, data. It maintains a centralized customer information database that is updated in real time with every registration at any one of its far-flung motels. Analyzing and accessing this data have resulted in reallocation of resources to services that customers actually use and to marketing aimed at higher-probability customers. Accessing the database at reservation or registration time makes it possible to enhance personal service for repeat guests. The result has been lower operating costs and higher repeat rates. Journey's End thus illustrates the adoption of a customer-driven company strategy—configuring the products and services offered to the needs of individual customers. A similar approach to database marketing and analysis has been adopted by commercial real estate management companies and automobile manufacturers and large dealerships.

Global Production Networks

No markets anywhere (for profitable products, at least) are domestic anymore, and no producer need be a domestic producer only. The addition of high-capacity information and communication systems to existing global transportation systems opens every market to any producer for whom the economics is attractive. Furthermore, it is increasingly easy to integrate design, production, marketing, and distribution resources distributed around the world into a coherent "virtual" production facility. As a result, every company has the potential for linking some portion of its capabilities with complementary capabilities of other companies regardless of their location. If a company whose strength is design recognizes an opportunity in a distant market but lacks local production facilities or distribution or marketing channels, the company no longer faces an obstacle to entering that market.

In 1991 the *21st Century Manufacturing Enterprise Strategy* report envisioned a resource that would be routinely utilized by U.S. industry in the year 2006, called *Factory America Net (FAN)*. FAN was to be an international, cross-industry computer network and database system that would make electronic commerce routine. It would provide instantaneous access to detailed information about the capabilities of hundreds of thousands of companies, about the cost and availability of their expertise and facilities, and about their terms for participating in collaborations.

In 1994 Enterprise Integration Network (EINet) began operations with precisely these goals, through the initiative of the Microelectronics and Computer Consortium (MCC) in Austin, Texas, and with funding from industry and the Advanced Research Projects Agency of the U.S. Department of Defense. EINet is linked to the Internet, which provides truly global coverage and an astonishing rate of growth of penetration into the total world community of computer users. The electronic commerce dimension of EINet is managed by Sprint. EINet's databases are steadily expanding, and as they do, the existence of routine global production networks comes closer to reality. EINet has a growing number of competitor-allies as well: CommerceNet, developed by Palo Alto–based Enterprise Integration Technologies, Inc.; ECNet, developed by an Arizona State University–led consortium to give small and medium-size southwestern companies networked production capabilities; and AgileWeb in northeastern Pennsylvania.

As with the democratizing effect of progressively more functional, smaller-scale, and less expensive production equipment (discussed earlier), these networks create many new opportunities for small and medium-size businesses. Quite apart from offering new products based on the use of the network, through the medium of the network companies can monitor opportunities for selling to customers anywhere in the world and can participate in joint ventures anywhere in the world.

Globalization is also bringing about the integration of the internationally distributed facilities of a single company into a truly coherent global production resource. The commitment of the Ford Motor Company to this goal is a case in point. In 1993 Ford announced that it was electronically merging its seven automotive design centers—in the United States (Valencia, California, and Dearborn, Michigan), England (Dunton), Germany (Cologne/Merkenich), Italy (Turin), Japan (Hiroshima), and Australia (Melbourne). Then, in 1994, CEO Alexander Trotman announced that Ford was merging all its activities, distributed among 30 countries, into a single global operation. Vehicle development will be divided among five centers by vehicle type (small cars and light trucks, mid-size cars, etc.), not by national or regional market.

Each center will develop particular types of vehicles for global marketing and will have comprehensive responsibility and authority for the entire vehicle development programs in its domain. Purchasing operations will be centralized to eliminate redundancy and to obtain greater leverage through larger-volume purchases. Trotman's objectives are for Ford to be able to develop a wider variety of vehicles, for a wide range of niche markets, more rapidly and at much less cost than it can today. (The budget for developing Ford's Mondeo world car ran to $6 billion.) Centralization of vehicle development should help in this regard, because 40 percent of new vehicle development costs come from changes required after the prototype is built.

AT&T has installed the Global Information Systems Architecture (GISA), which standardizes its business manufacturing systems world-wide. The objective is for AT&T to improve its ability to compete in all lucrative telecommunications markets wherever they may be located. With GISA in place, concurrent product development is possible, using whatever corporate resources are required regardless of their physical location.

Simultaneous Intercompany Competition and Cooperation

To a degree unprecedented in American business history, companies are entering into partnerships, joint ventures, and collaborations of every imaginable kind, including the formation of virtual companies. Some of these relationships aim at creating economies of scale by merging similar capabilities in order to avoid the costs of adding capacity. Some aim at joint development of new "back-office" capabilities, and some cooperating companies work on the development of new generic technologies, even as they plan to compete with one another for the end user. Some companies aim at achieving vertical integration, or at creating economies of scope, by synthesizing physically distributed complementary capabilities within or among enterprises. This is, of course, the essence of a virtual organization structure.

What is particular striking in all these forms of joint venture is the increasing frequency of participation of direct competitors. It would be wrong to conclude that we are witnessing a return of late-nineteenth-century trusts, cartels, and price-manipulating monopolies. Rather, there is a growing recognition that the basis of interenterprise cooperation is totally different with agile competition from what it was with mass-production competition.

In the mass-production paradigm, competition was one-dimensional and centered on price; hence the pursuit of the lowest unit production cost. The competitive environment was dominated by long-lived, standardized products. Cooperation among competitors inevitably took the form of, or at least raised the suspicion of, price- and supply-fixing as a means of increasing profits above the levels that lowest unit costs and an excess of supply would allow.

In the agile production paradigm, competition is multidimensional. Price remains important, of course, but the value of physical products is a function of the individualized combinations of information and services the products provide. The opportunities for adding value to agile-era products is thus much greater than it was for mass-production-era products. In addition, agile-era products are typically much shorter-lived and require for their creation a broader range of expertise, the currency of which must be maintained, usually at considerable expense. Paradoxical though it may sound, the complexity of these knowledge-based products provides a *competitive* foundation for their *cooperative* development!

GM, Ford, and Chrysler were unwilling to develop catalytic converters cooperatively in the 1970s. As a result, each company spent hundreds of millions of dollars developing essentially the same product. Today, the three firms have joined a multifaceted consortium, USCAR, which will permit the joint development of technologies, materials, and components ranging from structural plastics to batteries to electric vehicle-control systems.

Hitachi has been a major competitor of IBM in the mainframe computer market, but now the two companies are becoming partners. In the future, Hitachi will buy mainframe CMOS processing chips from IBM and will build and market (under its own name) IBM-architecture mainframe computers, the technology for which will be provided under license from IBM. In addition, Hitachi will adopt IBM variants of the PowerPC chip developed by IBM, Motorola, and Apple for new large computer system and workstation models and will also buy some high-end computers from IBM and resell them with the Hitachi label.

The IBM collaboration with Apple and Motorola to develop and market the PowerPC chip and operating system effectively ends DOS-Mac software exclusivity and links two competing microprocessor chip manufacturers, who also compete in the workstation market. Furthermore, IBM has formed its Power Personal Division which, working jointly with Motorola, has developed a PowerPC reference design. This is intended to *accelerate* the emergence of a PowerPC clone industry. To that end, IBM's Microelectronics Division has prepared design kits that make it almost as easy to build a PowerPC clone assembly facility as it is to build a PC clone facility.

Why would IBM want to encourage the rapid emergence of a PowerPC clone industry, given its experience with the PC clone industry? Because the only PowerPC "pie" worth getting a slice of has to be a large pie, larger than IBM, Apple, and Motorola can create on their own—quickly. Only if the pie is large will developers create software, and without the software, even a superior computer has no chance of cutting into Intel's PC market dominance.

IBM's Ambra subsidiary illustrates one form of a virtual company. It leveraged the core competencies of a group of cooperating companies to produce an in-house IBM PC clone. One of Ambra's major advertising themes was the extraordinary custom configurability it offered at no extra cost to the customer. Ambra headquarters were in Raleigh, North Carolina, where 80 employees coordinated activities at five companies that integrated facets of their overall operations in order to create, produce, market, distribute, and service Ambra computers.

Singapore-based Wearnes Technology provided engineering design services and subsystem development as necessary, and it either manufactured or contracted for the components needed to assemble Ambra PCs. SCI Systems manufactured the PCs from these components in its assembly plants on a strictly build-to-order basis, receiving digital customer order data from AI Incorporated. AI, a subsidiary of national telemarketing company Insight Direct, handled all Ambra orders through 800-number telephone lines. Its operators could respond to almost any customer request for computer system configurations with precise price and delivery quotations, because they had access to the vast catalog of third-party software and hardware supported by Merisel Enterprises, which handled Ambra order fulfillment as well as customer delivery. Finally, another IBM subsidiary handled field service and customer support.

To broaden its user base, CompuServe prepares and distributes to interested companies detailed technical specifications of its proprietary software and hardware so that they can more easily develop products that provide access to CompuServe's on-line information services. For example, Motorola, working with General Magic and River Run software, was able to incorporate into its Envoy handheld wireless communicator simple, automated access via CompuServe to E-mail functions, stock and financial market data, and news.

Xerox Corporation's Open Document Service depends for its success on the willingness of many other companies to observe the information exchange standard of its core software, DocuSP. Xerox's strategy in releasing this product, which allows remotely distributed printers and computers to be linked in a way that is both hardware- and software-independent, required creating a broad alliance. Xerox succeeded in signing agreements of support with more than 50 companies (including AT&T, Adobe Systems, Sun, Novell, R. R. Donnelley, Andersen Consulting, and Ernst and Young) in advance of the announcement of the product. Similar consortia dominate the developing markets for interactive video products and telecommunication services.

Sematech is a pioneering effort by U.S. companies to develop new infrastructure technologies collaboratively, independent of product applications and marketplace competition. It was stimulated by national security concerns over the reliance on foreign manufacturers for state-of-the-art computer chips. Sematech was bankrolled for five years at $200 million per year on a dollar-for-dollar matching basis by industry and Congress, which also legislated its legitimacy. After a difficult adjustment to the requirements of sharing people and proprietary knowledge, Sematech has begun to fulfill its promise of restoring competitive advanced chip-making capabilities to U.S. companies.

Large companies are not the only beneficiaries of cooperation. Networks of small companies are an increasingly popular strategy for competing in rapidly changing markets or for adding value to the supplier needs of large agile competitors. Since 1991 scores of such networks have been formed in the United States. The Kentucky Wood Manufacturers Network, Inc. makes it possible for its members, no one of which employs more than 40 workers, to pool their production resources. As a result, four firms won a Disney World contract for $2.5 million worth of wood products; they divided the design, manufacture, and assembly operations on the basis of their respective core competencies.

Indiana's cross-industry FlexCell Group makes it possible for member companies to form limited-lifetime, vertically integrated production capabilities, in effect, to form "pocket" virtual companies. In one case, a manufacturer of metalworking patterns and tools, a mechanical engineering firm, a producer of plastic injection molds and tools, a prototype machine shop, and a contract machine shop were able to work together to satisfy a contract that no one of them could have satisfied on its own.

With federal funding, a network of northeastern Pennsylvania machine shops called *AgileWeb* has been established. The goal is a coordinated, electronically integrated, competitive alliance of small shops capable of opportunistic exploitation of synthesized economies of scale and scope. The shops can continue to compete with one another for small-scale business, if they choose to do so, but they can also create appropriate mix-and-match combinations of shops to bid on large-scale contracts.

U.K. Fine Chemicals is an umbrella organization for ten British fine chemicals manufacturers. Direct competitors most of the time, the ten companies have formed an innovative joint marketing effort. They have been traveling across the United States, marketing themselves to U.S. chemical companies as a virtual single company, prepared to configure their collective expertise in whatever ways an application might require. As far as customers are concerned, they deal with a single supplier entity. With a contract in hand, the U.K. Fine Chemicals member companies distribute the work to be done in accordance with their competencies and prior agreements.

Distribution Infrastructures for Mass Customization

The competitive value to producers of goods and services of actively engaging their customers in the production process, and their growing ability to do so, threatens mass-production-era advertising, media, and distribution infrastructures. Mass production entailed mass consumption and thus the creation of distribution infrastructures and forms of wholesaling and retailing products that had no place in a craft production–driven system of competition. The most famous of these infrastructures, perhaps, was the department store, but mass-circulation daily newspapers and national radio and TV networks are just as much an expression of mass-production distribution requirements as department stores are. The distinguishing motif of the mass-market distribution infrastructure, in whatever form, was its appeal to average, or typical, customers.

Agile competition rests on individualized products and interactive customer relationships. Inevitably, product distribution mechanisms are emerging (among them, direct marketing by producers of goods and services) that reflect the characteristics of individual customer-centered production. These mechanisms link producer and consumer more interactively than mass-market stores did. Mass-market stores provided relatively passive shopping experiences. Customers sought out the ready-made item that came closest to satisfying their needs or desires. By contrast, people who had the financial means played a far more active role in the production by specialty shops of the custom-made, craft-produced, goods, and in the provision of the services, they required.

Agile-era shopping will incorporate many of the features of premium-priced, premium-product, customized merchandising of goods and services. There may be direct connections between producers and consumers, for example, when the producer does its own marketing and sales. New service opportunities are opening up for adding value for customers by helping them define what it is they want—telemarketing; cable TV shopping channels and computer network shopping services; car buying services; "boutique" banks (and one day perhaps car dealerships) in supermarkets, department stores, and within company, government, and college or university buildings; and two-way or interactive media.

In 1993 Americans bought $60 billion worth of goods through direct-marketing channels. This amounted to just under 3 percent of retail sales, but all signs point to dramatic increases ahead as people become increasingly familiar with the experience, the techniques, and the technologies. It is not long since no-frills "warehouse" retailing went from being an oddity to a $33 billion dollar a year business! Home Depot alone accounted for more than 20 percent of that total in 1993.

Compu-U-Card International operates a range of home shopping services that have more than 30 million subscribers who in 1993 paid more than $800 million in membership fees for unlimited 800-number access to the company's database of 250,000 products. Subscribers can use the information they obtain as a convenient form of comparison shopping, or they can place an order that CUC relays to vendors for home delivery to the shopper at the best discount prices.

Corporate Reorganization Frenzy

Because of the intense competitive pressure they experienced during the 1980s, American companies began implementing a wide range of initiatives in order to improve profitability, stem the loss of market share in established markets, and achieve competitive advantage in emerging markets. These initiatives included statistical process control, just-in-time logistics, flexible manufacturing, computer-integrated manufacturing, learning organizations, cross-functional teaming, concurrent engineering, enterprise integration, flatter managerial hierarchies, disaggregation, work force empowerment, continuous improvement, total quality management, reinventing the company, reengineering, quality function deployment, manufacturing resource planning, and so on.

All these initiatives were relevant responses to the marketplace challenges companies were confronting. Although relevant, however, they were, separately or together, only means. They did not include the ends for the sake of which companies needed to implement them. Ends need to be supplied by management independent of the change processes called for by these initiatives.

In addition to obvious cost-cutting measures—reducing the blue- and the white-collar work force, pressuring suppliers for lower prices, reducing the rate of wage increases, and installing new technologies to improve the efficiency of operations—companies have introduced a number of programs that are altering traditional managerial relationships. These programs are also altering the flow of compartmentalized command and control that was characteristic of the mass-production-era corporation.

Achieving the kinds of productivity improvements promised by total quality management, continuous improvement, and benchmarking required motivating personnel to take independent initiative and to challenge established procedures. Three kinds of initiatives are of particular importance for pushing companies toward agile business capabilities:

1. Distributing decision-making authority, often called *empowerment*
2. Enterprise integration
3. Concurrent operations

The novelty has worn off the concept of organizing a company's operational work force into empowered cross-functional teams. Large and small companies are making a commitment to the concept. In the process, they are discovering the collateral organizational implications of this transformation and learning the requirements for implementing it in their settings so as to realize the benefits it promises. Distributing decision-making authority to operational personnel, flattening the managerial hierarchy, creating an open internal information environment, increasing investing in continuous education and training for all personnel, and making customer service and sales everyone's responsibility are correlated initiatives. Companies are learning that all these initiatives must be implemented, and in a coordinated way, if the impact of any of them is to be lasting.

Over an 18-month period, Texas Instruments' Defense Systems and Electronics Group moved from 26,000 employees, seven levels of management, and $2 billion in revenues to 13,500 employees, every one of whom was in a cross-functional team, supervised by four levels of management while maintaining the same level of revenues and significantly improving earnings.

After the merger of Asea and Brown Boveri, CEO Percy Barnevik fractured the combined companies into more than 1300 quasi-independent business units and 5000 profit centers. At the same time, he cut the combined headquarters staffs from 4000 to 200!

Corning Glass operates as if it were a collection of hundreds of 10- to 15-person microcompanies, each making contracts, buying supplies, producing products, and finding internal and/or external customers.

Gould Precision Optics is a seven-employee, family-owned New York State business in which everyone is cross-trained in everyone else's job, the company's books are open to all for a monthly review, and everyone has a clearly understood stake in the company's competitiveness.

TRW's Auburn, New York, plant, a unionized facility, manufactures keyless remote-entry systems for automobiles. In four years, the company has grown from $40 million in revenues to $120 million and employment has more than doubled in spite of intensive automation. Sony two-arm robots assemble transmitters in 4.4 seconds, 24 hours a day, 6 days a week (1 day is reserved for service and maintenance). The union accepted the automation as necessary for competitiveness and has also accepted, for the first time, a deferred compensation agreement for a portion of wages.

For its part, management has implemented full-time best practice teams, made up of union and management personnel, that roam the plant, benchmarking operations and looking for ways to improve them. It maintains an open information "wall," modeled after Ford's, that contains weekly updates on such data as the company's profits, return on assets, inventory, delivery times, and so on. It also provides training to help employees understand a corporate balance sheet. TRW's keyless entry system is an industry-leading product, but its contracts with auto makers mandate 12 percent annual price reductions. The open information environment creates a sense of urgency among management and labor to improve productivity and develop a new generation of products even while the current product is still extremely profitable.

The concept of teams is hardly new. What is new is the undermining of traditional notions of managerial prerogatives—control, privileged access to information, decision-making authority—that follows when teams are made the norm for organizing personnel rather than being used as a way to handle special projects or solve crises. Lockheed Aircraft's "Skunk Works" has an extraordinary 50-year record of achievement in special projects for the U.S. Department of Defense, but it remains a special-projects effort. When activated, the Skunk Works has repeatedly displayed the kinds of capabilities described here as agile—rapid product development, interenterprise cooperation, leveraging resources within Lockheed and among partnering companies, leveraging knowledge and the impact of people on the project's goals, and accomplishing bold goals. But this type of team remains the exception, even within Lockheed, not the norm for company operations.

The positive impact of teaming on a company's organization and management is fully experienced only when teaming is made comprehensive across the company and coordinated with the delegation of decision-making to operational personnel and the flattening of the managerial hierarchy. Teams need to be cross-functional, have a common goal, and be supported by an open information environment and expanded education and training programs.

The cost of information continues to decrease, and the value of information to productivity improvement, and as a product in its own right, continues to increase. It is hardly surprising, then, that companies are creating seamless information-exchange environments, internally and with suppliers and collaborators. Companies are discovering that integrating the functionally separated divisions of a company, and thereby overcoming the linear business processes that this separation encourages, pays big dividends.

Michael Hammer has made the stories of concurrency in Kodak's development of the single-use camera and of the reform of IBM's credit operations familiar to business audiences. A 1992 Agile Manufacturing Enterprise Forum (AMEF) field study of new product development successes at 11 companies revealed a unanimous judgment that concurrent development was the decisive determinant of those successes. Once called *concurrent engineering,* concurrency now extends to everything that is relevant—an integration of design, engineering, manufacturing, purchasing, production scheduling, finance, marketing, supplier relations, and postsale customer service and support.

Companies are increasingly requiring electronic data interchange (EDI) capabilities from their suppliers. The steady growth of PDES, Inc., commercializing a Product Description Exchange Standard promoted by the National Institute of Standards and Technology, is symptomatic of the recognition of how vital digital three-dimensional product description standards are if interenterprise integration and routine virtual manufacturing capabilities are to become a reality.

The size of the investments being made in multimedia hardware and software networking technologies make evident the vision that industry holds of its future. The goal is networks that make it possible for people who are distributed worldwide to work together on the same files with simultaneous real-time audio and "video-in-a-window" images of the participants. Robust groupware is being rushed through development. Desktop hardware is rapidly becoming a commodity, as Macintosh, PC, and low-end workstations are offered, at very small price premiums, with microphones and video cameras built into the keyboard and monitor cases. Network speed and bandwidth are already a reality, and access is growing.

Pressure to Internalize Prevailing Social Values

Competitive pressures, such as the ones described above, that have a direct impact on a company's bottom line are "pulling" a transformation of business practices. At the same time, societal pressures are "pushing" business practices in the same direction. Environmental concerns are the most obvious and the most insistent source of pressure—air, water, and land pollution; the use, transportation, and disposal of toxic and hazardous substances; and atmospheric ozone depletion and global warming.

Energy concerns, natural resource depletion and recycling, workplace safety, work force diversity, quality of work life, and the community impacts of commercial operations are sources of pressure second only to environmental concerns.

Finally, there are the economic corollaries of business change—pressure on companies to accept significant responsibility for job loss and job creation, for regional economic development, and for work force training.

The pressures for change flowing from these sources take several forms. There are the traditional forms, for example, regulation by federal, state, and local governments, legislation, and litigation. But there is also a new form, namely, pressure on companies to assimilate prevailing commerce-related societal values into their internal decision-making processes. The public is, in effect, pressuring companies to be their own watchdogs, in principle obviating the need for regulation, legislation, and litigation. The elimination of external watchdogs is the carrot; the intensification of protests, litigation, and regulation, the stick.

At the federal level, the Environmental Protection Agency, the Food and Drug Administration, the Occupational Safety and Health Administration, the National Highway Safety and Transportation Agency, and the Department of Labor pose a formidable challenge to industry. Beneath superficial differences, however, it is a challenge very similar to the one posed at the turn of the century by antitrust legislation and the creation of such agencies as the Interstate Commerce Commission, the Federal Trade Commission, and the Federal Power Commission. In both cases, governmental action reflects deep societal fears of abuses of economic power by industry and a belief that corporate behavior can be shaped from the outside by threats and punishment.

The marketplace pressures that are pulling the emergence of agile competition are simultaneously creating a very different climate of interaction between social and commercial institutions. Like mass-production-based competition, agile competition is neither philanthropic nor virtuous. Unlike mass-production competition, however, it *is* inherently conscious of, and sensitive to, the social context of its operations. The mind-set of sensitivity to the values of current and potential customers, for example, is part and parcel of being an agile competitor. On quite pragmatic grounds, then, such a mind-set mandates a relationship with the communities in which a company operates that reflects a commitment to integrity in dealing with those communities and to respect for their values. Agile competitors thus find it in their own best interest to unlearn the inherent insensitivity and reactive posture of mass-production competition toward prevailing social values.

Management of an agile organization is most effective, therefore, if it incorporates into its ethic a proactive posture toward operations-relevant societal values. These values will be assimilated into decision-making processes companywide and at all levels, automatically shaping socially responsible behavior, and doing so nonadversarially.

WHAT IS AGILITY?—REVISITED

The ability of producers of goods and services to thrive in rapidly changing, fragmented markets—in other words, the ability to be agile—is not simply a matter of technology *or* of organization structure *or* of personnel utilization. Furthermore, no one feature of agility, taken by itself, is an innovation unique to it. For years, customer-centered companies serving rapidly changing, fragmenting markets have been attempting to push beyond the increasingly manifest limitations of the mass-production system. They have been very slow, however, to appreciate how fundamental are the differences between traditional mass-production markets, that is, mass markets for uniform products, and high-volume niche markets for individualized products. This difference is particularly marked when the primary value of physical products to the customer is their delivery of services or access to information.

The ability of companies to fragment markets, to build to order in arbitrary lot sizes, to widen their product ranges and change models frequently, to customize mass-market products, and to market information has undermined the competitiveness of the mass-production system. The acquisition of these abilities is an expression of industry "backing into" agility, unwittingly.

The vision of agility that has been developing during the past three years, on the other hand, is that of a deliberate, comprehensive response to the constantly changing requirements for competitive success in current and emerging markets. As a comprehensive system, agility defines a new paradigm for doing business. It reflects a new mind-set about making, selling, and buying, an openness to new forms of commercial relationships and new measures for assessing the performance of companies and people.

Working Definition of Agility

Agility is dynamic, context-specific, aggressively change-embracing, and growth-oriented. It is *not* about improving efficiency, cutting costs, or battening down the business hatches to ride out fearsome competitive "storms." It is about succeeding and about winning: about succeeding in emerging competitive arenas, and about winning profits, market share, and customers in the very center of the competitive storms many companies now fear.

Agility is dynamic and open-ended. There is no point at which a company or an individual has completed the journey to agility. Being agile demands constant attention to personal and organizational performance, attention to the value of products and services, and attention to the constantly changing *contexts* of customer opportunities. Agility entails a continual readiness to change, sometimes to change radically, what companies and people do and how they do it. Agile companies and agile people are always ready to learn whatever new things they need to know in order to profit from new opportunities.

Agility is context-specific. Markets pull the acquisition of agile business capabilities, and differences among markets limit the generalizability of detailed rules for becoming agile. In the end, the transition to agility is justified by the promise of sharing in highly profitable markets for information- and service-rich products configured to the requirements of individual customers. The profitability of these products rests on marketing and pricing strategies based on customer-perceived value, as will be discussed and illustrated in the following pages. Successful agile competitors, therefore, not only understand their *current* markets, product lines, competencies, and customers very well, they also understand the potential for *future* customers and markets. This understanding leads to strategic plans to acquire new competencies, develop new product lines, and open up new markets. As a result, the implications of agile competition are highly dependent on the competitive contexts within which individual companies operate.

Agile companies aggressively embrace change. For agile competitors—people as well as companies—change and uncertainty are self-renewing sources of opportunities out of which to fashion continuing success. Thus, to an unprecedented degree, agility is dependent on the initiative of people and on their skills, knowledge, and access to information. An agile organization is one whose organizational structures and administrative processes enable fast and fluid translations of this initiative into customer-enriching business activities.

Agility is aggressive in *creating* opportunities for profit and growth. Agile competitors *precipitate* change, creating new markets and new customers out of their understanding of the directions in which markets and customer requirements are evolving. Although agility allows a company to react much more quickly than in the past, the strength of an agile company lies in proactively anticipating customer requirements and leading the emergence of new markets through constant innovation.

Agility is a comprehensive response to a new competitive environment shaped by forces that have undermined the dominance of the mass-production system. Chapter 2 puts these forces into their social and historical context in order to explain why *agility* has emerged as the successor to mass production and why the strategic principles of agile competition that we describe in Chapter 3 are indeed the correct ones for companies to adopt.

2

The Emergence of a New Industrial Order

During the era of mass-production-based competition, the center of adding commercial value lay in manufacturing products. The terms *production* and *manufacturing* were, in fact, effectively synonymous. Similarly, a *product* meant something physical, a piece of hardware that did something. Services were very different kinds of things because they were personal and intangible, and so were placed in a category of their own. Information was not, even by extension, a product; it was a raw material used by producers of goods and by providers of services in the course of doing their work.

A New View of Production

A sign of the transition to a new era of competition is the widespread recognition that production is of much greater scope than manufacturing and that services and packaged information are also products, in spite of their intangibility. Today, *production* means everything it takes to create and distribute products, which with increasing frequency take the form of variable combinations of hardware, services, and information.

This implies that design is integral to the production process. But so are purchasing, inventory management, marketing, finance, accounting, sales, legal affairs, aftersale service and customer support, and supplier and customer relations, along with manufacturing. Conversely, the wider production process is also integral to each of these activities. No activity can be performed well without taking into account its contribution to the total spectrum of interrelated production processes.

The acceptance of a new interpretation of production is not the result of an intellectual breakthrough. It is a *fact* that, in the marketplace, the center of product value has shifted from manufacturing toward services and information. Inevitably, we find ourselves thinking differently about production and about the role of manufacturing in production, about products, and about services and information as products in their own right.

An *agile company* is one that has fully assimilated the new understanding of production and the implications of the shift in value toward information and service products. Such a company is thus able to pursue two concurrent marketing and product development strategies: the proactive creation of new customer opportunities, and a rapid reaction to unanticipated opportunities. To implement these strategies, a company must be able to develop new products much more quickly, at much lower cost, than it has done historically for its markets; and the products must provide high customer-perceived value through individualization.

For agile competitors, the ability to individualize products comes at little or no increase in manufacturing cost. It does, however, exact a cost: It requires major changes in organization, management philosophy, and operations. These changes include new personnel utilization and evaluation policies and new approaches to interenterprise cooperation. It may also require substantial investment in enabling technologies for manufacturing, information processing, and communications. It will certainly entail higher costs for work force education and training.

Inevitably, the question arises, what was wrong with mass production? Who, or what, undermined the viability of a system that had defined competitiveness for well over 100 years?

Agility in Context

We have lived so long with the mass-production system and with the forms of industrial competition adapted to it that we take them for granted. They seem part of the natural order, as do the metrics—the financial and management accounting metrics, for example—that we use to evaluate their performance. Typically, these metrics were one-dimensionally price centered. They reflected a market environment in which:

Lowest unit cost was the decisive determinant of competitiveness.
Efficiency was a function of direct inputs—the cost of materials, labor, and manufacturing processes.
Product value was fixed in the form of standardized pricing.
Sales took the form of single-instance transactions in which individual customers were relatively undifferentiated.

Agile competition metrics, by contrast, are multidimensional. They incorporate variable pricing strategies, reflecting the differential value provided for individual customers. In the course of an extended relationship, the physical, information, and service value dimensions of the original purchase will have changed substantially. Companies will therefore have unpredictable opportunities to add value for existing customers in new ways, even as they attract new customers, in part *because of* their ability to continue adding value for old ones. That is, what customers will increasingly value in a company is its ability to create, *and to continue creating,* mutually beneficial relationships with them.

It is not only producers who are unsettled by an environment of constant and unpredictable change. For customers, too, forming relationships that provide some shelter from constant change is valuable.

It becomes a strong justification for choosing one company's products over another, not so much because of the characteristics of the products as because of the character of the company.

The fact that agile competition entails displacing—at least from their position of dominance—activities, definitions, and performance metrics sanctioned by the weight of history may weigh against taking agile competition as seriously as it needs to be taken. But forms of industrial competition, *and* their performance metrics, are historical phenomena. As Robert S. Kaplan and H. Thomas Johnson have described in their book *Relevance Lost,* and as Johnson has illustrated more recently in his *Relevance Regained,* today's accounting metrics are recent additions to the counting room. They were invented to deal with the managerial requirements of late-nineteenth- and early-twentieth-century mass-production manufacturing enterprises. The identification and segregation in these systems of direct and indirect costs, for example, and their assignments to a company's various products and business processes, involve a chain of arbitrary assumptions. These assumptions were functional in the context of mass-production competition, but they have become increasingly dysfunctional since the 1970s.

It is useful, therefore, to place agile competition in historical perspective, the better to appreciate its character as a new production system, one that heralds the rise of a new industrial order, and with it a redefinition of the parameters of good business practices.

The emergence of agile production marks the onset of the fifth form that commercial competition has taken in Western societies since the Middle Ages. For each form of competition, there developed over a period of time a mutually coordinated set of production technologies, business practices, markets, and supportive social institutions. Each transition from one form of competition to another is characterized by changing markets and changing technologies, as well as by changes in social institutions and business practices. Which of these is cause and which is effect is open to debate, but it is unquestionable that they are inseparably intertwined. No one of them ever changes without the others changing as well, and in coordinated ways.

1. **The guilds.** The first form that industrial competition took in Western Europe was linked to guild-controlled production of goods. The craft guilds began their rise to dominance in the twelfth century. A sharp increase in agricultural productivity and in population surely had something to do with this, as did the explosive spread of water- and wind-powered machinery. William the Conqueror's survey of his new English domain found over 3000 water-powered mills in the late eleventh century. Life in western Europe at this time was marked by increasing urbanization, heightened industrial activity, and the expansion of local commerce and long-distance trade.

The craft guilds exercised their control, which varied considerably in effectiveness from one as yet weakly defined "country" to another, with the help of various social, legal, and economic institutions:

> The newly created universities, which spread literacy and numeracy, producing clerks for merchants, bureaucrats for the embryonic nation-states that were forming, and lawyers who expanded the scope of civil and commercial law
>
> Alliances among widely dispersed merchants, for example, the Hanseatic League traders in northern Europe; Venice's network of exotic partnerships that brought luxury goods (spices and silks) to Europe from Arabia, China, and India; and many alliances that crisscrossed the Mediterranean involving Christian, Jewish, and Muslim merchants
>
> Central governments, which regulated commercial activity
>
> Double-entry bookkeeping (borrowed from Muslim merchants) and (fragile) international banking services
>
> Liberalized attitudes toward lending money at interest
>
> Intensive technological innovation and the beginnings of standardized production, for example, of ships in the Venetian arsenal

2. **Mercantilism.** Slowly, production began to elude guild control. Beginning in the sixteenth century, as commerce with nonlocal markets

grew, and as cities continued to grow in size—perhaps, too, as a result of the depopulation and labor shortages caused by the Black Plague—guild-based industrial competition gave way to more open competition among entrepreneur craftspeople. Competition based on entrepreneurial craft production steadily displaced the guilds during the course of the seventeenth and eighteenth centuries. The entrepreneurs acquiesced in some of the guild-era institutions and values, for example, the master-journeyman-apprentice hierarchy, while agitating for the establishment of other institutions that would better serve their needs.

This was the onset of the age of mercantilism, in which, paradoxically, lie the roots of both protectionist and of free-trade policies. Fragile medieval banking services were replaced by robust financial, investment, and insurance services, both local and international; checks, drafts on foreign banks, stocks, and negotiable securities all existed. Use of the earlier invention of the commercial corporation as a "fictitious person" that could engage in business activities on behalf of "real people" who were thereby sheltered from many liabilities expanded. The scale of industry and commerce increased dramatically as western European nations became global powers. Modern technology and modern science arose in the sixteenth and seventeenth centuries, respectively, and began their long, complex relationships with industry and the state.

3. The factories. During the eighteenth century, entrepreneurial factory-based production began to challenge the dominance (though, of course, not the continued practice) of craft-based production. With the introduction of mass-production machinery and increasingly effective steam power in the late eighteenth and early nineteenth centuries, the dominant form of industrial competition shifted from craft production to factory-based industrial production. Again, social, political, legal, and economic values and institutions changed in ways that protected and reinforced the emerging forms of production, distribution, and consumption—above all, of consumption.

4. The modern corporation. Near the close of the nineteenth century, with the craft production tradition rapidly becoming marginal, entrepreneurial factory-based production was challenged by the rise of the modern industrial corporation. New forms of competition were made possible by the integration of improved versions of existing production, power, communication, and transportation technologies into this new organizational invention. The results were truly spectacular. The history of the twentieth century, in every one of its facets, is entwined with the domestic and global adventures of these corporations, their competition for markets, and their pursuit of profit.

The goal of the modern industrial corporation was to do business in a new way, one that promised, and delivered, dramatic competitive advantage. Companies that were reorganized or were newly created to exploit the economies of scale made possible by vertical integration, central administration, and hierarchical organization became the economic, political, and social power centers of the twentieth century. The model was provided by the Swift Meat Packing Company, Standard Oil of New Jersey, U.S. Steel, General Electric, Dupont, and the Ford Motor Company.

Many of these new companies added economies of scope to vertical integration and economies of scale. They recognized that they could use existing resources to compete in new markets at little additional expense. Dupont, a good example, expanded from gunpowder to chemicals to synthetic fibers. So, too, were the German chemical companies that moved to exploit the invention of synthetic dyestuffs and then recognized that their research and production capabilities would support their entering the pharmaceutical and photographic chemicals markets.

The competitive advantages achieved by these companies came, not from new technologies per se, but from the systematic *coordination* of production, marketing, and distribution. This coordination, in turn, was made possible by rapidly maturing technologies of communication, transportation, and mass-production manufacturing.

Refined after World War II by such lean manufacturing techniques as statistical quality control and just-in-time inventory management, mass-production-based industrial competition has today become allied to new information, communication, and computer-controlled production technologies. In the process, it has created global markets for customized goods and services that cannot be served effectively by industrial corporations organized under the mass-production-system paradigm. The challenge to the dominance that these corporations have enjoyed for over a hundred years comes from the ability of agile companies to engage in new forms of industrial competition.

The Inertia of the Mass Production Corporation

A market environment of continual, rapid, and unpredictable change is the seedbed of agile competition. In the mid-nineteenth century, however, an environment like this led Karl Marx to prophesy the imminent demise of industrial capitalism. Indeed, modern commercial and industrial corporations were invented to suppress just this kind of competition. Today, such change is rapidly becoming the global norm, and it is occurring most rapidly in the markets for the most profitable products.

The modern corporation was invented to exploit competitive possibilities that were unavailable to individual owners, even of factories equipped with mass-production technologies. It was spectacularly successful, providing its management with large quantities of capital at low personal risk. The modern corporation overwhelmed both craft production and entrepreneur-owned mass-production factories. It redefined the terms of industrial competition through a distinctive synthesis of existing technologies and a novel corporate organizational structure—vertically integrated, hierarchically organized, and centrally administered. The competitive power of this organizational invention, supported by novel financing mechanisms that funded large-scale implementations of state-of-the-art communication, transportation, and production equipment, was enormous. Even after the introduction of antitrust legislation in the United States in the 1890s, the modern industrial corporation succeeded in stabilizing markets and limiting the ferocity of competition at a time of intensive technological innovation.

This stabilization was accomplished by the emergence of a small number of dominant producers, typically five or fewer, whose scale of operations anchored the stability of the markets in which they competed. These producers achieved their market position and prosperity by exploiting newly acquired economies of scale and of scope, together with new marketing strategies made possible by these economies. But the time scale of the market changes to which these new industrial corporations and their service sector analogues could profitably respond is far longer than the realities of today's and tomorrow's markets will allow. That time scale is set in part by the technologies available to competitors, in part by organizational structure and managerial philosophy, and in part by the roles assigned to their human resources.

In the mass-production system, all these factors pointed in the same direction: to long production runs of uniform products built to market forecast by passive workers organized into companies with centralized authority.

In the agile competitive environment these factors point in a very different direction: to short lifetimes for highly differentiated products created and produced by an active, highly motivated work force organized into companies that have widely distributed authority.

Large-scale operations and vertical integration promised dramatic economies and high profits. They delivered on those promises often enough to define the conventional wisdom of twentieth-century corporate management. To reap those profits, however, it was first necessary to recover the high investment costs and the high operating costs of large, dedicated production lines filled with inflexible, special-purpose equipment operated by a vast, passive, operational work force commanded by an army of middle managers. This recovery was accomplished by means of long, high-volume production runs of uniform (indeed, if possible, of identical) products. The "beauty" of the annual (cosmetic) model change, for example, introduced into the auto industry by General Motors CEO Alfred Sloan in 1925, was that it provided an illusion of change that could be exploited by the design, marketing, and sales departments. In spite of the restyling of bumpers, interior fabrics, or dashboard elements, the production lines remained unchanged for as long as possible.

One corollary of being dependent for profitability upon long production runs of uniform products was that production was based on mass-marketing forecasts. A second corollary was long product development times. No purpose would be served by investing in rapid development of new products that could not profitably be put into production as quickly as they became available. For similar reasons, the requirement of long production runs for profitability under mass-production-based industrial competition limited the number of truly different models of its products that a company could offer.

It made no sense to forgo the large profits latent in producing for mass markets and to use the same facilities and incur the same overhead and operating costs for shorter runs of products tailored to the requirements, or the desires, of niche markets. Niche customers, commercial and consumer alike, either had to adapt uniform, mass-market products to their particular requirements or had to shape their requirements to match the capabilities of available mass-market products. If they had the wherewithal, of course, they could pay very high prices for goods and services custom-produced to satisfy their individual needs.

Unraveling the Mass Production Corporation

During the 1980s the principles that had guided the profitable operation of modern industrial corporations for 100 years began to unravel. On the one hand, the mass-production system had become so robust that it could be implemented almost anywhere in the world where raw materials, labor, market access, or transportation costs yielded comparative advantage. As a result, it became increasingly difficult to earn large enough profits from mass-production-based operations located in "first-world" countries to offset the high operating costs, and to pay wages consistent with the quality of life expectations of workers, in those countries.

On the other hand, the guiding principles of the modern industrial corporation were undone by the capability of more and more companies to operate profitably with shorter production runs, to build to customer order instead of to marketing forecasts, and to achieve dramatic reductions in new product development time. These capabilities were made possible in part by the introduction of more flexible, eventually more automated, computer-controlled production machinery. In part, they were also made possible by the refinements of mass-production manufacturing that were pioneered at Toyota's automotive plants and that came to be known as *lean manufacturing.*

These refinements, introduced by Toyota, were quickly adopted by Japanese manufacturers in all industries. They were developed for practical, not theoretical, reasons. They were needed to overcome financial and technological constraints that precluded simply replicating U.S. manufacturing facilities. Japanese industrialists did not begin with a plan to leapfrog mass-production-based competition or with a vision of agile manufacturing as the core of a new, more profitable production system. To compete at all with U.S. producers, Toyota, for example, had to be capable of producing mass-market automobiles more efficiently and with much lower overhead costs.

The refinements Japanese manufacturers introduced to accomplish this—statistical process control, just-in-time logistics, empowered work teams, more flexible manufacturing processes and faster change-over times, total quality management, and continuous improvement— certainly improved the efficiency of mass-production manufacturing.

What undermined the rules governing the organization, management, and operation of the modern industrial corporation, however, was the decision not to reduce the unit costs of uniform mass-market products but instead to couple the refinements to a new marketing strategy—to offer a wider range of shorter-lifetime products and models aimed at smaller markets. Very quickly, as customers responded to this strategy by giving Japanese manufacturers growing market shares, the long production runs and limited product variety that tradition-bound mass-production competitors needed in order to earn a profit became a liability. The leisurely pace of new product development became insupportable.

The first blow that manufacturers, initially Japanese manufacturers, struck at the entrenched mass-production system was the improvement of the *quality* of mass-produced products at no increase in cost to the customer. The second blow, building on the lean manufacturing technologies and management techniques that had improved quality, was to offer customers much greater *choice* at no increase in cost. In market after market, for audio, video, and photographic equipment, for motorcycles, automobiles, and bicycles, for computers and office equipment, Japanese companies won market share, created new markets, and generated large revenues (the profitability of Japanese corporations is an elusive figure even for Japanese tax auditors!). They did this by fragmenting markets, sharply increasing both the number of models of each type of product they offered and the rate at which they introduced new or improved models.

At the same time, they aggressively pursued economies of scope, embedding new technologies in, and using new manufacturing capabilities to create, new kinds of products or to transform existing ones. The manufacture of high-volume, low-cost solar-powered consumer products, for example, calculators, toys, and watches, helped spread the cost of developing photovoltaic cell manufacturing capabilities for more sophisticated applications and both shortened and partly underwrote the costs of the learning curve for commercializing that technology.

The Evolution of Quality

Production is justified by sales. The ability of mass producers of goods and services to target smaller and smaller market niches, and to do so profitably, marked the advent of the era of agile competition. Consumer expectations rapidly shifted from finding *satisfaction* in reliable, uniform products to demanding *gratification* from products and services more closely matched to their personal requirements. Commercial customers began to demand that the goods and services they bought enrich them, by enhancing their ability to create value-added products of their own to sell. In the process, what producers, commercial customers, and consumers alike meant by *quality* evolved.

Until sometime in the 1980s, quality in mass-market products primarily meant reliability, along with a degree of attention to detail in design and materials to which mass-market customers were unaccustomed. Higher quality translated into higher levels of customer satisfaction, which increased market share and drove the first phase of the post–World War II Japanese economic "miracle." Like the shorter production runs, wider and more rapidly changing model varieties, and economies of scope, the added attention to design and materials was made possible by the techniques associated with lean manufacturing. The greater efficiency achieved by the refinement of mass-production processes lowered unit costs. But a bold decision was needed in order to give up some of the higher profits created by increased efficiency and to spend more on design and for materials than was traditional in mass-market products.

Beginning sometime in the mid- to late 1980s, however, reliability began to be taken for granted, and customer satisfaction no longer translated into rising market share. Reliability became the price of admission to markets for high-value-added goods and services. By the 1990s, merely being highly reliable was no longer enough to win new customers. In the words of Chrysler engineer Dennis Renneker, "a Six Sigma Yugo is still a Yugo." Quality began to be identified with choice, with the ability to select from so wide a range of products, models, and options that a mass-market customer could find a close match to his or her individual requirements or desires.

Mass-market customers began to anticipate receiving the kind of gratification from the goods and services they bought that was traditionally associated with custom-made products. In a 1987 book, *Future Perfect,* management consultant Stan Davis foresaw this emerging development, which has been the driving force behind the second phase of Japanese commercial success. He called it *mass customization.* The implications of this development were explored at greater length in a 1993 book of the same name by Joseph Pine.

Today, customer expectations in more and more markets are assimilating choice to the new levels of quality that over the past 20 years have rapidly become the norm for mass-produced, traditionally uniform products. Such products begin to seem less and less uniform as variety increases, apparently without limit. The resulting market fragmentation promises new opportunities for profit. Companies can pursue strategies of further market fragmentation, by multiplying model varieties still further, and by individualizing the packaging of services and information, thereby targeting smaller and smaller groups of customers.

Magazines move from national editions to regional editions to issues custom-printed by ZIP code. *Time,* for example, is incorporating weekly information on congressional voting by district for its subscribers and is supplying preaddressed forms so that subscribers can write to their congressional representatives. AT&T and MCI vie for personalized telephone service packages, between them spending more than $400 million a year on advertising campaigns to increase their share of a global $800 billion a year market for long-distance telephone services. Starbuck Coffee brews each cup to order, flaunting its "10 second pledge": If a shot of espresso is not used within 10 seconds to fill your personal order, it is discarded.

The customer opportunities represented by individualized mass production can be exploited, however, only if production flexibility continues to increase as product development cycles decrease. That is, the cost of flexibility must continue to decrease as new products are introduced more and more rapidly, because the smaller volume of individual products sold still must generate returns capable of paying current overhead costs and funding the next generation of product development.

The new system works because the pricing of customized goods and services becomes a function of customer-perceived value. The same candies, for example, are priced very differently in their different packages, which may be targeted to lunch boxes, movie theater candy counters, and corporate "goody" baskets. The prices are not a function of weight. The fare for one airline seat will vary widely, depending on booking circumstances, and in fact frequent fliers may pay no fare at all.

The principle is simple: With agile competition, the cost of manufacturing goods and delivering services is a dwindling fraction of total production costs. Producers must exploit this situation by investing in the creation of products whose principal value is their value to individual customers. The convergence of goods and services that is characteristic of agile competition further shifts the value added by producers from reliability to customer gratification.

Thus quality has evolved from *reliability,* which created competitive advantage in the 1970s and early 1980s, to *choice* through multiplicity of models and options, which created competitive advantage in the 1980s and early 1990s, to *individualization.* By the early 1990s, the range of choices that companies were offering to their customers had become confusing and even irritating. Today, competitive advantage is created by companies that are capable of shifting the burden of choice from the customer to the vendor. Instead of the customer telling the vendor what he or she wants, the vendor works with the customer to determine the combination of choices that will best serve that customer—and then configures the purchase accordingly. Caterpillar, for example, has installed software that allows customers to describe in English the features they want on the vehicles they order. The tedious task of translating these features into the myriad parts numbers in Caterpillar's catalog, previously performed by customers, now is performed by computers.

The Scope of Agility

The development of commercial organizations from the late eighteenth to the late twentieth centuries was driven primarily by the competitive advantage created by economies of scale. These economies made lowest possible unit costs the premier production virtue. The goal of lowest possible production costs in turn encouraged the design, production, and marketing of uniform products and services.

In the fragmented, niche (but still high-volume) markets created by shorter product life cycles and wider product variety, being the lowest-cost producer is of lesser consequence. The parameters of competitive advantage change decisively, however, in markets for which the economics of production no longer favor a lowest unit cost objective. To respond to the new marketing challenges posed by shorter product development cycles and greater product variety requires far more than simply installing flexible production technologies.

Without long production runs to use as a means of amortizing high sunk costs and underwriting high operating costs, the economic advantages of vertical integration and large-scale operation need to be reexamined. To continue to enjoy these advantages, the implementation of vertical integration and large-scale operation will take a different form from the one that evolved under mass production. Indeed, large vertically integrated companies are today searching for the degree of integration and the scale of operations that are right for them in the era of agile competition. The knee-jerk reaction of downsizing and spinning off divisions is not necessarily right. Smaller is always better than too large, but it is not always obvious how large is too large or how much smaller a company should make itself in order to improve its competitiveness.

One of Louis Gerstner's first moves at IBM was to halt what James Quinn of Dartmouth's Tuck Business School calls the *disaggregation* of IBM. Gerstner seemed to recognize that big can be good even in the context of agile competition, if the size translates into a broader spectrum of capabilities than competing companies have. Other companies, among them Kodak, for example, have identified strategic core competencies, committed new resources to them, and sold off businesses outside those competencies (in Kodak's case, chemicals and pharmaceuticals, among others). Thus Kodak sold its Sterling Winthrop division (except for nonprescription, over-the-counter products) to Sanofi, a health and beauty care products subsidiary of Elf Aquitaine, for more than $1.6 billion. Sanofi promptly split off the medical imaging branch of Sterling Winthrop, an area in which it had no competency, and sold it to the Norwegian firm Halfsund Nykomed, for which imaging is a core business area, for $460 million.

Nevertheless, as product lifetimes become shorter, and faster product development times become a competitive necessity, doing everything within a single company, *even in a core competency area,* is no longer automatically the best way to do things, as it was in the era of mass-production-based competition. It is competitively advantageous to a company if the resources required to exploit a new market opportunity are routinely configurable by operational personnel in coordination with management, regardless of physical location, within their own company or in other companies.

Thus, as United States and western European companies attempted to respond to the Japanese challenge during the 1970s and 1980s, what initially appeared to be Japanese competitive advantages deriving from a bag of superior manufacturing "tricks" turned out to be much more than that. The Japanese advantage was finally understood to be rooted in changes in the way companies, business processes, and work were organized, managed, measured, and supported.

General Motors was one of many companies that learned this lesson painfully. In the early 1980s it invested billions of dollars in "high-tech" production equipment: robots, computer-aided design and manufacturing systems, and computer numerically controlled machine tools. There was little productivity improvement to show for this investment. In GM's joint venture with Toyota, however, the refurbished Fremont, California, NUMMI plant, in which GEO Prizms are assembled and to which Toyota contributed managerial expertise, productivity nearly doubled with little investment in advanced technologies.

Agility and Society

Agility is not solely a matter of production operations, company organization, and marketing strategies. Agility reflects a competitive environment that links producers and customers far more closely than the mass-production environment did. A hostile social environment, whether it is internal or external to a company, precludes agility. A company cannot routinely reconfigure itself to meet changing market opportunities if it must continually fight battles over the environmental and community impact of its products and operations. It cannot achieve a culture of universal accountability and mutual responsibility for the company's success if unresolved workplace health and safety, or work life quality and job security, issues alienate its work force. It cannot routinely collaborate with other companies, sharing information and expertise, if it is not worthy of the trust that intensive collaboration requires.

Looking from the company outward, the ability to reconfigure physical resources and change production processes quickly and routinely presumes a supportive social environment. If a production process change entails public hearings, litigation, and hundreds of permits from local, state, and federal governments, agility fades to a dream.

Looking inward, a company cannot have agile business capabilities if the relationships among its personnel are adversarial. The dynamics of teaming and of team management, of creating a company culture marked by universal responsibility and mutual accountability for success, by universal "thinking like an owner" attitudes, values, and behaviors, demands relationships that reflect trust, respect, and concern. This implies proactive postures toward workplace safety issues, the quality of work life, and work force diversity issues, not a grudgingly reactive posture.

The opportunities for improvements that will benefit everyone are enormous. A U.S. Bureau of Labor Statistics 1991 study revealed that one-third of automobile assemblers suffered a work-related injury or illness, 10 percent of them requiring time off, and that 5 percent suffered from cumulative trauma disorder. The payoff from a small investment in reengineering work processes to emphasize health and safety is great.

Changing Core Competencies

If competitiveness is enhanced by routinely utilizing expertise and facilities distributed among a number of companies, how is job security within a particular company affected? Cooperative production (in the broad, agile sense of the term) is not the same as outsourcing. But it does raise potential conflict with efforts to create relationships of trust and commitment within companies. Similarly, keeping a company focused on changing core competencies can be good for competitiveness but can translate into higher work force displacement.

Until the introduction of the SX-70 camera, Polaroid manufactured only the positive component of its self-developing films; it assembled finished cameras. Every piece of every camera was manufactured for Polaroid by some other company, Timex, for one, and the film chemicals and materials were produced for Polaroid by Kodak. The core competencies that the first-generation Polaroid Corporation needed to maintain were in organic chemistry, mechanical design (of its line of cameras), and some photographic film chemistry and production.

With the SX-70, the company had to acquire a much broader range of product development and production competencies, from camera bodies to film packs. As Polaroid shifts, during the mid-1990s, to a focus on digital photography, it is building new core competencies, away from organic chemistry toward semiconductor device design and manufacture, digital imaging, and computer-related expertise. Kodak, of course, is making a similar transition to digital photography, and the board of directors' commitment to acquiring new core competencies is reflected in the hiring of George Fisher from Motorola to become Kodak's new CEO.

Identifying and prioritizing core competencies and sharing this information with all personnel are ways to maintain integrity and a sense of community. Continuing education and training for all are another means of sustaining work force commitment as core competency assessments and priorities change with changing markets and customer opportunities. Polaroid began offering courses in electronics and computer-related areas to personnel as soon as its management recognized the need to shift to digital photography. Nevertheless, focusing on core competencies has profound job security and job quality implications: downsizing in the near term and, by mass-production-era standards, premature skills obsolescence in the middle and long term.

Proactive Environmentalism

There is growing evidence that manufacturers are recognizing the value of taking the initiative on environmental issues. Today environmentally neutral manufacturing is the objective of growing numbers of U.S. companies, including the members of the Chemical Manufacturers Association (CMA), who account for more than 90 percent of chemical production in the United States. The CMA's Responsible Care program commits its members to meaningful public involvement in siting decisions and to rapid reductions in toxicity levels in wastes as well as in waste volumes.

Increasing numbers of companies are becoming proactive on environmental issues and are working together with leading environmental organizations. A joint effort in this area involves the Grocery Manufacturers Association, the New England Electric System, General Motors, Sun Oil Company, the Audubon Society, the Conservation Law Foundation, the Environmental Defense Fund, the Friends of the Earth, the Natural Resources Defense Council, the World Resources Institute, the Sierra Club, and even Greenpeace.

At Sandia National Laboratories, biodegradable terpenes (from citrus fruit rinds) have replaced toxic chloroethylenes as solvents in circuit board manufacture, and the water wash volume has been reduced by more than 90 percent. At Air Products' South Brunswick, New Jersey, polymer emulsion plant—a facility run almost entirely by operational personnel with managers serving as resources—recycling processes developed by workers have slashed annual sewage treatment costs, increased plant efficiency, and brought about significant annual savings. Saturn Motors routinely runs full-page ads, the theme of which is the environmental sensitivity of the company and its workers, identifying the programs it has established to minimize waste and recycle materials. Chrysler's Neon car brochures highlight the design objectives of "environmental harmony" and "green"-ness: recyclable parts, emissions-free paint coatings, fuel efficiency, and non-CFC refrigerants.

The political power of the European "Green" parties is reflected in increasingly stringent European Community packaging and recycling laws and in rising environmental standards. Spring 1994 elections to the European Community Parliament displayed yet again the broadening base of public support for Green party positions on these issues. In the United States, where there are no such parties, the pressure for reducing the environmental impact of commercial operations is channeled through the political and legal systems.

Ethical Decision-Making

Increasing sensitivity to the value of ethical decision-making reinforces the emergence of an agility-based management philosophy. In 200 of the 1000 largest U.S. corporations the senior management position of corporate ethics officer or senior vice-president for business practices has been created. This reflects a growing acknowledgment that unethical behavior by individuals, especially by managerial personnel, is commonly not a reflection of individual "bad apples" but, rather, a company's culture and the values promoted by that culture. Issuing moral edicts from the board or from the CEO, or denouncing actions that are criminal or that incite public protests, is of little value. It is very well established that individual behavior can be greatly affected by the functional context of that behavior, namely, the dynamics of the environment in which individuals find themselves.

The ethical values of a company must be assimilated into its organizational structure, its managerial philosophy, and above all, into its operational procedures. This is management's job. That there will be a consistent, strictly observed code of company ethics, and what that code will be, must be initiated from the top and expected of everyone from the top down. The existence of such a code of ethics has the perhaps unexpected benefit of liberating the moral instinct that motivates most people and causes them to police their own behavior.

An ethically managed company thus creates a self-reinforcing moral environment in which doing the "right thing" becomes increasingly natural as time goes by. As Lynn Sharp Paine of the Harvard Business School puts it (in the March–April 1994 issue of the *Harvard Business Review*), "ethics has everything to do with management" and a "management-led commitment to ethical values" in companies consistently improves competitiveness, morale, and—vitally for an agile competitor—the strength of relationships with other companies and with customers.

Doing the right thing is especially timely in the current political and competitive environment, for a number of reasons. First, of all, doing the wrong thing, especially doing the wrong thing deliberately, for venal reasons, can be very expensive for companies, quite apart from the morality of the action. Sears' problem with "overzealous" auto service center managers cost the company an estimated $60 million, not counting the intangible (and probably greater) cost of loss of business from the adverse publicity the case generated. Beech-Nut's losses from pleading guilty to knowingly mislabeling its apple juice as "100% pure" were an estimated $25 million (including lost sales). These losses pale by comparison with those suffered by Salomon Brothers and the Johns-Manville Corporation.

Without having violated any law, four senior Salomon executives were forced to resign for not responding in a timely way when they learned of improprieties by Salomon government bond traders. The company incurred losses estimated at nearly $1 billion. Johns-Manville was forced into bankruptcy in 1982, as juries learned of decades of evasion by management of what it had known since the 1930s: that asbestos fibers posed a mortal health hazard at the levels to which many workers were exposed. As a condition of its reorganization, in 1988, the company had to create a settlement fund of $150 million in cash, $1.6 billion in bonds, 80 percent of the company's stock, and 20 percent of its profits from *1992* until all claims were settled!

Bill Sells, at one time the manager of a Johns-Manville asbestos cement pipe plant and later president of its Fiber Glass Group businesses, watched the calamity unfold from the inside. Consistently wrong decisions were buttressed by a culture of denial that pervaded all levels of management in the face of mounting evidence that eventually overwhelmed the company. Sells finally came to believe that the "active acceptance of product and production responsibility" by management, what he now calls *product stewardship,* improves profitability and creates competitive advantage, in both the long and the short term.

Taking charge of fiber glass manufacturing in 1981, Sells successfully applied the lesson he had learned painfully in asbestos manufacturing to the production of yet another mineral fiber product of suspected carcinogenicity. The essence of that lesson was to be scrupulously honest and open in communicating with employees and customers, to communicate fully, and to be proactive on all ethical and health- and safety-related issues. It is not enough to satisfy the letter of the law. It is, Sells argues (*Harvard Business Review*, March–April 1994), necessary to anticipate what those who will bear the burden of a mistaken judgment deserve to know *from their perspective.* The rewards for such a policy are respect and trust, the raw materials of cooperative relationships, as well as sustained profitability. In Chapter 3, the centrality to successful agile competition of cooperative relationships among companies is discussed at length. The ability to form partnerships routinely and quickly, ideally by electronic networking, depends on the ability of people to trust one another across company lines. Ultimately, such trust will be earned through shared experiences. At first, however, it will rest on clearly formulated decision-making policies and value commitments that are motivated by the mutually reinforcing relationships of interdependency that agile competition encourages.

The Social Impact of Agility

Mass-production-based industrial competition profoundly affected a wide range of institutions in all societies that adopted it. Agile manufacturing will have an analogous social influence. Some of the changes that will take place can be foreseen, at least in part because they will be deliberate. Educating a work force capable of excelling in agile work environments, for example, will require fundamental changes in schooling at every level.

Market forces already are at work in the schools, promoting curriculum reform that exposes students to computer technologies, to working in teams, to a problem-oriented rather than to a subject-oriented curriculum, to performance-based testing, to routinely accessing remote information resources, and to acquiring the ability to learn how to learn by using the skills they possess, as opposed to amassing information and parroting it on demand. The top half, perhaps the top two-thirds, of primary and secondary school students will respond to these reforms and eventually enter the work force prepared for some level of participation in the agile workplace. A national effort is needed to prevent the bottom third from becoming a permanently alienated class of unemployable men and women.

To perform well in an agile workplace, people must have strong social and communication skills consistent with the intensely cooperative, team-based environment of agile competition.

Formal schooling provides one approach to credentials, but it is only a start. Personnel at all levels and in all job categories must be open to routinely learning new things and acquiring new skills. They must be willing to think about what they are doing, and they must be capable of coming up with improved ways of doing it. They must be flexible in the face of changing work assignments, they must be capable of participating in electronically networked teams when necessary, and, perhaps most important from management's perspective, they must be responsive to a corporate culture that encourages employees to think like an owner: to share responsibility for the success of the company and to behave in ways that reflect that kind of commitment.

Not everyone can function in this way. What employment opportunities will exist for those who cannot? How will we, as a society, provide the greatest opportunity possible for people to join the agile work force? Should young people in secondary and postsecondary schools, and the current work force as a whole, be educated about the social impact of the transition to agile competition? If so, how and by whom?

If the task seems overwhelming, it is worth recollecting that national compulsory public education was put into place substantially in response to, and in the service of, an economy then newly based on the maturing industrial revolution and the emergence of mass-production competition.

Some of the social changes that the transition to agile manufacturing will cause, including perhaps the most profound, cannot be foreseen. We have learned enough from the industrial revolution and its aftermath to know that, if there is gain in the future, the path to it lies through pain. Since 1990 insurance giant Cigna has reduced its work force by 25 percent, and a hard-pressed IBM has reduced by more than a third its once 400,000 employees. But a flourishing GE has reduced its payroll by more than 200,000 since Jack Welch became CEO. Procter and Gamble has reduced its work force by 12 percent while enjoying rising sales, and hundreds of thousands of jobs have been eliminated in an increasingly profitable U.S. auto industry. To be sure, many jobs have been created as well, at growing medium-size companies, in addition to the small companies that are so often touted as sources of employment. But the pain of unemployment is very real, and the opportunities represented by newly created jobs are often not available to the unemployed, or the new jobs may not offer wages and benefits similar to the ones in the old jobs.

During the past 130 years, since the end of the Civil War, the percentage of the U.S. work force employed in agriculture has plummeted from perhaps 50 percent to under 3 percent. Even this small figure is inflated by government programs that undermine market forces: 85 percent of U.S. agricultural output is generated by only 15 percent of the farmers, and even that amount exceeds domestic demand.

The extraordinary productivity of the agricultural sector of the U.S. economy is a major factor in the high quality of life enjoyed by the great majority of U.S. citizens. Americans spend a smaller fraction of their incomes on food than do the citizens of any developed nation. But although direct farm employment is negligible, the total number of people employed in the food industry as a whole is very large. Shipping, processing, research and development, regulation, inspection, packaging, production, distribution, marketing, advertising, merchandising, preparation, and wholesale and retail sales all offer apparently endless opportunities for employment and growth.

The substitution of anthracite coal for charcoal in early-nineteenth-century iron making caused many people who earned their living logging, hauling, and reducing trees to charcoal to lose their jobs. The expansion of the iron and coal mining industries, however, created many more jobs, and the need for iron rails for the new railroads created many more jobs still, as did the expansion of commerce that the railroads caused.

When steel replaced iron, and bituminous coal replaced anthracite, when the railroads replaced the canals, when automobiles replaced horse-drawn vehicles, and when diesel-engined buses and trucks took passengers and freight away from the railroads, displacements occurred that were traumatic for many people even as they offered opportunities for many others. As new technologies increase the efficiency with which goods and services can be produced, there is again a painful contraction of employment for many, especially for those directly employed in large-scale production processes. Fewer people are going to be needed to manage agile companies and to operate these processes.

At the same time, there is a growing need for design services, for research and development, for integration services, for customizing modules and components, for information services and information products, for marketing and customer support services, for new kinds of distribution channels. As a result, there will inevitably be a great deal of anguish as companies of all sizes struggle to find the right size to be successful agile competitors.

The transition to agility will, if history is a reliable guide, create many more, and eventually better-quality, jobs than will be lost. In many cases, these jobs will not be open to people who have lost mass-production jobs. The personal and social cost of the transition will be high, but the competitive challenge that industry confronts today implicates the future prosperity, quality of life, and security of every industrialized society. Only a response as radical as agility is promises to be adequate to meeting that challenge successfully.

CHAPTER 3

Agility: A Framework for Mastering Change

As agility becomes a condition of success in more and more markets, growing numbers of companies are confronting the challenges and the opportunities of agile competition. What we are urging most strongly in this book is a recognition of the systemic character of agile competition. It is as a *system* that agility holds the promise of long-term, strategic benefit for companies. Only as a system can it offer enduring competitive advantage in a rapidly changing and uncertain competitive environment. It is not enough to look at a list of the elements of agility and say, "We're doing that one and that one and that one, so we're all right." That approach will yield tactical benefits at best.

AGILITY IS A SYSTEM

The competitive power of the modern industrial corporation did not come from the technologies it exploited. Those technologies were available to all, and some had been available for 100 years. Its power did not come from its organizational structure, either. Feudalism, after all, had been hierarchically organized, centrally administered (at least in principle), and vertically integrated, and so was the powerful early modern nation-state. Its power certainly did not come from the exploitation of the talents of its work force; the modern industrial corporation went to great lengths to restrict the expression of talent by all but a handful of workers.

The competitive power of the modern industrial corporation came from the way that people, organizations, and technology were systematically coordinated with one another to form a new kind of business entity.

As management consultant Russell Ackoff puts it, having every single piece of your car in perfect working order arranged on your garage floor does not mean that you can drive to work. Not even putting all those pieces together will allow the car to perform the function you bought it to perform: carrying you from one place to another. To do that, all the pieces need to be assembled in a coordinated way. A car can perform its desired function only as the integrated system it was designed to be. Likewise, only as a system, all of whose elements are in place and mutually coordinated with one another, can agility enable a company to be an agile competitor.

THE FOUR DIMENSIONS OF AGILE COMPETITION

Constantly changing customer and market opportunities ensure that there can be no single, universal formula for mastering agile competition, no algorithm to follow and be guaranteed success. Every company must formulate its own, market-specific, dynamic program for becoming an agile competitor. But although there is no formula for such a program, there are guidelines that can help companies assess the potential impact of agility on their bottom lines.

Through intensive work over a period of months during the spring and summer of 1992 with one of the earliest focus groups of the Agile Manufacturing Enterprise Forum (a group charged by the forum's industry leaders with studying how to measure the agility of a company),* a small number of strategic characteristics that are common to agile organizations were identified. After two more years of interacting with scores of companies, we have distilled these characteristics down to four strategic dimensions that underlie the acquisition by any company, of any size, in any industry, of agile competitive capabilities. By conducting an audit that relates these dimensions to its current and anticipated future operations, a company can tailor to its own competitive situation a prioritized program for becoming agile. In Part 2 of this book, especially in the concluding chapter, we provide various tools that can help companies in conducting such an audit.

The crucial step a company must take, in our view, is to link the evaluation of agility directly to concrete corporate goals and to specific, *strategic* initiatives for accomplishing those goals. Not doing so almost guarantees only tactical benefits from agility and only incremental improvements over current practices and performance.

Briefly, the four strategic dimensions of agile competition are as follows.

1. Enriching the customer. An agile company is one that is perceived by its customers as enriching *them* in a significant way, not only itself. The "products" of an agile company are perceived by its customers to be solutions to their individual problems. The packages of goods and services that customers buy are only the means for implementing the solutions, for solutions are what customers are actually paying for—and they are increasingly aware of this. With the effective uncoupling of the cost of production from lot size, the goods and services an agile competitor produces for an individual customer can be priced on the basis of the value of the solutions they provide to

---

*The Benchmarking and Performance Assessment Focus Group, under the chairmanship of Len Allgaier.

that customer. This situation creates new marketing strategies for management to consider. At the same time, it demands a reconceptualization of what the company's products really are.

2. Cooperating to enhance competitiveness. Cooperation—internally and with other companies—is an agile competitor's operational strategy of first choice. The *end* is bringing agile products to market as rapidly and as cost-effectively as possible. One strategy for doing this is utilizing existing resources regardless of where they are located and who owns them. Cross-functional teams, empowerment, reengineering of business processes, virtual companies, and partnerships even with direct competitors are all *means* employed to leverage resources through cooperation.

3. Organizing to master change and uncertainty. An agile company is organized in a way that allows it to *thrive* on change and uncertainty. Its structure is flexible enough to allow rapid reconfiguration of human and physical resources. It can support multiple, concurrent organizational configurations keyed to the requirements of different customer opportunities. There is no single "right" structure for an agile company, and no single "right" size. It is organized in ways that enable personnel to apply all the resources that may be necessary to exploit changing market opportunities profitably.

The goal of very rapid concept to cash time implies innovative, flexible organizational structures that make rapid decision making possible by distributing managerial authority. Personnel who are motivated and knowledgeable enough to convert change and uncertainty into new opportunities for company growth are empowered to do so, routinely and rapidly.

4. Leveraging the impact of people and information. In an agile company, management nurtures an entrepreneurial company culture that leverages the impact of people and information on operations. It does this by distributing authority, by providing the resources personnel need, by reinforcing a climate of mutual responsibility for joint success, and by rewarding innovation. People—what they know, the skills they possess, the initiative they display—and information are *the* differentiators between companies in an agile competitive environment. Because knowledge-based products offer the greatest potential for individualization, continuous work force education and training are integral to agile company operations. They constitute an investment in future prosperity rather than a cost to be assigned to current overhead expenses.

ENRICHING THE CUSTOMER

Selling Solutions

One element of the shift in mind-set required to be an agile competitor involves rethinking what products are, how they should be made and sold, who buys them, and how much buyers should pay for them. The goal is strategic relationships with customers: stable, long-term relationships that can survive constant marketplace change. The means by which companies can accomplish this is by selling solutions to individual customer's problems, rather than selling products that then have to be fashioned into solutions by the customer.

Traditional sales transactions have a one-dimensional character. The product is purchased; the customer takes it away to use. Barring service problems, the customer comes back, eventually, only to buy a new product. The merchant has very limited options (if any) for adding value for the customer.

By contrast, solutions are multidimensional. They involve physical products *and* information *and* services that are adaptable to the changing requirements of a particular application.

Traditional products generate single-instance sales and form discrete product generations. When the product is used up or finally breaks down, the customer buys another or moves on to the new model, which replaces the old one. Repeat customers are important, but every customer represents the same kind of discrete transaction. There is no difference between selling a toaster for the first time to a brand-new customer and selling a replacement toaster to an old customer. The seller has nothing to sell but the one product at one time.

The selling of solutions creates relationships that can endure for long periods of time. These relationships are based on inevitable dependencies and interactions that arise when producer and customer come to understand one another well enough to create solutions together. At the same time, the possibility for continuous "solution product" generations—solutions that evolve over time in step with the evolution of the customer's problems—is created. Involving the customer in the production process, as Ross Operating Valves is doing with its Ross/ Flex system described in Chapter 1, or by interactively defining the mix of goods, services, and information that is of optimum value to each customer, is central to agile competition.

The marketplace reality driving this redefinition of *product* is the capability for high-volume production on a build-to-order, arbitrary lot size basis. This capability, in turn, is made possible by the information processing capacity to treat each mass-market customer as an individual. For many companies, this means bringing individual customer data, that is, specifying the particular product features *that* customer has ordered, directly to bear on the physical production process. This capability may take the form of computer-controlled production machinery, but it often takes the form of human assemblers performing their tasks armed with information about individual customers.

When the economic order quantity (EOQ) for a company becomes any amount the customer wants, that is, when a company can produce to order in arbitrary lot sizes, the doors open wide to producing a vast array of products in continually changing model runs. This makes it natural to repair "bugs," incorporate improvements, enhance performance, or add functionality on an ongoing basis. It also causes very short model lifetimes, because the pace of technological innovation is rapid and agile competition rewards companies capable of marketing a wide range of continually changing models. This circumstance underlies the new economies of scope in which the same basic technology is used to create broad product families that have varying functions: computers, pagers, portable telephones, and autofocus cameras.

On the one hand, this is leading to open-ended products designed to be improved by the end user, and upgraded and reconfigured rather than replaced. Continuous product generations are the result. Progressive releases of a software product—for example, a word processor or database program—present almost unlimited prospects for adding value to the original purchase by extending its capabilities or by adding collateral features: a visual aids preparation program or a program for generating graphics from data. Similarly, computer purchasers can change disk drives, processors, or memory capacity and add audio, video, and speech capabilities.

Indeed, as user demands or requirements change, if providers do *not* continually add value, their customers are certain to switch—to another word processor or database or to another brand of computer. The customers will then be lost to the initial vendor completely. Conversely, the more successfully a vendor has provided solution products that are thoroughly embedded in a customer's activities, the less likely the customer is to adopt a competing product, if only because of the pain of migration. Instead, the customer has a strong incentive to work cooperatively with "customer-friendly" vendors to define new generations of products that will meet his or her evolving needs.

On the other hand, increasingly flexible production capabilities that incorporate information about individual customers mean that companies really *can* provide solutions, not just products. For years the recognition of this *possibility* has taken the form of advertisements that have announced the arrival of a revolution: "Oh, what we're going to do for you!" Only recently has the revolution begun to take hold.

The emerging new reality is the growing number of companies that are saying to their customers: "What do you want us to do for you? Let's sit down and work it out together."

Selling solutions enables a company to adopt pricing and marketing strategies on the basis of customer values. Solutions are far more valuable to customers than generic packages of goods, services, and information that then have to be forced into solutions, on the customer's "nickel." What customers have always wanted, but have not been able to buy from mass-market producers, are solutions. They have had to settle for products. Now they do not have to settle.

It follows from these developments that:

1. Goods and services are no longer distinct product categories. Agile competitors always offer the most valuable mix of physical products, information, and services to the customer (and hence the most profitable to the vendor).
2. What companies really have to offer to their customers is the application of knowledge, skills, and information to the needs and problems of individual customers.
3. An agile company's most important asset, and its true production resource, is the set of core competencies it possesses, first in the form of personnel, and second in the form of technologies.

Unisys Corporation has recognized that its best opportunity to add value for customers will not come from selling them computers but from selling management- and operations-related information, data processing, and information-processing services. Unisys advertises its commitment to "customerization," its version of creating individualized solution product for companies with information management and management services problems. Such solutions require computer hardware and software, of course, but not necessarily hardware produced by Unisys.

The profitability of solving customer problems by means of individualized information- and services-based applications packages prepared by Unisys personnel dwarfs the profits to be gained by selling these customers Unisys hardware and *not* providing the applications packages. For similar reasons, IBM has reorganized the corporation by industry served rather than geographically, the better to sell service solutions; and so has Hewlett-Packard. All three companies recognize that the fact that they manufacture hardware no longer means that hardware is the most valuable product they can offer to customers.

NCR and AT&T advertise that knowing about customers individually can increase revenues by 15 percent. This conclusion is based on their experience in helping companies acquire the information processing and telecommunications capabilities necessary to extract such information from their databases. R.R. Donnelley and Sons advertise their expertise in creating revenue-producing products out of a company's archived customer information.

We referred earlier to computers and their software, to Sega and Nintendo game machines, to CD players and CDs, and to the Apple Newton, as examples of the shift in the center of value of industrial competition from physical products to the information and services for which those products serve as platforms. This means that the bottleneck for producers shifts from plant, equipment, and machinery to people.

The profitability of an agile company is determined by the knowledge and the skills of its personnel, and the information they have and have access to. The constraint is the ability of personnel to tailor combinations of goods, services, and information to the needs of individual customers, and the availability of the resources they need to do that. Once it becomes clear that an agile company's true productive resource is its core competencies, a rationale emerges for organizing the company in ways that permit bringing those competencies to bear on the creation of solution products as rapidly and as cost effectively as possible. Customer opportunities drive an agile company's organizational structures: typically, multiple, concurrent structures as the company pursues different kinds of customer opportunities concurrently. Too often the reverse is the case. The company's inherited organizational structure is taken as a given and allowed to determine what kinds of customer opportunities it can pursue quickly enough and cost effectively enough to succeed.

Organizational structures are functional if they enable personnel routinely to reach out to core competencies possessed by other departments or divisions, or by other companies, to find the best way to achieve the goal of producing individualized solutions for large numbers of customers. This is the criterion on which decisions about outsourcing, partnering, and forming joint ventures and virtual companies are based. It was the basis for reorganizing Unisys, IBM, and Hewlett-Packard so that the entrenched structure, reflecting a hardware product line, did not inhibit a product line keyed to information and services, access to which was provided by *somebody's* computers. As often as possible, of course, it would be nice if it were the solution provider's models, but not at the expense of selling the solution.

Rethinking Design

Implicit in the creation of solution products whose characteristics are jointly defined by producers and customers is a fundamental redefinition of *design.* In an agile competitive environment, design becomes part of the total production process. It is no longer a stage in a serial process that moves step by step through development and manufacturing to marketing, sales, and service. Instead, design *becomes* the production process, a concurrent, holistic process in which everyone with a stake, from suppliers to customers, participates on a peer level.

This kind of interaction played a key role in the success of the innovative vehicle development team structure—the cross-functional "platform" teams—that Chrysler adopted for its award-winning Concorde, Intrepid, and Vision large cars and the Neon subcompact. Suppliers were able to influence the specifications of the components and subassemblies they provided because they were empowered to suggest improvements to designs shown to them by Chrysler engineers. Chrysler provided all suppliers with uniform computer-aided design (CAD) software and also provided any training their personnel needed to use the software.

As circumstances dictated, supplier company personnel went to Chrysler to work on problems directly with Chrysler teams, and Chrysler personnel went to supplier companies when doing so helped solve problems. Bose Corporation has used this same strategy to remain at the leading edge of the audio markets in which it competes. In addition to the cross-functional character of the vehicle development teams and the interactive supplier relations, for the first time in recent company history at least, Chrysler engineers interacted directly with the people selected to test-drive prototype vehicles. This, too, led to design changes that resulted in customer-determined improvements in the final product.

These innovative vehicle development methodologies have transformed Chrysler's position in the U.S. auto industry. Although Ford continues to have a significant edge over Chrysler in the efficiency with which its production lines operate (and a very large edge over GM), the much lower costs of Chrysler's recent new vehicle design and development projects, relative to Ford's costs, have made it the overall U.S. leader in operational efficiency by a substantial margin.

The redefinition of design as the armature of the total production process goes even further. Design must be holistic from the product side as well as from the production side (*product* means here the richly variable mix of physical product, information, and services we have been discussing). The capabilities that distinguish a solution product from a traditional mass-production-era product must be designed into it. Extensive customer configuration options, user reconfigurability and upgradability, the open-endedness of information- and services-rich products that can evolve through generations, acquiring new functionality as they age, must be built into products from the beginning.

A growing number of portable computers are upgradable and reconfigurable by customers without the need for any special tools or technical expertise. This is a marketing strategy that NEC has exploited successfully with its Versa notebook line and that Zenith touts for its revamped Z-NOTEFLEX line. Monochrome screens can be exchanged for color. Memory can be expanded. Disk drives can be removed to make room for other options or can be replaced by larger-capacity drives. Even the central processor can be unplugged and a faster, more powerful processor, for example, an Intel Pentium, simply plugged in. Although NEC offers a familiar docking station option for the Versa for full desktop capability, the Z-NOTEFLEX is part of a modular system of desktop and portable components of extraordinary breadth. The almost universal adoption of an industrywide standard for portable computer plug-in peripherals—PCMCIA-slot modems, disk drives, flash memory, programs in ROM—testifies to the competitive advantage this design strategy offers.

Whether they are hardware, services, or combinations of the two, products can evolve in step with customer demands, creating new performance capabilities, if components can be added to the original purchase. For this to occur, however, products must be designed from the start to serve as platforms for a broad range of current and projected future enhancements. Instead of having to discard the original purchase to acquire these improvements, customers can, at far lower cost, modify the purchase. This is a familiar marketing strategy for computer software, but more and more hardware is being offered with this capability.

One expression of the computer industry's evolving appreciation of a product development strategy based on customer-perceived value is the sudden rush to bring true "plug and play" add-on products to market. Such products—for example, sound cards, video cards, CD-ROM drives, voice recognition software, modems, and communication software—contain programs that automatically configure the host computer and all previously installed hardware and software to work together with the newly installed equipment, ideally across the Macintosh and MS-DOS environments.

The durability of physical products today can be very long. It is many years in the case of aircraft, automobiles, and computers, for example, but it is also long for many consumer products such as TVs, VCRs, audio, video, and photographic equipment, and home appliances. While durable, however, the market lifetimes of all products gets shorter as the pace of performance innovations increases.

Consumer product models have a lifetime measurable in months. Automobile model lifetimes are at three years and shrinking under pressure from Japanese companies. Computer chip model lifetimes are down to two years, but because of a commitment to the original Intel design architecture, a huge global market exists for products and services supporting the tens of millions of 286, 386, and 486 machines (and tens of millions more PC and PC-XT "antiques") that will continue in daily use even as the Pentium is replaced by its successor, the P-6 chip, perhaps as early as 1995. Mainframe computer model life is now two years, but Boeing aircraft have long product lifetimes, measurable in decades. During that time aircraft will have been significantly reconfigured to meet the changing needs of the same customer, or a series of customers—the fuselage stretched, engines replaced, wings altered, cabin space altered, control systems replaced.

Appreciating Information

An agile competitor never loses sight of the value of information, as it is embedded in physical products and services and as a product in its own right. IBM undervalued the (ROM BIOS) information embedded in its original PC in the fall of 1981. As a result, the PC clone industry sprang into existence without benefiting IBM and, in fact, harming it. When IBM replaced the PC-XT with the AT class of 80286-based computers, it tried retroactively to recoup royalty fees for the information on which the clones were built, but it proved impossible to do this. Even IBM's attempt to introduce a proprietary "bus" architecture for accessory options as a means of increasing the value of the design of the AT machines failed. It failed because customers did not perceive the proprietary design to be as valuable to them as the open system bus, in the absence of broad developer support of the proprietary design.

The lesson is clear: Companies need to value and protect information, *and* they need to share it. Chip architectures embody information, as does the look and feel of a computer program. Intel, Apple, and Lotus, for example, have been vigilant in protecting the information dimension of their products from reverse-engineered competitive products. Agile companies pay much more attention to information than mass-production companies did. They are able to put a value—to themselves and to customers—on the information they are selling, both explicitly, as a product in its own right, as well as implicitly, embedded in other products. They have policies for selling access to proprietary information, for selling information outright, or for "renting" information, as Ross Operating Valves does with its proprietary valve design library and software and as a number of application-specific integrated circuits (ASIC) manufacturers are doing.

COOPERATING TO ENHANCE COMPETITIVENESS

Cooperation—within companies but especially among companies—is the key to the competitive advantage offered by agility. This may sound paradoxical, but it is not a fact of nature that competition and cooperation are mutually exclusive. It is a fact about Western culture and about the role that individualism has played in shaping our institutions, values, and self-consciousness. Explicitly and implicitly, in hundreds of formative experiences, we are taught that the most desirable solution to a problem is the one we think up ourselves and, if possible, execute ourselves, so that we can receive all the credit for it. The images of John Wayne in *The Sands of Iwo Jima* and in *True Grit;* of Gary Cooper in *High Noon;* and of James Bond, Rambo, and the "Die Hard" films are powerful cultural reinforcers of these individualistic values over a 40-year span of popular entertainment. Cooperation, by contrast, is what we are compelled to turn to when we are unable to solve a problem on our own.

The result of this attitude is a lack of cooperation even among departments, divisions, or subsidiaries of a single company. For the sake of the greater glory of doing it all by oneself, companies, teams, and individuals within companies turn inward for their solution strategy of first choice. The "let's invent it here" syndrome and the "not invented here" syndrome are two sides of the same coin. Agile competition simply does not allow the luxury of trying the individualistic approach first, and only after it fails turning to a cooperative strategy.

The Value of Cooperation

Four features of agile competition reinforce the value of cooperation.

1. Agile competition places a premium on very low product cycle times—measured as the time from the first articulation of an idea for a new or improved product to the time that cash flow from sales begins (hence "concept to cash" time), and it places a premium on the frequent introduction of new products and improved models of existing products. Together, these necessary but not sufficient conditions for competitive success in agile markets impose severe demands on business processes. The objectives are dramatic reductions in new product development costs, time to market, risks, and the consequences

of failure. Cooperation is a valuable means of accomplishing these objectives.

2. Agile companies are distinguished by the intensity of the intraenterprise and interenterprise cooperative relationships they foster and by the virtual organization relationships they create. Adversarial and control relationships do not work in an organization whose hallmark is cooperation. Routine intraenterprise as well as interenterprise cooperation requires a wholehearted commitment to an ethic of trust, reflecting the mutual dependence of partners on one another for joint success or shared failure. Cooperating companies deal with one another honestly and openly, with integrity, for the obvious moral reasons but also for pragmatic ones—betrayed parties cannot be expected to cooperate fully a second time!

3. Making cooperation the norm for intracompany and intercompany relationships accelerates technology transfer and broadens the resources available for solving problems. It also increases the probability of innovative solutions to problems. Cooperation, however, goes well beyond organizing personnel into cross-functional teams; teams alone are not the royal road to corporate success. Teams are not the automatic organizational choice for every operation in every company. When they *are* the best choice, however, they must be supported by investment in the communication and information technologies required for their members to work with one another, and with personnel and facilities distributed across the company, and in supplier and customer companies as well. Underlying and enabling all of these operations-level capabilities is a management commitment to sharing information to mutual advantage with customers, with suppliers, and with partners, including competitors.

4. Making interenterprise cooperation a solution strategy of first choice, one that is routinely available to a company's personnel, opens up dramatic new competitive possibilities. It poses a formidable challenge, however, because it requires formulating and implementing truly innovative management policies and procedures, among them:

Managing cross-functional teams distributed across companies

Evaluating and rewarding personnel on these teams

Creating an open information-exchange environment suited to the needs of a collaborative project, while protecting intellectual property and company security

Formulating clearly defined criteria for partnering with other companies

Implementing an interenterprise ethics code and ensuring the integrity of collaborating companies and their participating personnel

Protecting the company's legal and financial interests

Increasingly, physical products in the most profitable markets are valued because they are platforms for information and services. It is in the services and in information- and knowledge-based applications for physical products that the highest profit opportunities lie for agile companies. It is also the information and service products that "hook" customers and create long-term relationships that can provide stability in unpredictably changing agile competitive environments. Under these circumstances, it is far more effective, from both financial and marketing perspectives, for companies to form cooperative product development alliances than to attempt to go it alone.

By entering into cooperative relationships, each company can focus its efforts on those activities for which its human and technological resources best suit it. Alliances among companies with complementary resources and expertise reduce sunk costs and risks at the same time that they reduce development time. Alliances expand the pool of available human and physical resources. They increase the probability of success and create interdependencies on which to build future collaborations and continuing participation in the creation of multiple generations of successful product families.

The PowerPC processor is an excellent illustration of this strategy. Developed collaboratively by IBM, Apple, and Motorola, it was brought to market in less than two years because of a willingness on the part of the collaborators to share proprietary intellectual property. Concurrently, the three companies jointly developed the PowerOpen Environment, a set of operating system compliance standards for the PowerPC that will allow it to run DOS, Macintosh, and UNIX software concurrently. To accelerate the broad adoption of the PowerPC processor by software and hardware developers, IBM, Apple, and Motorola created the PowerOpen Association. The association disseminates PowerPC architecture information and invites customer participation in determining operating system standards. It aims to create as wide a support base for the PowerPC as possible.

Notwithstanding all this cooperation, at the product level IBM, Motorola, and Apple intend to compete with one another for hardware, software, and system integration customers, as well as with many third-party developers to whom they will themselves have disseminated PowerPC "secrets."

Virtual Organizations

The virtual organization or, more accurately, an organization with a virtual organizational structure, is only one of many forms that cooperation, both among companies and within a single company, can take. It is of special interest because it places the greatest demands on a company to cooperate to achieve collaborative production. If a company is so staffed, equipped, organized, and motivated that the option of creating a virtual organization structure for a project is routinely available to it, then by virtue of that very fact all the other elements of agility are likely to be present and functional in that company.

A virtual organizational structure is an opportunistic alliance of core competencies distributed among a number of distinct operating entities within a single large company or among a group of independent companies. The underlying idea is almost trivially obvious and far from new: Organize a group of people with relevant abilities into a team focused on a well-defined problem. Motivate these people, give them access to appropriate resources, reward them on the basis of the value of the solution they create, and then stand back!

On a special-circumstances basis—the Manhattan Project, Clarence Johnson's Skunk Works at Lockheed, the creation of Data General's Eclipse line of minicomputers chronicled by Tracy Kidder in *The Soul of a New Machine*—this approach is well known and has repeatedly achieved impressive results. But even at Lockheed, where the Skunk Works' track record since 1944 has been extraordinary, it has not become the corporate norm. And at Data General, only the head of the Eclipse project, promoted to a vice-presidency, remained with the company after the completion of the project. No effort was made to sustain the momentum, initiative, and creativity generated by the Eclipse design team. Its members felt underappreciated, underrewarded, and inappropriately challenged in their next assignments.

The lesson to be learned? Whether they are intraenterprise or interenterprise, virtual project structures that override entrenched compartmentalizations of expertise and resources can achieve striking results. That they have not become familiar reveals the extent to which historical prejudices limit company performance.

The differences between a company's experiences with special-project teams and its ability to form virtual organizations are very deep. The virtual organization structure does not seek to create a miniature traditional company within the confines of an existing or new physical plant. It integrates all the resources necessary to produce goods and services into a coherent operational unit, while leaving the resources intact as far as possible. In addition, the participants interact as peers, rather than being organized hierarchically, as they would be in a traditional company. This structure reflects the recognition that the people and companies involved are equal participants in an enterprise that no one of them wholly owns, or is owned by!

Large companies are not the privileged benefiters from the virtual organization strategy, nor are they in a privileged position to exploit it. As described in Chapter 1, scores of networks of small companies have been formed in the United States during the past five years. Some networks offer their members horizontal integration opportunities. Other networks offer a framework for creating limited lifetime vertically integrated companies, that is, virtual companies, in response to transient opportunities. Indiana's cross-industry FlexCell Group was cited in Chapter 1 as an example of a network that provides small companies just this capability: in one instance, linking a manufacturer of metalworking patterns and tools to a mechanical engineering firm, a producer of plastic injection molds and tools, a prototype machine shop, and a contract machine shop.

Identifying complementary core competencies, and then synthesizing them at low cost into a complete production capability designed to satisfy a particular customer opportunity, creates a powerful competitive weapon. It is rapidly becoming available to companies of all sizes as computer networks adapted to the needs of integrated, interactive electronic commerce grow. EINet, CommerceNet, AgileWeb, and ECNet, described in Chapter 1, are just four examples of such networks that are, or are becoming, operational.

Furthermore, while the virtual organization is opportunistic, its objective is to create solution products with lifetimes as long as the marketplace will allow. These products are expected to evolve, and as they do, so will the virtual organization's resource requirements. Some participants will leave to join other groups because their competencies no longer add enough value to be most profitably used in the virtual organization. For precisely the same reasons, others will join, because they can add value as the product evolves in one direction rather than another. Or, the virtual organization may disband, but only because the customer opportunity that called it into being no longer exists. IBM's phase-out of Ambra operations in the fall of 1994 illustrates this aspect of virtual organization very well.

There are important personnel implications in exploiting virtual organizations. These need to be addressed openly and in advance, if this strategy is to be of enduring value. As people are assigned to virtual company projects to which management has committed its "home" company, they need to understand the criteria by which they will be evaluated. Management support includes developing job security policies as virtual companies form and dissolve or as participants join and withdraw from long-lived virtual organizations. There are important management and financial accounting issues involved as well. These will be discussed in Part 2.

The lifetime of a virtual company, and the duration of participation of individual "actual" companies, is a function of the profitable market life of the array of goods and services the virtual company is capable of producing. For a product like the Boeing 777, the lifetime will be decades; for consumer product models, it will be quite short, today on the order of months; but for product *families*, it will be years, if they have been designed for agile marketplace longevity.

Why Create a Virtual Company?

There are six reasons for creating a virtual company, and all of them are strategic; that is, there are six strategic considerations that bear on the decision to adopt a virtual organization approach to a project instead of a more traditional collaborative approach, such as a partnership or joint venture. These considerations are just mentioned here. In Chapter 6 they are discussed at length.

1. Would forming a virtual organization to market a new product allow your company to share infrastructure resources, R&D, costs, and risk?
2. Would a virtual organization enhance product development opportunities for your company by linking internal core competencies to core competencies at other companies?
3. Would it reduce concept to cash flow time by integrating knowledge and skills across company boundaries in concurrent operations?
4. Would it increase the apparent size or scale of the operation—first, to the people involved (in terms of access to expertise and resources) at less cost than achieving this scale internally; and second, to customers, whose response to a product from a sixty-person company might be very different from their response to the products of what may seem, in effect, a 6000 person company?
5. Would a virtual organization give your company access to new markets through the partnerships it would form, and allow it to share in other companies' customer loyalty base, by adding value with them and for them via the new product?

6. Would a virtual organization accelerate your company's migration from selling products to selling solutions?

The virtual company model is analogous to a home audio system made up of components from different manufacturers, with one important difference. Imagine that, instead of these components being installed in your home, they all (except for the speakers and a control unit) remained in place on the different manufacturers' premises. Then suppose that you paid each of these manufacturers, or a convenient one-stop broker, a fee for linking together the units you wanted when you wanted to use them and a fee for renting access to program sources—CDs, cassettes, LPs—instead of owning a personal collection of them.

The digital processing and telecommunications technologies necessary to do this are available today, although it hardly seems an efficient way of listening to the CD of your choice while preparing dinner! Still, the principle lies at the heart of the IBM–Blockbuster Video initiative to create inventoryless music stores in which CDs could be downloaded from a central library and produced on site, on demand. It is integral to the efforts of AT&T, MCI, Time-Warner, and many other companies to create a digital video-on-demand home telecommunications capability. And there is a print version of this marketing-cum-production strategy in Xerox's OpenDocument system, which can download remotely stored text and print customized books on site, on demand in minutes.

The analogy can be pressed a little harder. Just as the listener to the output of a traditional audio system cannot "hear" the heterogeneity of the manufacturers of its various components, so the virtual structure of a company is invisible to its customer-users. The evolution of a virtual company would then be analogous to the reconfiguration of the elements of an audio system in response to new technologies, new listener interests, and new program sources.

Such a virtual structure is maintained for as long as it is supported by the marketplace. As the basis for reaping the marketplace benefits changes, the structure can easily be reconfigured to rest on the new basis. When the benefits cease, the structure loses its rationale. Because dissolution is relatively painless, the participants withdraw and the virtual structure disappears the way our laps do when we stand up.

Initially, the introduction of instantly plug-compatible audio equipment during the 1950s seemed to entail a loss for equipment manufacturers. It limited their opportunity to sell complete systems to customers. But the plug-compatible marketing strategy, which required adopting a range of explicit and de facto standards, shaped the audio equipment market into one that remains dynamic and profitable after decades of competition. The same thing happened in the computer and telecommunications markets, to name just two of many similar instances.

Bicycle vendors to all but the lowest-priced markets have created what amount to global "virtual" products. In every case, frame manufacturers configure finished bicycles by selecting from an enormous variety of specialty components manufactured by companies, located literally around the world, that have built reputations for excellence in wheel, tire, hub, brake, derailleur, handlebar, tire, seat, chain, and even spoke design and fabrication. The difference between bicycle and automobile assemblers is that bicycle advertising explicitly identifies the component manufacturers. Indeed, companies compete on the basis of the customer-perceived value of the components.

Furthermore, bicycle companies that manufacture a wide range of components sometimes mount their products on frames created by famous frame designers and then add the components they do not manufacture to create the finished bicycles. In between are many companies that manufacture nothing, but sell bicycles by mixing and matching frames and components and assembling them. The value these companies add lies in the expertise they bring to the selection process and in the volume discounts they can pass along to customers.

Like the market for consumer audio products, the bicycle market is made possible largely through the "plug compatibility" of the components and frames. And like manufacturers of audio products, bicycle manufacturers learned that there was mutual advantage to building "virtual" bicycles rather than complete systems. In short, only a small number of companies can succeed when they compete on the basis of *closed,* proprietary systems. A large number of companies can create an enduring win-win situation for themselves if they build a very broad customer base for evolving component technologies designed for *open* systems. In such systems, evolving component technologies can push successive reconfigurations of end-products for many years.

Interactive relationships among the participants; integration without duplication of physical locations; the market-dependent, uncertain evolutionary character of its development over time; acceptance by all participants of responsibility for the joint success of all aspects of the collaboration: these are the features that set the virtual organization structure apart from familiar interenterprise collaboration models, such as relationships between original equipment manufacturers (OEMs) and suppliers, joint ventures, partnerships, movie production companies, and prime contractor-subcontractor collaborations. Participants in the virtual enterprise share accountability and responsibility for the success of the enterprise as a whole, as well as for their particular portion of its operations. All participants are involved, more or less actively, in all of the virtual enterprise operations.

The benefit of adopting a virtual organization structure is not only the much greater speed with which new products can be brought to market and the lower cost but the better match the structure allows between resources and the specific requirements of a new market opportunity. The inevitability of the virtual organization structure as a routine option for management follows from the centrality of core competencies to success in the agile competitive environment. Core competencies need to be complemented and supplemented on a dynamic basis if productive resources are to be fashioned within the short time lines that determine success in agile competition.

Kingston Technologies is a $500 million a year company whose "product" is its ability to custom-configure large numbers of computers very quickly. In effect, Kingston sits at the hub of a network of responsive manufacturers of accessory equipment with whom it enjoys preferred customer status. If a large-volume purchaser needs to have computers configured to a particular memory, storage, display, or peripheral equipment specification, and needs them very quickly (typically a few days), Kingston activates its network (the manufacturers). Stable price agreements and long-term buying commitments justify the diversion of production by these manufacturers to support the service Kingston sells.

In the arena of agile competition, the ability to form virtual companies routinely is a formidable competitive weapon. The routine formation of virtual enterprises is possible, however, only if communication and information exchange technologies are in place that are capable of supporting the plug compatibility required by the organizational structure of the virtual companies. In effect, virtual organizational structures entail not only the complete integration of the enterprise but also extensive interenterprise integration as well.

Even more important, however, are the changes in managerial values, organizational structure, and prevailing corporate culture paradigms that are required. Work force empowerment, self-organizing and self-managing cross-functional teams, performance- and skill-based compensation, flatter managerial hierarchies, distributed authority, and point-of-problem decision making are all expressions of moving toward acquiring agile business capabilities. Together with investment in appropriate technologies, implementing enterprise integration, concurrent operations, and treatment of the work force as the central asset of the enterprise, they also define the necessary conditions for creating virtual enterprises.

What will make virtual enterprises commonplace is the adoption of organizational paradigms keyed to the positive value of intensive cooperation within companies and between companies—even between direct competitors. The fundamental value is cooperation, first of all within companies and, second, among companies. As the full value of cooperation is appreciated, the many modes of benefiting from it will be recognized as well, and action agendas for achieving these benefits will be formulated. Making the leap to virtual companies in the absence of this structurally more fundamental reassessment of cooperation will not create enduring benefits; in fact, there may be no benefits.

Substituting Bytes for Bricks

The emergence of agile competition has created the current interest in virtual organization structures. The premium placed on the rapid development of new products and the introduction of them into high-value-added markets, along with the unpredictable character of new market opportunities and evolving customer demands, makes it effectively impossible for any company to maintain world-class capabilities from one end of the production value chain to the other. Increasingly, even the largest companies can compete successfully only if they have accurately identified their own world-class competencies and are prepared to integrate them with complementary capabilities possessed by other companies.

The economics of vertical integration and large-scale operation exploited by mass-production-based industrial corporations still apply today, but they no longer imply ownership of the integrated resources. Both vertical integration and large scale can be effected cooperatively. For opportunistic collaborations, whose lifetimes are defined by the profitability of the market opportunities they were created to exploit, electronic integration reduces the burdens of ownership of human and physical resources. It lowers the threshold of profitability of a new operation. It promotes networks of mutually profitable cooperative relationships with other companies among which the necessary resources remain dispersed.

A company with a virtual organizational structure thus substitutes bytes for bricks. It achieves just the right degree of horizontal and vertical integration of just those resources and capabilities required by a particular product development effort. By integrating these resources virtually, leaving them in place physically but knitting them together electronically, the company reduces the need to construct facilities or to hire personnel dedicated to the new product. A number of important obstacles will be overcome as the ability to form virtual companies becomes routine:

The need to calculate the changing partial value of the total product added over time by each virtual company participant
Intellectual property protection issues
Antitrust and product liability issues
Virtual enterprise performance metrics
Accountability
Consensus decision making

Company identification and loyalty for personnel whose work lives are bound up with making a success of the virtual company's products

None of these obstacles is unique to virtual organization collaborations. All are obstacles to any form of routine, intensive, interactive collaboration among companies to create, produce, distribute, and market goods and services. The concept of virtual companies and the growing capability for creating them and exploiting the advantages they offer excite the imagination. This attention serves to highlight problems to their implementation, even if those problems are not unique to them, just as it highlights their promise for competitive advantage.

Global Competitors

All of the problems mentioned above are exacerbated by the need to be able to collaborate with companies possessing complementary capabilities wherever in the world they are located. Agile competition is truly global in the sense of being increasingly indifferent to the geographical location of facilities and expertise. The rapidly growing connectivity of people, databases and research, and of design, manufacturing, marketing, and service facilities means that any company anywhere is vulnerable to competition from remote agile companies that can extend their reach into local markets. This situation is analogous to the one that confronted local and regional manufacturing companies 100 years ago, when the modern industrial corporation inaugurated truly national marketing.

Conversely, it is becoming easier and less expensive for companies to enter markets anywhere they can identify customers. Furthermore, erecting commercial barriers around domestic markets in order to protect local producers is likely to be counterproductive—and sooner rather than later. There are strong grounds, both logical and empirical, for concluding that domestic producers are efficient global competitors in the areas to which they are exposed to global competition, however painful may be the achievement of the efficiency required. Conversely, domestic producers will be inefficient if they are sheltered from global competition. After all, if they were competitive, they would not need to be sheltered!

Agile production is thus intrinsically global production, whereas mass production was merely international. As the national identification of producers of goods and services becomes increasingly blurred, the current international industrial order will be replaced by a worldwide industrial order. This order will be capable of utilizing required resources regardless of their physical location, based on cost and suitability of facilities and services alone, driven by technologies that provide seamless access to dispersed facilities and expertise.

Especially in rapidly changing and fragmented high-value-added markets, the ability to bring together quickly the kinds of expertise required to design, deliver, and service new products can confer decisive competitive advantage. It is increasingly the case today that global markets are fragmented—reflecting the need to customize a "world" product to the specific performance requirements or customer preferences of diverse societies—and that high-value-added markets do place a premium on a continuous stream of new products and constantly improving existing product "families." Agility is the compelling strategic goal of any company prepared to see opportunities for growth and prosperity in these challenges, not threats to its survival.

The technologies now exist to synthesize geographically dispersed knowledge, information, operational facilities, and expertise. Furthermore, these technologies are becoming increasingly robust, widespread, and comprehensive. But the barriers to cooperation, even when it offers clear advantages, are many and substantial. Within a single company, there may be many obstacles to breaking through entrenched practices in order to "borrow" people, information, knowledge, techniques, and equipment. These same obstacles, and many more, exist if the resources are distributed among different companies—some of them traditional rivals. Nevertheless, the requirements for success in agile competition demand that these obstacles be overcome.

ORGANIZING TO MASTER CHANGE
AND UNCERTAINTY

The hierarchical organizational structure of mass-production-era companies was designed to optimize the managerial function. Authority, expertise, and initiative were concentrated in management, and the scope of their exercise was defined by each executive's location in the organization's structure. As management became accepted as a general science, a standard organization structure evolved, with command and control as its dominant motifs. Command and control mandated a reactive work force in which independence, initiative, and innovation were seen as interfering with the one-way flow of command and control—down—through the fixed managerial hierarchy.

The transition from an entrepreneur-owner–run company, however large (and some eighteenth- and nineteenth-century factory operations, in the iron and textile industries, for example, were very large) to a centrally administered, vertically integrated company with large-scale and far-flung operations, effectively mandated an organizational structure keyed to control. The hierarchical structure of the modern industrial corporation was one means of establishing lines of control, responsibility, and authority. Power and compensation corresponded directly to one's place in the hierarchy.

Concurrently, operations-level job descriptions were as specific as the control hierarchy was for managers. A corollary of the pervasive control mind-set was the necessity for commanding job performance from employees who could not be permitted initiative without undermining the entire control-responsibility-accountability rationale for the management structure that was in place in the company. Given the command-and-control mind-set of management, and the privileging of power, compensation, accountability, responsibility, and initiative in the managerial ranks, it is hardly surprising that adversarial relationships became the rule between management and labor.

By forgoing work force initiative, management gave up two important assets: (1) access to the total skill base of its personnel; and (2) the possibility of a universal sense of responsibility and accountability. The only thing that could *reasonably* be expected to matter to employees was their performance on the specific tasks that were assigned to them by their superiors in the hierarchy.

Giving up Control

The organizational structure of an agile company is based on very different principles. In a very general way, such a company is designed to optimize its ability to exploit rapidly and unpredictably changing market opportunities for information- and services-rich, high-value-added, short-lifetime products.

The functioning of an agile company is analogous to that of a state-of-the-art hospital emergency room—an analogy first suggested by Phil Weinzimer, a consultant for Unisys. In the emergency room, a pool of resources—human, technological, and institutional—is available and can be configured very quickly to meet the specific needs of people with diverse problems who appear in no particular order. On demand, skilled and knowledgeable personnel form themselves into teams defined by the requirements of individual patients.

The resources immediately at hand are dwarfed by the resources that are quickly and routinely available from many sources. Physicians can link remote resources to a patient-response team, beginning with ambulance or helicopter attendants who can establish voice and data links with personnel and with equipment located at the hospital. Among other linkages to sometimes far-flung medical resources are:

Access to specialized knowledge possessed by physicians associated
with the hospital or, increasingly routinely, by real and "virtual"
experts (medical databases) located almost anywhere in the world
Access to specialized expertise or equipment located elsewhere in the
hospital or in other hospitals
Extensive generic hospital facilities not dedicated to the emergency
room but routinely available to it

Although there are important differences, the relationship of the hospital emergency room to its patients offers illuminating similarities to the relationship of agile producers of goods and services to their customers. The primary objectives of management in an agile company, as in a state-of-the-art hospital emergency room, must be:

To maintain a work force rich in skilled, knowledgeable people

To provide those people with the resources they need to respond to changing market opportunities and the requirements of individual customers

To enable the routine reconfiguration of the organizational "walls" that traditionally circumscribe the distribution of resources in a company, as well as the distribution of control and privilege. This reconfiguration must include the ability to link resources internal to the company—people, technologies, and information—to appropriate resources distributed among other companies, even among direct competitors, in order to provide the best possible solutions to customer problems

The urgency of emergency medical situations creates a climate in which people with complementary expertise work together intensively, joining their expertise to achieve a common goal: restoring the patient's well-being. The agile competition analogue of the medical situation is to respond to the competitive urgency of a new customer opportunity by synthesizing the expertise required to do so, integrating access to the relevant facilities and knowledge wherever they may be.

Companies today do not operate in a way that allows this to happen. Except in special-project situations personnel are not given the authority to command resources and to reprioritize the allocation of these resources in the light of new market developments, not even within their own companies, let alone in conjunction with other companies. Yet creating new production resources in this way and, especially, creating "virtual" production resources by integrating the expertise, facilities, and functional capabilities existing in a group of companies can result in a powerful competitive weapon.

The upshot of these very general considerations is that the organizational structure of an agile company is deliberately chosen by its management. For each customer opportunity, management can answer the question, "What is the best way for us to be organized to exploit this particular opportunity?" A company's organizational structure is not an inherited given that determines in advance the form of its response to market opportunities. Instead, an agile company has an innovative and flexible structure that mirrors its strategic agenda: the need to deploy specific configurations of human and technological resources in a way best suited to profit from customer opportunities.

Chrysler, Goodyear, and Texas Instruments' Defense Systems and Electronics Group are just three examples of companies that have derived dramatic benefit from flattening the managerial hierarchy, making cross-functional teams pervasive throughout the company, and giving people with the relevant operational expertise the authority to determine how to meet the goals set by management.

Asea Brown Boveri and Corning Glass are two examples of companies that have adopted a policy of breaking highly centralized organizations into a vast number of independent business units, and an even larger number of profit centers, each with a significant measure of autonomy, as a means of stimulating perpetual internal entrepreneurship.

Sony, Hewlett-Packard, and Motorola are examples of companies that, for more than a decade, have sustained very high rates of new product introductions that anticipated marketplace developments and then cultivated generations of those products as the markets evolved.

Optimizing Opportunism

The driving force determining an agile company's competitiveness is the need to minimize the concept to cash time for creating and exploiting customer opportunities. The marketplace rewards companies that can do this routinely; and it punishes those that cannot. Four specific consequences of how companies that master change are organized follow from this shift in focus—from optimizing the managerial function to optimizing the exploitation of new customer opportunities.

1. Expertise, initiative, and authority are distributed as widely as possible in an agile company, limited only by the need to maintain a coherent, companywide, market-pulled operations strategy. To support

the effectiveness of this strategy, personnel must be trained to act locally but to think globally, that is, to think of the impact on the company as a whole of their local, project-specific actions. Maximizing the positive impact of local decisions must also improve the overall position of the company; the latter does not at all follow automatically from the former!

John Reed's reorganization of Citicorp's senior management structure in the winter of 1991–1992 was based on this one point. Under the management of his predecessor, Walter Wriston, Citicorp's 15 global division heads ran autonomous operations. They were encouraged to optimize their individual operations and were compensated accordingly. In January 1992, Citicorp chairman John Reed initiated a dramatic reorganization of what was at the time a deeply troubled bank.

Reed eliminated the executive committee buffer between himself and the operating division heads, scheduled monthly meetings with the 15 as a group, and gave them more authority but removed their autonomy. They were now expected to run their divisions in the best interests of Citicorp and were compensated as a function of Citicorp's performance, not of the division they headed. Reed's role was, and continues to be, to provide a middle-term vision for Citicorp and to set bold near-term goals, allowing the 15 to decide how best to meet the goals through a consensus process at their monthly meetings. In January 1994 Citicorp announced record earnings for any U.S. bank corporation, and its stock was selling at five times what it had been in January 1992.

2. Decision making is accelerated by replacing a rigid, multilevel, functionally divided organizational structure with one capable of supporting a flexible focus on providing routine, rapid access to the company's core competencies—the information, skills, and knowledge that are its ultimate productive assets.

Packaged in various combinations, typically complemented by competencies contributed by other companies, configurations of competencies are the "stuff" of which solution products are created. As a consequence, a primary responsibility of management is to conduct ongoing, market-pulled competency inventories to ensure that the company has, or through alliances has direct access to, the kinds of resources that make it possible to exploit a customer opportunity proactively.

Related management responsibilities are to maintain as open an information environment as is consistent with supporting the needs of innovative, entrepreneurial personnel and to share information to mutual advantage with partnering companies while protecting the information that is truly vital to the fertility of the company's core competencies.

3. To be capable of a flexible focus on evolving core competencies, an agile company supports multiple, concurrent, highly flexible organizational structures. These reflect the differing requirements of diverse development, production, and customer support activities. Internal teams, interenterprise teams, peer collaborations, hierarchical collaborations, lattice structures, and flattened pyramids all have applications that are appropriate *if they are the best means of achieving a particular project's ends.*

Individually, these are *tactics* for achieving particular goals. The ability to select the best tactic in a given situation, however, requires a *strategic* commitment to acquiring and maintaining the diverse infrastructures and resources on which those tactics rest. If an interenterprise team is the tactic of choice to exploit a new customer opportunity, it is too late at the time of choosing the tactic to begin to hire people with the requisite skills or to install the communication and computing technologies that enable interenterprise teaming.

The overriding objective is the creation of interactive customer relationships in support of long-lived solution products. This objective mandates minimizing the number of functional "walls" that need to be breached in order to respond to new, inevitably cross-functional opportunities to offer solutions to customers' problems. Concurrently, interactive customer relationships are mirrored in interactive relationships with suppliers and partnering companies.

Similarly, serial work processes are replaced by flexible combinations of concurrent, parallel *and* serial work processes, optimized to the requirements of each project. These, too, extend across supplier, partner, and customer companies in order to create multienterprise work processes, if these serve the project best.

4. Leadership, motivation, and trust replace command and control as the dominant motifs of management. Leadership manifests itself in defining strategic goals and in acquiring and maintaining the human and technological resources needed to meet them. The goal of motivation is the creation of an entrepreneurial work force, pervaded by a universal sense of responsibility for the company's success. This is reflected in work force assimilation of universal problem ownership and in independent initiative in offering solutions to perceived problems. Trust takes the form of creating mutual dependencies for joint success. In the words of Tenneco CEO Michael Walsh, "The main requirements of leadership are guts and judgment. To win trust, you have to make yourself vulnerable," which requires "guts," while strategic vision is only as sound as the judgments on which it is based.

Strategic Intent

The Strategic Intent planning model promoted by Gary Hamel and C. K. Prahalad captures the essence of agile management principles:

Formulating a clear vision of company principles and commitments that is communicated to all personnel

Setting bold goals that can be met only by leveraging current resources, not by making the most efficient use of the resources currently available

Avoiding micromanagement in favor of providing personnel with the necessary physical and cognitive tools and then allowing them to meet their goals, reviewing progress and adjusting the goals as necessary

Working to win universal buy-in to, and responsibility for meeting, corporate goals, in part by drawing all personnel into meaningful participation in the strategic planning process

In an agile competitive environment, management must present a rationale for the balance between compartmentalizing, and openly distributing, resources that is in place in the company at any given time. Centralized control dictates compartmentalization. Distributing knowledge, responsibility, and accountability improves functionality but requires trust, which entails giving up a measure of control. Whatever balance management may strike is dynamic, however. It is inevitably transient because of the rapidly changing agile competitive environment.

An agile company cannot have a *fixed* organizational structure, but it does have a structure. There are always organizational "walls" that define various configurations of the company's capabilities. Typical configurations will cut across functional capabilities and business processes and will support multiple concurrent organizational structures. The walls that exist at a given time will be redeployable as a matter of routine. They will be redeployed as needed in order to create new combinations of expertise, skills, and equipment that are "right" for the new jobs that have to be done.

Traditional functional walls segregated the possession and the exercise of expertise: design, production, purchasing, finance, distribution, and sales. In agile companies, functional systems are put in place—purchasing, billing, shipping, production scheduling, accounting—and then access is provided to whoever needs them.

Moving from mass-production-based industrial competition to agile competition is, in the first instance, a management problem. How can command and control management be replaced by initiative-inspiring leadership? How can much more of the problem-solving power of employees than today's organizational structures and management philosophies allow be liberated to serve the company's (and the employees') interests? Implementing agility will transform how companies select, organize, utilize, and manage human and technological resources, as well as how companies interact with one another and with their customers.

Management by Design

Solutions to the problems of how best to organize and to manage an agile company are like solutions to engineering design problems and unlike answers to scientific questions. Just as there are no uniquely correct solutions to design problems, there are no uniquely correct solutions to the problems of how to organize and manage an agile company. Like design solutions, solutions to agile management problems are context- and time-sensitive and are constrained by resource allocation and availability factors external to the design problem. No particular solution is likely to remain successful for very long, because the continual and unpredictable market changes characteristic of agile competition will require that new solutions be found.

If the organizational *structure* of an agile company is distinctive, so is its organizational *culture.* The culture must be entrepreneurial if the company is to be one in which change is embraced as positive, a source of new opportunities for profit and growth. The all-too-familiar alternative is to fear change because it might undermine the status quo, which is comfortable.

An agile company is marked by a sense of universal responsibility for the company's success, by the mutual accountability of management and the professional, technical, and operational work force for achieving the company's goals. The tone is set by management's adoption of the roles of leaders and resource providers, nurturing an ethic of cooperation and mutual dependencies that in effect inverts the traditional corporate pyramid.

Agile business capabilities come at a cost—organizational change. Inevitably, this change must come from the top. William Weiss, CEO of Ameritech, puts it well: "The best way I know to get people to accept the need for change is to not give them a choice."

LEVERAGING THE IMPACT OF PEOPLE AND INFORMATION

People and information differentiate competitors in the world of agile competition. What a company sells is its ability to convert the knowledge, skills, and information embodied in its personnel into solution products for individual customers. This ability is the key to success in customer-value–based competition. James Schraith, director of sales and marketing at computer manufacturer AST Research, argues that "price will disappear as a differentiator" as companies compete on the basis of information-rich, customer-enrichment–based products and services. "Companies will have to compete on something other than price, and those who can compete only on price will cease to exist." Chrysler CEO Robert Eaton echoes this conviction: "The only way we can beat the competition is with people." Organization, process reengineering, and technology are not enough to keep a competitive advantage, although they may briefly win one.

Physical products by themselves, and services by themselves—even customer-configurable products and services—are significantly less valuable than the integration of physical products and services into what customers perceive to be solutions to their problems. This added value is what makes people and information the competitive differentiators in agile markets. For an agile company, people are the core productive resource—not technology, not plants, not equipment. What customers are really paying for is access to people who are capable of synthesizing profitable customer-enriching products out of the knowledge they possess and out of the information and technologies their company makes available to them.

Enabling People

People and information are truly an agile company's most valuable assets. Leveraging those assets into sustained value-adding, profit-generating activity is the objective of the company's organizational structure and management philosophy. Very quickly, the raw materials, the production equipment, the production and the business processes, the styling, and the marketing techniques that are employed by a company that achieves a great market success are available to its competitors. What cannot become quickly available are the knowledge, skills, initiative, motivation, and dedication of its work force, from senior management to operational personnel. The first task of an agile competitor, therefore, is to create a company environment that leverages the impact of people and information on its bottom line.

An agile work force is composed of people who are knowledgeable, informed, flexible, and empowered. People who are expected to think about what they are doing, are authorized to display initiative, and are supported by management to be innovative about what they do and how they do it. People who are open to continuous learning and able to acquire new knowledge and skills on a "just-in-time," project-pulled basis. People who are committed to cooperation and able to work well on cross-functional intraenterprise and interenterprise teams. People who are open to cross-training, are technologically literate, and are able to utilize an open information environment effectively and with integrity. People who are willing to think like owners of the company, that is, people who are willing to accept joint responsibility for the company's success, accountability for meeting goals they have set, ownership of the company's problems as their problems as well, and a universal customer service role.

Creating an agile work force defines management's responsibility: to provide personnel with continuing access to the production, communication, and information technologies, and to the constantly changing information and knowledge resources, that are required if a company is to be competitive in an agile business environment. The demanding challenge to management is:

To maintain a company of the right size for the markets and product lines in which it competes

To create an open information environment

To balance the objective of work force motivation and concern for job security (itself a powerful motivator) with the demands of constantly changing customer opportunities

To integrate continuous learning into workplace activities and job performance expectations

To support continuous education and training as an investment in the company's future prosperity

To conduct ongoing core competency inventories and to invest in the new skills, knowledge, and technologies that these inventories reveal are necessary to create new market opportunities

To make a commitment to and investment in comprehensive work force communication

To pursue high standards of work life quality and to use appropriate reward mechanisms as an expression of support for the high levels of commitment, dedication, and effort expected of a "think-like-an-owner work force" and as a means of nurturing empowerment and trust

A management philosophy adapted to the requirements of agile competition centers on personnel, not equipment, as the company's core productive resource. Are personnel *required* to think in order to perform their jobs well? Are they *expected* to think for themselves, or are they really there just to listen to supervisors and do what they are told? Are they given the information they need and the access to the knowledge, skills, and physical resources they require in order to be innovative?

The reward structure is an important part of creating an agile work force, but only a part. Basing a portion of individual salaries on team and/or company productivity is a valuable tactic. Many studies, however, support the conclusion that nonfinancial rewards, in addition to well-conceived financial ones, sustain motivation and dedication. A powerful motivator all by itself comes from treating people with integrity: respecting their intelligence, cultivating it by sharing with them timely and valuable information, and authorizing them to act on it. Peer respect and the satisfaction derived from achieving a self-assigned goal are similarly powerful nonfinancial motivators.

There are only short-term gains, at best, to be derived from improving the efficiency of machinery alone in an agile competitive environment. Long-term gains will always lie in improving the efficiency of what people uniquely contribute to creating goods and services for individual customers.

Motivating People

The behavior of individuals in groups is strongly influenced by their understanding of how their performance is to be measured. The introduction into a company of cross-functional and interenterprise teams must be accompanied by cross-functional performance metrics that reinforce the team's positive impact on the company's success. Currently, the narrowly functional metrics used by companies sometimes force people in different divisions of the company into conflict with one another, to the detriment of the company. These metrics optimize local performance independent of its global impact. Evaluating manufacturing performance on the basis of equipment utilization rates, for example, can encourage growing inventories of unsold goods; evaluating financial performance on the basis of return on assets may be incompatible with quality control metrics; and so on.

Work force motivation is enhanced by distributing decision-making authority. This can take the form of vertical networks of mutual dependency between levels of the management hierarchy, or of horizontal networks among personnel distributed across functional specializations (design, finance, production, sales, etc.). The objective is to promote universal ownership of problems that affect the company's bottom line, in particular, to promote universal ownership of customer gratification as everybody's business. This objective can be achieved by bringing problem-solving authority as close as possible to the location of the problem and to the people for whom it *is* a problem. Ideally, these people know best how to solve the problem. If they can solve the problem on their own, so much the better. If not, they are invaluable contributors to defining the terms of the problem, the terms of its solution, and the resources beyond their own expertise and facilities that will be needed to solve it.

Nucor Steel, John Deere's Moline, Illinois, seeder plant, and TRW's remote keyless entry system plant in Auburn, New York, have successfully implemented programs that tie a percentage of income to performance. But, like Ford and Springfield Remanufacturing, among many others, they have at the same time introduced an unprecedented sharing of information with personnel about company operations. This extends to providing short courses for all personnel on reading a profit and loss statement and then releasing timely, detailed, and accurate information about the company's operations, including production costs, financial figures (for example, regular return on assets calculations), sales, marketing, distribution, and service costs, and the status of these costs and figures relative to competitors' costs and sales.

Magna Copper of Tucson, Arizona, signed a 15-year contract with its 4700 workers in 1989 and received an 8-year no-work-stoppage guarantee and approval of joint labor-management work process redesign teams and decentralized decision making. By the end of 1991, the smelter was operating at 107 percent of design capacity and production was up 30 percent.

At Corning's Blacksburg, Virginia, plant, 10 percent of the intensive, continuous training programs are on the employees' time, but there is a formal no-layoff policy and workers are responsible for continuous improvement of production processes. There are no time clocks, and workers can choose shifts of $12\frac{1}{2}$ or 10 hours for 3- or 4-day workweeks to obtain rotating days off.

At Chaparall Steel, where a no-layoff policy is in effect, all 935 employees are members of the "sales" department and empowered to respond to any customer request; they have open access to sales, billing, credit, shipping, and production scheduling data.*

Nurturing Competencies

The decisive determinant of long-term agile competitive advantage is the ability to create and sustain enduring, strategic relationships with customers whose requirements are constantly changing. An agile company does this by providing customers with multigeneration families of high-value-added products. It thus maintains accurate and current knowledge of the competencies available to the company and nurtures those competencies, for example, by supporting cross-training of managerial and technical, as well as operational, personnel. It becomes vitally important to know which competencies the company possesses in its own work force, which competencies it has access to through cooperative relationships with other companies, and which competencies it is likely to require access to in the future.

---

*The U.S. Department of Labor has compiled data on "high performance workplace" practices at 175 companies. A digital file containing this data is available from the Agility Forum. See Appendix: Resource Organizations.

In addition, management must continually assess which competencies the company needs to "own" and which it can contract for from other companies on an as-needed basis. The former competencies determine the levels of investment in the personnel who will constitute the company's core work force and in the learning and the technologies needed to support them. The latter competencies determine the company's need for temporary personnel, for contract employees—including managerial and technical professionals—or for cooperative agreements with other companies, either to outsource whole functions, such as engineering and legal services, or to borrow expertise to the mutual advantage of the cooperating companies. A clear outsourcing policy that is continually matched against the company's strategic objectives thus becomes a primary responsibility of senior management.

A surprisingly large number of companies lack a systematic inventory of the expertise its personnel already possess, the expertise it will need in order to move into the markets in which it needs to compete, and a map of how its personnel are to move from the expertise they currently possess to the expertise the company needs them to possess. A growing recognition of this ignorance underlies the current interest in core competency inventories and in continuous education and training programs. Too often, however, these programs lack a foundation in market-centered, customer-serving company operations.

An agile company cannot afford such ignorance . . . for long. Company-supported education and training should, whatever else it offers to personnel, be responsive to what the company needs to be able to do in the markets in which it competes. Those needs then define what personnel need to learn how to do in order to enable the company to acquire the capabilities it must acquire to be profitable. A needs inventory is not a "once and done thing." As the marketplace changes, and new customer opportunities arise while old ones evolve, what personnel need to know changes as well.

Exploiting Information

Finally, the agile competitive environment places a premium on rapidly evolving, information-based products. The processes required for identifying, creating, and bringing such products to market cannot be driven from the top down only. The initiative for changing existing products, or for creating new ones, comes from all levels of the company. Furthermore, once a decision has been made to change products and/or processes, these changes can be very rapidly implemented.

The cumulative impact of these competency requirements is that an agile competitor must be committed to continuous learning for all personnel, because information and people are *together* the most valuable asset of an agile company. People must be knowledgeable enough to exploit information innovatively. The bottleneck to higher levels of performance in an agile company is not equipment but information flow, internally and among cooperating companies. Information is already an increasingly important and increasingly valuable component of consumer and commercial products. Packaging information, providing access to information, and information "tools"—for example, design software and database search software—will become increasingly valuable products in their own right, as well as increasingly valuable elements of hardware products, such as automobiles. The act of collecting, evaluating, organizing, and distributing information becomes a decisive enabler and infrastructure requirement of agile product development and delivery.

Recognizing and exploiting the value of information is creating new classes of products. For the 1994 model year, the average value of the electronics content of automobiles sold in the U.S. market was almost $800, a figure higher than the value of the steel in an automobile. Furthermore, the value of the electronics is rising rapidly and is widely expected to reach 20 percent or more of the value of a car by the end of the decade. The information embedded in the electronics systems is both itself a product and the basis for creating new products.

In Japan, Honda sells a 250-cubic-centimeter motorcycle with a "key" the size of a credit card that not only unlocks the steering head and activates the electrical circuits, but contains the data needed for the electronic fuel injection, oil pump and exhaust valve controls, and ignition timing to operate. Thus the key is not just a security device. At additional cost Honda offers a variety of cards that dramatically alter the performance characteristics of this motorcycle. One card alters the valve, oil pump, fuel injection, and ignition settings, thereby increasing horsepower by 20 percent. The owner needs to make just one mechanical adjustment to change his or her motorcycle from a docile commuter bike to a sports machine. One card that is planned will optimize fuel consumption for long-distance trips, at a sacrifice in power, and another card will improve performance for racing purposes. By exploiting the role that embedded information plays in a physical product, Honda can offer a single motorcycle with multiple personalities!

Not surprisingly, growth in the automotive aftermarket industry is being seen in companies that offer performance improvements by reprogramming the electronics that control engine and transmission operating characteristics (in the near future, changes in computer-controlled "active" suspension systems will be available). Companies such as AutoThority and Adaptive Technologies in California, Hypertech in Texas, and RENNtech in Florida offer a broad spectrum of performance-enhancing chips that meet emission-control standards for cars ranging from the Chevrolet Lumina sedan to the Mazda RX-7 Turbo, in addition to Porsche, BMW, and Mercedes. Adaptive Technologies offers a unit with four engine-control PROM chips that the driver can select from the dashboard and that can alter performance significantly to meet varying situations—need for greater towing ability, more power, less power and/or variable top speed cutoff, and engine disabler.

Management's Challenge

To summarize, management's primary task in an agile company is to create and maintain an entrepreneurial culture of reciprocal responsibility for the success of the company. This entails adjusting the resources that are available to personnel on a running basis: monitoring progress towards goals and adjusting support levels—and even the goals themselves, if necessary—in response to personnel performance, evolving opportunities, and changing parameters of marketplace success.

Agile company personnel think about their work and make their own decisions about how it can best be performed as their work objectives change. They commonly work in teams, but are evaluated and compensated for their individual skills, *as well as* for how their team's performance affects the company's bottom line. The ideal is a company in which every employee thinks like an owner, in which problem ownership is universal, customer service is everyone's job, and responsibility for the company's success is shared by everyone. Such a company must be made; it will not just happen.

To make such a company, management must unlearn "truths" that were fellow travelers of mass-production-based industrial competition. Among these truths are:

- That dependencies are a sign of weakness
- That information is power and sharing it means losing power
- That succeeding alone is superior to succeeding through cooperation
- That breakthroughs are better than incremental improvements
- That if a company improves its products, markets will take care of themselves
- That standards are for others to observe
- That labor-management relationships must be adversarial and that the managerial function must be one of command and control
- That managers should focus on operations and let infrastructure requirements take care of themselves
- that managers know better than operational personnel what the latter should do and how they should do it

HIGHLIGHTS OF THE FOUR DIMENSIONS OF AGILE COMPETITION

1. Enriching the Customer

The agile company:

- Is capable of individualizable mass production, targeting many niche markets.

- Offers products because of the value that individual customers perceive those products to have for them.
- Knows enough about customers, collectively and individually, to identify what products will be of value to them and to estimate how valuable they are or will be.
- Adopts pricing and marketing strategies determined by customer-perceived value.
- Initiates interactive relationships with customers as a means of tailoring products to their current (reactive product development) and future (proactive product development) needs.
- Designs products to incorporate a variable mix of hardware, information, and services.
- Designs products to be customer-configurable initially, and to be long-lived in spite of rapid innovation, because they are easily customer-upgradable and customer-reconfigurable to accommodate new capabilities.
- Implements a total product life cycle design philosophy, from supplier relationships to eventual product disposal, in such a way that design is integrated into a holistic production process incorporating all the company's business processes.
- Adds value to products by giving customers access to relevant information in the company (production scheduling, service records, field experience) and in the products themselves.
- Sells the company's core competencies, not just individual products.
- Exploits new economies of scope by designing core products that can appear in a wide range of continually changing models, within a market and across markets.
- Sneakerizes: develops products that fracture markets, create new niches, and convert commodities into individualizable, specialty products.
- Anticipates the short profit lifetime, especially of highly successful products, as imitative competitors convert specialty products into commodities.
- Builds to order, not to forecast: the economic order quantity for responding to a sales opportunity should be "any."
- Makes rapid concept to cash the central impetus of product development processes.

2. Cooperating to Enhance Competitiveness

The agile company:

- Internalizes the message—at all levels of the company—that cooperation and competition are not mutually exclusive.
- Makes cooperation the solution strategy of first choice at all levels of the company—across departments, divisions, subsidiaries, and affiliates and across companies, including direct competitors.
- Creates a company culture that supports people routinely working together to solve what are perceived to be everyone's problems, so that the company functions in a manner analogous to the way that a hospital emergency room functions.
- Identifies win-win relationships as the strategic justification for intercompany cooperative ventures.
- Shares information to mutual advantage with suppliers, partnering companies, and customers.
- Develops clear intellectual property rights policies.
- Develops clear partnering criteria, both for cooperative relationships within the company and with other companies.
- Develops an explicit intercompany ethics code and sticks to it.
- Implements explicit criteria, and the necessary capabilities, for routinely initiating or joining virtual company ventures.
- Integrates by bytes, not bricks: Whenever it is advantageous to do so, it links complementary core competencies, business processes, and facilities across enterprises on an opportunistic basis limited by the profit lifetime of the product.
- Adopts standards that support interenterprise cooperation at all levels.
- Learns the lesson of the audio system, "virtual" bicycle, and PC markets: develop plug-compatible and component architecture product designs in order to participate in win-win multivendor end-user product systems and extend product longevity through reconfigurability.
- Develops plug-compatible and component architecture business processes as well as products, in order to enable routine cooperation with other companies.

- Communicates the benefits of cooperation: cycle time reduction, reduction of development and operating costs, reduction of scale of risk, acceleration of technology transfer, reduction of impact of (typically) short product profit lifetime.

3. Organizing to Master Change

The agile company:

- Chooses its company's organizational structure deliberately; it doesn't just put up with the traditional structure.
- Calculates the organizational forms that best match the requirements of customer opportunities, strategic goals, and alternative product development, production, pricing, and marketing strategies.
- Pursues multiple concurrent customer opportunities, if necessary maintaining multiple concurrent organizational structures dictated by their differing requirements.
- Maintains flexible and dynamic organizational structures as a primary means of profiting from change and uncertainty.
- Precipitates marketplace changes that can be manipulated to the company's special advantage.
- Precipitates change even in markets and operations that are currently profitable if future growth considerations tip the balance in favor of change.
- Internalizes the message throughout the company that change creates new opportunities *because* it destabilizes the comfortable status quo.
- Organizes around motivation, leadership, and the creation of mutually advantageous dependencies (trust relationships), rather than around command and control.
- Organizes in ways that nurture an entrepreneurial company culture at all levels of the company and a universal sense of shared responsibility, and accountability, for the company's success.
- Organizes around people as the company's main asset and primary productive resource.

- Keys resource allocation policies to knowledge and the ability to exploit information innovatively as the company's main asset.
- Creates an open information environment and invest in continuous learning, especially just-in-time learning, for all personnel.
- Conducts continuing competency inventories.
- Creates a widespread awareness of the competencies available in the company and of the new competencies required by the company's evolving strategic product and market goals.
- Implements enterprisewide information integration.
- Organizes in ways that facilitate concurrent, rather than serial, company operations.
- Diffuses authority: coordination does *not* necessitate centralization of authority.
- Enables all personnel to act locally, when they have the ability to do so, but teaches them to think globally, anticipating the possible wider impact on operations of their local action.
- Invests in internal communication aimed at helping all personnel to understand the company's goals, principles of operation, priorities, and commitments.
- Invests in worklife quality.
- Assimilates the Strategic Intent planning model (page 104).

4. Leveraging the Impact of People and Information

The agile competitor understands that:

- People and information are the differentiators of companies in agile competition.
- People are successful agile competitors if they are:
  - Knowledgeable, skilled, informed about the company, and flexible in adapting to the organizational changes and new performance expectations demanded by changing customer opportunities
  - Innovative, capable of taking initiative, authorized to do so, and supported appropriately

- Open to continuous learning, able to acquire new knowledge and skills just in time as requirements dictate, and technology-literate
- Capable of performing well in cooperative relationships, on internal and intercompany teams that may be cross-functional and require multiskilled members
- Willing to "think like an owner" and accept customer service responsibilities, acknowledge accountability, and accept ownership of problems and shared responsibility for the company's success

4

The Transition to Agility

The preceding chapters have presented a descriptive overview of agility. The chapters that follow treat agility from the more practical perspective of its implementation: the acquisition by individual companies of agile business capabilities. As we argued at the end of Chapter 1, however, the implementation of agility is highly context-dependent. No universal prescription, applicable to every company, is possible. That a company needs to become an agile competitor, and if it does, what it must do to become one are decisions that must be based on an understanding of each company's customers and markets, competitors and products, and competencies and resources.

It is nevertheless possible to bridge the gap between a broadly descriptive view of agility and a narrowly prescriptive, company-specific view. The objective of Part 2 of this book, "Thriving on Change and Uncertainty," is to effect such a bridge by way of a methodical treatment of the universal features of agile competition that every company must factor into its strategic planning.

To prepare for the shift in the perspective from Part 1 to Part 2, we offer in this chapter an imaginative scenario, one that may, on first reading, strain your credulity but is not nearly as implausible as it may appear. Following the scenario, we reveal a real-world development that parallels the scenario to a surprising degree. Then we provide more than 100 illustrations of corporate behaviors that converge on the goal of acquiring agile competitive capabilities. Most of them are "common knowledge," and the number could easily be multiplied severalfold by studying recent business literature and media business reporting with an "agile eye." Collecting these illustrations, and systematically relating them to the objectives of agile competition, illustrates the claim that agility marks the emergence of a new industrial order in commercial reality.

A WEEK IN THE LIFE OF AN AGILE COMPETITOR*

Prelude

Our company had to change its culture to become an agile competitor. In the past, we had been organized into functional departments. We made standard products, and everyone knew who they worked for and what they were supposed to do. Today, we have almost no permanent organizational structures. The company operates like a quick-reaction SWAT team, except that we change products, internal practices, and relationships with customers and partners proactively, on our terms, at least as often as we react to marketplace changes.

We have people who are permanent members of customer relations teams, always looking for new opportunities for the company by studying what our customers are doing. We have a permanent team

---

*This material has been adapted, with permission, from a scenario outline originally developed by Lt. Gen. James Abrahamson (USAF, ret.), Chairman of the Oracle Corporation, and Chair of the Industry Steering Group of CALS (an international effort to create standards for communication of product descriptions).

with rotating members that has the job of making the speed with which we do anything—and I mean *anything,* from answering the phone to prototyping a new product—even faster. We even have a group of people whose job it is to study what's going on in the business world outside our company, in order to identify core competencies that we might need in the near future. One of their jobs is to give us "early warning" of the need to develop new competencies internally. Just as important, they begin in advance of our need to qualify companies who already possess those competencies so that they are prepared to work with us, at a moment's notice—literally a moment, in this age of electronic commerce—if the need arises.

One of the biggest culture changes we went through on the way to agility was the change in executive attitude about the need for, and the ability of, employees to think for themselves and to make decisions on the company's behalf. In a major reversal of previous policies, management recognized that the success or failure of agile competitors rests on the competence of *all* the people in the organization. Now, they ask us not only to think about what we're doing but to think about what our customers are doing, so that we can come up with newer and better ways to enrich customers that will simultaneously be profitable for us.

Today, our executive team has the job of setting the company's direction, getting us to buy into really bold objectives, goals that we simply cannot meet with current practices and resources, and establishing metrics for successful operations. Our job is to figure out how to meet, and exceed, those objectives.

One tool that we use to do that is a weekly "mapping" of the four strategic dimensions of agility onto our operations. These dimensions are generic, of course, and need to be specifically assimilated by each company based on its changing circumstances, but it turns out to be very valuable to challenge ourselves to identify the match between what we're doing and these broad principles. It's like checking a compass on a wilderness trek: we check the "agility map" to make sure that we're moving in the right direction. So we ask every organizational unit, no matter how small or large, to identify for each agility dimension the top five objectives they intend to focus on. That makes it easier to chart and measure everything they do by relating it to those objectives.

We do have organizationwide measures of the overall health of our company that we also track. By far the most important of these has been the concept to cash measure. More than any other, this metric set the direction for agility in our company. By *concept to cash time*, we mean the time from when we first consider an idea for a product concept to when the customer is billed, which, with the spread of pay-on-use accounting and electronic funds transfer, usually means when the first payments are received. We used Federal Express as an example to challenge ourselves: a company that did what seemed impossible and created a market by a short concept to cash cycle.

When we first heard of the idea, our best concept to cash time was measured in years for truly new products and was six to ten months for new models of existing products. Initially, we cut new product introduction time in half, and we were proud of our accomplishments, thinking that we must be the state of the art. This was right around the time of the Persian Gulf War and coincided with the publicity that CNN received for its global dominance of war coverage. CNN used the same equipment and technology as its competitors, but CNN was organized differently—to thrive on change and uncertainty anywhere in the world. Field personnel were empowered to make rapid decisions and to commit the organization's resources in order to exploit unanticipated opportunities.

The lesson for us was that CNN trusted its employees to act on behalf of the company and that trust made CNN more agile than their competition, with its rigid decision-making hierarchies, was. The CNN and Federal Express stories convinced us that an opportunity existed to raise our profits and to enrich our customers simultaneously, if we could be really fast and proactive. CNN did it by distributing authority; Federal Express did it by creating new markets through speed.

Senior management set up companywide cross-functional teams to study our practices. We were amazed at the amount of wasted time that was built into the way we were organized and that could easily be saved just by reorganizing. Every group that handed off to any other group always put a contingency time in the loop. If we had six to eight functional organizations involved in a product, we had six to eight contingencies in the loop. Each of those contingencies took longer than we take today for many whole projects!

We had to admit that we had never even tried to make the product conceptualization process efficient. Our factory and production systems were efficient, but coming up with new concepts or creating new designs or design variants and converting them into products was never considered to be an area where efficiency mattered. Nor had we thought much about the time between steps, or tried to make the overall process of concept to cash efficient.

The scenario that follows is typical of how we do business now. The time periods vary, of course, and this is very nearly our best example, but it's not a one-of-a-kind miracle. This really *is* the way we operate.

Day 1

At 10 a.m. on Monday, a small, cross-functional customer relations team that spends most of its time in the field—doing what they call "living with customers"—initiated a multimedia voice-data-graphics conference call. They were excited about a new product concept a customer had developed with them. Working with the customer's operations team, they had seen a way to increase the customer's profit significantly. The new concept made it possible to gain access to, and use information embedded in, one of the customer's products. The cause of the excitement was that the customer saw the possibility of increasing its market presence by more than 15 percent.

Within an hour, a national multimedia network conference with a full initial solution development team (ISDT), consisting of experts in information systems engineering, design, production, purchasing, customer relations (from other customers), finance, testing, service, and research and development, was set up for a working lunch. Our central time zone location in Boise, Idaho, makes this easy: the westerners eat a little early, midwesterners, a little late, and the easterners have a snack to be polite. Much nicer than a working breakfast called by an excited east coast team!

What the customer relations team wanted was validation of their idea. If a full ISDT shared their excitement, that would constitute the support to pull together the resources needed to proceed with a product development plan.

At lunch, the discussion began with a presentation of the concept to the ISDT. The customer relations team explained the value of the proposed product to the customer whose operations inspired it, and its generalizability to a number of industries in which products are rich with currently inaccessible embedded information. There was the usual barrage of hard questions and sharp challenges: a couple of devil's advocate types from New York and Boston, and two guys in Seattle who saw an even richer possibility in the new concept if only we pushed the envelope a little harder. Everyone agreed that the simple first step had enough customer payback to warrant proceeding with it.

The discussion quickly shifted from concept to customer applications. The ISDT specifically valued the capability of the product to serve as a platform for a range of customer-configurable options and generations of upgrades through reconfigurability. The spreading excitement soon pushed the discussion to extensibility issues—the availability within the company of the technology and the skills needed to create and produce the product, and the external resources we would have to pull together to get the product to the customer in record time. As always, the shortest possible concept to cash time was our goal.

By 2 p.m. Boise time, everyone was contributing ideas to the design developing on the network. We rapidly accumulated pictures and specs of the existing product on which the new one would be based, sketches of what the modification would look like, figures on capacity, critical personnel, and resource availability, and partnering company profiles that would fit this project to a T. Obviously, the team had a winner; buy-in was not an issue. We agreed to go off line for three hours and reconvene at 5 p.m. (tough on New York and Boston!).

By 5, one team of engineers had laid out the new circuits and the interface to the existing circuits that would be needed. We really liked an idea they came up with for a multichip module that would lower costs and could easily become the basis for related customer solutions in the future. Of course, to get this much done so quickly, they had had to use on-line software tools rented from an engineering service bureau. The service bureau wanted us to use the tools in exchange for equity rights to the concept. Our assessment of the value of the intellectual property led us to pay the outrageous fee for a few hours rather than giving up equity on our intellectual property.

Concurrently, a second team of engineers verified buildability using our production facilities. And a third, cross-functional team had done a network search to locate companies with the complementary resources we were going to need and to determine their availability and the currency of their precertified partnering agreements within our virtual company web.

At the 5 o'clock meeting, things started to come together. The circuit designs showed that we could actually make a device with the capabilities the customer relations team had envisioned. The production people identified the components we were best at building, and we had a list of potential partners who could contribute whatever else was needed to create the finished customer installation. The finance people generated customer value projections, as well as a selling price based on these projections which met the return on expense (ROE) hurdle. We decided that this was a go, authorized the resources to make it happen, and informed the corporate operations center. Everyone worked on their own on Tuesday; the next, and probably final, ISDT meeting was set for Tuesday at 5 P.M.

The preliminary circuit designs were networked on Monday night to an electronics simulation service company for validation, done by proprietary software tools that can check both the circuits and the proposed multichip modules. Naturally, problems were discovered, including a few sneak circuits, but the simulation company worked interactively with our people to correct the design. They sent the corrected design to a silicon foundry—selected on the basis of past experience, costs, capabilities, and availability from our virtual web database—and notified the ISDT that the production of the prototype chip was only one decision away.

Day 2

On Tuesday morning, selected suppliers were sent a first alert, with full details of component, software, and services requirements. The foundry had been queried automatically about cost and scheduling upon receiving the circuit design. Because standard simulations were used, the plan took minutes to prepare, and because the numbers were within the range projected at the Monday evening meeting, only an additional hour was needed to approve the plan.

The authorization alerted the operations people to order the critical circuit elements, software modifications, and parts needed to make the system and to custom-configure the necessary mechanical components. We asked our suppliers for one-day delivery via Global Transpark Service as time was money to our customer. The programmers, who were based in India, used the network for instant communications, of course. Also, since the Asian suppliers had the 12-hour time difference working in their favor, only one European company had to use Express SST shipping.

Anticipating success, the ISDT began the transition to a customer installation team (CIT) to work with the customer to plan an immediately profitable use of the new product. A multimedia conference with management and personnel from operations that would be affected by the new product was set up for Wednesday afternoon, at which time a working system would have been assembled.

Day 3

On Wednesday morning, engineers and production people assembled the system. With the aid of a universal tester and operational environment simulator, the engineers performed systems tests. Because the ISDT team wanted everything ready for the presentation, there was a working lunch, a very familiar fact of life.

Not surprisingly, the system worked and the customer was delighted with the potential. At this point, we decided that the specific application for our original customer had the possibility of wider application and customization. Therefore, another videoconference was scheduled for Wednesday evening involving selected suppliers, other current and potential customers who had an appropriate interest profile, and several venture capitalists who proactively keep up to date on our projects. There wasn't much notice, of course, but because most business is conducted this way, people expect to participate in meetings like this and are available to do so, if they are looking for business! Entrepreneurialism means learning about opportunities as much as it does seizing them.

The videoconference included simulations of the proposed product in action, developed by the R&D people primarily, as well as live test results from the primary customer, and face-to-face discussion with the customer relations team and the CIT members.

During the videoconference, a marketing company from our web was chosen to run a combination analysis and market simulation. An automated business plan with targeted revenues and ROE figures was quickly developed, in time to join the videoconference. The customer relations team that had come up with the idea explained the genesis of the product, how it worked, and how it could be customized to suit particular needs. The emphasis, always, was on the value that it added for the customer.

During the videoconference, some participating customers agreed to schedule a customized on-line computer-integrated multimedia dem-onstration of the product system. A few asked to download simulation models and product data for analysis by their own personnel. These com-panies would be able to immediately integrate our new system into their own products, because the simulation models and product data observed international standards developed for this purpose.

More important, the customer relations teams began working di-rectly and individually with customers who gave us valuable sugges-tions for performance features and optional physical configurations. Most important of all, we received verification that our customers saw significant enrichment potential for their customers and verified our original concept.

Day 4

On Thursday, the product adjustments suggested by the customers were being dealt with by separate and concurrent CIT teams working at individual customer locations. A key to our success is the informal communications that exist across CIT teams to ensure that synergistic opportunities arise and are evaluated.

Back in Boise, a product system potential team was formed to extract the essence of this product system and to ensure that all appropriate customer relations teams were aware of the development. They could then seek ways to generalize the idea with their own particular customers.

As customers gain experience with the newly installed product system, each CIT will enter problems and resolution ideas in the corporate log for use by the product service improvement teams who audit all product service systems seeking improvement opportunities. This is an ongoing activity.

Suppliers were notified of the final design and list of requirements, along with the shipment schedules. Using the virtual company database of prequalified partners, the ISDT team made its selection of several international companies to partner with on Friday. This is a matter of routine, now that digital product description data observe universal standards.

Day 5

On Friday, the components were integrated, and the system was assembled and tested. The package included multilanguage electronic product description. This dynamic information package, complete with interactive simulation and a reconfigurable three-dimensional product model, was sent electronically to all customer relations teams in our own company and to those at our web partners whose interest profile places their customers in the system's market niche. Companies are, of course, able to respond interactively if they like what they see and/or have questions or suggestions for features that would make the product more valuable for them.

Day 6

On Saturday, some customers, including the one whose operations inspired the product, received the units we shipped Friday. Because the new product system was "pulled" by our customer relations team's intimate understanding of our customers' operations, the new system was immediately installed, and it performed as expected. At 8 o'clock on Saturday evening, the first approval triggered an automatic funds transfer to our corporate accounts. For the record, concept to cash time for this project was five days and ten hours!

Postmortem

That Monday, under the guidance of a continuous improvement team, the group again organized a multimedia conference. Functioning at a more leisurely pace, the group conducted a postmortem and made note of opportunities for improvement of the process. This was followed by a few days of well-earned rest, and a spell of self-education and training.

Are you doubtful? Don't think it can be done? Can't be done in your industry? In your company? Read on!

[TC²], the Textile/Clothing Technology Corporation, a 200-company consortium, demonstrated the evolving agility potential of the U.S. apparel industry at the September 1994 Bobbin show, held in Atlanta, Georgia. For the first time at a major industry trade show, a fully integrated virtual apparel manufacturing capability was operational. A blouse and coordinated skirt were designed, cut to customer order, printed, sewn, and distributed daily to customers at the show and at three remote retail sites.

A designer located at the Fashion Institute of Technology (FIT) in New York City and linked by two-way audio and video to [TC²]'s booth at the Bobbin Show in Atlanta designed the blouse print pattern interactively with customers at the Show, at a retail store in Cincinnati, Ohio, at EDS headquarters in Dallas, Texas, and at the National Center for Manufacturing Sciences in Ann Arbor, Michigan. Approval from customers for the print pattern, sizes, and colors was obtained by 3 p.m. on each day of the Show. The FIT designer then transmitted the designs chosen electronically to the show booth of Computer Design, Inc. (CDI). CDI translated the designs into digital screen print color separation data and digital garment pattern design data. The former were transmitted to a screen-making facility in Atlanta, the latter to computer-controlled laser cutting machines at the Show.

Concurrently, full-color posters displaying the designs being produced on the Show floor were printed, as were custom garment tags that accompanied each order to fulfillment.

The Atlanta screen print manufacturer produced the screens overnight and delivered them by 8 o'clock the next morning to the Show booth of Precision Screening Machine (PSM) for off-site printing of that day's designs. (Safety regulations precluded printing at the Show itself.) Concurrently, laser cutting machines at [TC²]'s booth used the digitized point-of-sale garment pattern and size data to cut garment pieces out of white fabric and deliver them to PSM for printing during Show hours. The printed pieces, collated by customer order for size, style, and design, were then shipped to two separate locations on the Show floor for assembly by flexible, cross-trained manufacturing teams: blouses by Sunbrand, skirts by Juki.

The sewing completed, the garments were then delivered to customers at the show and shipped overnight to customers at the remote locations.

Accomplishing this demonstration involved a partnership among 35 companies and the electronic coordination of four remote sites and five different locations at the Bobbin Show. To do all this—perhaps even more than the products that were created according to interactive customer specification—reveals how close the apparel industry is to possessing agile production, marketing, and distribution capabilities: producing customized products to order for traditionally mass-market customers, leveraging resources to cut product cycle time by means of intensive interactive cooperation among companies, and leveraging the impact of people and information by flexibility, empowerment, and mutually advantageous sharing.

Furthermore, the limited Bobbin Show demonstration is only a piece of [TC²]'s larger agile manufacturing effort: its Apparel on Demand demonstration project. For that project, [TC²] members have participated in the development of three-dimensional body scanning hardware and software, programs to translate this data into two-dimensional design data for printing fabric and cutting garment pieces using computer-controlled laser cutters, and high-speed computerized garment assembly machinery. Together with the software linking point-of-sale data to fiber, fabric, and garment manufacturers (software thoroughly proven by experience with Quick Response) true agile clothing production moves from imaginative scenario to imminent reality.

ILLUSTRATIONS OF AGILE COMPETITIVE BEHAVIOR*

The question we are asked more frequently than any other is this: "Can you give us an example of an agile company?" The best answer to that question seems like an evasion but is in fact a clarification. Agility is not an end point a company reaches, after which it coasts along on its established capabilities. Agility is a continual process of managed change, of constant adaptation of internal practices and external relationships to new customer opportunities.

The right question to ask, in our view, is: "Can you give us illustrations of agile competitive behaviors that companies are adopting?" The answer to that question is "Yes, we can!" We have organized about 100 of them alphabetically, for ease of reference. The real value of this list, however, lies not in the individual illustrations but in the cumulative effect of all of them. Together, they express the breadth of the shift in competitive focus that is going on in industry and the convergence of that shift to agility. Almost all the entries have been reported in the business press, and more are being reported every week. Reading them should provoke you to recognize evidence of the migration to agile

---

*These illustrations were compiled from personal interviews, primarily, and from the business media, secondarily, especially the *New York Times, Wall Street Journal, Business Week, Fortune,* and *Forbes.* Between June 1994, when this is being written, and September, when the book appears, as many illustrations again could be collected from a growing number of sources as agile business capabilities are implemented increasingly widely.

competition, or evidence of resistance to that migration, in companies that you know best but perhaps had not previously perceived as examples of new business paradigms taking hold.

ABB was created in 1987, when the Swedish Asea and the Swiss Brown Boveri corporations merged. CEO Percy Barnevik divided the resultant giant company into 1300 separate companies extending over 5000 autonomous profit centers. He flattened a seven-layer managerial hierarchy to four and cut headquarters staff from 4000 to 200. The task of top-level management is to motivate, set bold goals, and create an environment that promotes aggressive growth. In 1991 Barnevik set up a pilot program to reduce all company process times by half. The long-term goals, apart from achieving a 25 percent return on capital, are an entrepreneurial corporate culture in which risk taking is nurtured and rewarded, as long as it succeeds more often than not.

> Illustrates: flexible organization structures, macromanagement, coherent decentralization of authority, leveraging the skills and knowledge of people at all levels in the organization.

Air Products' South Brunswick, New Jersey, polymer emulsions plant is run by operational personnel; the plant manager, at the bottom of an inverted organizational pyramid, serves as a resource to the work force. Personnel have improved product yield and implemented a recycling scheme that has reduced waste disposal costs. These two steps alone have generated annual savings of about $500,000.

> Illustrates: leveraging impact of work force, management in leadership role, building motivation and trust in place of command and control, management as supporting operational work force.

Airfreight services were transformed by Federal Express, whose success opened up people's thinking about how they could create and exploit value by the speed with which products could be brought to markets where they commanded premium prices. Israeli growers harvest flowers at night and have them on sale in Holland's wholesale markets the next morning. South American growers fly melons to European cities in the deep of the northern winter. Long Island fishermen fly 800-pound bluefin tuna packed in ice overnight to Tokyo, where sushi restaurants pay $20 a pound for them in wholesale markets.

Illustrates: rethinking products; creating services based on customer-perceived value.

Ambra was an IBM subsidiary that marketed IBM PC clones using a virtual company organization structure. It was made up of about 80 people located in an office building in Raleigh, North Carolina who coordinated the operations of at least five companies, none of them dedicated to Ambra. These companies used their expertise and facilities to produce other products and services at the same time they did what they did for Ambra. Singapore-based Wearnes Technologies provided design services, and component manufacturing and procurement. SCI Systems assembled the PCs on a build-to-order basis only. AI, Inc. handled the telemarketing. Merisel handled order fulfillment and distribution. An IBM spinoff handled field service and customer support. The result was a computer that exemplified mass individualization. Ambra advertising trumpeted the theme, "You tell us what you want and we'll build it for you, at no extra cost for customization to your configuration of hardware and software options." When the benefits declined below IBM's threshold (in mid-1994), Ambra operations were phased out.

Illustrates: virtual company organization, build to order, customer-configurable product with wide range of options, mass individualization.

AT&T has hired L. L. Bean to handle the telemarketing of AT&T's 800-number services, because of the excellence of L. L. Bean's telemarketing operations.

Illustrates: exploitation of core competencies, selective outsourcing.

AT&T has implemented its Global Information Systems Architecture (GISA) to standardize its business manufacturing systems worldwide. The objective is to improve its ability to compete in all telecommunication markets, in whatever part of the world they may be. With GISA in place, concurrent product development, using physically distributed resources and bringing about a reduction in product cycle time and cost, will be possible. Originally developed by AT&T's switching systems business unit, GISA spread to the consumer products, microelectronics, network cable systems, transmission, and wireless business units. Now it is global.

> Illustrates: global production network, enterprise integration in support of rapid product development for global market niches.

Baseball statistics (and, inevitably, statistics for other sports) continue to generate new businesses. Fingertip for Stats allows Apple Newton owners to download comprehensive updates directly into its Newton baseball software every day of the season for about $1 a day, over and above the price of the initial software, of course. With a cellular modem in the PCMCIA slot, users can even update their statistics while at the ballpark. Microsoft's Complete Baseball includes (in addition to a CD ROM–based book) an on-line electronic daily baseball "newspaper" for $1.25 a day.

> Illustrates: information as a product, information product exploiting a physical product.

Bausch and Lomb, under CEO Daniel Gill, has moved from a glass lens and scientific instrument optics manufacturer to a vastly larger, more diverse, and more profitable company. Product development was determined by research that identified what people would buy *because* it was a Bausch and Lomb product. The results led to hearing aids, dental implant and care products, eye care products, and skin lotions. At the same time, Bausch and Lomb exploited the shift of the nonprescription sunglass market from a low-priced, mass-market commodity to a medium- and high-price (but high-volume) niche market specialty product. Its Ray-Ban line of fashion sunglasses and, more recently, its Revo line of premium sunglasses (in more than 80 frame styles and five lens tints) have contributed to the rapid expansion of the sunglass market to more than $2 billion in 1993, with the fastest-growing segment, fashion and premium models, accounting for more than 40 percent of sales. Expanding overseas, Bausch and Lomb formed an alliance with Beijing Optical to produce lenses for the Chinese domestic market; similar ventures were set up in India and Poland. Foreign revenues accounted for 50 percent of Bausch and Lomb income in 1993.

> Illustrates: customer value–based product development and pricing, exploitation of customer-perceived core competencies, "sneakerization" (fragmenting mass markets by transforming a commodity into a specialty product in many models).

BellCore scientist Arjen Lenstra created a limited-lifetime virtual problem-solving network that broke the RSA-129 encryption code. He coordinated the collective efforts of 600 volunteers in 25 countries, identified via a request he posted on the Internet. This virtual community committed 1600 computers available to them (ranging from PCs to Cray supercomputers) to working on a set of algorithms Lenstra provided. Lenstra and his colleagues at BellCore were thus able to break the notorious RSA-129 encryption code in eight months (in 1977 the prediction was that it would take millions of years to do this). The problem required finding the prime number factors of a 129-digit number. After the factors were found, the network dissolved.

> Illustrates: virtual organization structure, the power of digital networks and information technologies for locating resources and combining expertise and facilities.

Bicycle vendors to all but the lowest-priced markets have created what amount to global "virtual" products. In every case, frame manufacturers configure finished bicycles by selecting from an enormous variety of specialty components manufactured by companies spread around the world that have built reputations for excellence in wheel, tire, hub, brake, derailleur, handlebar, tire, seat, chain, and even spoke design and fabrication. The difference between automobile and bicycle assemblers is that bicycle advertising always identifies the component manufacturers. Companies compete on the basis of the customer-perceived value of the components. Furthermore, companies that manufacture a wide range of components sometimes offer finished bicycles by mating their products to frames created by famous frame designers and then add the components they do not manufacture. In between are many companies that manufacture nothing but sell bicycles by mixing and matching frames and components and assembling them. The value these companies add lies in the expertise they bring to the selection process and in the volume discounts they can pass along to customers. Like the market for consumer audio products, the bicycle market is made possible largely through the "plug compatibility" of these components and frames. And like audio product manufacturers, bicycle manufacturers learned that there was an advantage in sharing in "virtual" bicycles over competing on the basis of complete proprietary systems.

> Illustrates: virtual products, win-win alliances enabled by the "plug compatibility" of the components that make up a total system.

Boeing's 777 passenger plane was created by about 250 cross-functional teams, including members from supplier companies and airline customers, distributed over a number of locations. All were linked electronically and through use of common CAD software. For the first time, a commercial airliner was created and put into production on a virtually paperless basis, using computer modeling almost exclusively. This significantly reduced both the cost and the time of development. In addition, Boeing assembled the plane from components and subassemblies manufactured by an alliance of domestic and foreign manufacturers, including manufacturers of competing aircraft and of suppliers to such manufacturers. (Mitsubishi, for example, a potential future competitor, is the single largest value-adding supplier to the 777.) The 777 production system thus has something of a virtual organization character; it is managed by Boeing, which contributed design, assembly, and marketing expertise, but many other companies play an active peer role and will continue to do so, as appropriate, for the lifetime of the aircraft. Northrop pioneered paperless aircraft production at its El Segundo California plant. Beginning in 1989, Northrop replaced the 16,000 sheets of paper previously associated with the manufacture of each F-18 fuselage with PC terminals at each assembly station. With this one change, production costs dropped 30 percent.

Illustrates: integration of information technology and design and manufacturing processes, remote cross-functional teaming, peer-level supplier and customer interactive relationships, virtual organization structure.

Bose Corporation is a $500 million a year audio equipment manufacturer with a reputation for sustained technological innovativeness, especially in speaker design. In 1987 Director of Purchasing and Logistics Lance Dixon implemented a significant variation on just-in-time logistics. Bose offered to certify as preferred suppliers, and to enter into long-term contracts with, companies willing to station a senior executive at Bose. The executive's task is to identify proactively ways in which their company can enhance Bose products, production processes, or development teams by sharing expertise. These executives are empowered by Bose to place purchase orders to their own companies, to interact with Bose personnel, and to use Bose in-house information systems, including access to MRP data and concurrent engineering programs progress reports. In a market with very narrow product opportunity windows, this innovative approach to supplier relations saves time and money and enriches both Bose and its suppliers.

Illustrates: interactive supplier-vendor relations, leveraging resources through cooperation, sharing knowledge to mutual advantage, the value of trust-based relationships, managerial innovation as a means of reducing cycle time.

Carpenter Technology is a $600 million specialty steel products company with four plants on the east and west coasts and 3400 employees. Confronting growing global competitive pressure on its customer base and slowing domestic demand, management initiated a review of all company practices and processes in spite of the company's strong performance throughout the 1970s and 1980s. The focus of this review was to link strategic manufacturing objectives, to develop strategic capabilities to respond to changing market conditions, and to view cost savings as a benefit of change not the impetus of change (change should come about proactively, not reactively). Management implemented empowered, self-directed work teams, cultivated a cross-functional process orientation, created an open information environment, and treated the skill base of employees as its core growth asset. The managerial hierarchy was flattened, and investment was channeled into an infrastructure supportive of Carpenter's new strategic agenda, including synchronous manufacturing processes and a just-in-time information system. The results? On-time shipments more than doubled (to more than 90 percent), quality improved 75 percent, cycle time reductions of 25 to 75 percent were realized, and work-in-progress inventory was almost halved (from $130 million to $70 million).

> Illustrates: leveraging the impact of people and information, nurturing core competencies, focusing on processes, investing in infrastructure, embracing change proactively.

Caterpillar has, in just two years, doubled production per shift and enhanced customer involvement by exploiting information technology investments that had previously shown little bottom-line impact. Instead of burdening customers with specifying the Caterpillar parts numbers for the myriad choices involved in ordering an individualized vehicle, customers can now describe their requirements in English. Proprietary software then translates these statements into Caterpillar product codes and configures a production order. The improvement in productivity has had two sources. On the one hand, Caterpillar changed the company's organizational structure, moving from a functional (marketing, manufacturing, etc.) to a systems business unit structure (tractors, powertrains, etc.). At the same time, the information systems within the company were integrated, so that design, manufacturing, and production control systems are now all interconnected.

> Illustrates: enterprise information integration, interactive customer relationships, selling solutions, shifting from offering choices to providing individualized products, linking information systems and organizational structure to enhance the impact on production.

Chaparall Steel is a highly successful, technology-intensive mini-mill that is one of the five lowest-cost steel mills in the world. Each of its

935 employees is considered to be a member of the sales department. Sales, billing, credit, and shipping are implemented as universally accessible support systems. All employees are expected to handle any customer request that comes in, and they are empowered to respond to those requests. Chaparral focuses on products dictated by customer needs and pushes productivity by participatory management and supporting technology investments. Continuous learning is embedded in the corporate culture. At any given time, 85 percent of its personnel are in training courses, and all personnel are required to take an annual educational sabbatical that includes visiting customers' plants, universities, and other mills worldwide, and they are expected to incorporate what they have learned into their work on their return. Multiskilling and cross-training are the norm.

> Illustrates: customer-enriching products, leveraging the impact of the total work force, implementing service functions as universally accessible support systems, continuous learning, creating a company culture of universal accountability and shared responsibility.

Chrysler's recent product development success stories—the Chrysler Concorde sedan and its siblings, the Dodge Intrepid and Eagle Vision, and the Neon subcompact—resulted from the utilization of team organization techniques, cooperative peer relationships with suppliers, concurrent engineering, and attention to seamless information flow among product development team participants, including supplier companies (who provide more than 70 percent of the value of the sedans, for example). Both projects brought new vehicles to market in less than $3\frac{1}{2}$ years, far faster than the U.S. average, and at much lower cost than the GM Saturn or Ford Mondeo development projects. Team sizes were less than two-thirds the recent norm. Chrysler provided all suppliers with the same CAD software its internal teams were using as well as with training for those companies that needed it. Monthly cross-assembly team lunches generated a common understanding of the overall project and opened pathways for cross-fertilization of design and manufacturing problem solutions. Suppliers were able to recommend design changes that improved performance even at increased cost if compatible with trade-offs that kept the overall budget within specified limits. Engineers were incorporated into all phases of the project, including customer response to prototype vehicles, which, in one case, led to the redesign of the throttle linkage to provide full opening at well under pedal-to-the-metal pressures for a sense of greater power!

> Illustrates: validity of agile manufacturing concepts, especially interactive supplier relationships, concurrent operations, enterprise information integration, cross-functional team organization, and macromanagement: encouraging initiative by establishing what needs to be done but giving people latitude to determine how it can best be done.

Citicorp, under former CEO Walter Wriston, had been divided into 15 virtually autonomous fiefdoms whose heads were expected to optimize their own division's performance and who were compensated accordingly. For a variety of reasons, by the end of 1991, with John Reed the CEO, Citicorp was struggling financially. Reed reorganized Citicorp, requiring that the 15 division heads meet monthly, under his leadership, to make resource allocation decisions that would optimize the performance of Citicorp as a whole, as opposed to focusing on any individual division. Their compensation was to be indexed to Citicorp's performance. Reed's task was to create a strategic vision for Citicorp with well-defined, challenging goals. The task of the 15 was to utilize their distinctive expertise to achieve those goals. By early 1994, Citicorp stock had more than tripled in price, and earnings for 1993 were among the highest ever recorded by a U.S. bank, in part as a result of the reorganization.

> Illustrates: acting locally but thinking of the company as a whole, empowerment with coherence, the power of visionary leadership and macromanagement, shaping behavior by reward mechanisms.

CompuServe, to broaden its user base, prepares and distributes to interested companies detailed technical specifications of its proprietary software and hardware so that the companies can more easily develop products that provide access to CompuServe's on-line information services. For example, Motorola, working with General Magic and River Run software, enhanced its Envoy handheld wireless communicator by incorporating into it simple, automated access via CompuServe to E-mail functions, stock and financial market data, news, and so on.

Illustrates: sharing information to competitive advantage.

CUC International of Stamford, Connecticut, has more than 30 million members in its direct-dial telephone discount shopping services; in 1993 they paid $850 million in membership fees. Members have unlimited access through 800-numbers to operators from whom they can order products or get comparison shopping information. CUC's core asset is a database of over 250,000 product descriptions and prices. With no inventory of its own, it has relationships with merchandisers that allow members to place one order with CUC and have products shipped directly to their homes with all warranties intact or enhanced. (Refer to the section on Kingston Technologies later in this chapter.)

Illustrates: information as a product, distribution mechanisms better suited to agile competition than traditional retail stores, virtual warehousing, network of cooperating companies.

DEC, Broadband Technologies, Compression Laboratories, Micro Wave Systems, and Philips Consumer Electronics have created a vertical alliance for interactive TV equipment. Philips makes the TV set accessory boxes, Micro Wave makes software for the boxes, Broadband makes equipment for sending video and telephone signals through fiber-optic lines, DEC makes the processor chips and server hardware, and Compression Laboratories makes signal-compression software and hardware.

Illustrates: integration by bytes instead of bricks. *Note well:* These companies are not dedicated exclusively to this joint project; they are pursuing other business opportunities while devoting some part of a core competency resource to creating jointly a complete system product that no one of them could create as quickly or as cheaply on its own.

Eaton's Department Stores, a large Canadian retailer, has 3500 suppliers. More than 500 of these are Electronic Data Interchange (EDI) capable, and the percentage of the EDI-capable among those who will remain suppliers is growing very rapidly. In addition, Eaton's and Grand National Apparel (GNA) are linked by software that provides point-of-sale information in real time back to the fabric mills and forward to Eaton's management. This has allowed Eaton's to begin the implementation of an "automatic replenishment" policy for GNA's Haggar apparel lines. Eaton's and GNA are also using information technology to create cross-functional and cross-enterprise teams, whose members remain physically located in their respective companies, in order to optimize the interactions among Eaton's and GNA. Cross-functional and cross-enterprise teams have also been put in place in KMart Canada, Rubbermaid Canada, and Husky Injection Moldings and have achieved significant reductions in order processing costs, inventory costs, and delivery times.

> Illustrates: value of information networks, value of sharing information, interenterprise teaming, interactive supplier-customer relationships.

EDS and Sprint are exploring a merger that would unite the leading outsourcing information management services provider in the United States with a major national and international telecommunications company that has a large fiber-optic network already in place. If EDS and GM agree to separate (GM bought EDS in 1984) amicably, new strategic options and opportunities for major savings are open to EDS and Sprint management. GM is by far the largest customer of EDS, providing one-third or more of its revenues. GM has divested itself of the highly unprofitable National Car Rental. Letting go of highly profitable EDS while retaining its services is consistent with the GM policy of focusing on core competencies to return to profitability in its primary business: the North American automotive markets. Analogously, AT&T and Silicon Graphics have formed a joint venture, Interactive Digital Systems, that will design and build video and data networks capable of delivering multimedia and interactive TV services to businesses and consumers. Silicon Graphics will provide state-of-the-art hardware and software expertise, and AT&T will provide telecommunications network expertise. In addition, AT&T Switching Systems will handle Interactive's sales.

Illustrates: forging win-win alliances that cut costs and create new capabilities, focusing on core competencies.

Federated Department Stores, in the midst of profound corporate financial problems, has created a profitable business in its Sabre Group, selling information processing capabilities that centralize all back-office operations and manage inventory to retailers. American Airlines' reservation system, also called *SABRE* (but in capital letters), has been a "cash cow" for the company for decades, in some years generating higher profits than the airline operations themselves. In the summer of 1994, American initiated a lawsuit against Northwest Airlines for "stealing" its state-of-the-industry "yield management" software models, said to be worth $300 to $400 million a year in increased revenues.

Illustrates: value of information.

Ford recently reorganized its automotive operations into five global vehicle design centers, each responsible for developing specific types of vehicles for its world markets. Some of the objectives are cost saving from centralized supplier relations and purchasing (Ford purchases $37 billion a year worth of materials), true worldwide production scheduling, and integration and assimilation of front-end and back-end operations. Ford had already linked its seven design studios into a single studio network, capable of working jointly on design projects, including working around the clock to solve design problems if necessary. The goal of CEO Alexander Trotman: develop a wider variety of cars and trucks, aimed at more diverse market niches, faster, and at lower cost.

Illustrates: creation of a global production system.

Ford's Lansdale, Pennsylvania, electronics components plant reduced the time needed to manufacture and ship an order after receiving it from almost eight days in 1991 to just over one day in 1994 by implementing agile manufacturing techniques. This included redesigning the plant to highlight information flow, software control of production equipment, organization of the work force into teams, and an open information environment extending to operational personnel.

> Illustrates: validity of agile manufacturing concepts, centrality of information flow to flexibility of production, team organization and open information as means of achieving operational personnel buy-in to managerial objectives.

Grupo Azteca is the Mexican soft-drink bottling unit of Panamerican beverages. It has invested heavily in information and communication technologies that are driving its growth in sales in a market that seems oversupplied. Given Mexico's poor telephone system, Grupo Azteca has linked its 12 bottling plants by satellite, uses headquarters-based computers to track the action at its 180,000 distributors (including a semiannual distributor satisfaction survey), and is beginning to distribute handheld computers to its delivery truck drivers for real-time, on-site tracking of store-by-store inventory and product-by-product sales rates (in the manner of Frito-Lay distribution). Analogously, Nu-Skin, a Utah-based direct-sales company, uses a computer network to track the real-time activities of 300,000 independent dealers who sell their personal care and health products in eight countries. Dealers receive payment based on a complex arrangement of multinational hierarchical distribution of commissions, but notwithstanding the complexity, commissions are paid immediately by electronic funds transfer, creating instant reinforcement that drives sales efforts. University of California at San Diego Medical Center nurses and doctors all carry portable computers. Wherever they are, they can enter and/or access updated information on any patient. Laboratory test data are entered automatically into the computer network from test instruments, minimizing error and time.

> Illustrates: using information and communication technologies to competitive advantage, coupling management, marketing, production, distribution, and sales into a coherent, customer-pulled system.

Hamilton Bancshares, Ohio's second-largest bank, is converting 40 percent of its branch banks to unstaffed, automated facilities. A study of its customer usage patterns indicated that the bulk of its profits came from customers who were "ATM literate" (used ATM machines routinely and intensively). The new branches will be much smaller and much less expensive to operate than existing branches. They will have full service capabilities via 24-hour video connection to remotely located bank personnel for transactions that require human intervention. This includes extremely rapid processing of the great majority of loan applications. Similarly, Atlanta's Bank South Corporation has located 30 percent of its 143 branches in Kroger supermarkets. The branches cost $250,000 to open and become profitable during their first year, as compared to $1.5 to $2 million and four to five years for stand-alone branches.

> Illustrates: customer enrichment-based products, customer-centered provision of services, "democratization" of production facilities.

Harley-Davidson is an extraordinary example of a company that has sustained a product line driven almost entirely by development and marketing strategies based on customer-perceived value. Although its manufacturing operations have been modernized, and quality improved dramatically, since the Davidson family bought back control of the company from AMF, the product is still "low tech" compared to its competition. Harley's core strategy for more than a half century has been to offer a product that remains true to the Harley style and lasts for a long time. Changes, improvements, and options can be incorporated into older models. In addition, Harley recognizes the value of third-party accessory and custom component manufacturers, even when their products compete with options that Harley offers. Harley owners invariably customize and modify their machines, and in many cases the factory honors the warranty for custom components, even performance-enhancing ones, from approved manufacturers. The result is that new Harleys command premium prices (more than $20,000 for the top-of-the-line highway cruisers) in the face of lower-priced, better-performing competitors, and used Harleys command prices that often equal and sometimes exceed the prices for new models.

> Illustrates: pricing and product definition and styling and development strategies keyed to customer-perceived value, sharing products with after-sale, third-party component suppliers as a way of increasing product longevity and value.

Hewlett-Packard, like IBM and Unisys, is reorganizing to better exploit the rapidly growing and highly profitable market for computer services. As hardware profit margins shrink, with even the most technologically sophisticated physical products becoming commodities more and more quickly, high-profit markets for the information and services enabled by these physical products grow. Companies continue to outsource information management services at a rapid rate, with contracts doubling in value from 1993 to 1994. EDS, for example, has recently taken over information and computer systems management services for Bethlehem Steel and Xerox; in the case of Xerox there is a long-term contract worth $3 billion. Hewlett-Packard is counting on its reputation as a customer-centered company to break into an industry in which an understanding of applications is crucial to successful service. (See the IBM and Unisys entries.)

> Illustrates: shift in dynamics of industrial competition from hardware manufacture to information and services; value of system integration and information-based services.

Hitachi has signed an agreement with IBM to buy IBM's mainframe technology, including computer systems that Hitachi will sell in Japan with the Hitachi logo. Hitachi was motivated in part by the changing economics of the mainframe segment of the computer industry and in part by the accelerating rate of innovation—the state-of-the-art lifetime of mainframe computers has dropped from four years to two, and IBM holds important advantages in future mainframe technological innovations (for example, PowerPC–based machines and parallel processors). This agreement is particularly notable given the past tension between the companies, including the industrial espionage conducted by Hitachi personnel against IBM that resulted in embarrassment to Hitachi as well as the payment of a large cash settlement by the company.

> Illustrates: pressure of decreasing product lifetimes, power of core competency and innovation leadership, alliances among competitors to mutual advantage.

Honda markets a 250-cubic-centimeter "multiple-personality" two-stroke motorcycle (in Japan only, as of mid-1994). A magnetically coded card inserted into a slot in the steering head unlocks the steering head, programs the electronic engine management systems, and activates the handlebar-mounted data display. By inserting other, differently programmed cards, the rider can change the electronic ignition timing, oil pump, and fuel injection settings and the exhaust valve timing. With a single mechanical adjustment (to the jetting), the motorcycle can be a sedate or a sporty street machine, a racer or a fuel-economizing tourer. The security virtues of the system are real, but they are just a bonus to the new revenue stream created by multiple cards and allied products, together with the marketing advantage of a single motorcycle that can satisfy multiple needs and desires. An analogous industry is growing in the United States, exploiting the increasing quantities of digital information embedded in automobiles, with similar objectives of changing performance characteristics by reprogramming electronic engine management (and soon active suspension management) systems.

> Illustrates: value of information embedded in physical products, new kinds of information products and companies (reverse information engineering), need to protect information embedded in physical products and to exploit its value.

Hotel and motel chains, such as Canada's Journey's End, are building customer databases that permit mass customization of services—based on knowing each customer's preferred combination of accommodations, services, and special requirements or requests—and the identification of the facilities and services that are actually valued at each location by tracking their use. Auto dealership networks and large-scale property managers and real estate service companies are building similar databases for the same reasons.

> Illustrates: mass individualization of services, use of information technology to create customer-enrichment and discover customer values.

Hyundai, Kia, and Daewoo are being helped (for fees) by Mitsubishi, Mazda, and Honda, respectively, to develop luxury sedans for the South Korean market. South Korea sharply limits Japanese car imports, so this assistance is of little direct consequence to the Japanese manufacturers, but the potential is there for the South Korean manufacturers to be good enough "students" to challenge their Japanese "teachers" in foreign markets, as they have done in shipbuilding, steel, semiconductor manufacturing, VCRs, and computers. Why, then, are the Japanese companies helping? They are exploiting customer opportunities now, confident that creating new markets will eventually create new opportunities for them and that they will stay ahead of companies who are copying what they are capable of now.

> Illustrates: the aggressiveness of agile competitors, cooperation among competitors, the need to develop new core competencies.

IBM is reorganizing the entire corporation by the industry served rather than by geography. The objective is to focus on computer services and computer-based information services (especially software) that are enabled by hardware. Until now, IBM's Integrated Systems Solutions division was the mechanism for selling computer services, but now all salespeople are going to be expected to do much more than passively take orders; they are going to have to sell solutions to customer problems. Solutions cost more than hardware does, and the profit potential is much greater. (See the Unisys and Hewlett-Packard entries.) An early (June 1994) step taken toward this reorganization was IBM's creation of a Networked Applications Services Division. This division will be responsible for developing products for commercial, as well as consumer, network products that exploit IBM expertise in multimedia, Internet services, electronic financial trading, video conferencing, groupware, networked information services, and electronic publishing, as well as generic networking hardware and software. Efforts to produce CDs and videos on demand and on site, for example, through its Blockbuster Video agreement, would come from this division, as would information kiosks that could provide remote access to government services and to shopping. IBM is petitioning for reversal of a 1956 federal decree that limits its ability to be competitive in the computer services area.

> Illustrates: agile-era "products" are integrated physical product-information-services packages, the selling of solutions rather than products, customer-enrichment product and pricing strategies.

IBM has signed agreements with Cyrix and NexGen to manufacture rival Intel 486 and Pentium chips for those companies. In the case of the Cyrix agreement, IBM contributed a manufacturing facility and its chip manufacturing expertise; Cyrix put up the cash for renovating the facility. In addition to charging Cyrix for the chips produced, IBM reserves the right to manufacture one chip for its own purposes for every chip that it manufactures for Cyrix. Some companies with superior chip design expertise but with limited or no production facilities—Cyrix, AMD, and NexGen—suffer when demand increases and contract manufacturers (Texas Instruments and IBM, for example) use all their capacity for their own needs. Outsourcing all manufacturing thus poses a potentially serious constraint on cash flow and profitability, in spite of the high cost of production facilities and expertise. A parallel problem exists in the pharmaceutical and chemical products industries, especially the market for custom chemicals. The profitable lifetime of drugs and custom chemicals is steadily shrinking, yet the knowledge required to create valuable products steadily increases. More and more companies are choosing to maintain drug and custom chemical design expertise as their core competency and to outsource all manufacturing on an as-needed basis. (See the Molecular Design entry.)

Illustrates: focusing on core competencies, leveraging resources through cooperation.

Ideation is a company whose product is its expertise in a formalized, inventive, problem-solving methodology, applied primarily to complex engineering problems. Clients can hire Ideation to generate inventive solutions to particularly difficult problems that they have encountered or anticipate. Alternatively, they can send personnel to Ideation to learn how to use the methodology in which its staff is demonstrably expert. Ideation also offers innovative workshops of a broader scope, aimed primarily at enriching the design phase of product development.

Illustrates: knowledge as a product, making a product out of one's core competency.

Intel reported that the cost of developing the Pentium chip was between $400 and $500 million. Intel began work on the Pentium at the same time the 80386 went into full-scale production and the 80486 was in beta testing. By mid-1994, the Pentium and the 486 were in full-scale production, the Pentium's successor, the P-6, was in beta testing, and teams were finishing the design of the P-7. The lifetime of processor chips has dropped to two years, and the value of chip design tools has soared as the window for reaping high enough profits to fund the next generation chip has narrowed. Pentium and 486 chip clone manufacturers such as AMD, Cyrix, NexGen, and even Texas Instruments and IBM have become more sophisticated. Add the competitive threat posed by the higher-performance, less expensive PowerPC chip codeveloped by IBM, Motorola, and Apple, and Intel's June 1994 alliance with Hewlett-Packard makes a great deal of sense. Together, the two companies plan on developing a processing chip that will run earlier Intel chip software (Windows-based programs) but will be based on a totally different, PowerPC–like RISC chip design philosophy. Hewlett-Packard will contribute RISC design expertise and base its future hardware on the chip. Intel will contribute its own considerable design expertise, primarily in CISC chips, and its outstanding competence in high-volume chip manufacture.

Illustrates: leveraging resources through cooperation, short product lifetimes, criticality of fast product development, narrow windows for high-profit production.

Intelligent Manufacturing Systems (IMS) is the name given by Japan's Ministry for International Trade and Industry (MITI) to an effort it launched in the late 1980s for coordinated development of the next generation of computer-based manufacturing technologies. MITI organized a domestic consortium that quickly grew to more than 80 companies whose managements were already concerned that lean manufacturing was losing the ability to add enough product value to support operations in high-wage Japan. The Japanese invited U.S. companies and universities to join this venture, adding their software expertise and technological innovations to Japan's manufacturing expertise. The overriding objective of the Japanese was the establishment of international IMS standards that would create a unified market for the new technologies that were envisaged and would avoid the costliness of competing standards "wars," such as those fought between VHS and Beta or (more painfully for the Japanese) between various analog high-definition TV standards and the digital standard eventually set by the FCC (but only after the Japanese had spent hundreds of millions of dollars on an analog format!). After considerable debate inside and outside the Bush administration, the United States promoted a multilateral approach to IMS development. Today, teams from Japan, the United States, the EC countries, Canada, and Australia are engaged in cooperative first-generation, multinational, cross-industry pilot projects. The purpose of these projects is to identify the generic technologies and intellectual property rights policies needed for computer-controlled manufacturing of extreme flexibility and to establish a common international standard.

Illustrates: cooperation among competitors, sharing information to mutual advantage, leveraging resources through cooperation, the power of standards to create extended markets, the importance of intellectual property rights issues to cooperative development of new products.

John Deere's Moline, Illinois, seeder plant added agile manufacturing characteristics to its incorporation of the lessons of lean manufacturing. With very little investment in new technology, the plant was able to shift to a build-to-order capability, eliminating inventory and improving productivity, by reorganizing production processes, organizing the work force into teams, and providing operational personnel with production information and making them responsible for acting on it appropriately. (A percentage of each employee's weekly pay is a function of meeting team productivity goals.) Toshiba assembles all of its more than 20 models of portable computers on a single production line in batches of 20 (and can afford to handle batches of 10) per model, with only a notebook computer at each work point instructing personnel on how to build a model and how many of that model to build.

> Illustrates: value of rethinking production processes (not merely making existing processes more efficient), building to order instead of to forecast with little production technology investment, teaming, empowering operational personnel, giving them more responsible and authority, and sharing information with them.

Johnson Controls, Inc., was founded in 1883 and has been manufacturing heating systems controls, batteries, and automobile seats, among other traditional products, for over a century. In 1989 Johnson entered the facilities management services market. Group Vice-President Terry Weaver described the opportunities in managing the heating, lighting, and security operations of office buildings as "explosive . . . almost impossible to quantify, a market worth tens of billions of dollars in the United States alone." Johnson has therefore developed a core competency in facilities management, precisely because facility owners and tenants typically have poor competencies in that area. CEO James Keyes says that service now drives the entire corporation: "Most of our growth has come from the fact that we do more for our customers." And not just in management services. As the largest seat supplier to Detroit's Big Three, Johnson now adds much more value than in the past by providing production engineering and design services; traditionally Johnson passively followed the manufacturing instructions it was given by its automotive assembler customers. As recently as 10 years ago, Johnson had fewer than a dozen engineers in the auto seat division; today the company employs more than 500 engineers and uses their expertise to create profit opportunities.

> Illustrates: shift of center of product value from manufacturing to services, including manufacturing as a services-rich product, exploiting core competencies, developing new core competencies to exploit customer opportunities, leveraging the impact of people, knowledge, and skills.

Kingston Technologies' main "product" is its ability to custom-configure large computer orders very quickly. It does this through mutually beneficial relationships with peripheral equipment vendors who, in exchange for attractive purchasing agreements, give preference to filling Kingston's "rush" orders as they come in, almost always unpredictably.

> Illustrates: one form of virtual company, leveraging resources, value of customer-configuration services, independent of production capability.

Kodak's single-use camera was developed in 40 percent less time than the norm for new camera projects at Kodak through the use of concurrent rather than serial engineering-manufacturing development teams. Rapid concept to cash was particularly important for this product. It was positioned as a very-low-cost item, displayed at a checkout counter, with heavy potential sales through small kiosks and souvenir shops. In many of these outlets, there would be room for only one single-use camera to receive prominent display, and at least one competitor, Fuji, was also developing such a product. In addition to rapid product development, Kodak quickly saw ways to use the initial product as a base for a wide range of variations. At first, there were versions with different focal lengths (panoramic, close up, etc.) and then a waterproof version. Recently, Kodak offered a version of the camera for weddings and similar events, either to replace a professional photographer or to be a supplement. With one camera at each table, guests can take pictures of one another at their convenience and to reflect their own moods. When processing pictures from this model of the camera, Kodak annotates the finished photos with a brief description of the event (wedding, etc.), the people, the place, and the date. Finally, Kodak has increased the recycle dimension of the product, which is returned with the film for processing.

> Illustrates: value of rapid concept to cash, concurrent development, marketing strategies based on product variations, personalization and empowerment as customer perceived values, assimilation of environmental concerns.

Kodak's divestiture of companies not central to its photography business has accelerated since George Fisher from Motorola became Kodak's CEO. Kodak sold the prescription drug side of its Sterling Winthrop pharmaceutical unit for $1.6 billion to the French firm Sanofi, a health and beauty products company owned by Elf Aquitaine. Kodak also bolstered the strength of Sterling's nonprescription operations in anticipation of a separate sale of those assets. (Sanofi immediately sold the medical imaging division of Sterling Winthrop to the Norwegian firm Halfsund Nykomed for about $460 million; that division was not within Sanofi's core competencies.) Kodak had previously sold chemical companies it owned that were not directly related to photographic chemical requirements. Fisher is committed to building a world-class core competency for Kodak in digital photography. [See the Polaroid entry.]

> Illustrates: focus on, and evolution of, core competencies.

LARG*net will connect seven health care delivery institutions in the area around London, Ontario, Canada. The University of Western Ontario, Robarts Research Institute, University Hospital, London Regional Cancer Centre, St. Joseph's Health Centre, Victoria Hospital, and Fanshawe College are being linked by fiber-optic cable to create shared access to medical imaging databases, video teaching and training materials and programs, clinical experience and information, information resources, and research data. As it becomes part of the routine operation of these institutions and their personnel, LARG*net will emerge as a single "virtual" health care facility encompassing the expertise, experience, facilities, and knowledge bases of all seven participating institutions, as manifested in real-time treatment and decision making.

> Illustrates: leveraging resources through cooperation, sharing infrastructure support and costs, sharing information to mutual advantage, leveraging the impact of people and knowledge.

Legal Research Network, founded by Dov Seidman, is a Los Angeles–based, computer-linked pool of lawyers located all over the nation who do contract legal research for corporations and traditional law firms. LRN already has about 250 lawyers available for assignments, all of them with expertise and experience in particular aspects of law. By configuring the appropriate mix of this expertise, LRN can generate background legal research at a fraction of what law firms charge. Lawyers at LRN's hub analyze customer requests, identify the resources necessary, and quote a fixed price up front. Typical corporate customers include MCI, for a study of communications law issues, and Motorola, for a comprehensive survey of all 50 U.S. state court interpretations of a recent Supreme Court ruling. More generally, lawyers have made computer-based legal research services a routine aspect of case preparation. Of the law firms surveyed by the Center for Law and Computers (Chicago-Kent College of Law) and reported in *The American Lawyer*, 98 percent used Lexis court decision databases and 97 percent used similar Westlaw databases. Westlaw has a de facto monopoly on court decision data because of its copyrighted format for the pagination of such data: Virtually all judges require that citations be in Westlaw format. In addition to using software for legal research, 96 percent of the firms surveyed used specialized software to automate the legal document preparation process. Of the attorneys surveyed, 76 percent had computers on their desks versus only 19 percent as recently as 1988.

> Illustrates: value of information and information services, information as a product (in Westlaw's case, the format in which publicly available information is presented is the unique and highly profitable product!), computer information networks.

Lockheed's "Skunk Works" was created by Clarence Kelly Johnson in 1943 in response to an urgent Army Air Force need for an experimental jet-propelled fighter plane. The XP-80 first flew eight months after the contract for its development was signed. During a 51-year period, the Skunk Works has maintained an extraordinary record of accomplishment in developing advanced-technology aircraft and weapons systems quickly and efficiently, including the U-2 and the SR-71 "spy" planes, the F-104 fighter plane, the Stealth F-117, and most recently, the YF-22. Johnson's operating philosophy for the Skunk Works has been constant during that time and serves as a valuable model for a special-projects effort, one with features that are directly related to virtual organization structures and agile competition. The core of this philosophy incorporates interenterprise cross-functional teams, customer-centered and customer-involved product development, a very small managerial staff authorized to make all relevant decisions and devoted to coordinating and supporting with appropriate resources the activities delegated by the project team, a minimum of ritualized reporting and a maximum of shared information within the project as to the state of the project, and a universal sense of accountability for success.

> Illustrates: a special project version of a virtual company, internal teaming, interactive customer and supplier relationships.

MAC is the nation's second-largest ATM card. It is the "product" of Electronic Payments Services, a Wilmington-based corporation jointly owned by two Pennsylvania banks and one Ohio bank. The power of the MAC card derives from the fact that more than 1600 banks have issued their "own" ATM cards to their customers but have actually merged their ATM operations into a single seamless web that generates more than 92 million transactions each month.

> Illustrates: cooperative networking among competitors, the value of customer-centered services, shared infrastructure, the value of standards in enabling interenterprise integration.

Marketing (as opposed to financial and generic management) skills are increasingly being recognized as crucial even to high-tech product success. IBM replaced its PC division head (Robert Corrigan, who resigned) with a former Nabisco Foods marketing executive. NEC hired a Kraft Foods executive as its marketing manager. Steve Ballmer, the number two person at Microsoft, was once assistant brand manager for Duncan Hines baking mixes. The vice-president of marketing at Canon Computer Systems came from Procter and Gamble, as did the president of Intuit.

> Illustrates: agile competition is intensely marketing-sensitive precisely because it is centered on customer-enriching products.

Martin-Marietta's Moorestown, New Jersey, manufacturing plant (Government Electronics Systems) had been experiencing sustained outsourcing and steady downsizing for years prior to the winter of 1991. Under the leadership of Operations Director Jack Irving, the company and the union began a joint competitive initiative that has not only stemmed the outsourcing but continues to bring manufacturing back into the plant and has prompted tens of millions of dollars of investment in new and advanced manufacturing equipment. The initial commitments, strongly supported by the union and its members, were to reduce cycle time by 50 percent by mid-1993 and costs by 25 percent by the end of 1993. Both goals were met, and surpassed, ahead of schedule. Working closely with operational personnel, the company organized the work force around "high-involvement" empowered teams, consolidated 26 job categories into 4 job "bands," won union support for voluntary out-of-seniority layoffs for people who could not function in the new environment, and achieved total work force buy-in to the competitive initiative and the work center design team mode of operation. These teams are now aiming at the next goal: a 40 percent reduction in scrap and defects per unit. Management estimates that the dollar value of these improvements is more than $112 million—and counting!

> Illustrates: leveraging the impact of people, leadership, macro-management with constant monitoring and mentoring, universal buy-in to a company's strategic goals, universal accountability and shared responsibility for company's success.

Matthew Outdoor Advertising is at the leading edge of enhancing the value of a very "trailing edge" advertising medium—billboards. Matthews owns only 2,000 of the 390,000 billboards in the United States, but it offers clients videotapes of the billboard "in action," showing the site, the look of the ad, and the traffic flow at different times of the day and season. By a quite natural extension, the videotape images can be linked by PC graphics software to show existing clients how ads could look in a new location, by superimposing the ad designs on "real" billboard images. Or this technique can be used to show new clients how their ads would look at various sites. Gannett Outdoor operates 40,000 billboards and uses a PC technology called *PosterVision* that creates computer-generated billboard images, without the real-world dimension of Matthew's combination of site-based videotapes and computer graphics. In 1993 billboard revenues exceeded $1.5 billion and are growing.

> Illustrates: fusion effect of coupling information technologies to traditional products in innovative ways, exploiting customer-perceived value, adding value for customers (by bringing the sites they're paying for to them!).

McKesson Corporation, a distributor of products to drugstores nationwide, based the automation of its Spokane distribution center (stocking 18,000 different items) on the embodied wisdom of its veteran warehouse workers. They were the central members of the design team that created a handheld scanner-equipped computer, linked by radio to a minicomputer, that personnel use as they handle orders. Similarly, when Paine Webber introduced a new trading and information system for its 5200 brokers in 264 offices, replacing the existing Quotron system, it began with user requirements, attitudes, and anxieties. The result was a multiple-personality system with a color-coded keyboard that allows brokers to replicate the Quotron system features, to access Windows-based applications, or to use newly developed advanced features—depending on the brokers' levels of "literacy." In both companies, productivity improvements reflected immediate usability, which in turn reflected basing the design on what personnel know and do rather than requiring that personnel adapt what they know and do to newly introduced technologies.

Illustrates: recognizing and utilizing the centrality of people to processes, leveraging the knowledge of the work force.

Molecular Design and Schnyder Consulting are two Swiss firms whose only product is information—chemical and pharmaceutical manufacturing information. By creating and continually "growing" expert databases, these companies save chemical and pharmaceutical manufacturers a great deal of time, money, and effort. On the technical side, they can identify alternative approaches involving less dangerous, less toxic, or less energy-intensive reactants and reactions. Commercially, they can add value by locating potential customers for substances that need to be disposed of and for substances that would otherwise be waste products requiring treatment or expensive disposal. Procedurally, they maintain a centralized database on environmental, workplace safety, and drug and process approval regulatory requirements in various countries and on the procedures that need to be followed to meet them. Schnyder specializes in safety and environmental impact data about materials and processes.

Illustrates: the value of information as a product.

Monterey, Mexico, newspaper publisher El Norte has invested heavily in product- and customer-pulled information technologies and services, based on the conviction that the key to being a "first-world" country and company is information sophistication. The company routinely targets individual households to receive special sections of the weekend edition of the paper based on personal preferences (including multiple copies, if desired, of popular sections). It has created a network of papers throughout Latin America that share news and feature stories and a communications satellite-based on-line information services subsidiary, Infosel, that provides access to business articles and statistics. Its extensive internal computer network is entirely PC-based in a highly distributed mode.

Illustrates: mass individualization of information, value of networks and information.

Motorola is developing its Motorola Integrated Radio Service (MIRS) as a rival to the cellular telephone, in spite of the high profitability of its cellular telephone operations, which are subject to (and limited by) the FCC's duopoly philosophy: two companies per metropolitan area. MIRS—which combines cellular phone, pager, and two-way radio capabilities into a single compact unit—bypasses this regulation by exploiting specialized mobile radio frequencies that Motorola already "owns" through its Land Mobile Products division, a two-way radio manufacturing and services operation. Motorola has exchanged these frequencies for a stake in a national network to be constructed by MCI and Nextel, who have agreed to base the network on Motorola hardware. Motorola's Plantation, Florida, two-way radio manufacturing plant had suffered from very poor productivity, and Motorola had switched to an offshore source. Today, because of teaming and an investment in new manufacturing and information technologies (à la the Bandit pager plant in Boynton Beach, Florida, which provided a valuable technology learning experience), Plantation builds to order only, assembling any one of 500 variations in two hours as opposed to ten days as recently as 1990.

Illustrates: power of agility, openness and growth orientation of agility (deliberately opening up new product lines and markets when existing product lines are still profitable), teaming.

Motorola's MicroTac cellular phone was priced at $2500 when it was introduced in 1989. Five years later it was retailing for less than $150 and is often given away free as a bonus to new subscribers by cellular telephone service providers.

Illustrates: shift of dynamics of industrial competition from physical products to information and services, rapid "commoditization" even of high-tech physical products.

NCMS, the National Center for Manufacturing Sciences, is a not-for-profit collaborative manufacturing research consortium of about 200 U.S. and Canadian companies, founded in 1986. NCMS members have conducted hundreds of projects exploring a wide range of manufacturing technologies, processes, materials, and practices. Its Teaching Factories program erects prototype state-of-the-art manufacturing facilities across the United States, with a special view to hands-on learning by small and medium-size companies. Through its Manufacturing Information Resource Center, it has made tens of thousands of relevant documents available to its members and provided easy, central access to hundreds of manufacturing-related databases. It has developed a comprehensive self-assessment tool that companies can use to identify those areas in which they most need to develop improved capabilities in order to enhance their competitiveness.

> Illustrates: leveraging resources through cooperation, collaborative infrastructure efforts, networking, sharing information to mutual advantage.

Networks of small companies are an increasingly popular strategy for competing in rapidly changing markets and as a means of adding value to the supplier needs of agile competitors and virtual companies. Since 1991 scores of such networks have been formed in the United States. The Pacific Wood Products Cooperative centralizes purchasing for its 185 member firms, sharply reducing costs. The Metalworking Consortium in Chicago provides participating small shops with an opportunity to do collaborative marketing and production on a scale no one of them could manage. [See the U.K. Fine Chemicals entry.] AgileWeb was created in 1994 with funding from the Advanced Research Projects Agency (ARPA) to link northeastern Pennsylvania machine shops into a coordinated, electronically integrated, competitive network with expanded metalworking capabilities. The Kentucky Wood Manufacturer's Network, Inc. allows its members to pool their production resources. For example, four firms won a Disney World contract for $2.5 million worth of wood products; they divided the design, manufacture, and assembly work. Identifying a core competency and then complementing it with core competencies at other firms to synthesize a complete production capability results in a competitive advantage. Indiana's cross-industry FlexCell Group allows its members to synthesize vertically integrated production capabilities; in a typical case, a manufacturer of metalworking patterns and tools was linked with a mechanical engineering firm, a producer of plastic injection molds and tools, a prototype machine shop, and a contract machine shop.

> Illustrates: leveraging resources through cooperation, value of establishing and exploiting core competencies, use of information exchange technologies and standards to allow networking.

Nikon, in 1994, entered the high-profit, rapidly expanding market for premium nonprescription sunglasses, products with retail prices of $50 to $250. Its strategy was a form of "sneakerization": transforming a mass-produced, low-priced, low-margin commodity to a high-priced, high-profit, high-production-volume specialty product. Nikon offers more than 30 frame styles in five lens types keyed to the distinctive sun-protection requirements of five different sports activities: shooting, flying, fishing and water sports, hiking, and skiing.

> Illustrates: fragmentation of markets, customer-enrichment-based product design and pricing, mass individualization.

NCR advertises that its highest-value-adding product is providing companies with the capability of treating their customers as individuals. This capability alone, the company claims, has repeatedly resulted in revenue increases of up to 15 percent for these companies. The product NCR offers to accomplish this "mass individualization" is a variable combination of information processing hardware and software and expertise in collecting, interpreting, and moving information, locally and globally (exploiting its purchase by AT&T). For its part, AT&T runs its "Get, Move, and Use [Information]" ad campaign that depicts its Global Information Solutions division as uniquely able to tie computing and communication together and thus help companies learn the most about their customers.

Illustrates: customer-enrichment product strategy, treating customers as individuals, agile-era products as variable combinations
of physical products, information, and services.

Nintendo and Sega game machines generate cash flows to these companies, but all their profits come from game software. Because of
the intensity of competition in their markets, machines are sold at cost,
at best. Corporate strategy then contracts to a choice of either develop
ing games in house, and incurring the very high overhead of maintaining a staff of programmers, or buying games from independent developers. Nintendo management prefers the first option, which gives
Nintendo all the profits from successful games. Sega management
prefers the second option, which gives it only a share of the profits but
saves it the cost of large numbers of staff programmers. Analogously,
Apple contracted with Sharp to manufacture the Newton, in spite of
the fact that Sharp was permitted by the agreement to bring out a rival
machine, the Expert Pad. For Apple, the highest profits are to be
realized from licensing fees and royalties derived from applications
running on the Newton, or the Expert Pad, or any other Newton-com-
patible Personal Digital Assistant. Sony's profits from its CD music
business are far higher than those from its CD player manufacturing
business. A similar situation exists in the computer industry, at all
levels, with hardware profits typically much lower than those for
software and services.

Illustrates: shift in dynamics of competition from physical products to their information content, physical products serving as
platforms for high-value, high-profit information and services;
physical products, however sophisticated, quickly suffering from
commodity competition and pricing pressures, whereas informa
tion and services more readily sustain specialty or customized
status.

Otis Elevator has installed OTISLINE, a centralized dispatching center
linked to an integrated corporate database including customer data,
customer service histories, all service mechanics, field offices, and

constantly updated field service experience with Otis products. Its 24-hour customer hotline handles a half-million calls a year, and all calls received are tracked to closure. Management can monitor product performance data in real time. Field offices can follow all service activity in their region or in other regions to see emerging problem patterns. A major selling point of this system is the ability to show potential customers "raw" product performance and service response data. The system has eliminated paper service reports. It is being extended to handheld computers for all service mechanics linked by radio to a private network, to routine distribution of service data to engineering departments for product performance improvement and ideas for new product capabilities, and to installation of remote elevator monitoring sensors and diagnostic technologies for proactive maintenance and response to problems before they are reported!

> Illustrates: customer-enrichment focus, enterprise integration, seamless information flow within a company, value of real-time information at multiple levels for different purposes.

Outsourcing: Thirty percent of Fortune 1000 industrial corporations outsource more than 50 percent of their manufacturing. This amounts to between $100 and $250 billion a year. These 1000 companies account for 60 percent of the contribution of manufacturing to the U.S. GDP (23 percent of GDP in 1993).

> Illustrates: need for networking, opportunities for interactive supplier relationships.

People working at home or from home are a rapidly growing social phenomenon and market. Approximately 12 million people currently work full time at home, 12 million work part time, and 7.6 million telecommute. This represents a $25 billion a year home office equipment and services market. For example, Hewlett-Packard discovered that 40 percent of its ink-jet printer sales are to home offices. Canon discovered that home office buyers are *not* looking for low-priced, bottom-of-the-line equipment but high-performance models. Virtually untapped markets exist for services catering to home workers and telecommuters.

Illustrates: changing nature of work, centrality of computers, information services and networking to work.

Polaroid entered manufacturing with its SX-70 camera, introduced during the early 1970s. Until then, all Polaroid cameras, and all the film except the positive print elements, were manufactured by other companies and assembled by Polaroid into finished cameras. The company's core competencies at that time were in the organic chemistry that underlay the instant developing process and film packaging, and in mechanical design of the camera mechanism. For the SX-70, Polaroid needed to develop a wide range of new core competencies in all aspects of film and camera component manufacturing that it had previously contracted out, while cultivating its organic chemistry expertise to remain a leader in instant-developing features. By the early 1990s, electronic photography loomed as an increasingly serious competitor to traditional film, and Polaroid began the process of acquiring new core competencies in this area. The personnel implications, in particular, the implications for technical professionals, of such a reorientation of Polaroid's product lines, were profound. One phase of building the new core competencies needed in computer science, digital imaging, charge-coupled device (CCD) design and manufacture is education and retraining programs of progressively greater depth to help personnel willing and able to make the transition do so. During the 1970s, the company made what initially appeared to be a calamitous product development decision, PolaVision, its instant movie film and camera, a marketplace failure in competition with the earliest video cameras. The lessons learned from PolaVision were applied to creating new products for new markets, especially instant 35-mm slides for medical, industrial, and commercial applications. This was not only a successful product in its own right, but it gave Polaroid experience with 35-mm photography markets. That led to new 35-mm camera products, including the successful Captiva, a compact instant-development camera in which the exposed and developed film remains inside the camera until the user wants to see the photographs.

> Illustrates: evolution of core competencies, the need for regular core competency inventories to match current and developing products against market opportunities, personnel implications of changing core competencies, proactive creation of new markets, including imaginative applications of knowledge acquired from "failed" product development projects.

PowerPC is the name given to the central processing chip developed jointly by IBM, Motorola, and Apple. This alliance among direct competitors was announced in the fall of 1991, and the PowerPC chip began shipping in quantity by the winter of 1993–1994. Apple's PowerPC–based Macintosh computers were on sale in the spring of 1994, with IBM's PowerPC–based PCs to follow in the fall. The three companies collaborated on the development of the chip and an operating system that exploited its power and allowed it to run software for DOS and Macintosh machines, as well as variants of UNIX. They shared hitherto proprietary technical information about their hardware, software, and manufacturing techniques. IBM and Motorola even collaborated to promote the emergence of a PowerPC clone industry. Through IBM's Power Personal Systems division, they offer potential manufacturers a wide range of reference design services and, through IBM's Microelectronics division, even kits of components to ease manufacturers' entry into PowerPC computer manufacture and assembly. At the same time, all three companies expect to compete with one another—and with the clone manufacturers they are encouraging—for customers for their respective implementations of the PowerPC chip, operating system, and applications.

> Illustrates: concurrent cooperation and competition.

Production equipment in many industries is being reduced in scale and in cost while retaining very high performance capabilities. This is also true for the production of services. Thus, desktop publishing, digital audio and music, and digital video production studio services of high quality cost a small fraction of what they did even five years ago. Yamaha's DX-7 synthesizer, based on FM synthesis technology, was a major product success, with more than 20 million sound board chips sold. Today, waveguide technology offers even greater capabilities, and Yamaha already has commercialized it: its $5000 VL1 waveguide-based synthesizer is on the market. The "Toaster" made desktop video production possible and affordable. Minibakeries can be found in many supermarkets and department stores. (See Hamilton Bancshares entry.)

> Illustrates: scalable, modular production equipment, "democratization" of production, new opportunities for small-scale producers and entrepreneurs, pressure of competition from niche producers.

Quick Response is the name of a software package that is transforming retail fashion sales. Developed with support from Milliken Industries and the North Carolina–based textile consortium [TC²], Quick Response automatically feeds point-of-sale data back to garment and even fabric producers. In place at many large retailers and a growing number of medium-size ones, Quick Response dramatically reduces inventory requirements and eliminates the need to guess a year in advance what fashions, colors, and styles the public will respond to. In a few days, or at most a few weeks, manufacturers can replenish shelves with precisely the merchandise that is selling the fastest, in the sizes and colors that are moving most quickly. Similar software is being used at WalMart, J. C. Penney, and KMart to send checkout data directly to suppliers, simplifying ordering and inventory management. Bar code readers at supermarket checkout counters may or may not have made the checkout process faster, but they have been very valuable in exactly the same way: reducing the cost of inventory management, tracking what people are buying, and reducing the time needed to restock and the costs of ordering by providing suppliers with sales data on a daily basis. Frito-Lay has used a similar system for several years. It has allowed field salespeople with handheld computers to relay sales data on a store-by-store basis for daily analysis. As a result, even stores in the same neighborhood can be stocked with different mixes of Frito-Lay products as a result of buying pattern differences. Spalding implemented universal bar coding of all products as they are manufactured and integrated the coding with a centralized database that links production, inventory, order processing, billing, and shipping. The time needed to respond to customer orders and the processing costs were reduced dramatically. Kao Corporation is a large Japanese producer of soaps and cosmetics serving a national chain of 280,000 mostly small shops in addition to its own wholesale channels. Its average order size is just seven items, but it is able to deliver within 24 hours, thanks to an integrated information system analogous to the one Spalding installed. A flexible company and effective use of information are the bases of agility, not necessarily flexible manufacturing facilities.

> Illustrates: information as key to rapid response and flexible production of goods and of services, enterprise information integration, power of sharing relevant information with suppliers and customers, interenterprise information integration.

Ross Operating Valves is an established manufacturer of hydraulic valves. Its headquarters plant is in Madison Heights, Michigan, and it has plants in Lavonia, (Georgia), Tokyo, and Frankfurt. Ross has achieved extraordinary market success from converting its Lavonia plant to what it calls the *Ross/Flex valve manufacturing system*. Using proprietary computer-based valve design software and a digital valve design library, Ross offers customers the opportunity to codesign custom valves with Ross "integrators," engineers and skilled machinists at the Lavonia plant. Designs are downloaded to computer-numerical control (CNC) machine tools, and prototypes are completed within one day at a typical cost of $3000, a tenth of the previous cost and time. After the prototype is tested, customers can request modifications to improve performance, can get additional prototypes, and when satisfied, can order the final design to be put into production. Ross has chosen not to charge extra for this customization feature but to use it to win and keep customers. Beginning in 1994, Ross offered customers with in-house engineering capabilities the option of remotely accessing its design software and library, for a fee, designing their own valves, and downloading them to Ross production machinery for manufacture. All

Ross/Flex personnel are cross-trained in all skills required to work with customers to design and produce valves, and all are responsible for sales, design, production, delivery, and customer service.

> Illustrates: value of customization, integration of information and flexible manufacture, value of providing access to proprietary information, working with customers to define products, winning and keeping customers by creating interactive relationships with them, leveraging human resources through cross-training and continuous education for all.

Roto-Rooter had great brand name identification, but by 1993 it held only 17 percent of the drain cleaning market and 2 percent of the plumbing market. Management went on the offensive by offering service 24 hours a day, 7 days a week. All employees were trained in customer relations as well as in plumbing and pipe and drain cleaning. At the same time, the company moved into general maintenance, which now accounts for more than 40 percent of revenues. ServiceMaster, of Downers Grove, Illinois, has grown to a $2.3 billion corporation specializing in home and commercial building services. ServiceMaster cares for gardens and plants, cleans, dusts, exterminates pests, or performs any other related services the owner or tenant may require. ServiceMaster "teammates" are carefully chosen and go through extensive training that emphasizes self-respect, commitment, and an appreciation that a core "product" they are selling is peace of mind and security.

> Illustrates: selling solutions, emphasizing service, leveraging the impact of people, changing core competencies, repositioning a company within an agile competitive space.

Scitex is a $600 million a year company, a leader in color image communication systems serving the publishing, broadcasting, and paper and textile printing industries worldwide. Much of its development and production (70 percent) are carried out in Israel; there are distribution and maintenance centers in Boston, Brussels, Tokyo, and Hong Kong. Users of Scitex systems routinely share files among distributed personnel linked by computer networks, and each system is configured to the work requirements and information environment of individual customers. Scitex operates its own global computer network that enables interaction between customers and Scitex sales personnel, product developers, production scheduling, management, and all other functions of the company. Documentation for its system is accessible from any location by customer personnel via the Scitex network. Maintenance is facilitated by direct communication between the customer's system and the nearest maintenance center. Customer application experts maintain a database of customer problems and the impact of proposed solutions that all can share via the network. [See Otis entry.]

> Illustrates: global competitor, integrating customer's production requirements and information environment, global vendor information network as asset to customers and to vendor's personnel, interactive customer relationships through sharing information and providing access to company resources.

Sematech is a consortium of U.S. semiconductor manufacturing companies that is jointly developing advanced processes, materials, and equipment with the aim of restoring U.S. global leadership in this area. Because of the defense implications of depending on other nations for the most advanced semiconductor devices, Congress and the Department of Defense agreed to fund half of Sematech's first five years of operation; the rest of the funding comes from consortium members. Sematech operates a proof-of-concepts prototype production facility but does not produce chips for sale; its members do not jointly develop commercial semiconductor devices. Through the Semiconductor Research Corporation, Sematech supports university-conducted basic research, and through the Centers of Excellence program, it supports university-based applied manufacturing research. Analogously, the Microelectronics and Computer Consortium (MCC) provides a mechanism for 100 corporations, public agencies, and universities to collaboratively develop high-risk, high-impact technologies by pooling expertise and eliminating duplication of effort. Its mission is applied research, rapid transfer of new technologies to industry, and rapid deployment of new end products. MCC supports the development of standards that will enable the achievement of these objectives, and it played a leading role in the creation of Enterprise Integration Net (EINet), which has the goal of developing the means necessary for full electronic commerce among distributed companies.

> Illustrates: leveraging resources through cooperation, sharing competencies to mutual advantage, networking.

Shell owns a lubricant manufacturing plant in Brockville, Ontario, that has been reorganized so that three self-managing, mutually collaborating, cross-functional teams whose members rotate between teams and between jobs on the various teams operate the plant. The teams are bulk processing, warehousing, and packaging. They are linked to other teams, on site and at other locations, but they share responsibility for administration and even for marketing. The primary role of management is to promote the self-sufficiency of these teams and to support them with the necessary resources. For example, an open information environment was implemented, and all control and information systems integrated, so that personnel could routinely access production, financial, sales, and customer information. Work processes have been deliberately designed so as to amplify the direct contacts that personnel at all levels will have with customers. Compensation is performance-based and a function of how many different skills an employee has acquired at various levels of competence. The result has been improved profitability and productivity and a work force culture with universal accountability and shared responsibility for the company's success.

> Illustrates: organizing to leverage human resources, value of empowerment, management as leadership and resource provider.

Sony and Philips, who have been direct competitors in a number of markets, are collaborating on the development of a new generation of 120-minute digital video CD players. Sony owns Columbia Pictures and what had been Columbia Records. Philips owns 75 percent of Polygram Records and Films. Time-Warner and Toshiba (which owns 5.6 percent of Time-Warner Entertainment) are collaborating on a rival video CD player. Matsushita, which owns MCA studios, is already marketing a digital video CD player in Japan, but it is capable of only 74 minutes playing time.

> Illustrates: power of cooperation, cooperation between direct competitors, compatibility of cooperation and competition, power of standardization (both Sony and Philips have been "burned" by not reaping the profits from new products they introduced because a standard was set by others, e.g., Sony's Betamax versus VHS).

Sprint Corporation has formed an alliance with Deutsche Telekom and France Telecom to create integrated broadband telecommunications networks across the markets served by those companies. The objective is to move vast quantities of digital data seamlessly in support of business services—especially internal networks linking the facilities of multinational companies (see the Ford global reorganization entry)—and electronic business in what is the single largest and richest market block in the world. MCI and British Telecommunications have already formed an alliance with the same objectives. An AT&T–led consortium that includes a Japanese long-distance carrier and Singapore Telecom is forming an alliance with Unisource, a consortium owned by the Swiss, Swedish, and Dutch telephone companies; other countries are expected to participate. (AT&T had wanted to ally itself with France Telecom and Deutsche Telekom, but European Community regulators did not approve of the alliance.)

> Illustrates: creation of global production networks, enterprise integration, value of information infrastructure, alliances as the competitive strategy of choice.

SprintNet, one of the largest public data networks in the world (by contrast, EDS's network is private), is now accessible wirelessly, for example, via cellular modems in portable computers. AT&T's PersonalLink is also accessible via cellular modem. In addition to sending data "back home" while traveling, the user of this service can easily download on-line information services. (See the CompuServe entry.)

Illustrates: value of information and information transfer infrastructure.

Starbucks Coffee is frequently cited as having triggered the current resurgence in U.S. coffee drinking. Its nationwide chain of coffee shops and minishops, for example, those at airports, not only feature high-quality coffee but affirm the company's "10 Second Pledge": If a shot of espresso is not used to fill an order within ten seconds of being poured, it is discarded. Every cup of coffee is a specialty product that is built to order to meet each customer's requirements. At the same time, price is kept comparable to what other vendors pour from carafes sitting on heaters until customers come along.

> Illustrates: enhancing the value of a commodity by customizing it, converting a commodity into a specialty product, customer-perceived-value marketing, building high-volume products to order, pricing to create new customer opportunities.

Taco Bell has evolved in ten years from a $700 million regional fast-food company with 1,500 outlets to a $3.9 billion multinational food delivery company with over 15,000 "points of access," from kiosks to sit-down restaurants. Management reconceptualized the company from being in the fast-food business to competing for a "one-third share of [everyone's] stomach." Local managers were given incentives to find or create new business opportunities consistent with the company's new objective, from "manufacturing of food" to the food service business. Hierarchical command and control were replaced by teams running outlets, with many teams working without any manager. Regional managers who previously saw themselves as factory-style supervisors became business school graduates who saw themselves as entrepreneurs in the food business. By the year 2000, Taco Bell plans to increase the number of its worldwide points of access by a factor of 10—to 150,000.

> Illustrates: power of reconceptualizing "product," leveraging the impact of people, migrating from selling products to selling product-based solution services, coupling product definition, production, distribution, and marketing.

[TC²] stands for the *Textile/Clothing Technology Corporation,* a consortium made up of more than 250 U.S. soft goods and equipment manufacturers, clothing industry associations, and academic institutions (plus 16 offshore organizations). At its Cary, North Carolina, headquarters, [TC²] operates a state-of-the-art real-time manufacturing facility as a teaching factory for its member companies. It has played a major role in the spread of Quick Response software to U.S. retailers. (See the Quick Response entry.) In addition to Quick Response, the teaching factory, and its research and education activities, [TC²] is combining "agile" clothing manufacturing capabilities and Quick Response into "apparel on demand": three-dimensional body scanning information obtained from customers in real time, converted into two-dimensional pattern design and cutting data for downloading to ultra-high-speed laser cutters, with the garment parts then assembled at a flexible manufacturing facility. The elements of this system all exist and have been demonstrated, separately and in subsets of the whole. When fully realized, it will permit very rapid delivery of custom-made garments on a high-volume basis at little or no cost premium over off-the-rack garments.

> Illustrates: agile manufacturing, alliances among cooperating and competing companies for mutual advantage, sharing information to mutual advantage, mass individualization, value of information integration along the value-adding chain, interactive supplier relationships.

Texas Instruments' Defense Systems and Electronics (DS&E) Group is a $2 billion a year business of growing profitability employing more than 13,000 people; there are four levels to its managerial hierarchy. Every employee is a member of one of four types of cross-functional teams, from manager-led to self-managed. This includes the former president, Hank Hayes, who in December 1993 converted his position into the office of the president team, made up of himself and his two senior vice-presidents. Best-practice benchmarking across industries is epidemic in the company. Product development times and production costs have decreased dramatically, and productivity has risen. All of this happened in less than three years. Back in 1990–1991, the Defense Systems and Electronics Group was a $2 billion a year business that had more than 25,000 employees and seven levels to its managerial hierarchy. In 1994 all personnel, managerial and operational alike, are expected to work smarter and faster, to display initiative and innovativeness, and they are empowered to do so.

An illustration of the power available in the work force is the impact of teaming on the production of the HARM missile by the DS&E Group. Prior to the implementation of cross-functional empowered teams, 25 missiles were produced each month at a unit cost of $1 million. With no new technology, no renovation of the production facility, and no loss of jobs, output was increased by a factor of ten and unit costs were reduced by a factor of five. The difference was leveraging the knowledge possessed by personnel by sharing comprehensive production-related information and letting them tell management what they needed in order to work faster, smarter, better.

> Illustrates: leveraging human resources through teaming and empowerment, flattening the managerial hierarchy, distributing decision making.

Times-Mirror Company has agreed to sell its currently profitable cable operations to Cox Enterprises for $2.3 billion, partly for cash and partly for a 20 percent stake in a new cable and TV services operation to be created by Cox. Times-Mirror management decided that its expertise was information and entertainment content, not delivery systems. Given the growing intensity of competition in the cable TV and telecommunications networking industries, the right posture for each company is to focus on its core competencies, even though the delivery operations happen to be profitable now. In Cox's hands, they may remain profitable for a long time, in which case Times-Mirror benefits through its equity stake. If not, Times-Mirror will save the huge amounts of money that it might have committed to promoting its cable operations had it held onto them. Similarly, NeXt made the painful decision to stop production of its innovative but marginally successful computer in favor of concentrating all its resources on its much more marketable NeXtStep operating system, incorporating full object-oriented programming virtues. In the summer of 1993, Imperial Chemical converted its pharmaceutical manufacturing division, Zeneca, into an independent company, separating it from Imperial's chemical manufacturing operations, Kodak sold off its drug division, and Thorn-EMI management wrestled with converting its two major divisions into stand-alone companies: Thorn-EMI music and Thorn furniture manufacturing were both profitable, but the former on a rising note, the latter on a trailing one.

Illustrates: focus on core competencies.

TRW's Auburn, New York, keyless remote automobile entry systems plant tripled its employment and quadrupled its revenues between 1991 and 1994. All devices are assembled by Sony two-arm robots working around the clock six days a week. Sony engineers resident at the plant work with TRW engineers to ensure that new product designs are matched to the manufacturing capabilities of these highly flexible robots. Management has created a cooperative work force environment that has internalized best-practices benchmarking, universal accountability, and shared responsibility for the company's success. A Ford QOS-style information "wall" is updated on a weekly basis with company financial and production information. A permanent Best Practices team, made up of operational personnel and one manager, roams the plant soliciting ideas for improvements and authorized to pursue their implementation.

Illustrates: integration of production and design processes, value of open information environment, leveraging human resources, value of manager-led work force culture based on shared responsibility for success.

U.K. Fine Chemicals is a consortium consisting of 11 British fine chemicals manufacturers, most of which are direct competitors of one another. They formed the consortium as a means of creating a united marketing effort, primarily in the United States. Visiting U.S. chemical manufacturers and industry association meetings and conventions,

U.K. Fine Chemicals offers potential customers the combined competencies of the 11 companies in any combination required to produce what a given customer needs. At the same time, the apparently greater scale of operations and scope of capabilities of U.K. Fine Chemicals vis-à-vis its individual member companies is also an advantage. The customer is buffered from the details of working out which of several capable companies will produce what.

> Illustrates: a form of virtual organization structure different from Ambra or Kingston Technologies, value of enhancing the appeal to new customers and sharing in new business rather than trying to get it all for oneself.

U.S. West, Nordstrom, and J. C. Penney are collaborating on an interactive home shopping channel that will allow viewers to browse catalogs and to make purchases. It is expected to begin operation in 1994. The test vehicle will be Time-Warner's Orlando interactive TV test bed. Nordstrom is simultaneously collaborating with Bell Atlantic on a similar project, and Time-Warner and Spiegel already have a noninteractive TV shopping service currently reaching 400,000 households.

> Illustrates: leveraging resources through cooperation, the compatibility of cooperation and competition, cooperating with companies and competing with them concurrently.

Union Carbide has a large and very profitable polyethylene manufacturing division. It constantly pushes the leading edge of manufacturing technology, which is the basis for its own operations while licensing slightly older technologies to rivals. In the area of ethylene glycol manufacturing (an intermediary in the manufacture of polyester garment fibers), Union Carbide has entered into joint ventures with Japanese and Taiwanese fiber manufacturers and a Kuwaiti petroleum refinery company. These partners put up the bulk of the billions of dollars required for new plants in exchange for guaranteed markets for raw materials and supplies of intermediary materials.

Illustrates: aggressive, self-confident attitude toward core competencies, potential for sharing costs and risks through cooperation.

Unisys, under CEO James Unruh, is adopting "customerization"—individualized solutions to customer products that are worked out jointly with customers—as its leading product. It is moving to become a provider of computer, information planning, and management, process redesign and strategic management services. It will also manufacture the hardware needed to provide these services. But it is prepared to provide the services using other manufacturers' hardware if that is the customer's preference. (See the Hewlett-Packard and IBM entries.)

Illustrates: the shift in dynamics of competition from hardware primarily to information and services primarily, customization, selling customer-defined solutions rather than products.

Williams Companies is a natural gas transporter that exploited its low-tech pipeline network and rights-of-way by running fiber-optic cable through them and now owns the fourth-largest U.S. fiber-optic network. It transmits digital audio, video, and music signals for production studios and rents out capacity to MCI, LDDS, and others, on an as-needed basis. Williams recently rejected a $2.3 billion offer for this digital transmission network. In a similar way, Sprint began as the internal communications function of Southern Pacific Railroad, which, like Williams, used its rights-of-way to create an instant large-scale fiber-optic network on a budget.

Illustrates: new version of economy of scope, value of information and information services.

Xerox's announcement of its Open Document System in the spring of 1994 promised to transform publishing as profoundly as desktop publishing software and hardware did. With Open Document, even very large files, incorporating text and graphics, can be transferred across networks and phone lines to be printed out at remote sites. With high-speed broad-bandwidth transmission facilities that are increasingly available to everyone, whole books can be printed out in minutes on high-speed copiers. The genius of the Xerox contribution is the breadth of its hardware and software independence. Users can create files using their favorite word processor and have them transmitted, received, and printed out without concern about the intermediary hardware and software. Xerox was able to accomplish this by forging an alliance based on mutual benefit among manufacturers of computers, copiers and telecommunications equipment, and software developers. All agreed to abide by the standards needed to achieve the performance objectives of Open Document while continuing to compete with one another for customers.

> Illustrates: win-win alliances keyed to acceptance of a common standard that allows a new market to be created, power of cooperation, giving up a small slice of the systems-only sales "pie" in exchange for access to slices of a vastly larger component sales pie.

Thriving on Change and Uncertainty

CHAPTER 5

Leading, Learning, and Thinking

W hat an agile competitor *really* sells are skills, knowledge, expertise, and information in a relationship over time. The enrichment value provided to customers derives from the skills, inventiveness, and knowledge of the people who work *for* the company and *with* the company, at its partner companies and suppliers. These people encode their expertise explicitly or implicitly into the products and services provided to the customers. Recognizing that the ability to enrich the customer is derived from the role played by people is a key to success in agile competition. It is the essence of the fourth dimension of the agile competitive "space," leveraging the impact of people and information on a company's bottom line.

Our Wealth Is in the Knowledge of Our People

At a White House conference, on the "Future of the American Workplace," President Bill Clinton, Secretary of Labor Robert Reich, and

Secretary of Commerce Ron Brown all agreed that the nation's wealth is in the nation's people; that people really are the secret to our economic success. This is a major departure from the era of mass-production-based competition, when plant, machinery, and equipment were our most valuable assets. Committing a company to the centrality of people to its strategic success will have a significant impact on the way it organizes for agility and on the role it assigns to its leadership. This chapter deals with the implications of this commitment.

LEADERS

Perhaps the most dramatic role change for people is in what the agile organization asks of its leaders. In the old days, leaders were asked to be "doers," to tell the people "below" them in the managerial hierarchy what to do, and to police their performance, making sure that employees actually did what they were told to do.

In today's emerging agile world, many firms send executives to school to learn how to coach and to lead and to learn how to bring out the best in employee teams. The days of the "doer-manager" are over, says Goodyear Senior Technical Vice-President Fred Kovac.

Dennis Pawley, Executive Vice-President of Chrysler Manufacturing, agrees with him. In a 1993 speech in Traverse City, Michigan, Pawley said, "The success of Chrysler was in part due to all the wonderful technology they had, but mainly due to the people. People at Chrysler are now given the authority to meet the goals and objectives set by management." Pawley indicated that, "Chrysler has reduced the number of levels in the [corporate] hierarchy and [decided] that management's job [from now on] was to set, simplify, and refine goals and objectives letting the people whose job it was to accomplish them figure out how to meet them."

The job of leaders is to determine what businesses the organization should be in, to assess its competitive situation, to develop resources and strategies, and to set appropriate goals and objectives. Many firms have set up so-called dream teams to assess core competencies and customer opportunities and to position the company for success in agile competition.

The pyramid of authority typical of mass-production-era companies and many other organizations won't work for agile competitors. The pace of decision making in a pyramid is inherently slow, and communications are "noisy," cumbersome, and frequently distorted. Decision making in a pyramid organization can be compared to a herd of elephants heading toward a moving target. The elephants go where the moving target was, with little or no chance of hitting it. An organization using the pyramid of authority will have trouble with agile competitors.

There are companies whose accumulated inertia prevents them from adapting to changes in their markets even when they have as much as a year's advance warning of those changes. Most companies found themselves in that position entering the 1980s, but many are now removing layers from the bureaucratic pyramid, knocking down organizational walls, and distributing decision-making authority. The Greek philosopher Democritus said, "A fool can learn from his own experience; the wise learn from the experiences of others." Today, companies are proud of learning even from their own hard-won experience, because so many others have painful corporate experiences and seem to learn nothing from them.

Removing multiple layers from the organizational hierarchy and switching to macromanagement, in which top executives set goals and objectives for large numbers of independent business unit managers who have profit and loss (P&L) responsibility, are important steps in speeding the pace of decision making for an agile competitor. The agile macromanaging leader sends out a memo saying, "We need to be more entrepreneurial." The mass-production micromanaging leader sends out a memo saying, "We need to be more entrepreneurial, and here is how we are going to do it. . . ."

The key point is that the people who have the responsibility to meet goals and objectives know best how to meet them. Senior managers lead by setting direction and objectives. Mid-level managers lead by finding the best way to meet goals and objectives given their current situation. Although the motivation to change to a distributed authority model is based mainly on the need for increased speed, many people find that it opens up significant economies and new opportunities as more people throughout the organization are allowed to make decisions.

Alcoa CEO Paul O'Neill established the "office of the chairman" and eliminated several senior corporate executive positions from line management. The office of the chairman is populated by several counselors who used to be division senior executives. Their advice and service are now an optional resource to a large number of smaller division presidents. Each Alcoa president reports to the CEO, who sets broad-based P&L objectives. The presidents have wide latitude in how they choose to meet those objectives.

Texas Instruments (TI) Defense Systems and Electronics Group has moved to empowered, cross-functional teams so completely that its president, Hank Hayes, converted his own position into a three-person office of the president, filled by him and his two (former) senior vice-presidents. This capped the conversion of the group's entire work force to a team organizational structure. Whereas in 1990 there were 25,000 people in seven managerial levels generating $2 billion in revenues with TI losing money, today there are 13,000 people, four management levels, the same $2 billion in revenues in spite of declining defense budgets—and the Group is making money.

It is not at all coincidental that, in 1993, TI's Defense Systems and Electronics Group won a Malcolm Baldrige Award for its commitment to quality in the enterprise. Interestingly, when restricted to a small number of attendees at the award ceremony with President Bush in Washington, D.C., TI chose to bring mainly people from the shop floor—the people, Hank Hayes said, who made it happen. Recognizing and rewarding the role and contribution of people at all levels of the organization are important aspects of agile organizational leadership.

Generically, there is a shift in organizational structure from a hierarchical organization to a network of variously structured organizations operating concurrently within a single company. A few layers of management share leadership duties and set broad-based goals and objectives for clusters of semiautonomous P&L units. Many large multinational organizations, among them Asea Brown Boveri, are creating an internal web of smaller organizations. Each of the smaller organizations typically has P&L responsibility and the authority to act on its own, along with access to a variety of infrastructure support services and information sources. These services are offered on a fee basis and not as allocated costs. Similarly, traditional vertically integrated firms are now creating independent business units and allowing each unit the freedom to partner with, or purchase components from, world-class suppliers. Although some preference for sister organizations remains, because of shared culture, goals, and objectives, most people agree that without the option to buy and sell to outsiders it is difficult to be a world class competitor or supplier.

The Role of People and the Need to Think

Agile organizations compete on the basis of their core competencies. They need to be people-centered. They need to value learning. They need to evaluate skills carefully. Most important, they need to be dynamic, thinking organizations. The role of people and the need to think are dramatically different for an agile company than for a mass-production-era competitor. The mass-production adage "Don't think, just do what you are told" won't work if you are going to be a successful agile competitor.

LEARNING AND THINKING

We don't do a very good job of preparing people to think. Starting in kindergarten, we tell people what to do; we don't help them to figure it out. Lehigh University recently changed its objective from being a teaching institution to a learning institution. Although some faculty members thought of this as an exercise in semantics, Lehigh Provost Alan Pense explains it as a serious and significant switch in philosophy, from "the jug and the mug" or "the sage on the stage" to "the coach in the corner" or "the guide on the side." In the jug and mug model, students bring empty mugs to class and professors fill them from their jugs of knowledge. No thinking required. In making fun of such a teaching environment, one artist drew a picture of a big tape recorder playing back a lesson while a collection of smaller tape recorders in the student seats recorded the lesson. This is not a learning environment. It does, however, remind us of the mass-production paradigm, remnants of which exist not only in universities but also in businesses at all levels. Although business leaders have recognized the need to shift to being the coach in the corner or the guide on the side, employees at many organizations still see the sage on the stage type of leader.

During 1994, we informally surveyed businesspeople from a variety of industries. We asked them: "What percentage of their time do you think people in your organization spend thinking, learning, and innovating?" The answers cluster rather strongly in the range of 5 to 15 percent. There were a variety of responses to the follow-up question, "Why don't people think more?", including:

- Most technical professionals have been paid, promoted, and rewarded for doing what they were told. Now, suddenly you are asking them to think! They are afraid to think and act on their ideas. What will happen if they are wrong?
- Most people are embarrassed at the thought of anyone knowing that they were wrong or made a mistake. The possibility of punishment for "thinking mistakes" only exacerbates this perception.
- They don't believe that you seriously want them to think and act on their own. They have no model for when to act and when to ask!

Most large organizations have systematically stamped out entrepreneurial behavior because it disrupts mass-production harmony. Now, suddenly, because the old ways no longer work, we are asking people to be more entrepreneurial and to think. They wonder, "Are you serious? Do you trust them? Will you really let them do it the best way they can? Or are you in that category of leader who says that we need to be more entrepreneurial—and here's how were going to do it?"

It is important to explain the context of the data-gathering process used in obtaining these answers. In most mass-production organizations, with a pyramid of authority, *change* was and is disruptive. It is common practice to discourage new ideas, different ways of doing things, and so on. People who work in those organizations eventually

© 1993 Iacocca Institute • Lehigh University • Illustrator: Gene Mater

discover that *thinking* about their jobs and about how to do things differently or innovatively is not desired, appreciated, or rewarded. Inevitably, they stop thinking and innovating and just do what they are told to do. There are, of course, professions in which discouragement has not occurred and therefore has not dampened the rewards of on-the-job thinking: academics, doctors, lawyers, and researchers. The data and the answers discussed in this chapter came primarily from people in the discouraging type of organizations.

You need to ask yourself about your organization. Are people asked to listen, or are they really expected to think? What kind of culture have you set up, and what is the environment you are putting in place? Trust is a major part of that environment. You can't ask people to think and get them to do anything effective if you don't enable them to act by trusting them.

It's important to recognize that thinking faster, smarter, or better, about how to do what we used to do more efficiently, is good only for a while. Thinking about how to do different things, including how to do things previously thought to be impossible, opens up enormous opportunities for *sustained* success. Without innovative thinking on the part of its personnel, a company will quickly lose its competitive edge in an agile business environment.

If it is true that organizations sell the skills, knowledge, and expertise of the people who work for and with them, and if it is also true that those people think, learn, and innovate only 5 to 15 percent of the time, then it seems possible to triple the effective output of an organization by moving the effectiveness in thinking, learning, and innovating from 15 to 45 percent. What can we do to motivate people to move in that direction and significantly increase the organization's profitability?

Part of what needs to be done involves addressing how people benefit when they do the "right" thing for the company's success. What reward structure is in place in the company? How much of their salary and compensation is based on their bottom-line impact? Are they aware of their bottom-line impact?

At Springfield Remanufacturing, a company that rebuilds truck engines, everybody in the plant has been trained to read a P&L statement and is given a copy every time it comes out. Lunchroom conversations at all levels of the organization focus on the P&L results and what each person can do to make the P&L statement even better the next time.

NuCor Steel pays every employee every week a salary that is based on the performance of his or her unit that week. NuCor does it by the week so that the employees won't lose sight of what they did that week that made a difference. NuCor employees report that if they bring home a check for $1,000 this week and one for $800 next week, they've got some explaining to do!

Tom Malone, President of Milliken, said, "If you are not measuring it, then you can't be serious about it." The corollary is that employees know how they are measured and behave accordingly. If you want to foster a type of behavior, you must make the behavior clear, measure results, and provide rewards when appropriate—especially if you are trying to inspire employees to change cultures and behavior patterns.

It is important to create an atmosphere that encourages people to take appropriate risks. It does not take any great effort to reward risk takers who succeed. To have an organization that takes appropriate risks, however, it is necessary to reward risk takers who do not succeed. It is tempting to say "risk takers who fail," but that description seems to push most CEOs a bit too far. However, they will, and should, reward those who take appropriate risks and don't succeed.

The CEO of one small company tells the story of a senior engineer who came to him and explained that he had spent $40,000 trying to find a way to make a process more reliable, only to conclude that it wasn't possible to do so. The CEO decided that he would have done the same thing and gave the man a raise for trying!

When is a risk "appropriate"? The answer is, of course, based on the situation, the benefit, the cost of not succeeding, and so on. How then can an executive set the proper tone? Without a formula, the best way we have seen is by example and with lots of dialogue. Of course, the reward part will play a major role in an employee's mind. Rewards are, in fact, the ultimate measurement. But culture also plays an important role.

Those of you who have visited Japan have occasionally heard the statement, "We got that to work on the fifth try." Think of Mazda's persistence with the Wankel engine through years of weak oil seals, poor fuel economy, and emissions-control problems. Today, a twin-turbo Wankel powers the prestigious, much admired, and very successful RX-7 sports car. Why don't we hear such stories in the United States? The typical answer is, "You don't get five tries in the United States." Think of the Corvair, the Vega, and Fiero automobiles. If an organization is to be innovative, self-controlling risk-taking behavior is needed.

CNN won the news war during the Persian Gulf conflict because it could be depended upon to have late-breaking news on the air first. Often within minutes of an event, CNN was on the air live. Not just the second the war broke out, when they had an open phone line, but consistently throughout the war CNN was first—when Scud missiles fell in Tel Aviv and so on. CNN had no equipment advantage over the other networks, nor did it have any other technological edge. Rather, CNN asked its employees to be entrepreneurial, to think, take some risks, and make decisions for the good of the organization. Field staff at CNN had more authority than their counterparts in the other networks to make decisions without needing to ask for permission. CNN is an agile news network, and it won the concept to cash war in Desert Storm.

The key here is not promiscuous empowerment, but to give those responsible for carrying out tasks the power to make decisions and take actions and risks that will improve their performance. That's a very important part of the role of leadership.

Will entrepreneurs survive in your organization? Entrepreneurs are the people who think, learn, and take the risks needed to give you a competitive advantage. In mass production, such people were the disrupters and had to be confined and restricted, or they would have destroyed the system. In agile competition, thinkers are the basis for success; it is the nonthinkers who can destroy the system.

Are employees aware of the state of the company's bottom line? Do they understand how their performance affects the bottom line, positively and negatively? What part of employee compensation is based on bottom-line performance?

To succeed as an agile competitor, you must create a thinking and learning environment. Thus it is important to ask some questions: Are people, skills, and knowledge treated as core competencies and assets, or are you focused on plant equipment and machinery? Are you benchmarking and investing in your core competencies? During the era of mass production, when we had a few products and sold them over and over again, we could categorize an organization by its products. With agile competition, in which products and services are mingled in a relationship over time, an organization is more likely to be categorized by its core competencies. These are the capabilities that attract agile customers, can be leveraged in virtual organization relationships, and can even be sold directly as product services. Core competencies become a major focus of agile managements' concern. They represent the organization's most precious assets and determine its profitability.

Core competencies are, of course, based on the skills and expertise of the people the organization can tap. Agile competitors will focus on identifying critical core competencies in which they must maintain world-class skills in order to succeed, and they will acquire ancillary core competencies as needed from partners, suppliers, and so on. Deciding which core competencies are critical is the task of leadership, to be undertaken in consultation with customers who know what it is about an organization they value and what causes them to do business with it. One way to gain access to ancillary world-class core competencies is through virtual organization relationships. This is the focus of the next chapter, where virtual organizations are given an in-depth treatment.

EXPERIENCE WITH AGILE COMPETITORS

Perhaps the best advice to provide with respect to leading, learning, and thinking in the context of agility and agile competitors is to share what has been learned from others who have thought about these issues. Seminars and workshops on the principal dimensions of agility have generated valuable data on becoming an agile competitor and on using agility to achieve strategic goals and objectives. In the following sections, the answers of several hundred executives to three seminal questions are summarized. These questions are:

1. Why is there no prescription for agility?
2. What is new or really different about agile competition?
3. How can a company benefit from agility, and how would the company know that it had benefited?

Why Is There No Prescription for Agility?

- The agile concept of doing business is still new; success is situation-specific and market-opportunity-based. Agile strategies need to be people-, company-, and product-dependent to be useful.
- Success with agility depends on your goals and objectives, and on the agility "fit" to your organization. Each organization's ability to succeed with agility is based on different situations and skill sets.

- Customer needs are different, markets vary, and customer perceptions of value are different.
- The situation is different in each industry and in each company. The cultures of corporations are different. Customers and organizations have knowledge differences, and technical capabilities vary. In short, because the situation is different for each company and customer, no single prescription or formula is possible.
- The competitive environment is different and constantly changing. In an agile environment, the constraints change and customers needs constantly change; we are dealing with a moving target. It is an entrepreneurial environment with many market forces driving it in a variety of directions.
- Beyond differences in situations, there are different opportunities, different competitors, and different time frames. Further, the degree of organizational change needed differs from one company to the next.
- Agility is New Frontier–based, the idea is still in development, and there are many descriptions, too many variables, and a great deal of uncertainty. A formula or prescription is not possible!
- We have limited flexibility and information availability in our organization; we are not ready to be opportunity-specific and to treat our customers as individuals. Nor can we follow any other prescriptions. We need to proceed at the pace and in the agile direction which is right for us, not for somebody else.

What Is New or Really Different about Agile Competition?

- The focus on survival because of the volatility and increased rate of change. The need for recognizing change and dealing with it.
- That the change from a production focus to a customer service focus is the leading edge of the change from mass production to mass customization.
- The concept that the customer is king, that we must proactively deal with changing customer needs and demands. The need for a organizationwide commitment to enhancing customer value.

- The recognition that we are selling knowledge that is implicitly or explicitly encoded into products and services. That customers do business with us because of our core competencies.
- That we enrich customers when we provide solutions. That a solution is an opportunity-based combination of products and service in a relationship over time. That solutions have different values based on the customer context and benefit.
- The continuing increase in demand for customized solutions, despite the significant increase in product variety available on the market. That, when the degree of customerization goes up, the value of information also goes up, and sharing proprietary information becomes an important issue.
- The need for open-mindedness in seeking opportunities in a different way. The need for collaboration out of necessity, even collaboration among competitors. The greater extent of cooperation based on balanced mutual strengths and flexibility.
- That cooperation can enhance competitive capability. That competitors can cooperate and compete. That partnering should not be a last resort. The utility of teams and partnerships to enhance and build on core skills and the need for trust. The ability to spread risk across organizations and to open opportunities which otherwise are too risky to try.
- The need to establish a risk-taking environment. The need to reward risk takers who succeed. The significant need to reward risk takers who took appropriate risks and didn't succeed.
- The market demand function is different. Speed is an important competitive factor, as are flexibility and short life cycles. The importance of knowing the customer. Knowing that what you sell must be opportunity-based and customer-focused.
- The benefit in sharing markets, leveraging core competencies, and teaming up and bringing the best resources together. That we need help in meeting all the customers needs.
- That pooling resources brings about increased ability, flexibility, and speed in adapting to customer requirements.
- The importance of people as an asset base. That assets are not just physical. The value of information as an enabling resource. The value of information in product and service solutions to enrich our customers.

- The destruction or removal of most levels from the pyramid of authority. The need for trust, teams, and empowerment to succeed.
- The wide variety of new technologies that are opening new opportunities. The greater need for education to use new technology and to see new opportunities.
- The activities of our competitors, who are reengineering the way they do business and how they interact with us. Overseas competitors are cooperating and competing with each other.
- The importance of waking up and focusing on how to obtain competitive advantages. The need for humility. The need to solve problems by looking outside as well as inside. A willingness to change—to be entrepreneurial.
- The global market created by distribution and information systems. Customers and suppliers work together in a global network environment. With globalization come blurred trade functions and more governmental concern with the competitive capabilities of a region. In addition, more societal interest and a focus on people and education as economic resources of significance exist.
- The overcapacity of production capability tends to reduce arrogance and increase the recognition of the importance and relevance of being customer-oriented.
- Nothing is really new here! You are just using new names and terminology.

How Can a Company Benefit from Agility, and How Would the Company Know That It Had Benefited?

- Agility can shrink the concept to cash time. When speed is the key competitive factor, increased customer satisfaction and higher customer retention accompany a significant reduction in concept to cash time. An additional benefit can accrue in lower inventory needs and a reduction in the cost of goods sold.

- For a company with a short concept to cash cycle, being first to market makes "leadership pricing" possible. In addition to increased profits on the bottom line from using leadership pricing, the stock price of the organization can increase.
- Agile competitors who invest in employees see reductions in employee absenteeism, increased productivity, better work force utilization, and higher employee morale.
- Agile employees who care about their organization's customers provide an important differentiating capability. This can result in more value-based products, happier customers, increased customer renewal rates, more new customers attracted, and increased market share.
- Agile competitors invest in people and quality and are using cooperative and agile partner relationships to gain access to world markets through virtual organizations. This results in significant positive impacts on profit potential.
- Agility makes better asset utilization possible, which in turn results in less capital required and improved ROA/ROI results.
- Agility offers an increased competitive capability, and thus fewer competitors are equal to your abilities.
- With the higher-value products and solutions made possible through agility, comes a new way for a company to distinguish itself from its competitors. This can be translated into new market opportunities and an increased probability of survival.

HIGHLIGHTS OF CHAPTER 5

An agile organization sells the skills, knowledge, and information of the people who work for it, partner with it, and sell to it.

Removing multiple layers from the organizational hierarchy and switching to macromanagement, in which top executives set goals and objectives for large numbers of independent P&L managers, is an important step in speeding the pace of decision making for an agile competitor.

Agile organizations compete on the basis of their core competencies. They need to be people-centered, they need to value learning, they need to measure skills carefully, but most important, they need to be dynamic, thinking organizations. The role of people and the need to think are dramatically different for an agile competitor. The mass-production adage "Don't think, just do what you are told" won't work if you are going to be a successful agile competitor.

Although business leaders recognize the need to shift to being a coach in the corner or a guide on the side, employees at many organizations still expect to have the sage on the stage type of leader.

Most organizations have systematically stamped out entrepreneurial behavior because it disrupts mass-production harmony. Now, suddenly, because the old ways no longer work, we are asking people to be more entrepreneurial and to think. They wonder, "Are you serious? Do you trust them? Will you really let them do it the best way they can?"

It's important to create an atmosphere that encourages people to take acceptable risk. The key here is not reckless empowerment, but to allow those who are responsible for carrying out tasks the ability to make decisions and take actions and risks that will improve their performance. That's a very important part of the role of leadership.

To succeed as an agile competitor, you must create a thinking and learning environment.

CHAPTER 6

Virtual Organizations

INTRODUCTION

In agile competition, unlike mass production, things change rapidly and are opportunity-based. The virtual organization is a dynamic organizational tool for agile competitors. It is at once neither temporary nor permanent. Designed to be opportunity-based, the virtual organization is a pragmatic organizational tool for competitors who are seeking a strategic concept to use in an environment of change and uncertainty. Virtual organizations reflect and facilitate three major motifs of agile competition:

- The virtual organization model expresses the need of agile competitors to create or assemble new productive resources very *quickly*.
- The virtual organization model expresses the need of agile competitors to create or assemble new productive resources *frequently* and *concurrently* because of the decreasing profitable lifetimes of individual products and services.

▪ The virtual organization reflects the *complexity* of today's most profitable products, which often require access to a wider range of world-class competencies—research, prototyping, manufacturing, design, marketing, distribution, service, and within each of these many, more specialized competencies—than any one organization can afford to maintain "in between" customer opportunities or can identify in advance of unanticipated opportunities.

The virtual organization is a complex strategic weapon in the hands of an agile competitor. Companies have already found six different rationales for using virtual organizations. We expect that virtual organization strategies will continue to evolve as we make the transition to full agile competition.

Based on the cooperation dimension of agility, the fundamental strategic option behind the use of the virtual organization is sharing in a multiwin arrangement to accomplish goals not otherwise achievable.

Indeed, we find that a virtual organization can accomplish tasks that could not be done by each of the competitors working sequentially or even in tandem. There is no magic here, but rather the virtual organization is formed by integrating core competencies, resources, and customer market opportunities. *It is dramatically better than business as usual for a network of companies sharing a business opportunity on a product and service basis.* For the purpose of analogy, consider the capabilities of an all-star team formed in some sport. Assume that the team members have overcome the difficulties of learning how to work together and compare their abilities to those of any of the teams who contributed to the all-star team, or compare their abilities to those of all the other teams working as a cooperative group. The virtual organization *integrates* core competencies and resources into an all-star world-class team.

Virtual organizations are the business equivalent of all-star teams. Imagine the power of an all-star team for every business opportunity, tailored to the challenge of that opportunity and that competitive situation. In this chapter, the concept of a *web,* to facilitate forming teams and to eliminate the problems of rapidly forming an all-star team and expecting the players to function as a team as soon as they start playing, is introduced.

In addition to sharing core competencies to be world-class, there are strategic reasons for using the virtual organization model. These concepts are introduced below. Later in the chapter they are formally categorized and examples of them are provided.

- To share facilities and resources and perhaps core competencies in order to increase the apparent size or geographic coverage a competitor can offer to a customer, that is, to have critical mass or to be a world-class global competitor.
- To share the risk and infrastructure cost of qualifying to compete. The cost of entry for large and small competitors is growing rapidly. Sharing the expense of precompetitive technology, facilities, and resources leaves more resources to spend on customizing product features and services that provide for competitive advantage. Consider, for example, an all-star research group consisting of the best talents from all the competitors in the United States.

Competitors are increasingly forming virtual organization relationships to take advantage of this synergy and maximize the resources they can use to distinguish themselves with customers. This type of virtual organization gives rise to the advantages competitors can get by cooperating and competing.

- Agile competitors must deal with rapidly opening and closing windows of opportunity for products and services. In agile competition, it is reasonable to expect that a firm may use a virtual organization not because it could not make a particular product, but because it could not make it fast enough to exploit the high-profit opportunity window. In this case, a firm would form a virtual organization to work on a product or service concept concurrently with other firms and meet the window of opportunity in time for high profits to be generated.
- Although exact figures are not available, most people would agree that a portion of the profits in the entire window is far more

valuable than all the profits in the second half of the window. Furthermore, it is unlikely that any firm that missed the first half of a product window could capture even a majority of the profits in the second half of the window.

▪ Although it may seem unthinkable to mass producers, agile competitors will more and more use the virtual organization concept to strategically share markets, customers, and market loyalty. The concept of cobranding is but one example of this type of strategic sharing of markets and market loyalty. In a virtual organization marketplace, knowledge, customer loyalty, and market contacts are core competencies to be shared for mutual strategic benefit.

▪ The virtual organization concept allows skills and services to be combined into unique customer solutions. It allows small entrepreneurial firms to compete on the same scale as giant corporations in terms of one-stop shopping and providing solutions to customers. Of course, it allows large firms to organize as collections of smaller entrepreneurial firms and to use the virtual organization concept internally as well as externally to meet unique and special solution opportunities. Thus, the virtual organization concept can be used to assemble from skill-based providers a critical mass of capabilities to provide customers with value-based solutions whose enrichment values they can see and measure.

Although it may be easy to encourage the use of the virtual organization concept, it is not yet simple to form and operate a virtual organization. Some of its advantages give rise to its most significant implementation difficulties. For example, there is no inherent reason for the parts of a virtual organization to be in physical proximity. Indeed, eventually we will routinely use the information superhighway as a mechanism to facilitate cooperation between members of a virtual organization. However, today this is not yet easy to do. Although some people advocate focusing on the information superhighway as the enabling technology for virtual organizations, it seems to be only a facilitating mechanism, albeit an important one. When the information superhighway arrives, things will be better, but few companies, are waiting for it to be in place before using the virtual organization concept to strategic advantage.

VIRTUAL ORGANIZATION CHARACTERISTICS

In a cover story on the subject (Feb. 8, 1993), *Business Week* defined a *virtual company* as a new organizational model that uses technology to dynamically link people, assets, and ideas. We emphasize that, although technology will be an important facilitating mechanism for the virtual organization, in the long run, it will not be an essential requirement.

Business Week identified several other key characteristics of the virtual organization, described below and summarized in Figure 6.1.

- The virtual organization must be the ultimate in *adaptability;* it must be agile in its internal organizational structure, rules and regulations, and so on. A virtual organization is an *opportunity-pulled* and *opportunity-defined* integration of core competencies distributed among a number of real organizations.

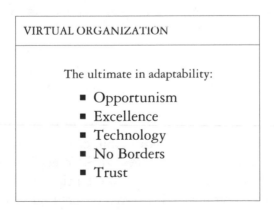

VIRTUAL ORGANIZATION

The ultimate in adaptability:

- Opportunism
- Excellence
- Technology
- No Borders
- Trust

FIGURE 6.1   Characteristics of a virtual organization.

Unlike other organizational structures commonly used by business, the virtual organization is formed to meet an opportunity and disbanded when its objective is attained. Opportunities can and will last tens of years, as is the case with the Boeing 777 airplane, or they can be short windows lasting only a few weeks or months.

- The virtual organization is assumed to be world class and *excellent* in its core competencies, having obtained these competencies in the all-star team fashion.

- A virtual organization is assumed to offer *world-class technology* in its product service solutions. The organization acquires this technology the same way it acquires its core competencies.

- What makes the virtual organization concept exciting today is the growing ease with which physically distributed, complementary competencies can remain dispersed and still be synthesized into a coherent productive resource, one whose synthesized character is invisible or *borderless* with respect to the customer.

A customer buys an Ambra computer, a Ford automobile, or a compact disc and is never made aware of the fact that the Ambra was produced by a network of cooperating companies extending from Southeast Asia to North Carolina, each of which devotes only a selected portion of its operations to that effort; that a virtual design studio, made up of designers pulled together electronically from Ford's seven design centers literally around the world, was responsible for the automobile's style; that the musicians on the recording either played together in separated studios linked by fiberoptic cable or played at different times in different places and had their contributions combined electronically into a single performance.

It is the seamless synthesis that appeals to the customer; there is no reason to hide the membership of the virtual organization. A growing number of airlines—USAir and British Airways, Northwest and KLM, United and Lufthansa—are integrating their flight operations so that travelers can be offered a wider range of flights and destinations, as if they were dealing with a single airline.

THE VIRTUAL COMPANY

© 1991 Iacocca Institute • Lehigh University • Illustrator: Gene Mater

- The members of the virtual organization team must behave toward each other in a *trusting and trustworthy* manner. If mutual trust does not exist, they cannot succeed and customers will not do business with them.

What makes a virtual organization valuable are the reduction in time, costs, and risks and the increase in product service capabilities and relationships achievable when the participants integrate core competencies and resources while collaborating intensively with the customer throughout the concept to cash cycle.

These characteristics are familiar to us from special task forces formed in response to urgent situations or inspiring challenges: the Manhattan Project, Lockheed's Skunk Works, the Apollo Program, and more recently the deciphering of the RSA-129 encryption algorithm by a "virtual" computer made up of 1600 actual computers ranging from PCs to Crays. It is now practical to make the formation of "special" task forces ordinary by integrating the ideal resources required to accomplish a well-defined goal without uprooting the members of the task force. *It would be like assembling an all-star sports team every day tailored to the challenge posed by that day's competitors.*

VIRTUAL ORGANIZATION MECHANISMS

The concept of the virtual organization and the mechanisms used to form virtual organizations are not in themselves new. Nor is the idea of cooperation new; but the degree of use and intensity of cooperation are new. As with much of agility, old concepts are put together in new ways, to deal with new and emerging market realities. Cooperative, collaborative relationships among companies, and even among distributed core competencies, are familiar enough in the form of partnerships, joint ventures, strategic alliances, consortia, and royalty or licensing agreements. The prime contractor-subcontractor model employed in the movie, construction, and defense industries, for example, links core competencies to achieve a particular goal: to produce a film, to build a home, an office building, or a power plant, or to develop a weapons system. For a time limited by their common goal, a group of people with specific skills, and the complex of equipment and facilities they need to exercise those skills, are assembled into a single productive resource.

It is not necessary to have a new legal structure in order to form a virtual organization. Although someday we may find a need for new legislation to recognize some special requirements of virtual organization formation and operation, this is not the case today. The key is in acting like a single-source provider, with full accountability to the customer. Each example of a virtual organization uses one or more of the existing organizational mechanisms such as:

- Partnership
- Joint venture
- Strategic alliance
- New corporation
- Supplier subcontractor
- Cooperative agreement
- Royalty or license
- Outsourcing contract
- Web

Of these organizational forms, only the web is a new concept, and it is explained later in this chapter.

COOPERATION ENHANCES COMPETITIVE CAPABILITY

Recognizing that cooperation can enhance competitiveness is a powerful motivator for the virtual organization.

The growth in the number, and the aggressive agendas, of industrial consortia during the past 10 to 15 years is symptomatic of how widely this recognition is spreading. Consider these examples: Sematech and the Microelectronics and Computers Consortium (MCC); the National Center for the Manufacturing Sciences (NCMS), with its growing network of teaching factories and manufacturing technology "extension" centers, and the clothing industry consortium [TC²]; USCAR, pooling the efforts of Chrysler, Ford, and General Motors, and CAM-I, Computer-Aided Manufacturing, International.

At the same time, there has been a parallel growth in the rate of formation of small business networks, within single industries and across industries, for purposes of vertical as well as of horizontal integration, and there has been an explosive increase in the number of corporate collaborations of all kinds. Apple partnered with Sony to bring its Macintosh PowerBooks to market more quickly and more efficiently than Apple could have done on its own. For similar reasons, Apple partnered with Sharp to manufacture the Newton. IBM, Motorola, and Apple jointly developed the PowerPC chip and operating system. IBM and Toshiba jointly developed the flat-panel displays in their competing notebook and subnotebook PC products. IBM, Toshiba, and Siemens are jointly funding a 256-megabit DRAM chip production facility because the $1.5 to $2 billion price tag makes it an unreasonable investment for any one of them.

Cooperation is the foundation on which virtual organizations rest, and cooperation entails trust. Although some people say that trust in business cannot be achieved, there is ample evidence that trust, in the form of mutually reinforcing dependency relationships, emerges when it is a necessary condition for shared success. Stock and commodity trading are familiar examples of trust and of honoring commitments that are maintained in the face of extreme competitiveness.

The stage is certainly set today for routine access to virtual organizations becoming a central tool in a company's competitive arsenal. To protect the trust relationships that underlie that access from abuse, models for sharing intellectual property to mutual advantage will be needed. The multilateral Intelligent Manufacturing Systems initiative, for example, described in Chapter 4, has had an Intellectual Property Committee examining just these issues.

SIX STRATEGIC REASONS TO USE THE VIRTUAL ORGANIZATION CONCEPT

Many people claim to see the value of the virtual organization concept. Some report that they are already using it because it is just good, common business sense. Our experience, however, is that common sense is not all that common and that there is a wide gulf between recognizing a concept in the abstract and understanding its concrete implications.

We find six strategic reasons that motivate companies to use a virtual organization model. We have no reason to believe that there are not other good reasons. What makes these six valuable is that they focus on the strategic benefit to the company of adopting this model of cooperation.

1. Sharing infrastructure, R&D, risk, and costs.
2. Linking complementary core competencies.
3. Reducing concept to cash time through sharing.
4. Increasing facilities and apparent size.
5. Gaining access to markets and sharing market or customer loyalty.
6. Migrating from selling products to selling solutions.

Sharing Infrastructure, R&D, Risk, and Costs

The first strategic consideration is the value of sharing risk, infrastructure, R&D, and/or the costs of resources, human or technological, that a company would otherwise not be able to afford or could afford only by taking funds away from more productive uses. For a small company, access to specialized manufacturing equipment might be justification enough to join a virtual organization. For a large company, it might be R&D that it cannot afford to do on its own because current operations absorb all its investment capital. Sharing R&D or generic resources still leaves room for competing on the basis of how the partnering companies use the resources or the results of the R&D.

One type of virtual organization, then, is motivated by the need to do things that a company could not, or should not, do at its own expense. Lee Iacocca has said that he never sold a single car because it had a better catalytic converter than its competitors had. In fact, each of the Big Three developed catalytic converters on their own, at a cost to each of about $250 million in mid-1970s dollars. Sharing the cost would have freed valuable resources for activities that could have created competitive advantage (which may have been GM's reason for *not* sharing, given the "depth of its pockets" at the time!).

Later, GM and Toyota created New United Motors Manufacturing Incorporated (NUMMI) out of GM's Fremont, California, Pontiac plant for the mutual advantages it provided. Chrysler and Mitsubishi formed Diamond Star Motors in Normal, Illinois. Ford and Mazda jointly developed a production facility that they share in Flat Rock, Michigan. Today, Chrysler, Ford, and GM, together with various government agencies, are active members in the USCAR consortium and are cooperatively developing a wide range of generic automotive technologies.

Among other examples of sharing infrastructure facilities and costs are:

- The Steel Research Institute, jointly operated by several steel companies for their mutual benefit. Organized to share the cost of steel research—considered to be shared precompetitive generic research.

- Sematech, as discussed earlier in this chapter, set up to share the development of semiconductor manufacturing technologies plans.

- The National Center for Manufacturing Science (NCMS), carrying out several hundred million dollars of annual research and development activities for its member companies. This organization receives matching government support for R&D needed by its members and the Department of Defense, and it develops standards, demonstration projects, and proof of concept experiments in manufacturing-related projects of interest to its members.

- The Agile Manufacturing Enterprise Forum (AMEF), organized to serve as a vehicle for exploring the strategic benefits of agility, provides a common infrastructure for developing, exploring, and sharing knowledge with respect to the strategic dimensions of agility with more than 200 participating organizations.

- "Incubator facilities" for new and small entrepreneurial firms, such as the one operated by the Ben Franklin economic development program in Bethlehem, Pennsylvania. This incubator provides for low-cost rent and shared infrastructure items such as phones, faxes, copiers, and cafeterias. In addition, such facilities provide access to legal, accounting, and financial services from professionals.

- A food court, condominium association, or other organization designed to share common areas and resources.
- Most industry associations designed to leverage a group's common interest such as in lobbying Congress and setting standards.

Linking Complementary Core Competencies

The second strategic reason to use the virtual organization concept is the most generic and will have the most variants. The goal is to unite complementary core competencies in order to serve customers whom the separate companies could not serve on their own. Each member of the virtual organization is chosen because it brings something unique that is needed to meet a customer opportunity. It follows that an agile company will position itself so that it is chosen by others to participate in the virtual organizations that they initiate. If no one ever seeks a company's participation, the company is limited to the opportunities it can develop on its own. AgileWeb, discussed below, is an example of a virtual organization pool out of which clusters of prequalified core competencies can be pulled together quickly, as needed to meet a customer opportunity.

Examples of this type of virtual organization include but are not limited to:

- The joint development of Hewlett-Packard HP-100 palmtop computer with a built-in Motorola pager.
- The way Ambra competed in the PC clone market. Linking 80 employees of its own to those of five other companies that had complementary capabilities, IBM was able to create a competitive PC clone company of its own in the face of bitter cost-cutting competition among already established rivals.
- AT&T contracted with L. L. Bean to market its 800-number service for it, because of the excellence of Bean's telemarketing competence.
- AgileWeb, whose "product" is the ability to form focused virtual organizations quickly out of an amorphous pool of resources.

- Toshiba and IBM, which had jointly developed generic flat-panel display technology for small portable PCs, partnering to meet the special needs of a Toshiba customer for a more sophisticated flat-panel display.

Reducing Concept to Cash Time through Sharing

A third reason why a virtual organization is valuable is the ability for multiple companies to operate in parallel, performing many tasks concurrently. In the process, speed of development is increased, and concept to cash time—and cost of development—reduced. Design should be included here as integral to the production process, but concurrent production places great demands on cooperating companies for cultural, technological, and business process compatibility. Why bother? In order to:

- To reduce time to market
- To increase quality
- To decrease cost

In the commercial world, concept to cash time is an important measure of a company's agility. In a virtual organization, this time is reduced, in part by not having to build new facilities or to find, hire, and train new people and in part by concurrent operations involving multiple partners. Extending the lessons learned from concurrent engineering experiences to concurrent "everything," that is, to eliminating serial processing to the fullest possible extent, the virtual organization model enables a group of companies to create a concurrent enterprise composed solely of world-class competencies for the particular product desired.

Examples include but are not limited to:

- Apple asking Sony to work with it in order to bring out its PowerBook line in a shorter time.

- Motorola, Apple, and IBM getting together to bring out the PowerPC chip.
- The Boeing 777 airplane: Some team members were included to complement core competencies, some were included for their ability to operate concurrently, and some were included to provide access to non-Boeing markets.
- Chrysler's cross-functional vehicle development teams, covering all aspects of new car development from initial concept to final manufacture and market introduction.

Not every virtual organization needs to have the biggest player in charge. As its first product, a small company called Telepad manufactured pen-based computer-input devices. It later expanded to multimedia input systems. It uses well-known design firms for product design and IBM for manufacturing. With 28 permanent and 4 temporary employees, this small firm introduced 4 successful new products in 12 months.

The virtual company concept was intuitive with Telepad founder and CEO Ronald C. Oklewicz. After *Business Week* interviewed him and gave a name to what his company was doing, Oklewicz and his staff were able to make significant advances just because they were operating with an explicitly defined concept. This highlighted concurrency as a key enabling factor in their success. As a result, on their first consciously virtual company product development project, they used a design house they were quite satisfied with; on their second, they contracted with another design firm.

Why? Because the first product was not yet finished when the second project began and they did not want to diminish the intensity of the first effort by starting a second project with the same studio. Instead, they had the first design firm advise the second firm on a consulting basis, while it prepared to design Telepad's next product.

This is exactly the methodology used by Intel with internal design and development teams: leapfrogging generations of 80X86 chips to sustain concurrent product development momentum. "Without partners, and without working concurrently, we could not have achieved the success that we have," says Oklewicz. Telepad is willing to trade equity for innovation, and its partners understand and welcome the opportunity.

A special benefit to small firms of using large partners is the reception the small firm gets in banking and client circles. "When I say IBM manufactures our products and that we have business relationships with other major firms, we gain significant credibility in financing our business and having clients know we are serious contenders and will be able to deliver what we promise," says Oklewicz. Telepad is now producing multimedia, client-configurable, high-speed computing devices. It credits the virtual company concept for its ability to achieve its objectives.

Increasing Facilities and Apparent Size

The virtual organization is a way of leveraging your ability to satisfy and enrich your customer. For small organizations, serving the customer through a virtual organization allows you to show depth of backup, additional breadth of capability, and the financial ability to deal with what the customer may view as a large-firm opportunity. The need to increase apparent size, facilities, and scope is not limited to small companies competing for larger opportunities. As a truly global economy emerges, with customers scattered all over the world and companies needing to provide a worldwide interface for customers, the ability of a virtual organization to serve the customer anywhere in the world becomes an important competency in its own right.

Examples of increasing apparent size include:

- AgileWeb, an example of the cooperative efforts of small companies who need, on occasion, to provide a critical mass of capability to secure business.
- Rosenbluth and other travel agencies that have become world-famous through global affiliates that act as a single agency when an overseas client has a problem or needs service.
- Extending the salesforce of an organization by using a representative In some cases the representative actually sells for the

client; in others, the representative qualifies leads and the home company finishes the sale. In both cases, the representative extends the apparent size of the organization. Similarly, newspapers and wire services employ stringers who make it seem that there are reporters in every part of the world, waiting for news to break.

Gaining Access to Markets and Sharing Market or Customer Loyalty

Market access and product loyalty are two very valuable core competencies of an organization. Nevertheless, in a virtual organization relationship, they may be shared.

Examples include but are not limited to:

- The variety of franchise operations and what they really offer to the franchisee. In generic terms, a *franchise* is a formula for doing business on the basis of an established positive set of customer expectations. Consider the hotel franchises offered by Hyatt, Marriot, Holiday Inn, Comfort Inn, and Motel 6. Each of these conjure up a set of different expectations in terms of service, facilities, and price. To join such a virtual organization is to gain access to a set of market expectations that are well defined.
- Another example of shared market access and product loyalty is that of *cobranding*. Ben & Jerry Ice Cream makers sell an ice cream flavor called Heath Bar Crunch, thereby taking advantage of the brand names of both companies. Betty Crocker sells cakes with Reese's Pieces in them.
- Intel successfully made the public aware of its name by having its customers label their computers as having "Intel inside." The idea of the end user being aware of contributing organizations will spread significantly as virtual organizations become more common.
- Sears' products are made by many manufacturers under a single name. Sears' reputation for product quality and service allows many original equipment manufacturers (OEMs) to participate

with it and share Sears' markets. At the same time, every Sears store has a Brand Central department, where shoppers who prefer other brands can find them, even if these companies manufacture the same appliances with the Sears name.

Migrating from Selling Products to Selling Solutions

The sixth reason to use the virtual organization has to do with moving to a clear and unambiguous perception of value as determined by the customer. The same product may have different value to different customers at the same time. As discussed in the next chapter, the value of solutions is contextually dependent on what of significance the customer is able to do or to avoid doing. The main point here is that the virtual organization is an enabling mechanism for the enrichment dimension of agility. Some examples of value-based pricing:

> Universities that provide scholarships for the difference between tuition and what a student's family can afford to pay have long been using a form of value-based pricing. The price of tuition at such a university varies from zero to the quoted tuition.
>
> Lawyers have used a variety of value-based pricing policies in contingency-fee cases.
>
> Real estate transactions, and tips for service, are typically based on some percentage of value provided to the customer.

Virtual organization opportunities provide an occasion for a company to consider moving to value-based pricing. The underlying assumption is that charging a customer a percentage of the value provided is a natural extension of providing customized products and that customers will respond appropriately by attributing greater value to the product. A corollary is also true: A customer who gets little value from a product or service pays correspondingly less for value-based product and services.

The customer does not see a solution, and therefore the value, in all product and service offerings. One needs to get over some minimum threshold of sophistication for the customer to see a product and service as a solution. For example, although it may be difficult to see hoses and valves as solutions, engines containing hoses and valves can be perceived as solutions that have an intrinsic value to the customer. Thus it is sometimes necessary for skill-based product or service suppliers to join in a virtual organization with other skill-based providers under what we call the *general contractor principle.* A general contractor synthesizes the skills of a group of skill-based providers into a solution-based product with known value to the customer.

Examples include:

- Home builders play the role of a general contractor. How much do buyers pay for a house, compared to what they would pay the plumber, the electrician, the carpenter, and others, if they were their own contractors? There is an expectation of buying something with a perceived value and once that happens you're willing to pay a value-based fee for it.
- IBM performed the general contractor role in its initial development of the PC. IBM took a collection of hardware and software components available on a skill-based pricing system and created a PC with considerably higher perceived value on the part of the customer. In fact, the perceived value was so significantly higher than the cost of the components that the PC clone market was launched.
- A Hollywood movie company typically is a virtual company of the general contractor type.
- The health maintenance organization (HMO) concept is sometimes also implemented as a virtual organization of this type.
- The establishment of performance-based compensation for the teaming of one or more organizations set up to achieve a common goal is also a form of this type of virtual organization. Notable examples are sometimes called *outsourcing.* For instance, EDS has entered into a strategic relationship with Bethlehem Steel. The fee to EDS is in part performance-based, for it is computed on the value EDS provides to its virtual organization partner, Bethlehem Steel.

- Ideation is a small California-based firm that specializes in solving difficult but important engineering problems for its clients. It prices its services as a percentage of the value it provides to its customers. Ideation works in tandem with the customer to develop solution options and to share the risk. The relationship Ideation has with its customers is a virtual relationship of type six.

THE VIRTUAL WEB CONCEPT

The success of the virtual organization model is tied to the ability of "real" companies to form virtual organizations rapidly to meet an emerging time-based opportunity. The ability to work intensively with other organizations and to be able to trust them from the start of a project is enhanced by prequalification agreements based on company attributes and contractual commitments. Prequalification is a static means of meeting an agile competitor's needs, however. It would be far more advantageous to also have a dynamic basis of prior agreement on the ways in which companies are prepared to interact with one another.

The concept of partnering in a virtual organization is relatively new. It must accommodate the likelihood that a company will be a member of several virtual organizations at the same time and will have a broad range of current and future partners. The intensity of opportunity and the depth of potential cooperation and collaboration in a virtual organization suggest the possibility of a more dynamic means of facilitating virtual organization formation than prequalification agreements, and these are called *organizational webs*.

The web is an open-ended collection of prequalified partners that agree to form a pool of potential members of virtual organizations. One can imagine organizing a large number of supplier companies into a resource pool from which to draw the number of companies, and the kinds of companies, that would be required to provide comprehensive customer services in any industry and that would compete directly with the largest single companies in that industry. U.K. Chemicals, described in Chapter 4, is a small-scale instance of that very strategy. For each customer, a unique combination of companies is pulled into a virtual relationship because of the distinctive requirements of that customer.

The Japanese *Keiretsu* are webs with a fixed membership. As we envision them, however, webs have an open-ended membership, with companies joining and leaving opportunistically. Webs can be informal, with little or no structure; or they can be formal, with significant structure. The key to their successful utilization is the ability to form a virtual organization quickly to meet specific market opportunities.

The North American Advertising Agency Network is a 63-year-old web, of a sort. Its members share methodologies as well as core competencies, but the web is narrowly focused and has a fixed membership of prequalified agencies. The web has a minimal infrastructure. It was designed to be a flat network of peer organizations with floating leadership and is administered by a two-person office that uses members to accomplish common-interest tasks as they arise. The value of the web lies in the ability of members to form opportunistic alliances to compete for contracts no one of them could win on its own.

A more aggressive web would have a floating rather than a fixed membership, with its members extending across industry sectors to expand the customer opportunities its members could create or respond to. However it is organized, an effective web must have a way of identifying the evolving core competencies of its members as well as of its changing membership. It must have a means of projecting the changing "grand competencies" that the web as a whole can support by synthesizing them out of the smaller-scale, more limited competencies of its members. Multiple vertical integration patterns can also be configured out of the competency pool of the web.

The way a web identifies and qualifies opportunities for a virtual organization instance is also critical to its success. Webs may use central or distributed marketing capabilities, but when a market opportunity is identified, the mechanism for choosing partners must be clearly established. Similarly, whether the web benefits financially or otherwise from the virtual organization activity it generates, how liability issues are handled, and other, similar matters must all be addressed.

With the web, there is a unique opportunity to establish model relationship methodologies to be used as virtual organization opportunities arise. As we gain experience with webs and virtual organizations, the need for such models will decrease. However, currently a web or other mechanism will have an important role to play in facilitating some significant portion of virtual organizations.

Finally, the role of the giant corporation in the agile competitive world has been questioned. This is indeed an important point in the light of the trend for large corporations to be broken into smaller collections of corporations, each of which is responsible for meeting goals and objectives set by the parent organization. In a very real sense, the parent organization or large corporation is a web of organizations. In fact IBM, AT&T, and other large corporations report that they have been using the virtual organization concept internally as well as externally. If we think of a web as a group of prequalified organizations with a shared organizational culture and one or more opportunity areas of excellence, then perhaps we have defined the distinctive role of large corporations in the future, namely, as webs.

Regardless of the amount of structure used in creating a web, the key goal of a web is to permit a virtual organization to be formed very quickly. The web is designed to be a virtual organization—enabling mechanism.

AgileWeb

AgileWeb is a network of small businesses in northeastern Pennsylvania that have agreed to prequalify each other so that they can combine their collective core competencies to serve clients whose needs exceed the capabilities of any one of them. AgileWeb was formed with federal funding assistance by the Lehigh Valley office of the state-supported Ben Franklin Partnership, an economic development program that acts as AgileWeb's facilitator. The companies involved view their principal strategic benefit to be new business opportunities.

It was a revelation to AgileWeb's members when they realized that pooling competencies was not the same as pooling product offerings. That is, the individual members had thought that they were gaining access to additional markets for which they would continue to quote prices as they had in the past. It was an important insight to recognize that the web was more powerful as a whole than its member companies were. In particular, it was a revelation that web clients might get core competencies from more than one source while no one web member made any whole subcomponent. (Web materials developed to help web members understand the evolving concepts are shown in Table 6.1.)

Although AgileWeb has decided to market competencies to its customers, it is still learning how to do business this way. It is easy to suggest that organizations pool their competencies, but at this time there is no standard lexicon for expressing what those competencies are. AgileWeb has decided to work with its customers to determine a set

---

TABLE 6.1

AWeb Offers
Unique single access to a broad-based array of companies, competencies, and resources capable of optimizing and producing electrical and mechanical components and systems.

Features of Web Relationship With Customers
1. Web *teams* with its customers
   - No finger pointing
   - Customer appears and acts as if it has enhanced internal resources
2. Web takes minimal to full responsibility for product/service optimization/engineering and production.
   - Web acts as a partner and assumes manufacturing management function if desired.
   - Web emphasizes entire system versus a collection of components, thereby providing minimal systems costs and increased reliability of product/service system to the customer's customer.
3. A web team is a subset of the web membership who have both the interest and the capabilities/competencies necessary to fulfill a web opportunity. Teams include only competencies/resources that enrich the customer.
   - Offers competencies not normally for sale.
   - Provides both needed competencies and protective capacity in depth and breadth should need arise.
   - Other members of the web provide additional backup support.

BOX 6.1
WEB RULES FOR SHARING PROFITS

- All virtual organization members benefit when any member does a better job.

- All web members who contribute to a job (even backup services) are on the team and share in the profits.

- Share of income to each member is determined by the base cost (to provider with out indirect charges) plus share of split web profit.

- Profit to be split on the basis of the number of chits held by each team member. Chit distribution to team members is worked out on the basis of equalizing value of contributions.

- A standard internal working agreement with details of proportions and roles is filled in for each web virtual organization team formed.

---

of competencies that the web might offer collectively. AgileWeb has set up guidelines for forming a virtual organization in response to a web opportunity.

Benefits to Customers

- Access to skills and experience of many different manufacturing approaches (initially and over time)

- Focus on the system versus components
  Higher reliability
  Better quality and consistency
  Lower cost for given functionality
  Lower internal development costs

- Flexible access to resources
  Variable production quantities
  Pay only for services needed, with backup access as needed
  More robust partnering

AgileWeb has identified a 14-step model for developing and qualifying virtual organization opportunities for the web to pursue. Table 6.2 is the first iteration of an evolving situation. The major elements of the 14-step procedure are the identification of a prospect and the selection of a neutral qualification and marketing team whose members check the customer's needs, match web competency capabilities, and qualify the opportunity for success against the web members' objectives for return on effort.

Each step in the procedure is accompanied by details describing what must be considered and done. For example, the qualification described in step 2 consists of three parts. First, the web team qualifies the web itself to determine whether it has the required competencies to meet

TABLE 6.2   MODEL FOR EVALUATING OPPORTUNITIES

1. Customer opportunity is identified and initially screened.
2. Neutral web client qualification team is formed.
3. Meet with customers to explain the web.
4. Work to qualify the customer for the web.
5. Web qualification team makes go or no-go recommendation.
6. Recommendation and details of process made electronically available to entire web membership.
7. In the case of a no-go recommendation, any member may still decide to organize a web response.
8. In the case of a go, an organizer for a web response is appointed.
9. Any interested web members are invited to meet and form the web response team. This team then takes the steps necessary to create a web proposal for the customer.
10. A set of memos of understanding among the web team members is filled in based on a generic model. Similarly, a generic customer memorandum of understanding (MOU) is filled in.
11. Response team meets with customer to explain proposal and MOU.
12. Customer responds to proposal and steps 11 & 12 repeat until either agreement is reached, or the response team decides to abandon the opportunity.
13. Customer signs the agreement.
14. Customer and Web member joint team begin working on the project in a virtual organization.

the customer's needs. The web may solicit participation by organizations in the web's outer core, that is, companies whose core competencies are occasionally needed to complete the web's ability to deliver world-class core competencies in all aspects of an opportunity.

The second part is qualification of the customer. This step includes determinations as to the customer's ability to partner with the web. Is the customer culturally and organizationally ready? Of note here is the web's preference for medium- rather than large-size partners, reflecting the assumption that medium-size organizations are more likely to be able to deal with the web team as a partnership and not as an arms-length set of independent suppliers.

The third piece of the qualification procedure deals with the opportunity itself. Once the web believes that it is qualified and has qualified the customer, it must determine whether the resultant opportunity will yield enough profit for the virtual organization to satisfy the web's expectations. Is the opportunity robust enough to justify working through the web, as opposed to doing business as usual? How probable and likely are the projections of success, and what can web members on the team expect in both the short and the long term in the event of a success?

A particularly interesting step is number 9. It is broken into two parts. The first deals with the development of a proposal to meet the customer opportunity or needs. In effect, the second part of step 9 is worded: "and then a miracle happens and we know who will participate, who will lead the web team and how profits will be distributed." It is noteworthy that the web members are aware that these issues will be difficult to resolve in the first few instances, but that models to use as reference are available and that the effort to find a way to succeed is worth it because of the potential benefit from operating in a virtual organization mode.

Finally, it is worth noting the web members' faith in the development of a generic agreement that can be used over and over again by just changing some of the details for each virtual organization opportunity they encounter. Before returning to the strategic advantages of using virtual organizations, we point out to the reader that a history of the AgileWeb is being generated as it progresses. Future editions of this book will document progress as it is made.

EXPERIENCE WITH VIRTUAL ORGANIZATIONS

Through seminars and workshops on the strategic use of the virtual organization concept, we have collected valuable data for those who might want to form a virtual organization. In what follows, we have integrated the answers of more than 200 executives to the following questions. Readers may wish first to determine which questions are relevant to their own circumstances and then answer those questions *before* reading the answers generated by other executives.

Questions

1. What are the essential characteristics of a virtual organization?
2. What are the significance and major benefits of the virtual organization to business, especially to medium and small business?
3. What are the business trends that have given rise to the virtual organization?
4. What would you do to make sure that you were gaining strategic advantage from participation in a virtual organization?
5. What is the most important reason for your organization to consider the virtual organization relationship?
6. What should you or your organization do in order to be selected to participate in a virtual company by others?
7. Under what conditions would you not want to use the virtual company? Why?
8. What is the relationship between the virtual company organizational model and reducing the concept to cash time?

Answers

1. What are the essential characteristics of a virtual organization?
   - The virtual organization must be customer-focused and opportunity-based, and it must have a clear and agreed-upon set of

objectives. Through the combination of the core competencies of all its members, it must establish a set of world-class core competencies to meet each opportunity.

- The relationships among the partners in a virtual organization must include trust, open and honest communication, and compatible management styles. The organization must be able to make decisions quickly and to disband relatively painlessly when the opportunity that occasioned its creation has passed. It must have been organized because no one member could have met the opportunity alone. It may be designed to be joined very easily, to operate in distributed mode, to exploit concurrency, or to include competitors.

2. What are the significance and major benefits of the virtual organization to business, especially to medium and small business?

- A small business can appear to customers as if it were, and it can act like, a big business because of the access to complementary competencies that it has in a virtual organization. A small organization can look big while retaining the entrepreneurial nature of being small, thereby enjoying the best of both worlds.

- Regardless of size, the virtual organization offers to its members access to expanded markets, the ability to combine resources for new markets, and the ability to cut the concept to cash time through concurrency.

- The virtual organization has the ability to combine a disparate set of core competencies and offer advantages to customers in terms of systems reliability and capability. For example, the combined set of core competencies can exceed the capabilities of the member organizations acting either alone or in a nonintegrated network. A virtual organization of small companies can collectively take on systemic tasks and be responsible for the manufacturing function of a customer firm, as is done by AgileWeb.

3. What are the business trends that have given rise to the virtual organization?

- The development of a worldwide communication and transportation system enabling worldwide sourcing and selling. This, in turn, has created increased global competition, borderless economies, a need for worldwide operations in businesses such as airlines and telecommunications.
- The development of sophisticated production and service capabilities that can create products and services in arbitrary lot sizes. This, in turn, has fostered a demand for a shorter life cycle and a faster time to market, and has made it possible to deal with shorter finite windows of market opportunity and distributed niche markets.
- The development of the information-handling capacity to treat customers as individuals instead of as statistical averages. This, in turn, has made possible a change to increased product customization. Increased customization requires an increase in the complexity of process technology and material logistics, as well as a convergence of technologies in products. Increased customization also requires extended core competencies—the acquisition of skills inside or outside the organization.
- An increased information-handling capability puts information technology in the role of a key enabler of enhanced communications. Intellectual capital in the organization also gains in value. These assets can assist in coping with the decreasing resources, company downsizing, and the high pressure to reduce cost, improve quality, and deliver quickly for reduced-life-cycle products.
- More sophisticated stakeholders, customers, stockholders, and others demanding all these capabilities and complexities in rapidly shrinking windows of opportunity foster the development and use of the virtual organization to share the risk and rewards in development efforts and to provide the ability to deliver on stakeholder expectations to be an agile competitor.

4. What would you do to make sure that you were gaining strategic advantage from participation in a virtual organization?

- Pick opportunities and partners wisely—make sure that they make sense. Examine the quality of commitment and the synergy between potential partners, competencies, and resources. Carefully determine the customer needs that define the opportunity. Define a clear set of objectives and stay focused on them. Keep sight of any downside risks and make them explicit.
- Negotiate at the highest level. Keep the agreement simple and make sure that it's clear who owns what and what is to be shared with respect to customers and technology. Share risks, rewards, and benefits. Ensure that individual organizations understand and focus on their value to the virtual organization and on satisfying the customer. Partner with the customer and place significant weight on the customer's feedback.
- Develop performance standards measures and metrics for internal and external milestones. Metrics must apply to both ongoing and final results. Benchmark the competition to maintain an understanding of your strategic advantage.

5. What is the most important reason for your organization to consider the virtual organization relationship?
    - Because of the fit with our organizational strategy, business plan, and culture.
    - Because it would provide increased customer loyalty, market share, sales volume, margin, profit, and/or value to the customer.
    - Because of the adverse consequences of not entering the relationship.
    - Because companies can no longer afford to do everything by themselves, by combining core competencies and market knowledge, they can reduce capital requirements and achieve a variety of benefits such as cost savings, shared resources, increased speed, combined skills, and increased pace of growth. They can also enhance competitiveness and increase profits by increasing customer satisfaction without adding cost to their infrastructure.

- To leverage core competencies and create better solutions for customers by the efficient use of complementary partner skills to deliver a more comprehensive solution focused on a well-defined customer opportunity, for example, to enable our customers to better meet the needs of their customers.
- To presell our basic core competencies to other companies.
- Because of the need to be perceived as world-class or as best in class in all aspects of the business, organizations are willing to trade equity for world-class competencies and innovation in a virtual organization, for example, to pursue a market opportunity you cannot otherwise realize, to allow movement into new markets, and to provide integrated value-based solutions to your customers—in short, to be proactive in the marketplace.

6. What should you or your organization do in order to be selected to participate in a virtual company by others?
   - Demonstrate core competency and have a unique skill or knowledge. Make that uniqueness known to your industry and to complementary industries. Be committed and up-front. Be selective in your partners.
   - Create a vision of what you can add. Show how your contribution adds to the overall value offering. Actively market your assets to web members or partners.
   - Be willing to share risks equal to the economic benefits you seek.
   - Conduct your regular business dealings in a trusting, trustworthy, and reliable way. Keep your promises, follow through on your commitments, and show that you are willing to share. Be known for total quality management (TQM) and as a world-class performer.
   - Hire the best people you can. Understand your core competencies and values. Identify and market your core competencies.
   - Identify potential partners and prequalify them. Make sure that potential partners are aware of all the skills you can contribute. Develop or participate in an organizational structure for partnering or a web. Solve legal problems ahead of time.

- Network with others in person and electronically. Be capable of and effective at being electronically linked to customers, suppliers, or partners.
- Publicly announce that you have adapted the virtual organization as a corporate strategy. Advertise your success rate in meeting customer needs and your knowledge of how to be a good partner, team member, and so on.
- Take on projects independently and seek other partners. Make it happen and actively organize, and participate in the organization of, virtual organizations. Be proactive; don't just wait to be selected.

7. Under what conditions would you not want to use the virtual company? Why?
   - When it diverts your attention from your company's strategic growth path.
   - When you have the competencies or skills required to satisfy a market need on your own.
   - When the risk-to-benefit ratio is poor, or when there is no clear benefit or advantage, or when there are no well-defined objectives.
   - When there are incompatible management styles and philosophies. When adequate levels of trust and openness cannot be achieved. When your intellectual property would be at risk or lost.
   - When the ability of the virtual organization to produce a quality product or service would be in question. If the core competencies don't match well, if your potential partner can't meet volume or schedule requirements, or if the logistics are not right.
   - When the opportunity has not been qualified. When incomplete specifications or requirements prevent a proper evaluation of the opportunity. When success will not provide appropriate benefits.
   - When there is an inadequate legal framework, or when something about the arrangement is illegal.

8. What is the relationship between the virtual company organizational model and reducing the concept to cash time?

- The virtual organization can eliminate steps, can reduce the need for temporary hiring and training, and can provide for coordination, flexibility, and increased speed in reducing the concept to cash time.
- It can facilitate concurrent development and therefore can achieve quick access to markets and resources. It provides for infrastructure needs and capabilities to be shared, thus avoiding costly delays and shrinking development time.
- It forces a company to identify its own core competencies and to see the efficiency that comes from being focused. It reduces some capital requirements and the need for other resources to meet customer opportunities effectively. It helps remove internal company organizational walls and helps focus on shrinking the concept to cash time while increasing customer satisfaction.

HIGHLIGHTS OF CHAPTER 6

The existence of a global market, with increasing demands for customized products, is forcing the development of the virtual organization as a dynamic mechanism to focus on time-based customer opportunities.

The virtual organization is based on the fact that cooperation enhances competitive capabilities. Even competitors can cooperate and still compete.

It is necessary both to protect and to share intellectual property. Good legal models for this are still under development and only beginning to emerge.

The virtual organization is an opportunity-based dynamic organizational structure. It can and should be used to bring pieces of a variety of organizations together to meet a worthwhile opportunity.

When the opportunity is over, the virtual organization should be disbanded and celebrated. The virtual organization can exist for a period of months or for many decades.

A web is a form of virtual organization used to incubate or otherwise facilitate the development of other virtual organizations. At a minimum, the web is a set of prequalified partners; or it may be a very formal organization that facilitates cooperation and the formation of virtual organizations. One can easily draw an analogy between a web and a Japanese *Keiretsu,* though there are important differences between them.

There are six strategic reasons to form a virtual organization. They are overlapping, but each has a primary focus of benefit to the bottom line.

Organizations that form virtual companies must be able to identify the primary strategic purpose in doing so in order to ensure bottom-line impact. The six strategic reasons are:

1. Sharing infrastructure and risk.
2. Linking complementary core competencies.
3. Reducing concept to cash time through sharing.
4. Increasing facilities and apparent size.
5. Gaining access to markets and sharing market or customer loyalty.
6. Migrating from selling products to selling solutions.

The use and role of virtual organizations are subtle and evolving. Although some firms may intuitively happen upon the virtual organization concept, true strategic benefits will accrue most easily to those who link their virtual organization efforts directly to measurable bottom-line impacts.

Pick opportunities and partners wisely—make sure that they make sense. Examine the quality of commitment and the synergy between potential partners, competencies, and resources. Carefully determine the customer needs that define the opportunity. Define a clear set of objectives and stay focused on them. Keep sight of any downside risks and make them explicit.

Develop performance standards, measures, and metrics for internal and external milestones. Metrics must apply to both ongoing and final results. Benchmark the competition to maintain an understanding of your strategic advantage.

7

Enriching the Customer

The accepted philosophy in mass production was, "If we can make it, they will buy it." Organizations were limited in the amount of profit they could make only by the market and the capacity of their production facilities. Agile competitors are limited by the speed with which they can determine customer needs or opportunities and convert them into product-service combinations. Thus the marketing function must be reinvented. It moves from being the third or fourth most important company activity to the first. Whereas in the past a company might first develop a product concept, make a prototype, and then market the prototype or a production model, now the comprehensive production process begins with the marketing function. As with other mass-production concepts, the name remains the same but the function must be reinvented: it changes fundamentally, not just superficially.

The marketing challenge switches from convincing customers that they need a preconceived product or service to determining how to provide product-service combinations to customers that uniquely meet their needs or allow them to pursue new opportunities. We call this reinvented form of marketing *solution-based marketing.* The key to success rests with determining how to create customer-valued solutions.

PRODUCTS VERSUS SOLUTIONS

From the perspective of commercial customers, a *product* (in the traditional sense of the term) is a purchase whose impact on their bottom line is indirect. Before it can have any impact, it must first be integrated into a customer's operations, and that, as a rule, is done at the customer's expense. A solution, by contrast, has a direct, and therefore easily evaluated, impact on the bottom line. Whereas for products a customer will pay a fee based on materials, labor, cost of production, and a market-based profit, for solutions the fee can be a function of the value that the vendor and customer agree can be attributed to the solution. The customer enrichment dimension of agile competition thus suggests that if a company knows its customers well enough to provide them with solution products, it also knows the enrichment value of those products to the customer. In such a context, it makes good marketing sense to charge the customer some fraction of that enrichment value.

Solutions, then, are product-information-service combinations that have a known bottom-line enrichment value to the customer. This enrichment value need not be known exactly. As Robert Kaplan of Harvard put it in another context, knowing the first digit and the number of zeros is close enough.

This chapter explores the concept of providing enrichment value to the customer in greater detail than Chapter 3 did. It suggests a variety of strategies by which vendors can migrate from selling either products or services to selling customer value-based solutions.

Solutions Have Contextual, Not Absolute, Value

It is customary to think that the same product or service should have one price for everyone, that it is "not fair" to sell it at different prices.

This idea may have been valid for products, but it is not valid for solutions. The value of a solution is contextual even to the same customer, and will vary according to the varying circumstances of their purchases. It is very likely that the same solution has different enrichment values for different customers under the same circumstances.

Consider, for example, the value of an airplane seat. Airlines have taken advantage of the contextual value of airplane seats for years. They charge businesspeople who want to decide at the last minute when and where to fly more than they do vacationers, senior citizens, and others. A family that is planning pleasure travel can choose flights with cheap seats available. Traveling to meet a client to close a multimillion dollar deal, however, makes the price of the airplane ticket a negligible consideration: you need to get there fast, and any price may be worth it.

In setting fare prices, airlines do not treat passengers as individuals; instead, they treat them statistically. In some abstract way they assume that the class of business travelers is homogeneous and that all business travelers will pay almost arbitrarily high fares. This is not agile value-based pricing.

Businesspeople are the best customers airlines have with respect to repeat business or frequent flying, but they receive the worst deals in terms of value. This makes sense only if all businesspeople always consider airfare to be incidental compared to the value of the business deals that flying generates. This is clearly not the case, as is demonstrated, for example, by the contract the General Services Administration (GSA) has with airlines on behalf of the federal government and its traveling employees.

Although at one extreme airlines charge most businesspeople the highest prices, the airlines do negotiate with the government and some corporations for what appear to be commodity-based prices. Airlines are suppliers to businesses, in the same way that producers of raw materials and components are suppliers to manufacturers. Therefore, airlines should negotiate value-based deals with customers, on an individual company basis, that fit the context of that particular customer organization in a relationship over time.

Other examples of the contextual value of solutions can be found in the cost of restaurant meals, the price of automobiles, and the charge for hotel rooms. If one is eating to survive, buying a car for basic transportation, or staying in a hotel room for shelter, then one chooses very different ways of satisfying one's needs than would someone who was eating to celebrate a business success, buying a car to impress clients or friends, or renting a hotel room for a luxurious vacation. The value of a product or service has always been contextual for the buyer. During the mass-production era, companies targeted a pool of stereotyped customers—business class, coach—and charged them all one price regardless of the individual circumstances of their purchases. In an agile world, companies deal with customers as individuals, and pricing reflects the variation of contextual value experienced by those individuals as customers.

Such value-based pricing schemes are familiar, for example, in percentage-based fees. Why does the waiter who served a family an inexpensive meal get a smaller tip than the waiter who served the couple at the next table a gourmet meal? Because service by waiters is contextually valued by the price of the food ordered. The real estate agent who sells a family a $300,000 house gets a larger commission than one who sells a $200,000 house. Did the first real estate agent work harder to sell the more expensive house? Did this agent provide more service to the customer than the other agent did? Was the cost for the agent of selling the house higher or lower? These questions are routinely considered irrelevant with respect to the fee, for the fee is contextually set by the value of the transaction.

Banks charge customers a variable fee based on the amount of money a customer needs to borrow. In fact, the exact percentage is in some sense inversely proportional to the need of the customer to borrow it. Healthy business customers who have positive balance sheets and whose businesses are in sound financial condition pay less than those at the other end of the spectrum. Those who most need the money and who might have the fewest choices of banker or banking relationship pay the highest fees! In addition, although banks typically charge fees based solely on the amount of money borrowed and in various accounts, they pride themselves on the spectrum of business services and advice they provide to their customers.

Most large commercial banks have staffs of specialists with expertise in a variety of industries, markets, pension plans, and a broad-based spectrum of areas in which they offer services in the form of investment advice, guidance, and reviews. Although many banks began hiring people with such expertise in order to evaluate the risk of doing business with various clients, it is clear in today's banking relationships that banks are selected in part for the nonfinancial services they provide as well as for the financial terms and conditions attached to their client relationships. In this environment, banks are giving away skills, knowledge, and expertise in a relationship over time. They are paid a potentially value-based fee for these services as well as for their money-lending and money-handling services by fees set on the basis of the amounts of money in play. As banking services increase and real partnerships between banks and their clients grow deeper in agile relationships, banks will begin changing to value-based fee structures. These will more accurately reflect overall value to the client in place of charging fees based solely on the amount of money in play.

Value-based pricing is hardly a new concept. In most value-based exchanges, however, a fixed percentage is established for a defined level of transaction. The idea that the contextual value may vary substantially with individuals and not be statistically fixed is far less common. Restaurant tips to waiters, for example, are usually stated as a range of percentages, say, 15 to 20 percent of the bill. But unless there are extreme circumstances, most people want to leave the "normal" percentage. Barbers commonly receive average tips for routine service. But if they stay open late for a customer, fit in a customer when the schedule is full, or otherwise obviously go out of their way to meet the needs of a customer, tips may go up by as much as five times the normal amount.

As a graduate student in an economics class, the founder of Federal Express wrote a paper about the value to business clients of one-day delivery of packages anywhere in the country. The professor gave him a D for such a foolish idea. No sane businessperson would pay $14 to send a package that the U.S. Postal Service would carry for a few cents, said the professor. The professor did not understand value-based pricing as well as his student did, and we all know the rest of the story. The message here is that, under special circumstances, a service with a known value can be worth an order of magnitude more than the usual amount. It all depends on the context of the customer's circumstances. This is as true at the personal level as it is for selling to businesses.

Many U.S. universities charge value-based fees, but in a strange and ineffective way. They set a maximum tuition, and then say, "We will not turn any student away for a lack of ability to pay." A third party statistically evaluates student family finances to determine what they can afford to pay. This amount becomes the price unless it exceeds the stated tuition ceiling. Thus, with the exception of students who pay full tuition, the fee is assumed to be "individually value-based," indexed to a statistical formula designed to set a level of sacrifice equal to the value of private college education for the student's family.

Once individual financial statements and applications have been evaluated by individuals in the finance office, it seems silly to use statistical evaluations by a third party to determine the tuition. In practice, most middle-income families do not estimate value in the same way that statisticians do. As a result, private universities are beginning to see two populations of students, the poor and the rich. The middle class has been eliminated by a model of the value of a private university education to middle-class families developed by statisticians. The lesson here is that, if you want to charge value-based prices, know or ask your customers the value they perceive your product to have for them; don't use a statistical pool to determine value.

Unisys is now seeking ways to help its customers with *their* customers. Unisys perceives this as a way to provide value to their customers by increasing existing markets and opening new markets for their customers.

AT&T routinely advertises in newspapers (similar to Figure 7.1) that treating customers as individuals can increase revenues by 15 percent. AT&T has the right idea, but the percentage increase may be even higher.

The upshot of these observations is that a fair price for solutions in the agile world will be contextually based as a function of what the solution is worth to individual customers under the circumstances in which they make their purchases.

FIGURE 7.1 Treating Customers as Individuals Increases Profit.

Enriching and Pleasing Customers

The definitions of many commonly used terms will need to be changed from their mass-production usage to be applicable to agile competition. One of the most difficult terms to redefine is *added value*. In mass production, added value meant "increased cost." The use of an expensive resource or specialized machinery or a highly skilled individual in producing a product was considered to be a high-value-adding activity, because it increased the cost of production.

In the agile competitive world, value is added by increasing the bottom-line enrichment to the customer. It doesn't matter whether the greater enrichment solution has a higher cost basis. The customer sees value in terms of the solution's bottom-line impact, not by calculating the cost of the supplier's operations. Companies can enrich their customers in two fundamental ways: They can lower the customer's cost of operations, inventory, or other infrastructure items; or they can enhance the customer's market penetration, market share, or ability to open up new markets. Clearly, enriching the customer suggests a closer coupling of supplier and customer than the arm's-length transactions we sought in mass-production.

Beyond the simple form of enrichment defined above, is the indirect enrichment that comes from facilitating an event that will enrich the customer. Thus airplane seats needed to close a multimillion dollar deal are worth more in the context of getting to the place where you can close the deal. The airplane seat does not provide the value directly; it facilitates getting the deal which has the enrichment value. Similarly, the Federal Express concept of charging $14 to deliver a package in one day does not have intrinsic value or directly enrich the customer. However, there are lots of circumstances in business when the reliability and speed of Federal Express facilitate valuable returns to businesses that make the difference between $14 and a few cents for postage stamps trivial.

Mass-production thinking suggests that products and services have their own intrinsic value independent of the customer and the use of a product or service. In an agile world, with mass individualization–based products and services, understanding the context of a customer's purchase, and the variable value of your products and services to that customer, will be a marketing imperative.

VALUE AS CONSTRAINT AVOIDANCE

From the business point of view, there are always constraints on the amount of profit a business can earn: number of contracts, clients, stores, factories, engineers, capital equipment. Or we might consider market share, product lines, and value of the company's stock in financial markets. There are, of course, an unlimited number of possible constraints. The point is that, if a business has an opportunity to alleviate a serious constraint, one that will measurably affect achieving a significant strategic goal, then any activity that ensures the opportunity's probability of occurrence is contextually increased in value. Consider, for example, the value to a customer of *not* bouncing a check. A business operating in survival mode must work closely with its bank. Not covering an overdraft of $1100 drove one firm with more than a $1 million line of credit out of business, because the bank decided to bounce small overdrawn payroll checks throughout their operation. The lack of $1100 of credit began a chain of events that caused the operation to close down.

The use of a fax machine has become so important a part of doing business that, for a fee, hotels now offer rooms equipped with fax machines to businesspeople. The fee is value-based, not on the cost of amortizing a fax machine but on the value to a busy executive of having a fax.

Activities undertaken to change a constraint are a function of the value of either avoiding or achieving the constraint, depending on which outcome is the desired one. It is worth spending $50,000 to prepare a $1 million proposal; it is worth chartering a plane to avoid missing an opportunity in which the cost of the charter is small. Organizations will spend significant amounts of money to avoid adverse publicity, lawsuits, or embarrassing important clients because of the still greater losses that the occurrence of these events could cause.

On a personal level, activities that constrain us or take on significant value in our lives cause us to be willing to pay contextually more to achieve or to avoid such an opportunity. Consider the ransom price for retrieving a kidnapped child or relative, or consider the fees we are willing to pay for a doctor, lawyer, or dentist when we are seriously ill, under arrest, or have a toothache. On a personal level, the value of professional services is frequently constraint-alleviating and contextually value-priced. More pleasantly, the amount of money people are willing to spend to celebrate weddings, special anniversaries, and other once-in-a-lifetime occasions reflects contextual valuation.

People have always understood contextual pricing abstractly, but before agile global competition, they were not able to put it to work routinely in business. Today, people have to understand the contextual value of having or not having various products and services, in order to deal with customers as individuals, in order to price solutions appropriately, and because all businesses are also customers for context-sensitive products and services. Naive customers and suppliers alike will miss opportunities by ignoring this important aspect of the changing nature of competition, pricing, and relationships.

The Agility Forum's Supplier Support Focus Group developed a graphic means of displaying the degree of interaction between customer and supplier. The horizontal axis of Figure 7.2 expresses the degree of cooperation between supplier and customer on product definition. The zero point represents a catalog of products offered by the supplier to the customer and thus no interaction at all. The far right of the axis represents shared development with the customer of products designed to enrich the customer's customer. Points along the way represent varying degrees of collaboration and interaction in defining product and service concepts that suppliers will provide to their customers.

The horizontal axis can thus be called the customer-*enrichment axis,* but it deals only with creating value-based solutions for customers. The vertical axis expresses the financial arrangements between supplier and customer. The zero point of the axis corresponds to fixed-price products or services, and thus intersects the zero point of a catalog relationship on the enrichment axis. As suppliers work more closely with customers to provide greater value, moving up the vertical axis represents a greater risk for the supplier, and this is reflected in revenue-sharing arrangements. Intermediate points along this axis express cost recovery and minimal profit sharing, royalties, licenses, usage fees, and so on. The vertical axis is called the risk and *reward axis,* and it represents financial arrangements ranging from zero risk, low reward, fixed-price product relationships to high-risk and high-reward sharing relationships.

The third axis expresses the degree of business process linkage between supplier and customer. On this axis, zero indicates interaction via phone, mail, fax, and purchase order. It corresponds to catalog sales at fixed prices on the horizontal and vertical axes, respectively. The far end

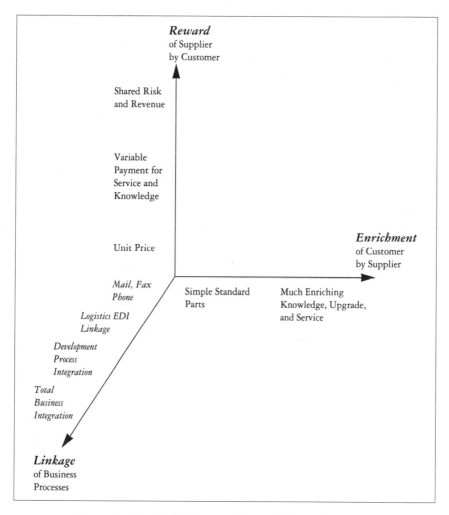

FIGURE 7.2 The Enrichment-Reward Linkage Diagram

of this axis includes linked networks of workstations, shared databases, tools, and facilities. Intermediate points reflect the use of EDI (Electronic Data Interchange), E-mail, wide-area networks, and so on. For obvious reasons, this axis is called the business process *linkage axis.*

This graphic is useful for envisioning the "space" of interrelationships between customers and suppliers. It is discussed more fully in Chapter 8 in the context of supplier-customer relationship strategies. High values on the enrichment axis cannot be achieved without movement along the business process linkage axis. In a similar fashion, having moved along both of these axes, one can expect corresponding movement on the risk and reward axis.

The rest of this chapter focuses on the enrichment axis and on continuing to understand the process of creating customer-valued solutions. The enrichment concept applies to the end user or consumer as well as to the customer. Consider the purchase of a house from a general contractor. Houses whose construction has been finished by a general contractor have a value significantly higher than what we expect we would have to pay the collection of skill-based service providers such as carpenters, masons, and electricians who would build the house if we acted as our own contractor. The general contractor provides the customer with a solution that has a significant apparent value. IBM acted like a general contractor when it developed and introduced the original PC, as did Polaroid for all of its instant cameras prior to the SX-70 model. These companies created products that had significantly higher perceived value than did the sum of their hardware and software component costs.

For the consumer, value-based solutions relate to perceived enrichment of life style rather than the bottom line, but this perception, too, is context-based and highly variable from consumer to consumer. The perceived enrichment offered by owning a fancy sports car, a sailboat, artwork, or good seats to the Super Bowl suggests that knowing one's individual customers is central to providing them with value-based solutions.

American Express offers a platinum credit card to selected customers for a fee of $300 a year. No credit card, regardless of the color, could be worth that much to everyone. American Express packages a high level of services with this card. In effect, the card provides a 24-hour worldwide "virtual" concierge service. In addition, card members get one free first-class or business-class ticket for overseas travel on a variety of airlines when they buy a seat of similar value. A very valuable benefit, for some. American Express has learned the value of customized service, and it uses computer databases to arm its virtual concierges with personal profiles and a history of the services requested by and provided to individual card members in real time, as they deal with their latest requests.

WHAT BRINGS CUSTOMERS TO YOUR BUSINESS?

The core competencies of your organization are in fact what you sell to your customers. The skills, knowledge, and experience of your employees, and those of your partners and suppliers, allow you to create the goods and services you provide to your customers. This was true in the mass-production world as well, but it was harder for customers to know this as explicitly as they will in agile competition. Customers' perceptions of the value of these core competencies cannot be assumed to be the same as the companies' own assessment of their value. It is therefore imperative to know the customers' perception of the value they are being provided.

Obvious as it may sound, it is important for companies to know the business they are in and how and why their customers value their capabilities. Navistar personnel thought that their company sold trucks, but they discovered that they were providing a means of moving heavy loads from one location to another; the trucks were only a means. Unisys, IBM, and Hewlett-Packard are reorganizing to emphasize selling customers information-integration solutions for which hardware is a means. EDS provides Bethlehem Steel and many other client firms with strategic information on which they base critical business decisions. EDS is not in the business of selling networks but, rather, information utilization solutions. Andersen Consulting, Deloitte and Touche, Peat Marwick, CSC, and other systems integrators have all realized the value to be derived from understanding their customers' needs. They are now organized to sell solutions whose value lies in the strategic benefits they yield.

Knowing what your customers value in your core competencies is a valuable insight and cannot be limited to the senior executive and marketing departments alone. People throughout the organization, at all levels, need to understand who your customers are and how you enrich them.

The following questions are designed to help stimulate the development of action plans with respect to how your core competencies enrich your customers.

- What core competencies bring our customers to us?
- What customer problems, needs, or opportunities are affected positively by doing business with us? That is, what do we really do for our customers?
- What do our products or services do to enrich our customers' bottom lines?
- Is the customer aware of and measuring these enrichment benefits?
- What areas would our customers say we most need to improve in order to be world class? Why?
- Do all the people in our organization who need to know the answers to the above questions know them?

CAUSING CUSTOMERS TO SEE INCREASED VALUE IN PRODUCT AND SERVICE RELATIONSHIPS

When competition is based on what solutions do for the customer, it becomes important to consider all aspects of the relationship between customer and supplier.

Pay-on-Use Sales

Hammer and Champy (1993) reported on a company that, in re-engineering its accounts payable effort to streamline the cost of infrastructure, eliminated invoices by agreeing to pay suppliers on receipt of an order. Having discovered the concept of event-driven electronically initiated payments, the company then went further and began experimenting with a pay-on-use concept. Suppliers were given access to the master build schedule and they shipped just-on-time. When the part was used in production by the company, a signal was created that generated a payment to the vendor. This type of pay-on-use relationship has several novel aspects to it. First, the customer has effectively provided an incentive to the supplier to be a just-in-time supplier. One executive misunderstood an explanation of the concept and suggested that suppliers put parts at the company on consignment, and then when the company used them it would make payment. That arrangement is, of course, not the intent. The company does not want the part, nor to make the payment, before they need it. The supplier gets paid automatically, and knows exactly what to make and when by being electronically linked into the customer's master build database. It is a welcome relief for the supplier to build to the real schedule, rather than the rapidly changing, hardly ever accurate, build *forecast* they used before. The new efficiencies benefit both organizations by eliminating wasted actions and delays in payment. Suppliers are more and more considering the customer's perception of the added value provided by the supplier's capability to sell on a pay-when-used basis, and are turning that perception into competitive advantage.

Integrating Data Systems and Customers

When Federal Express announced that it would allow customers to track packages from their office computers using Federal Express's data system, some people thought that this was just a sales gimmick. Others thought that Federal Express was cleverly reducing its cost of answering customer inquiries by transferring work from their staff to the customer. In fact, Federal Express was inviting customers to tie their database systems to that of Federal Express.

It is now possible for a FedEx customer to program its own database to automatically generate a phone or E-mail message to staff members, informing them that, within the last ten minutes, the customer has received the package they sent. FedEx has thus begun to help FedEx customers in dealing with *their* customers. When customers perceive that their linkage to your database helps them better interact with their own customers, they may see strategic value in that linkage. Once customers are electronically "hooked" to your data system, it becomes harder for the competition to dislodge them. Price alone will no longer do it.

Some companies have used the open-data relationship as a means of strengthening the bond of trust between customers and suppliers, thereby facilitating closer relationships. Would your customer view an open-data relationship from you as the supplier as increasing the value or your products and services? What new benefits could an open-data relationship provide to your customer?

ON TREATING CUSTOMERS AS INDIVIDUALS VERSUS TREATING THEM STATISTICALLY

Treating customers as individuals instead of treating them statistically is appealing and seems like good sense. How can you treat your customers as individuals? Although the answers will vary according to different industries and according to the organizations within an industry, the issues and strategic opportunities have some similarity.

People resist treating customers as individuals because, they say, there would be too much data to handle, there would be chaos with systems, procedures in place for decades would be upset, and it would be unfair. Or: Why change now?

True, most businesses have not been organized to treat customers as individuals; there are rules in place to prevent it, and it does represent a new way of doing business. In the past, the unavailability of relevant information on a timely basis made treating customers as individuals difficult. This is changing for most businesses. Information processing, networks, databases, and expert systems software combined with various special-purpose data-collection, data-recording, and data-handling equipment make it possible in many businesses to treat customers as

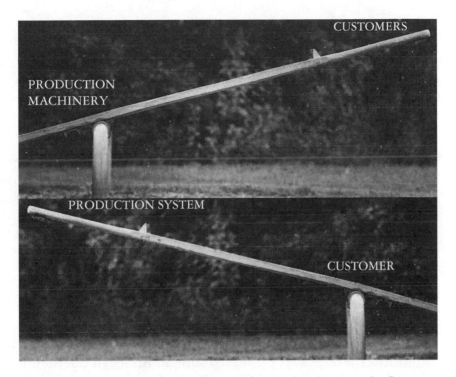

FIGURE 7.3   Mass Production Puts Production Machinery at the Center.
Agility Places the Customer at the Center.

individuals. Examples of this at the consumer level are companies that keep detailed profiles on their customers.

The travel agent knows what airlines you prefer, where you want to sit, and what special meals you like to order; the agent makes sure that your frequent-flier number is in the record when you ask them to book a flight. Similarly, car rental companies, hotel chains, and a variety of other service-oriented businesses keep a profile on your preferences and try to please you by respecting and acting on your preferences.

Using profiles to treat customers as individuals is but one way of meeting a customer's individual needs. Ross Operating Valves, described in Chapter 4, allows customers to use its design equipment to design the products they plan to purchase from Ross. Boeing prides itself on the degree of customization they provide to airplane customers. Ambra, the IBM PC clone company, allowed customers to configure their PC clones from among a wide variety of options. The customers not only chose their options, but were informed of any delay in shipment or of price impacts of their choice. Thus customers play an active role in configuring their own products and setting their own priorities among product features, cost, and timely delivery.

The idea of individualized products and services will mature and grow with the spread of agile capabilities for product and service generation. Today we can see some amusing examples of anomalies as we make the transition to individualized products from statistically sized products. Some wedding dresses are made to order for the bride, but the standard practice is for the bride to order a standard size that is the closest to her size. Then, after the dress is made to a standard size in an order quantity of one, the dress is altered by the bridal shop to provide an exact custom fit to the bride's figure. Interestingly, the technology is in place to make the dress to measure, but that's not the way it's done, today!

Table 7.1, based on initial research by Rudy Gedeon, follows the transition of products from commodity to mass individualization. Table 7.2 provides the correlated pricing transitions. Although the work is very much still in progress, it is valuable even in its current form. The concept of mass individualization suggests that we look first at the enrichment axis of our customer-supplier relationship diagram (Figure 7.3). As mass individualization becomes a commonly available method of product and service generation, the infrastructure for and method of ordering and delivering product services will change. What will happen to the market demand and prices of product services in the first three or four columns of Table 7.1? Will the infrastructure for delivering them remain in place or be dual use? We address some of these issues in the chapters that follow.

TURNING COMMODITIES INTO SPECIALTIES

Not too many years ago, sneakers were either high-top or low and came in two colors, black or white. They were clearly commodity

TABLE 7.1

Type of Market

Type of Product	Commodity	Commodity with Supplier-Selected Features	Commodity with Customer-Selected Features	Niche Market with Customer-Selected Components and Features	Mass Individualization, Possibly One of a Kind, One-Time Only Solution
Home entertainment, TV	Basic color TV	Stereo, color TV, cable-ready with remote control	Choice of picture, built-in VCR, monitor features, etc.	Large screen, custom-configured; possibly laser disk, VCR, Surround-Sound, stereo	Audiovisual engineer visits customer's home, interviews customer, and designs system and selects components to achieve desired performance criteria selected by customer
Electric drill	Basic drill	Drill set includes basic drill, popular bits, and screw bit	Choice of speeds, horsepower, home or professional model, portability, and assorted accessories	Designed for concrete work, steel, or heavy construction; various models to suit different professional and end users	Custom-designed and built for specific applications—outer-space usage, military applications, automotive, aerospace, and microelectronics

TABLE 7.1 Continued

	Type of Market				
Type of Product	Commodity	Commodity with Supplier-Selected Features	Commodity with Customer-Selected Features	Niche Market with Customer-Selected Components and Features	Mass Individualization, Possibly One of a Kind, One-Time Only Solution
Material-handling equipment	Basic forklift truck	Forklift truck with extraheavy lift or height	Choice of battery systems, special gearing, and physical reach	Forklift truck operates in unmanned mode as AGV, with selectable features	AGV designed for specific factory material-handling applications or as farm tractor transport
Jewelry	Basic ring in costume jewelry department; one or a few sizes fit all	Ring offered in standard sizes, and a few configurations that include glass or stones of crystal color	Ring customer has choice of settings, precious stones, and type of precious metal	Customer selects stone, design of ring, settings, and has ring engraved with message	Ring is designed and sized for the customer beginning with drawings and specifications

TABLE 7.2

Type of Market

Pricing Methodology	Commodity	Commodity with Supplier-Selected Features	Commodity with Customer-Selected Features	Niche Market with Customer-Selected Components and Features	Mass Individualization, Possibly One of a Kind, One-Time Only Solution
	Cost plus small markup	Cost plus market-based markup	Cost plus wide market-based markup	High-end market-based prices not related to cost	Value-based prices or very high-end market prices; definitely not cost-based pricing

items, and they sold for low prices in variety stores like Woolworth. Then, a "miracle" took place. What had been a low-priced commodity market became a high-priced specialty product market. Sport shoes are sold in boutique shops and are matched to their distinctive uses. Buyers frequently need three or more pairs if they are at all active athletically.

The question arises for companies competing in other commodity markets. Can you perform the sneaker miracle? The nonprescription sunglass industry has transformed itself in that way, and so have suntan lotions in response to the thinning of the ozone layer and concern over ultraviolet radiation. What, if anything, could be done to your products to specialize their performance? Do different users encounter different weather conditions, such as snow or sand, or cold or hot? Can the commodity be optimized for increased performance in different applications?

Another useful transformation for a commodity is to make a version that the customer wears both for its functionality and as jewelry. Perhaps the best examples of this are watches and pens. At one end of the spectrum, they are inexpensive and are useful in telling the time or writing. The president of the Rolex organization was asked about the condition of the watch market. He replied that he had no idea—he was not in that business. He said that his organization made jewelry. Judging by the prices of Rolex watches, he is, of course, right. In a similar vein, the makers of Cross pens, and more particularly the Mont Blanc line of writing instruments, really sell jewelry. It is worth asking whether your customers might consider wearing some version of your product. What might that do to its commodity status?

Could you enhance the value of your commodity products by adding information or service?

In Japan, the 7-Eleven stores decided that they were selling convenience, not commodity products. They organized themselves accordingly, collected data on individual customer preferences, and stocked each store according to neighborhood trends. Inventories changed more than 70 percent a year, and they now offer photo developing, copying, and other convenience services their customers asked for or indicated they would use. In their view, convenience is a service they offer. They determine what convenience means on a store-by-store basis with extensive data collection, interviews, and so on. Profitability went up 42 percent, with the change from offering a commodity to offering convenience.

Several years ago, American Hospital Supply put a computer terminal in the office of customer purchasing agents to make it convenient for them to order goods. The response was a significant increase in business. Convenience can be translated into increased value for both customer and supplier.

Caterpillar's automated ordering programs now accept ordinary English-language statements of requirements from its customers, selecting the engine that best meets the customers' needs. Caterpillar software then automatically connects the order with a scheduling system and releases the order to manufacturing. Customers see easy, convenient ordering and rapid build and delivery.

Service at a car dealership used to be treated as a kind of commodity, involving only parts and mechanics. Lexus has changed the standard. Its waiting rooms offer business facilities for use by the customer, various refreshments and amenities, or a free loaner car if you can't wait.

A surprising conversion of a commodity into a specialty market has been achieved by the long-distance phone companies. Long-distance service would appear to be a commodity. The phone companies have nevertheless turned it into a fiercely competitive and lucrative market by creating a complex rate structure on which to compete. Things are so complicated that several phone companies can each legitimately claim to be lower-priced than the others. The truth lies in the fine print, of course. The companies appeal to customers who have friends or enemies, families, or overseas relatives; they have established a wide variety of other customizable categories to offer the customer money-saving plans. Simply put, they have cleverly taken what should have been a commodity market and arbitrarily created pricing schemes and discounts that offer perceived value to customers. Could your commodity industry play this game? We expect to see it being played in the electrical power industry once it is deregulated.

ON VALUING INFORMATION ASSETS

The agile competitor values information as a corporate asset of significance, as described in the leveraging people and information dimension of agility. This is essential first, because of the value of information in making the operation of an organization agile. However, information has a second dimension of potentially greater value to the organization, and that is its value in enriching customers. Today, AT&T charges for information services that had traditionally been free. A challenge to all businesspeople is to identify, value, and sell information previously given away or not shared at all. Can you, in fact, find in your business an analogy to the AT&T experience, in which for years the company gave away what turned out to be millions of dollars of potential revenue.

AT&T has a perfect infrastructure in place to allow other companies to sell information. It created the 900-number service. Customers call a 900-number, and AT&T connects them with your business, which sells information to the caller. AT&T provides the infrastructure needed to connect with the customer and also handles billing. The 900-number calls are billed and are collected by AT&T's long-established and widely effective long-distance billing system.

The challenge to other businesspeople is, now that AT&T has made it easy for you, what information do you have that customers would pay for through access on the 900-number service? A sampling of 900-number services reveals that a wide variety of information products are being offered. There is a whole class of computer-based services; that is, you make the call using your Touch-Tone phone or computer and your request is handled by a computer at the other end. Information is provided to the customer directly by the computer in digital or simulated voice form, as you might expect, but some clever variations are also available. Some purveyors offer their customers fax responses to queries, and still others use the fax as a form of automated data entry system. We know of one PC hardware and software distributor located at the hub of an express service that will take your order for hardware and software products until 2 A.M. and deliver your order the same day. Still other purveyors of value-based information services on 900-numbers simply connect you to a conference call involving other people who want to discuss similar topics. An interesting question to consider is, Would your customers pay for a 900-number what you pay for an 800-number?

The amount of commerce for information-based products and services rises quite significantly as more and more organizations discover the contextual value of information to current and new clients. This phenonemon will grow even more with the advent of the national and international information highway, the merging of PC, video, voice and communications systems, and the multimedia home- and office-based devices embodying this technology. In place now, at a variety of locations equipped with fiber-optic cable TV systems servicing the information highway, are experimental systems linking businesses at different locations so that they can share live and on-line voice, remote video, and data systems. In these experiments, team members at disparate locations use the systems to integrate their work without having to get together. As these techniques mature and develop, they will be utilized routinely to integrate customers and suppliers, first only business customers, but then for advanced consumers, and eventually for everyone.

Thus the challenge to businesses is, how can this emerging information technology allow you to offer value-based products and services that previously were not possible? Providing the same old product but faster and cheaper will not give you a competitive edge for long.

Consider as an example the impact of universal product codes (UPCs) and the installation at supermarket checkout counters of UPC code readers. These information technology systems were installed and justified in the beginning mainly because of their ability to increase the speed and accuracy of the checkout counter, to provide the customer with an itemized bill, and to make it harder to steal from the store. But the real value of these systems has not been to the consumer, whose service they certainly improved; rather, the real value came from unforeseen benefits to supermarkets and their suppliers and distributors.

The database tailored to each individual store and soon to be customer-based, allows for analyses that permit the store to be proactive with its customers and accurate with its suppliers in offering shelf space and ordering products that customers are looking for. It has been possible to eliminate or drastically reduce wastage of products that spoil, increase varieties and shelf space for products when individual store demand indicates the need, and avoid chain-based average statistics, which have huge variances in accuracy across stores. The database is used to vary the store contents and inventory based on the individual store and neighborhood. Further, instantaneously available data can be used to tell the difference between a sale that is attracting new customers and one that is resulting from stocking up during big price reductions. Of course, the inventory control, automated reordering, and other inventory benefits you would expect are achieved, but the statistics are now based on individual stores. Imagine what will happen when the customer identity is also available—and that is coming.

It used to be true that business could operate successfully without much use of sophisticated information and databases. This is less and less true today and will effectively disappear as we become agile and compete on the basis of mass individualization.

Consider for a moment the change in information requirements between mass production and agile competitors. In mass production, there was a fixed and reasonably steady-state array of products and product configuration variables. Sales and marketing people could communicate with customers and the product service generation organization by using quantities, names, and/or catalog numbers. The producing organization set the specifications and assigned a simple product code to reflect the name of the product. The product code was varied in a limited number of ways to allow the customer to specify the exact nature of the standard product.

In an agile world, with mass individualization, the sales and marketing people report back with a description of the precise customer need or opportunity, instead of saying that they want 100 No. 2781 without flanges, and paint them red. The amount of information involved is several orders of magnitude larger, and it is incomplete. In most cases, a team of people needs to be formed to develop a product service concept and then, working with the customer, to refine it into a design. The volume of information in the agile business environment creates an entirely different work context. The difference is not limited to the marketing and sales teams. Every part of the organization dealing with the concept to cash cycle will be dealing with information that must be carefully maintained and updated to provide an accurate record of what took place in meeting the customer's needs or satisfying the customer opportunity.

Consider the implications of this for product service and documentation. If there are no more mass-produced products, then it may not be possible to distribute the same manual with each item sold. Can a company afford to write a different manual for each customer? Information technology will have to facilitate the development of self-documenting products and services. This is possible and appearing more and more with computer-based information systems. Expert system tutors built into word processors, spreadsheets, and mail-handling programs are examples of this capability. These information systems examine the context of what the user is trying to do and make suggestions as to how the product can be used to achieve the user's desired ends. It may sound like science fiction, but it is an emerging capability that will be greatly enhanced as more and more businesses rely on it to assist their customers with operating and configuring products and services.

Databases begin to be an important tool for a business in dealing with customers. Appliance manufacturers and many firms with call-in help services now use the customer's phone number or account number to consistently connect the customer with the same service provider. They use a customer history database to improve their ability to help and personalize their service. Local pizza vendors use their customer databases to configure special offers based on individual buying patterns and frequency. How might you use data to customize what you offer to sell, or to know what your customers might want?

The use of databases becomes an imperative in the agile world of mass customization. Although most products will be custom-built for individual customers, they will frequently be assemblages of modules, each of which has specific capabilities. Organizations currently custom-building products for their customers reuse modules frequently and develop more than 80 percent of a customized product with previously created modules.

Customization can and will come from configuring and reusing existing modules in new and unique ways. In this type of environment, the corporate database of information modules and their capabilities becomes an essential design tool. Knowing which modules were used with which customers and for what purpose, a company is in a position to exploit the benefit to customers of redesigning old modules to give them new capabilities. Similarly, a company can do focused and accurate recalls of any products that went out with defective components. Currently, car companies go through massive publicity campaigns and lots of negative publicity, in part because their databases do not contain information about which specific car got the faulty or potentially dangerous components. Thus, if only 1 or 2 percent of your customers have faulty components, with the proper use of a database you could reach exactly, and only, the affected customers in a private communication.

Table 7.3 shows an information product as it moves from being a commodity to generating individualized value. As you review Table 7.3, consider again the Ideation Company. Its product is teaching and exploiting its own expertise in a generic problem-solving methodology called *TRIZ.* Ideation offers to solve its clients' most difficult and important engineering problems. Its product service clearly falls into the category shown in the far-right column of the table. Ideation asks clients to define constraint problems from which there will be significant potential value when solved. It represents the first wave of agile competitors who have figured out how to get their clients to identify value-based opportunities for the firm's product services.

Can you find a way to get your clients to be as clear in identifying their high-valued solution opportunities for your information product?

How would you answer the following questions?

- What is the role of databases in your business?
- Who generates, uses, and owns the database information?
- What is the trend with respect to the information content of your product-service offerings? Why? What is it worth to your customers?
- What asset value does information and intellectual property have in your organization? Is this value appropriate?

TABLE 7.3

Type of Marketplace

Information products	Commodity	Commodity with Supplier-Selected Features	Commodity with Customer-Selected Features	Niche Market with Customer-Selected Components and Features	Mass Individualization, Possibly One of a Kind, One-Time Only Solution
	Book	Specialty book (e.g., handbook of chemistry or physics tables)	Book of the Month Club	Rare book collection	Using information systems designed and built for organizational needs and circumstances (Merrill Lynch worldwide information system)
	Telephone information service	CD ROM with encyclopedia	Data service that answers inquiries	Member of CompuServe	Custom software system created by EDS and Sybase for 1994 World Cup soccer games
	Computer program	On line to database system using SQL query language	On line to a database server with large number of databases	On line to Internet using Mosaic or WAIS	Military information systems for national security applications
	Data on disk		American Airlines Sabre system	Wide-based business usage of client server applications software configured to the needs of organization	Information tools (TRIZ) to solve important engineering problems
			Customer configurable software interfaces	Geographic and demographic focused data and databases	
			On line to service such as Prodigy		

On Valuing and Selling Core Competencies That Have Not Been Products or Services in Your Business

In the age of agility and virtual organizations, core competencies become an important explicit organizational asset. In that context, it is worth exploring why an organization would have world-class core competencies and not sell access to them. In the old days of focusing only on products, many core competencies were needed to be able to formulate, design, plan, and produce the products. Yet companies sold only the finished product. In an agile world, organizations combine core competencies in virtual organizations and combine products and services to create new value-based, individualized solutions for customers. In this context, all core competencies have a market potential and value as an income-producing asset.

Consider the case of L. L. Bean, now reported to be profitably sharing its competence in telemarketing with AT&T. It is gaining value from a core competency it developed in order to be world-class in its primary business. Prudent business leaders are now reexamining their core competencies and thinking about what their organization is prepared to sell or provide access to. A major consumer goods company discovered that it had built a world-class capability in machine design. Developed solely for internal need, the capability is now marketed by the firm.

A good indicator of a company's ability to sell or profitably share previously internally exploited core competencies can be found from the results of successful and comprehensive benchmarking exercises. Good benchmarking practice suggests that you benchmark all core competencies in your business. It further recommends that you look outside your competition's competence area to see how you rank against the world's best.

When the results show that you have a world-class competency, better than others inside and outside your industry, there should be a market for that competency in the organizations you benchmarked who were not as good as you were in it. Looked at in this way, benchmarking becomes a way of indirectly generating customers for your world-class competencies and a way of gaining partners for competencies in which you are not world-class.

What do you have a world-class core competency in that you have not been selling or providing fee-based access to?

HIGHLIGHTS FROM CHAPTER 7

In creating customer-valued solutions, the marketing function must be reinvented in an agile company, reflecting the fact that solutions do not have an absolute value: they have a contextual value based on the customer's situation.

For both consumer and business markets, the contextual value of commercial exchanges generally reflects the presence of a constraint that the customer must overcome.

Enriching your customer is perhaps the most important dimension of agility. Enriching customers confers sustainable competitive advantage.

Customers in both the commercial and the business-to-business sectors value enrichment-based products and services. For business customers two generic opportunities for enrichment are represented by cost containment and revenue-enhancement metrics.

With respect to consumers, enrichment is linked to prices, yet individual consumers can feel enriched by solutions that raise the quality of their life, such as medical procedures or luxury products and services.

Core competencies explain why customers do business with suppliers. Organizations sell the skills, knowledge, and expertise of their employees, irrespective of business or industry sector.

Companies can cause customers to see increased value in their product and service relationships through pay-on-use systems, information connections between customer and supplier, and treating customers as individuals.

The tabular method of examining the change of product services from a commodity through to mass-individualization-based products and services was used to chart the change in perception and degree of customer involvement with product/service offerings.

Understanding customer opportunities and needs is critical to developing the ability to provide mass individualization, for example, by turning a commodity market into a specialty market to enrich customers with solutions derived from commodities.

Sell convenience by adding special features.

Add information, and services to effect the commodity transformation.

Information itself is a valuable commodity, and its value for enriching the customers must be explored.

Sell access to core competencies that were not developed to be products or services.

8

Customizing Agile Business Strategies

A company that is agile deals with change as a matter of routine. In an agile company the strategic plan deals not with product but with enhancement of capability, which in turn leads to products and services that are unpredictable at the time the plan is made. If the move to agility is perceived only as a move to improve the fulfillment of customers' currently perceived requirements, then agility is not being used to gain strategic advantage. One does not install a high-bandwidth communication channel only to improve the quality of a telephone conversation, but to open up entirely new methods of interaction and commerce. Similarly, planning a move to agility starts with a perception, even vague and approximate, of the new and qualitatively different mixes of products and services to be offered. To start off only with the currently perceived requirements is to set the aim too low to be of strategic significance.

Who is the customer? For most companies, the customer is another company, so that focusing on a customer means focusing on other companies. Fewer than 10 percent of industrial companies and service companies have end-user consumers as their customers. For most companies, the agile outlook of enriching one's customers is by helping those customers help their customers.

A strategic plan is made relative to a goal, using a methodology to define the goal and how to get there. The goal should be clear from all that has gone before in this book. This chapter will describe a useful model to be followed for planning, based on a model developed by a group of industry executives and academics (Preiss and Wadsworth 1994). There are other approaches to customizing a move to agility. Some companies start by setting up self-empowered teams and independent profit centers. Some prefer a less structured approach, establishing a flatter and entirely different organization, while training employees to be entrepreneurial. Many organizations have moved to being more agile by motivating their people and having them find the directions and opportunities for a company. That approach does not suit every organization; some prefer a more structured approach. One should not hesitate to use whatever approach suits the temperament and the circumstances of the company.

A MODEL FOR AGILE RELATIONSHIPS

Agility is all about relationships—relationships between end users of products and services and their suppliers, relationships between companies in the value-add chain, and relationships between employees and their company.

Products, Services, and Enrichment of Each Customer

For generations, companies and employees have identified themselves by the products they produce. The age of mass production saw the physical product as its aim, and marketing organizations saw the one-time sale event as their success. "What does your company do?" "We make widgets for gadgets."

Today, a company wanting to succeed breaks out of the thought pattern of generating income from products sold in one-time deals to seeing income opportunities over the entire life of a product. What can these opportunities be? They are defined from the perspective of enriching the customer and include:

- Individualized configuration and packaging to meet evolving needs and opportunities
- Upgrade components to increase the utility and value of a product
- Automated remote monitoring and maintenance
- Environmentally benign decommissioning, and reuse or recycling

The income to be generated from services over the life of the product can be much higher than from the one-time deal in the original sale. That being so, it is sensible to think of the product not as an item to which one adds services as a secondary consideration but to define the primary purpose of the product as a platform for upgrades and value-added services. The services and upgrades become primary aims, and the product specification and its design and manufacture follow from those aims. When the development, production, and distribution costs of a product and the profit to be made are considered, the lifetime money-making opportunities may even make it worthwhile to decrease the initial product price, so as to provide upgrade and service opportunities. The cellular telephone has evolved in this way, from being sold as a device to being given away in order to sell service.

*An agile **product** is a platform for profitable upgrade components and enriching services over its entire lifetime, not an object sold for a profit in a one-time deal.*

Many people define their company, and their job, in terms of product. A predefined catalog-type product is the focus of most relationships between suppliers and customers. The implications of the new concept of a product as the basis for ongoing enrichment are that the product and services form the basis for ongoing relationships with customers in a changing world. This concept will rearrange the basics of industrial society—from relations between companies; to new jobs that will be created; to old jobs that will disappear; and to advertising, retailing, and every aspect of industrialized life. The new concept is of special importance to teams that define and design a product. They will need to unlearn many approaches and familiar truths if they are to maximize the advantage deriving from the concept of a product as a platform for customer solutions, rather than as an object of a one-time sales transaction.

Having considered that a product is an opportunity for ongoing customer relationships based on enriching services and upgrades over its lifetime, a company next needs to make a conscious decision about where it wants to locate itself on the spectrum of such services. The producer of the product needs to plan proactively which services it will want to provide and, of these, which will come from internal resources and which will be provided through arrangements with other companies. This decision will determine which competencies are to be expanded and which will be reduced. A significant effort will be invested in promoting teams and entrepreneurial workers and in establishing an organization that constantly changes itself as the business environment changes. Planning the changes is preferable to reacting to fortuitous,

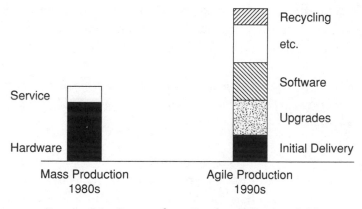

FIGURE 8.1   Income from Goods and Services Sold

haphazard events, for planning will guide decisions as to which opportunistic situations should be pursued and which would be beyond the company's ability to exploit. In summary: *The supplier company moves from selling product to selling capability; the customer company moves from buying product to buying a solution.*

It follows that the concepts of a customer, a supplier, and a sale change:

- **A customer** is no longer the recipient in a one-time transaction but a subscriber to the solutions of the supplier.
- **A supplier** no longer hands over goods in response to an order but is a long-term supporter or partner of the customer.
- **A sale** is no longer a one-time event, but an ongoing transfer of products and services, and of payment, between the supplier and the customer.

Figure 8.2 is from Preiss and Wadsworth (1994), referred to in Chapter 7. It creates a three-dimensional space within which any company may be located and is thus useful for analyzing the relationship activities of a company. On the horizontal axis is the total value add conferred on the customer by the supplier company—the *enrichment* of the customer. Simple, predefined parts with no value-added service are near the origin. Moving to the right, the customer receives much more before-sales and aftersales information, knowledge, and other enriching services (discussed in Chapter 7).

The vertical axis represents the financial arrangement used to determine the flow of revenue from customer to supplier—the *reward* of the supplier. Near the origin, the customer pays the supplier a fixed price per quantity of products or parts. Further up the axis, the customer pays the supplier a fixed price per quantity of products *plus* a variable price for some level of service and knowledge provided (just-in-time delivery, maintenance, warranty, special design, etc.). At the end of the axis, the customer shares risks and revenue with the supplier. One can observe that the closer to the origin the supplier is, the more the supplier will be treated like a classical mass-production supplier. As the payment basis goes up the axis, the more the supplier will be a "partner," possibly

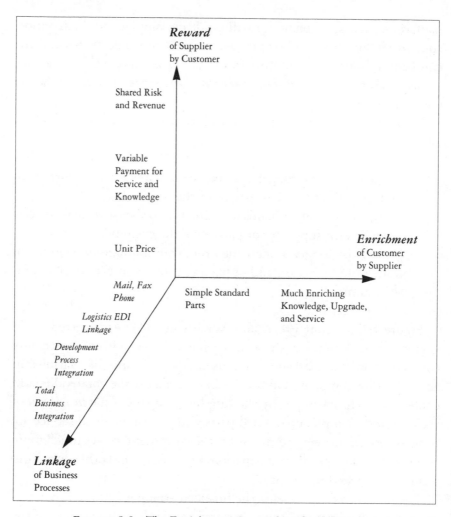

FIGURE 8.2   The Enrichment-Reward-Linkage Diagram

in a virtual arrangement. Chapter 6 discussed alternative virtual company arrangements.

In order to do business, companies interact, whether by personal meeting, mail, phone, fax, or computer network. The third axis in Figure 8.2 shows the continuum of the business process linkage between supplier and customer—the *linkage.* The traditional mass-production systems of simply taking orders is near the origin. Going along the axis, the process linkage between supplier and customer becomes tighter. Chapter 10 will discuss various systems that enable business process linkage.

In summary, the three axes show the following aspects of a relationship:

- **Enrichment**—the products, services, or other items passed from supplier to customer
- **Reward**—the revenue or other reward passed from customer to supplier
- **Linkage**—the business process linkage between customer and supplier that enables them to work together

Figure 8.2, which describes customer-supplier relations, is hence known as the *enrichment-reward-linkage* diagram. It provides a convenient means of understanding a company's relationships, both as a supplier to its customers and as a customer to its suppliers. It is a useful tool for planning strategic changes in those relationships, and will now be used as a model for planning agile business strategies. Since it is difficult to visualize a three-dimensional diagram, the discussion will continue with two two-dimensional diagrams, the *reward-enrichment* and the *linkage-enrichment* diagrams.

Consider the *reward-enrichment* diagram, shown in Figure 8.3. The collection of enriching upgrades and services over the life of the product cannot be predicted at the time the customer-supplier agreement is negotiated, and so the cost to the supplier of providing that high enrichment cannot be known ahead of time. If much enrichment is to be provided, but the customer insists on paying on the basis of a fixed unit price of product, a dysfunctional relationship that will not survive over time will be established. The region in the diagram of high *enrichment* but low *reward* is hence an untenable location. On the other hand, if the supplier were to supply simple product with no lifetime enriching services, then establishment of a complex arrangement of risk and revenue sharing would be much too complicated for the simple transaction involved. The region in the diagram of low *enrichment* but high *reward* is hence also an impractical location. Figure 8.3 shows the

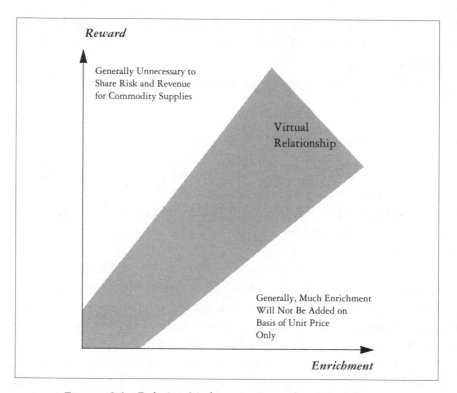

FIGURE 8.3   Relationship between Reward and Enrichment

region of compatible relationships. As the supplier moves from passing simple product to passing increasing enrichment to the customer, the method of computing revenue changes from a simple unit cost for product, through a variable formula for product and service, to a method of shared profit and product, possibly a virtual company relationship.

Consider the *linkage-enrichment* diagram, shown in Figure 8.4. The products and services with a high value of *enrichment* but a low value of *linkage,* outside the shaded area to the right, are not achievable because the lack of sufficient linkage will not enable the high levels of enrichment to be supplied quickly enough. On the other hand, if a supplier supplies simple unit product, but the supplier and customer have a tight linkage between their business processes, the investment of time,

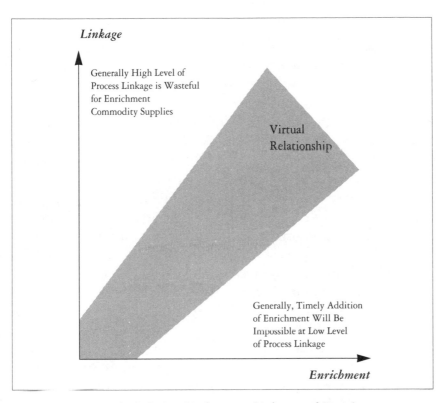

FIGURE 8.4   Relationship between Linkage and Enrichment

training, and equipment in that linkage is wasted. The region of low *enrichment* but high *linkage* is also an undesirable location.

So we see that the *reward* to the supplier and the *linkage* between supplier and customer should increase hand in hand with the *enrichment* created for the customer by the supplier and not get out of step. At low values of enrichment, where product is provided with little value-added service and information, a unit price transaction and simple linkage methods suffice. As enrichment increases, the relationship becomes more agile, requiring sharing of profit and risk, and closer linkage of business processes. Hence, the enrichment-reward-linkage diagram gives a concise picture of agile business relationships.

As information, knowledge, and services increase and become more customized, more continuous interaction is needed between people in the customer and supplier organizations. It is not feasible to maintain close working relationships with many suppliers, and so the customer reduces the number of its major suppliers. Many customer companies have established a target of retaining no more than 5 to 25 percent of their suppliers as they move away from classical mass production. The reliability of both supplier and customer then becomes critical, because if the supplier's operation stops, it is likely that the customer's operation will be forced to stop as well. This illustrates the change in perception of suppliers by agile customers. Mass production is product-focused, and the supplier is chosen on the basis of quality, speed, and price for product only. Agile business is process-focused, and the supplier is chosen on the basis of core competency, organizational quality and reliability of all its business processes and relationships.

Both customer and supplier companies in the agile relationship need to establish a balance between dealing with too many suppliers or customers and dealing with too few. This puts a premium on the selection process, on the reliability of a supplier, and on the continuing reliability of the customer. This mandates all the aspects of agility: empowered teaming, openness in financial and other data, and mutual dependence and hence trust, cooperation, and visionary leadership. Note that a company is both a supplier to its customers and a customer to its suppliers. It will have many relationships at many points in the spectrum, as both supplier and customer. However, experience shows that a business unit can manage to operate profitably over only a limited range of the enrichment axis.

Business units do not usually manage simultaneously to be both low-cost commodity suppliers and competitive, high-enriching leading-edge knowledge service providers. It follows therefore that a company should understand which portion of the enrichment axis each business unit covers and should make a strategic decision as to where they should be located on the axis. This decision will be based on markets, competition, external environment, and internal strengths and weaknesses, and it will form the basis of the plan of how to move the company to agility. The purchasing, development, production, financial, sales, and all other processes should be aligned to support the overall business strategy, and they can be pushed to the left or right on the *enrichment* axis in the diagram. It is better to know where you are and where you want to be than to let the changing world and your competitors force you into a position they choose for you.

The Enrichment Chain

Goods and services pass from one company to another up the "food chain" in the worldwide economy until they finally reach the end user. Each company in the process adds value or enrichment to the product or service involved. In mass production, it is common for a company to plan in terms of the products it can make and the customers who buy those products. For agile business, the context of planning is expanded to visualizing the entire enrichment-adding chain. Figure 8.5 shows a small part of such a chain, to illustrate the principle.

A company usually thinks of its market segments as only those categories of customers to which it currently sells its product. In doing so, the company implicitly agrees to locate itself at particular points in the enrichment-adding chain, but often without analysis and explicit

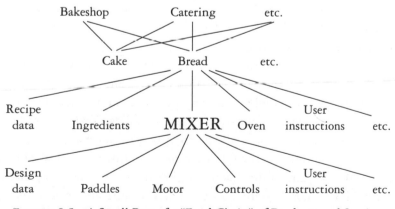

FIGURE 8.5   A Small Part of a "Food Chain" of Products and Services

decision as to why it should be there. That approach suited the old days, when a company considered itself a supplier of a product for a one-time sale. It should now think of itself as a supplier of customer solutions that comprise products, information, and services and that include solutions that use the products as platforms. To achieve agility, the people in a company need to constantly rethink where the company is located on the value-added chain.

Which information and services? Why should they be limited to those needed by the customer that takes the product directly and passes it along as part of its own activity? If a company can offer a service needed by a customer further up the value chain, why not do so? To quote Unisys, the aim becomes helping your customer help their customer. An example of a company moving from the focus of product only to product and service, and doing so at new locations on the value-added chain, is Johnson Controls, which moved from supplying control systems to both supplying control systems and providing extensive maintenance of facilities.

When a company moves in the direction of agility and progresses from supplying product to supplying solutions, it may find profitable opportunities at points in the value chain other than where it was accustomed to operating. Bernard Marcus, CEO of the successful chain Home Depot, tells his staff, "You can never do enough for a customer." In the world of agility, never doing enough means not only doing what you can in the context of existing products and services but opening other locations on the value chain, expanding the products and services offered, and making alliances with other companies, whatever can create profitable business opportunities.

There is already one widely required service—the recycling service. Laws are in place in Germany and other European countries, and will be introduced more widely, that require the manufacturer of a product to recycle it, reusing whatever subassemblies can be reused. The only practical way to do this is to disassemble the product into components and send each to its own manufacturer for disposal or for testing and reconditioning. Each supplier down the chain repeats the procedure for its components, and so on. This introduces another new concept. There is no final "end user" anymore. In the days of mass production, there was an end-user who bought a product and then junked it. Today, when products are recycled, everyone passes a product on to someone else, and so the open chain of material supply has become a closed loop.

Planning the Move from Providing One-Time Product to Providing Customer Enrichment

Customer enrichment is attained by providing a continuous flow of upgrades and services. The move away from the concept of product only to a product with allied services is a strategic move that needs planning, care, and prioritization. Whatever the plan, the issues are important enough to warrant checking before moving into implementation. Whether the conclusion of the planning exercise is to do nothing, to do little, or to undertake a big change in the orientation of a business, it is important that a systematic procedure as outlined here be followed. It is important to leave a paper trail documenting the steps, with the reasons for decisions along the way, so that the conclusions can be checked independently. It is easy, and dangerous, for a person doing this work to be carried away by preconceptions that warp the conclusions, and so independent checking is usually needed. This section describes a systematic procedure which minimizes the risk in making the move.

It is important, in planning the move to agility, to look beyond today's capability. To plan with only today's capability in mind is to aim behind the moving target. One should avoid the trap of assuming that what was always will be. The well-known story of IBM's missed opportunity with the Xerox invention (Hammer and Champy 1993) illustrates the point. At one time, IBM was offered the rights to the xerography technology but declined. Why? Because a group of experts estimated the market for copying by calculating the amount of carbon copies made at the time, which was minuscule compared with the size of the copying market today. They could not imagine the entirely new demand that would be created by the invention of xerography.

The story of Alexander Bell's invention, the telephone, illustrates the same point. He offered to sell the patent rights but was turned down. The reason given by the committee of experts at the time was that, since information was adequately distributed by telegram, there was no real need for the new invention. From their perspective, the telephone was a toy, requiring many miles of wires with attendant maintenance problems that overshadowed the marginal market value. They, too, could not imagine the entirely new markets and opportunities, indeed, the entirely new way of living, generated by the invention of the telephone.

The trend to proactively choose locations on the "food chain" of enriching services and products, then to design solutions for customers at those locations, is a natural extension of modern industrial philosophies. Dick Dauch, the engineer's engineer who rebuilt Chrysler's manufacturing capability, writes (Dauch, 1993):

> The favorable impact on the quality of your end product is a 100:1 return in product design, 10:1 in process design, and only 1:1 in production.

The point is not the accuracy or inaccuracy of the factor 10, but that the further upstream you go in making improvements, the higher is the factor by which you improve competitive standing. Agility pushes us beyond decisions relating to the design of a product to the realm of decisions about which products and lifetime services to offer, and at which points in the value-added chain a company should position itself to do that. To paraphrase Dauch, these decisions produce another tenfold increase in value as perceived by the customer and enable a company to make even more money than before. Typical trends can be seen in the approach of Johnson Controls, which expanded from a company which supplied only controls to one that supplies maintenance service; in Otisline, which provides on-line monitoring of its elevators; and in the cellular telephone industry, which has moved from selling phones and communication equipment to selling services using the cellular phones.

The starting point of the plan to move to agility is evaluation of products, services, and the enrichment-adding chain.

CUSTOMIZING THE AGILE BUSINESS STRATEGY

Analyze the Company

1. The first step is to form a good picture of the company and where it stands. A useful technique is an agile WOTS-up analysis, which evaluates the:

> Weaknesses—the weaknesses relative to competitors and changing market environment
>
> Opportunities—the opportunities created by the changing market environment
>
> Threats—the threats to present success from changing competitors and markets
>
> Strengths—the company's strengths, particularly definition of its core capabilities

This analysis not only counts the facilities and machines in the company but pays special attention to the capability and motivation of the people. Note that all four items in the analysis involve evaluating the company relative to its markets and competitors.

Overall Opportunity Analysis

2. For the capabilities of the company, list in general terms the enriching services, as well as product, that the company could offer. Don't be limited to items that the company can deal with as currently configured. Doing this requires some creative thinking and techniques

of brainstorming or otherwise breaking set ways of thinking. It also may require talking to current customers or reading about products and activities of customers several levels above in the enrichment-adding chain. This stage may lead to ideas for new products and services and new market niches.

3. By looking at the capability of the company, and the changing markets and competitors, estimate the growth potential for each enrichment opportunity. Remember that, over the life of the product family or service, many unpredicted upgrades and service opportunities will occur, and allowance must be made to take advantage of them.

4. Analyze the company's current ability to provide each upgrade or service. List the in-house abilities available, and estimate the cost and effort to be incurred if the skill and equipment needed to provide the service were to be acquired or developed. Obviously, some skills or equipment may be obtained by outsourcing, partnering, or by a virtual company arrangement. These options should be considered from the perspectives of price and reliability as well as whether the capability required is a part of core capability, in which case there is a premium in retaining it in the company.

5. After completing the analyses, evaluate each option and eliminate the opportunities for which predicted reward is so low as to warrant forgoing them. This may include moving capabilities which have been in the company for a long period to partners or suppliers. In making such a decision, one must be careful not to outsource a core competency, because doing so can build up a competitor while weakening oneself.

Comparison with Current Products

6. Revisit the current product or service offerings, viewing them as opportunities for upgrades and services of value to customers. Take note of capabilities and untapped entrepreneurship of the people in the company. Identify new service and business sectors and changes in the

product that may enhance those business opportunities. Plans at this stage can deal with no more than general considerations, since specific solutions will be developed with specific customers. The current product and service offerings thus develop into a plan of what types of customer solution to provide, looking beyond the current list of products and services.

7. Revisit steps 1 through 5, improving them with the new plan of customer solutions in mind.

Initial Plan of Market Presence

8. Identify the enrichment-adding chain into which the proposed solutions could enter. Look at the entire chain of current customers, the uses to which they put the solutions and products, the services they buy for the product, and the companies to which they sell solutions and pass products, including the recycling stage.

9. Note the company's current locations on the enrichment-adding chain.

10. For all the solutions, products, services, and upgrades, select the points on the enrichment-adding chain at which a presence is needed to supply them.

11. For each such location, plan how to be there, either alone, or as will be more usual, in cooperation with other companies. For each such presence, estimate the moves, time, and costs needed to establish a presence.

Refine the Plan

12. One never has enough time or resources to check out every possibility. The information from step 11 enables the prioritization of

the work of surveying customers, checking the correctness of cost and income estimates, checking the potential for each enrichment opportunity, and planning of negotiations with potential cooperating companies. This stage of the effort will focus and crystallize the opportunities that should be followed, in order to establish new presence in the enrichment-adding chain.

Analyze the Barriers to Change

13. The plan derived above establishes where one wants to go, and by which stages. This is a move into a regime of new methods of working and interacting with suppliers, partners, and customers, very different from the methods that were common for mass production and commerce. Moving on and reaching the goals require overcoming many barriers; the major ones are outlined in Chapter 9. Those companies that do not recognize the barriers to change or do not deal with them, will face stronger and stronger competition, becoming low-value-added organizations competing against cheap labor from around the world. Those that do recognize the barriers and deal with them successfully will become the high-value-added successful companies of the twenty-first century.

Plan the Internal Realignment of the Company

14. Implementation of the move to agility will require a realignment of the company. This will include changes in the organizational culture and internal structure of the company, will often require changes or investments in the systems supporting work in the company, and will require deep changes in the methods of interaction with customers, suppliers, and partners in virtual organizations. The *enrichment-reward-linkage* (Figure 8.2) model is useful for this, as is the description of the infrastructure components in Chapter 10.

STRATEGIC PLANNING DEPARTMENTS' NEW ROLES

In the past, strategic planning in a multidivisional corporation evaluated which businesses the corporate center should buy or sell. For a division or single-sector company, the strategic planning department would recommend new market sectors or product lines for the company. In the world of agile enterprises, such initiatives devolve from centralized corporate control, to teams and points of initiative throughout the organization. The rate of change of every factor in the business environment has increased. As a result, questions that used to be far out on the time horizon, such as which products to make or evaluation of business opportunities, are now close in time and are part of the regular operational work of tactical teams. Issues that never were considered before, such as locating the company on the enrichment-adding chain and others discussed in this chapter, need to be dealt with systematically. Strategic planning now has to deal with these new and far-reaching issues that previously did not need attention. They include:

- Evaluating what the core competencies of the company are
- Evaluating the directions in which the core competencies of the company should develop
- Constant evaluation of the skill base of the employees in the company and checking to ensure the compatibility of these skills with the designed core competencies of the company
- Recommending how to position the company as a more desirable partner to others looking for alliances and partnerships of all types
- Finding potential partners and devising an efficient method for evaluating them
- Constant analysis of the value-added chain as it changes and fragments from year to year
- Constant search for profitable business opportunities at every location in the chain, particularly at newly developing locations and locations neglected by competitors
- Constant review of the new services and product packages and upgrades offered by competitors

- Prediction, based on monitoring of technology and marketing developments, of which services and products packages are expected to be provided by competitors.

Agile competition thus offers much opportunity for enterprising managers of strategic planning departments.

NOTES ON CHAPTER 8

In many interactions with varied groups of people, we have found that the material in this chapter serves various purposes. A company may find the material in this chapter useful in the following ways:

- To customize the steps outlined for the company's specific circumstances.
- To evaluate how to deal with the planning process.
- To analyze which steps can be dealt with adequately by using internal resources and the steps for which outside people should be brought in as a guide or "sanity check."
- To consider how the company would set about getting started to customize a company-specific strategy.

Some example projects for a course are:

- Review the methodology suggested, finding ways to improve it.
- Evaluate the barriers and difficulties in carrying out any of the planning steps.

Public or elected bodies may find the material in this chapter useful in the following ways:

- To check whether existing systems and regulations are barriers or aids to businesses in the region that would undertake the effort to plan a move to agility.

- To analyze the locations on the enrichment-adding chain of the markets for businesses in the region and to determine whether these businesses compete in low-value-added sectors or whether they are moving to high-value-added agile markets. In this analysis, the implications of the conclusion arrived at on social and economic planning should be considered.

9

Barriers to Assimilating Agility

$\mathbf{B}$ecoming more agile is difficult, not only because change itself is inherently difficult but also because all the administrative and legal systems, as well as the habits and thought patterns of people, date back to the era of mass production and mass marketing. The concepts of agility have yet to be incorporated into commercial systems, measures, laws, customs, and habits.

The barriers to assimilating agility can conveniently be described as financial barriers, and barriers internal to, and external to, an organization, although items from each category obviously influence the others. Good leadership can address the difficult barriers within an organization but not those barriers external to an organization, which are due to government regulation or societal attitudes. Addressing external barriers is laborious and long-term, but any country or society wishing to maintain competitive ability over the long run must do this. The surest way to competitive extinction is to resist change within while circumstances change without.

The commonly used financial accounting system is cited as a special case of a barrier, not only because it is important but because it is an example of a method that was reasonably accurate for classical mass production but is unsuitable for agile commerce.

The first section of this chapter gives the history of cost accounting, a detailed explanation of why it is now unsuitable, and a discussion of some alternative methods. This illustrates that the difficulty with this barrier is not a matter of personal attitude or of not trying hard enough to overcome it but is a fundamental problem that requires application of systematic modern analysis. Similar problems are likely to exist with other methods and management practices. Investigation will undoubtedly identify those methods which need to be completely rethought for agility.

The discussion in this chapter covers the more important barriers that must be dealt with effectively by a company, government, or other organization wishing to become more agile. It is adapted from a list of barriers compiled by the industry executives who contributed to the Iacocca Institute report *21st Century Manufacturing Enterprise Strategy* (Goldman and Preiss 1991).

OUTDATED MANAGEMENT ACCOUNTING SYSTEMS

Generally Accepted Accounting Principles (GAAP)

The universal and most important measure in a business is money. Every decision is evaluated in terms of the financial cost and benefit, and management accounting is an influential performance-measurement system. Surprisingly, the methods commonly used for management cost accounting have become fatally flawed. This is what two foremost authorities say about current accounting procedures (Johnson and Kaplan 1987).

> Today's management accounting information, driven by the procedures and cycle of the organization's financial reporting system, is too late, too aggregated, and too distorted to be relevant for managers'

planning and control decisions. [This system can lead to] misguided decisions on product pricing, product sourcing, product mix, and responses to rival products (Johnson and Kaplan 1987).

Experience with many manufacturing companies shows that this indictment, serious as it is, is an understatement. In many cases current cost accounting methods lead companies to abandon profitable products, to pursue unprofitable ones, and to drive themselves into serious problems. This is because management accounting systems, which once were useful, suffer from a fundamental theoretical flaw in cost allocation. As companies are forced by competition to move to agility, the problems caused by the flaw in management accounting systems will become even more serious.

To understand how such a state of affairs could develop, we need to look back over the development of industrial society. Early businesses were run by owners who paid for raw material themselves, who sold product themselves, and who paid for labor on a piecework basis. The conversion efficiency of the business was known to the owner day by day and was governed by market rates. As businesses became larger and acquired significant investments, owners hired salaried managers and workers who were paid by the hour. They needed methods to measure the efficiency of the business. Textile mills, railroads, department stores, metalworking businesses, and others developed suitable measures such as cost per ton-mile, cost per yard of cloth, or cost per ton of steel.

The concept of depreciation was not known in any of these early organizations. All expenses incurred by a plant during a period were applied to that plant for that period. No expense was allocated to products, and there was no need to do so. Andrew Carnegie's steel-producing organization made use of detailed data on direct operating costs but made no use of capital depreciation or return on investment (ROI) calculations. Also, there was no demand that the financial numbers reporting profitability to external authorities and investors be consistent with the measures used to monitor and improve internal operations.

By the late nineteenth century, managers of many metalworking companies had developed formulas to accumulate and analyze costs and efficiencies for converting raw material into product; they had also developed standard measures and standard rates in order to plan the most efficient work flow for a factory. Costs were divided into direct labor and indirect costs. The indirect cost, mostly overhead labor, was allocated to a product based on the direct labor time invested in its production. The engineers used the formula in factories that produced few products, and in those factories overhead resources were used by each product at about the same rate. The accountants adopted the formula for use in general, including situations that were dissimilar. The evaluation by Church, a contemporary of Frederick Winslow Taylor, and quoted by Johnson and Kaplan, of the averaging procedures is note-worthy.

> . . . it is very usual practice to average this large class of [overhead] expense, and to express its incidence by a simple percentage either upon wages or upon time. . . . As a guide to actual profitableness of particular classes of work, it is valueless and even dangerous . . . in the case of a machine shop with machines all of a size and kind, performing practically identical operations by means of a fairly average wage rate, it is not alarmingly incorrect. If however, we apply this method to a shop in which large and small machines, highly paid and cheap labor, heavy castings and small parts, are all in operation together, then the result, unless measures are taken to supplement it, is no longer trustworthy.

Holden Evans, a naval contractor around the turn of the century, described how even then cost accounting practices were driving businesses into difficulties:

> In some of the large establishments with numerous shops the expense burden is averaged and applied on the basis of direct labor—notwithstanding the fact that in one shop the shop expense percentage is nearly a hundred while in another it is less than twenty-five. Frequently such establishments are called on to bid for work which is almost exclusively confined to the shops where the expense is low,

and by using the higher average rate the bids are high and the work goes to other establishments where costs are more accurately determined. Thus profitable work is often lost.

This identical source of error persists today. According to H. T. Johnson (1992), in the early days of the semiconductor industry, plants made low-density chips. Low-density chips use little overhead, compared to high-density chips, which are more complex, requiring many expensive skilled people. In plants that came to make both low- and high-density chips, the accounting system allocated overhead charges, not on the basis of which products in fact used the overhead skills, but according to the direct labor input. Low-density chips thus appeared to be more expensive to make. In fact, the computation carried the hidden implication that the low-density chips subsidized the high-density chips. Market prices, however, followed actual cost, not computed cost. Hence many U.S. manufacturers who made both high- and low-density chip products, upon finding that the calculated costs of low-density chips was higher than the costs incurred by their competitors, concluded that their manufacturing cost could not compete with the market price of the low-density "commodity" chips. During the late 1970s and 1980s many large semiconductor manufacturers with mixed lines surrendered what they thought were unprofitable lines to foreign companies. That process eventually led to a serious loss of U.S. industrial capability.

The inventors of cost accounting methods knew that the methods could be applied only to similar operations in single-activity companies. It is interesting to follow how cost accounting methods became part of modern society in spite of the flaw in the principles underlying them.

Costs were then, and still are, considered in two categories, direct and indirect. Direct costs are the costs of raw material and direct ("touch") labor; indirect costs are all other costs. Indirect costs were once a small fraction of direct costs. For instance, in the Lyman Mills Corporation in the 1850s, the ratio of indirect cost to total cost at a plant was 10 percent, and for the whole corporation it was 23 percent, where indirect cost included all nondirect labor, plant, and equipment acquired in the reporting period, at purchase cost, and sales discounts. In the automated industry of today, direct labor can be 5 percent or less of the total cost. This entirely undermines the validity of cost-allocation procedures, which were developed for a very different industrial environment (see Figure 9.1).

The methods described above, which were developed for single-activity companies, were inadequate for the multiactivity corporations which developed during the first decades of the twentieth century, such as DuPont and General Motors. As DuPont developed, it expanded into diversified divisions, and corporate DuPont was faced with making choices of capital allocation among the different divisions. In order to choose the better candidates for use of capital, between unrelated businesses, they invented the ROI measure. This measure was used only by top corporate management, but not within operating divisions. As companies increased in size and diversity of operations and products, new measures were needed to enable rational choices between disparate opportunities. Managers of operating units were made responsible for profitability and capital allocation, and the ROI measure became commonly used as an internal measure *within* these operating units. Its use gradually trickled down to all levels of management who used it to justify investment decisions to themselves and their superiors. By 1925, all the major characteristics of today's management accounting systems were in place.

In the early days of
classical mass production

In agile production

FIGURE 9.1 The Proportion of Direct to Indirect Labor Costs

The system of allocating costs based on the direct labor input had an interesting corollary. Material was assumed to "absorb" cost, as it went through the production process, in proportion to the direct labor time spent on dealing with it. Material, semifinished or finished, was considered an asset, for it was implicitly assumed that what was not sold today would be sold tomorrow. That assumption may have been reasonable when products were long-lived and when producers governed markets. It certainly is wrong for the agile world, where product life is short, products are individually configured for customers, and markets are governed by customers, not producers.

At the time these internal performance measures were developed, they were a separate system from the external financial reporting system. In subsequent decades, auditors and regulators, aware of their legal responsibilities in preparing financial reports, needed objective, verifiable, and unambiguous numbers. When measuring cost of goods sold and the value of inventory, they used the verifiable numbers in the firm's books. In addition, the auditors based the income statement and the balance sheet, which defined a company's worth, on the identical transactions and events used to manage the company internally. These transactions and events were measured and recorded, and the documents were traceable and verifiable. No estimates, which would need justification and argument, were required of the auditor by any authority or creditor. This led to the reverse practice—of internal management decisions being based on the numbers used for external reports! The fact that internal management decisions were based on distorted inventory costing procedures or cross-subsidized product costs was overlooked. In companies with few products and dedicated product lines, the approximations were not significant; in agile companies, they are serious.

Although many people saw the defect in cost allocation as it developed over the years, and many different cost accounting methods have been suggested to deal with it, the method used with the GAAP is to allocate all indirect costs proportionally to direct costs, without analyzing the real impact of these numbers. For that reason, the method, although faulty, became widely used, both for financial reporting to investors and authorities outside a company and for internal management decisions.

When financial systems became computerized in the 1960s, the systems that had been formed a half century earlier were embedded in computers. Today's systems deal with millions of numbers and give the appearance of accuracy, but the systems are fundamentally flawed. The flaws are two:

- Measurements useful for single-activity companies with long-lived products made on dedicated production lines are still being used today, when product mixes change continuously, when production resources are shared by many products, and when a product's window of opportunity in the market is short
- The measures used to report a company's performance to creditors, owners, and regulators are used to prioritize operating decisions internally, leading to erroneous management procedures discussed later in the chapter.

Modern managers run a company "by the numbers." But the numbers are fatally flawed! The adverse effects of the arithmetic error in conventional cost accounting will become more serious as competition becomes more agile. Conventional GAAP cost accounting is not suitable for management of an agile organization. What will take its place is as yet unclear.

Activity-Based Costing (ABC)

In traditional cost accounting systems, the only costs attributed directly to a product are direct labor and materials. All other costs are allocated based on one approach or another, usually in proportion to the direct labor content of the product. As we have seen, the indirect or overhead costs, which once were less than the direct costs, are today the overwhelmingly major part, as much as 95 percent or higher, of the total labor cost. *Activity-based costing (ABC),* attributed to Kaplan and Johnson, categorizes all costs of all kinds in terms of activities and then relates each activity to the product or project to which it contributes. Costs are counted for a product or a project only to the extent that the activity in fact contributes to it (Lewis 1993).

Some companies have adopted ABC with success. The Harley-Davidson Motor Company faced bankruptcy in 1981 but then fought back with many wide-ranging changes. As the company became more customer-focused, using techniques of just-in-time, statistical process control, and employee empowerment, it became clear that the conventional accounting system was a cause of many management problems. The introduction of ABC was a key to the successful turnaround Harley-Davidson has made (NCMS newsletter Dec. 1993).

ABC has enthusiastic supporters and also vigorous critics. In support of ABC, it seems more sensible to use what appears to be accurate data rather than to allocate overhead arbitrarily. On the other hand, much work and expense are involved in setting up the systems needed to collect the data, and even then the data are often insufficiently accurate for informed decision making. Another, more subtle but very important problem with ABC is that even ABC does not take into account the availability of internal company resources to carry out a project or to make a product. In the classical world of mass production and dedicated production lines, there was never a conflict over use of shared resources, so the question never occurred; in the world of agility, this is a necessary consideration. It is hence unlikely that ABC will be the method universally suitable for agility.

Time-Based Costing (TBC)

Time-based costing (TBC) is a system that does take into account the ability of an organization to perform a task. It is currently at an early stage of development, but since it is based on a mathematical understanding of a system, it is potentially a powerful method for estimating costs and for management decision making.

TBC makes use of a little-realized fact of systems theory, that if the demand for the use of any one resource exceeds the available capacity, the whole system behavior changes. This is analogous to driving a car: Under usual road conditions, we turn the steering wheel in the direction that we wish to go. However, on ice, when there is no friction under the tires, the car goes into a skid and must be steered in the direction the car is moving, not in the direction the driver chooses. This is counterintuitive. It is an example of a change in a system parameter creating an entirely new set of rules by which to operate the system. Similarly, if in a work system one resource becomes overloaded, the rules by which the system must be managed change fundamentally. This is the message of the well-known book *The Goal* (Goldratt 1984), although the message many readers of that book remember is that one must locate bottlenecks in order to overcome them. That is true, of course, but emphasizing the overcoming of bottlenecks obscures the more important message—that an organization with a limitation on internal capacity must be controlled by rules that are different from those in an organization with no internally constraining process. Management of a company with a constraint (alternatively named a *gating*, or *controlling, process*) is as yet understood by only a small group of managers, but those who do understand it do remarkably well; those who do not understand it find themselves trying to manage a company skidding out of control, but without sound and suitable management principles for such a situation.

The Fully Utilized Balanced Line Fallacy

The attachment of cost to material based on the time material spends in a process leads to a goal set by cost accountants, that each resource in an organization or a factory, be it machine or department, be utilized 100 percent of the time, all the time. It seems intuitively correct that if the line were designed so that the capacities of each station were balanced, each station would be utilized for an equal amount of time. In fact, that is not possible, because small statistical effects are enormously magnified in such a line. For example, imagine a customer order processing system, where at the first station we see a group of people (or a computer system) taking orders, then a station processing the payments, then a station scheduling the orders, then a packing station, and so on. Even if the capacities of each station were exactly matched, inevitably there would be a statistical variation of capacity with time at each station. Different orders require different amounts of time to process, machines and computers break down or malfunction temporarily, the pace at which people work changes, and so on.

A well-known game illustrates this. Have ten people sit in a row, each holding a dice. Their job is to pass something (a match, say) from one person to another at a preset pace, for instance once every 30 seconds. A player may hold no more than one match at a time. Each person is given one match to start with, and new matches are supplied at the beginning of the line. However, before passing a match, each person rolls a dice. If the number 6 shows, the person does not pass the match along. The number 6 will come up one-sixth (16.7 percent) of the time. You can expect that if a match is passed into the line every half minute, after 30 minutes the number of matches passed out of the line would be $60 \times \frac{5}{6}$, which is 50. Try it and see.

We can calculate the outcome of this game. The average utilization of each station is $\frac{5}{6} = 83.3$ percent. The maximum number of units of work a perfectly operating station could process in 50 minutes is 100; so this station will process on the average 83 units in 50 minutes.

Workstations will have delays and breakdowns at unrelated times. When a workstation is down or delayed, it will starve the subsequent station, which is capable of working but will not have material fed into it and hence will not be able to produce. The time lost is never recovered, because the starved station will not be able to produce at a capacity exceeding 100 percent when it resumes working. The temporarily starved station will have lost some production, which will never be recovered. As a result, the capacity of the whole process will be reduced and will be lower than 83.3 percent. What will be the capacity of the system of ten stations? To compute that precisely is exceptionally difficult, but we can find the lowest possible value of the capacity, which is called a *lower bound*. The lower bound is the time during which all the stations will definitely be working, and the line will surely be producing. For a ten-station line, with each station working at 83.3 percent capacity, the lower bound is $0.833 \times 0.833 \times 0.833 \ldots$ (ten times), in other words, 0.833 to the tenth power, or 0.833^{10}, which is 0.16.

So, if in a 40-hour week any one station is functioning for $\frac{5}{6}$ of the time (or 33.3 hours), the whole line will be productive for some value of time between 0.16×40 (6.4 hours) and 33.3 hours (the result is in fact about 20 hours for the data used here). This explains an enormous frustration of managers, that a work system as a whole is much less efficient than any one process in the system.

It is interesting to note that Henry Ford, the entrepreneur of mass production, knew this well. At the River Rouge plant, a classical mass-production plant, each process was arranged so that it operated at less than 100 percent of its individual capacity, in order that the flow in the total process would not be impeded. For Henry Ford, the timing of the individual flows, so that the entire process was coordinated, was more important than the efficiency of any single activity. This is a far cry from today's requirement often applied blindly by cost accountants—that each process be 100 percent utilized.

As Henry Ford knew, statistical variation was unavoidable, even when many identical copies of a single product were produced. When a constantly changing mix of products and services is being produced, variation will be even more prevalent.

Both conventional cost accounting by the GAAP and ABC seek to allocate costs to material as it goes through the work process and to monitor the efficiency of the conversion process by monitoring costs at points along the process. The approach of TBC is fundamentally different from both of these methods and *does no cost allocation at all.* In this, it is similar to the method of *economic value add (EVA).* (Tully 1993). This derives from the observation that there is no practical significance in differentiating direct from indirect labor cost. In most companies today, as production loads vary, the only variable cost is the raw material for the products produced. Neither direct labor nor indirect labor is hired and fired as production varies. This is even more true in the world of agility, where workers are regarded as valuable assets. Operating expense is constant over the time period for which the product mix decision is made, and it does not change with product mix. It is therefore unnecessary to measure money values as if they were attached to products within the production process. Whatever the product mix, operating expense (which excludes truly variable costs) will be constant.

Smart companies are beginning to notice the validity of this observation. In its September 20, 1993, issue, *Fortune* magazine reported that abandoning old-style cost measures and using EVA computations for performance measurement and bonus payments had given large bottom-line returns at Coca Cola, AT&T, Quaker Oats, Briggs & Stratton, CSX, and other well-regarded corporations (Tully 1993).

TBC goes a step further than EVA and takes note of the fact, mentioned above, that a balanced line capacity is not feasible. Systems that are capacitized "exactly" for the work needed are therefore in fact capacity-controlled. The inevitable conclusion is that every practical system will at any point in time have one resource utilized more than all the others. This most-utilized resource is potentially a gate. As will be shown later, if the flow required through the gate exceeds the capacity of the gate, management prioritization decisions need to be quite different from what they would be if there were no gate.

Many conclusions follow from these two observations. Most of them seem surprising because they are contrary to the management practices which have evolved around the GAAP costing method.

When TBC is used on a system, where the system may be a corporation, a division, a plant, a production line, or a project set up as a virtual corporation, the only parameters that are needed to measure the conversion efficiency of that system are:

- The rate of income generated by the system from actual sales less the true variable cost (TVC) associated with each sale. This is the throughput (T), in dollars per unit of time
- The constant operating expense (OE) needed to keep the system working, which includes direct labor, manufacturing overhead, selling and administrative expenses (all expenses other than the truly variable expenses), in dollars per unit of time
- The one-time expenses incurred to develop a product or to improve the system, the investment (I)

As we see, when used for TBC, these terms have different meanings from what is usual in other cost accounting methods.

COST ACCOUNTING EXAMPLE

This is an example of a truly profitable project that would have been rejected using conventional cost allocation methods. The company considered whether to make and sell a product, given the following data.

Market research concluded that the product should have a list price of $240 per unit and that annual sales would be 150,000 units. A decision was needed on whether to go ahead with the project. No internal resource of the company would be fully utilized to do the work, and the internal company system would therefore not be capacity-constrained.

General financial guidelines from the holding company were that the minimum required gross margin be 50 percent.

The standard manufacturing cost structure for the company was:

Material and outside processing = 65%
Labor   7%
Overhead for manufacturing   28%

Every dollar spent on direct labor is thought to incur four dollars of overhead.

Projected one-time expenses for the project were:

Research and development = $1,000,000
Tooling and fixtures $2,000,000

Projected nonmanufacturing additional annual expenses were:

Marketing and product introduction   = $1,000,000
Sales (6 regional sales managers plus support) $1,000,000

Annual manufacturing operating expense for the project were predicted to be:

30 direct labor at $25,000 each = $750,000
6 indirect labor, made up as follows:

  2 manufacturing engineers = $125,000
  2 technicians $75,000
  2 material handlers $50,000

Indirect material, freight and other cost of goods sold = $1,500,000

Total = $2,500,000

Net sales price to the company = $180 per unit

Unit costs were predicted to be:

Material = $100 per unit
Labor $3 per unit
Overhead $12 per unit (using the factor of 28/7 = 4, from above)

(continued)

On the basis of the above data, the anticipated gross margin is calculated.

Total manufacturing costs = $115 per unit
Gross margin (sales price − manufacturing costs)/sales price = (180 − 115)/180
= 36%

Based on conventional cost accounting, the project is rejected. The usual response of a company may include "right sizing" to reduce staff or a plan to move to a region with cheaper direct labor. Yet that conclusion is erroneous. This is a very profitable product as is shown by TBC.

TBC dealt with the costs in the following way:

Sales income = 150,000 × $180 = $27,000,000
Truly variable material cost = 150,000 × $100 = $15,000,000
T = ($27,000,000 − $15,000,000) = $12,000,000
OE = ($2,500,000 + $1,000,000 + $1,000,000) = $4,500,000
Net profit = ($12,000,000 − $4,500,000) = $7,500,000
Return on sales = 7.5/27 = 27.8%
Investment = ($1,000,000 + $2,000,000) = $3,000,000
ROI = $7,500,000/$3,000,000 = 250%
Time to repay the investment = $3,000,000 × 12/$7,500,000
= 4.8 months

We see that this project would make a profit of $7.5 million per year and repay the investment in 4.8 months, which is in fact very worthwhile.

We follow with a sensitivity analysis, to determine whether the project would be profitable even if the assumptions were optimistic and the numbers less successful than predicted.

Assume that sales turn out to be half of what the optimistic project proposers predicted, but all the staffing remained the same:

Sales income = 75,000 × $180 = $13,500,000
Truly variable cost = 75,000 × $100 = $7,500,000
T = ($13,500,000 − $7,500,000) = $6,000,000, as before
OE = ($2,500,000 + $1,000,000 + $1,000,000) = $4,500,000, as before
Net profit = ($6,000,000 − $4,500,000) = $1,500,000
Return on sales = 1.5/27 = 5.6%
Investment = ($1,000,000 + $2,000,000) = $3,000,000, as before
ROI = 1.5/3 = 50%
Time to repay the investment = $3,000,000 × 12/$1,500,000
= 24 months

The project still makes money.

(continued)

Now assume that the original project plan predicted sales correctly but that the annual expenses were double those predicted.

The only change in the original numbers is operating expense (OE), which will now be $9,000,000 instead of $4,500,000.

Net profit now is ($12,000,000 − $9,000,000) = $3,000,000
Return on sales = $3,000,000/$27,000,000 = 11.1%
ROI = $3,000,000/$3,000,000 = 100%
Time to repay the investment = 3,000,000 × 12/$3,000,000 = 12 months

The project is still profitable.

Acknowledgment is made to Technology Systems Corporation, Bethlehem, Pennsylvania, for use of this example.

The cost accounting example, from a successful manufacturing company, shows that the tradition of costing that developed for single-product-family, single activity organizations and which is now applied to multiactivity and multiproduct organizations leads to incorrect decisions. This is just as predicted by the inventors of the methods, who understood the limitations a hundred years ago. Correct management decisions can be obtained by not even trying to locate costs within the system but by measuring money flows into and out of the operation, at its boundaries, as done by TBC. Using allocation and average formulas of cost divisions within the system often gives wrong answers. Prudence would lead to the conclusion that, because the regular cost accounting method is found to lead to wrong decisions in one project, it should be considered an unreliable basis for management decisions in all projects. It *is* unreliable, and it should not be used for management decisions in agile enterprises. It can be used for external financial reports to investors and to the Securities and Exchange Commission (SEC) and other authorities who may require its use, but as an aid to management decisions it is unreliable and potentially hazardous.

We come to the second principle of TBC, and that is the influence of a gate, or flow control point, on system behavior. Consider the work system shown in Figure 9.2. Material flows from one station to another and is processed at each station. As explained above, it is not feasible to have each station working at 100 percent capacity all the time.

Station	A	B	C	D	E	F	G
Capacity (units per hour)	20	15	25	8	12	20	20

FIGURE 9.2 A Flow Process with Seven Stations.

Figure 9.2 shows the capacity of each station as the work flows from station A to station G along a process line. The operating expense for this line is $10,000 per week. The cost of raw material is $50 per product unit, the line works for 40 hours per week, and the sales price of a unit of product is $100. The market for the product is larger than the quantity that can be made, so the limitation is production capacity.

Q. What is the maximum capacity of the whole line?
A. It is the capacity of the slowest process in the line, station D with a capacity of eight units per hour.

Q. If one wanted to increase the flow of work in the line, at which stations should the effort be made?
A. To increase the rate of work through the entire process, only the slowest station need be speeded up, that is, station D in Figure 9.2.

Q. If the line worked at its maximum capacity, what would the utilizations of the various stations be?
A. The utilizations would be as shown in Figure 9.3.

Q. For the process line in Figure 9.2, what is the maximum throughput and the maximum net profit?

Station	A	B	C	D	E	F	G
Utilization	$8/20$	$8/15$	$8/25$	$8/8$	$8/12$	$8/20$	$8/20$
	40%	53%	32%	100%	67%	40%	40%

FIGURE 9.3 Utilizations of the Work Processes.

A. Maximum throughput is the income from sales less the truly variable cost. In this example the maximum possible throughput is:

8 units/hour × 40 hours/week × ($100 − $50) = 8 × 40 × 50 = $16,000 per week.

Net Profit = Throughput − Operating Expense = $16,000 − $10,000 = $6,000 per week.

Q. What will be the result of a management decree to have every station work at 100 percent utilization?
A. The result will be to accumulate excess, undigestible inventory or work in process at various locations in the line, leading to real waste.

Q. What is the impact on the whole system if the gating resource is less than 100 percent utilized?
A. The impact is to lose production of the entire process. Each hour that the gating station is not working is an hour lost to the whole line.

Q. What is the impact on the whole system if a nongating station loses some work time?
A. Provided the utilization is such that it has time to catch up with the work, there is no impact at all.

Q. What is the impact on the system if the gating station is starved and waits for material?
A. The time that the gating station waits for material is productive time lost to the whole system.

Q. What is the real financial cost if material along the line is spoiled?
A. This depends on where the spoilage happens. If the material is spoiled before the gate, then the stations preceding the gate will have time to replace the material before it is needed at the gate; the cost will be the replacement cost of the material only. The time to reprocess the

material will lead to no real cost. If the material is in the gate station, or beyond it, the loss of the spoiled material is not only a loss of material but a loss of time to the entire system. If material at or beyond the gate is spoiled, the time required to replace it is equivalent to a loss of time for the whole system. This leads to an understanding of the value of inventory or work in process in a gated system. Before the gate, inventory has a low value, equal to the replacement cost of the material. Inside the gate and beyond it, the material has a high value, equal to the throughput of the whole system. Material in the system will have one of only two values, low before the gate and high everywhere in and beyond the gate. This is a markedly different result than for conventional cost accounting. It runs directly counter to the commonly accepted but erroneous concept that inventory accumulates value as it passes through a work process.

The implications of the observations above are many, and pervasive. For instance, if a company is producing without having any internal gating station, management must work hard both to increase markets and to reduce expenses. The company is then run in "normal" mode. If there is a gating station, the company has to decide which projects or products are to be preferred, since there is not enough capacity to produce the entire market demand of every product. Traditional cost accounting bases the choice of preferred product or project on gross margin, but using gross margin for this decision is erroneous. The parameter for prioritizing the choice is the throughput dollars produced per unit time of constrained resource used by the product or project. The company is then run in "skid" mode. This simple rule, understood by only a few managers who had previously prioritized products by gross margin, has yielded millions of dollars in real profit to their companies.

TBC is in an initial stage and is used by few companies. It has theoretical appeal, but it is as yet unclear that it will be the method of choice for the management of agile organizations. What is clear, however, is that the system of management accounting used with success for generations of mass production needs to be completely rethought for agile commerce.

INTERNAL BARRIERS

Performance Measurement Systems

People behave according to how they are measured and rewarded. The tradition of a hundred years of mass production has been to divide and subdivide each job into minutest detail, to control each job hierarchically, to give each worker precise instructions, and not to allow any worker to question the details.

In most companies, the result of this practice is to have different measures for different functions. Consider a manufacturing company. The product design group may be measured by quantity of products designed per year; the manufacturing group by percent-on-time delivery; the quality assurance group by warranty claims; the financial group by return on assets; the sales group by total sales recorded (which may exclude discounts). This list is an invitation to conflict. Product design is motivated not to waste a single day, even to save cost or time in manufacturing. Manufacturing is motivated not to waste a single day, even to improve quality. The financial group is motivated not to approve the purchase of equipment that would improve the measured performance of the manufacturing or quality assurance groups. The sales group is motivated to report sales, even if there are many cancellations, discounts, or returns later.

Teams are important components of an agile organization. However, what is called a team in a company is often not a team at all. A *team* is a group in which one player may excel but in which loss or victory is shared by all the members. People in most organizations owe their loyalty to the person who signs off on the annual evaluation and who influences hiring and firing decisions. This is usually the department manager, but it may be some other authority, possibly the union leader. As noted above, performance measurement systems can force departments into conflict. The department representative on the "team" may find herself or himself not in a proactive position of wanting to solve the problem at hand for the sake of the whole company but in the defensive position of ensuring that any decisions or recommendations do not adversely affect her or his department. Teams, which are formed to eliminate dysfunctional organization, often perpetuate it. Eliminating adversarial relationships and the ensuing dysfunctional organization requires visionary leadership which ensures that a common goal is perceived by all the people in the extended organization, including customers and suppliers. Federal Express gave a good example of a well-communicated, measurable goal with personal meaning for every worker and customer: "We will deliver the package by 10:30 next morning." However, stating a well-understood common goal is not enough for the success of a team. The goal is not achieved unless traditional performance measures are adapted.

In the earlier era of long-lived products and dedicated production lines, in a producer-push system, fragmenting performance measures did indeed lead to efficiency. Each component, each player, developed a deeper, better-honed specialty. The individual had no need to know anything about anyone else's work or about the whole organization. Each worker was a pawn, moved by a manager. Today's world of agile competition requires exactly the opposite performance measure. This change has occurred dramatically and almost overnight. Today's worker needs to see a companywide goal and to be measured relative to it. It is no exaggeration to say that companies, workers, and trade unions who do not find a way to change entrenched performance measurement systems will eventually find themselves on the sidelines.

Nondefinition of Core Competency Knowledge

The approach of most organizations to knowledge derives from the days of the product-centered, producer-push system. It is "everything is secret unless decided otherwise." In the constantly changing world of agile competition and dynamically self-reconfiguring virtual organizations, one has to decide in detail which core competency knowledge can be shared—and with whom. Deciding that all knowledge is to be kept secret makes one an undesirable partner and will lead to the organization being shut out of joint ventures. A secretive organization will not even be given the chance to turn down business opportunities. On the other hand, not *all* the knowledge a company has can be made available to everyone. On balance, agile companies share much more data and knowledge than did mass-production companies. The Ross Operating

Valve Company, IBM's series of agreements with companies including previous competitors, Bausch and Lomb's new markets, Federated Department Stores, the Williams companies, and many others attest to the growing importance of rethinking what one's core competencies are, and when to share and when to protect them.

Budgeting Procedures

In the days of mass production, producers would make a production plan based on a sales forecast. The plan would allow some leeway for producing more or less quantity, but the products to be made and sold were defined, and no allowance was made in the budget for unanticipated products and projects. The budget was prepared to suit the annual plan, and the plan was fixed for the year. Once the budget was approved, changing it was intentionally made difficult, since the budget was the means by which hierarchic control was maintained. Budgeting today has become more responsive, empowering managers at a level lower than before to make changes, in order to enable more rapid reaction to opportunities. However, a lengthy budgeting cycle causes difficulties. As time goes by, agile organizations find ways to deal with budgets on several time scales. An annual budget is a declaration of intentions, not necessarily a plan of action. A time horizon of a few months can be used for updated budget plans, and then actual decisions on resources allocated are made with very short notice. CNN outdid other news organizations during the Gulf War in 1991 largely because of the authority given lower-level managers to authorize hundreds of thousands of dollars for the deployment of technical and other resources without waiting for higher-level management permission. A company using an annual budget cycle with strict control would struggle to deploy an agile response.

Dysfunctional Organization and Information Systems

Today, information systems are central to many organizations. The development of such systems during the past 30 years has been fragmented for two major reasons. The first reason is external to the organization. Rather than agreeing on standards, suppliers of information systems software and hardware have tried to outdo one another with technically incompatible systems. The other reason is internal. Knowledge is power, leading to serious conflict over who decides what data is needed, who stores it, who analyzes it, who updates it, and who distributes it. These discussions are often accompanied by detailed reasons from the group wanting to retain power, as to why the proposed retaining of their power locally is for the good of the whole organization. The thought pattern that assumes that information is controlled and supplied by an information department is a producer-push mind-set deriving from the days of producer-push mass production, when computers were relatively expensive and information sparse. In the world of agility, information is plentiful and distributed and is made available by user pull.

This poses some interesting technical challenges that are being dealt with in development projects. If one does not know where in a network information is to be found, "mole" or "burrowing" programs can search throughout the network and find the information. Also, problems can occur when copies of the same nominal data are held in more than one place or when different data entries refer to the same item but at different times. Intelligent interface programs will deal with these problems. One solution is to have only one keeper of the data. This becomes impractical as databases spread out to many locations in networks. In the agile world, users of data develop tools and expertise needed to evaluate the reliability of the data.

All executives who have dealt with problems of coordinating activities within and between businesses emphasize the difficulties in coordinating information systems and in controlling the quality of the data. There are many examples of ad hoc, poor solutions for this problem. For instance, in industries where there are a few strong assembly and marketing corporations, as in the automobile industry, it is common for each customer to insist that its supplier companies use the same information systems it does. As a result, some supplier companies keep data on their products on as many as 30 different systems, to satisfy each customer. Obviously, this creates a significant overhead in entering data and maintaining the quality of that data on all the systems. Efforts are being made in various industries to establish common standards so that one information system can be used all through the supplier chain, but progress in these matters requires many years of work and coordination.

Betrayal of Trust

In the product-centered world, competitive advantage was gained by the delivery speed, quality and price of the product. That world was driven by the producer. The customer could decide to buy the product or not, but was not part of the specify-design-build-deliver-service process. In that world, trust was less significant than it is in the agile world. If a supplier had a good product at a good price, the customer bought it. Similarly, in the "food chain" of industrial products, price for the product was the determining factor in customer-supplier relationships.

In the world of virtual organizations and agile competition, product and service offerings are short-lived. They are highly customized and take advantage of fleeting opportunities in the face of worldwide competition. Since there are no long-lived products, no one has a long production run of unchanged components. A supplier provides capability and process, from which a continuously varying mix of product emanates. Under these circumstances, a supplier gains reputation not because a particular product is competitive but because of the capability of its processes and people. Entrepreneurial companies become active everywhere in the world. A company that betrays the trust of its suppliers or customers will not be able to rely on a superior product to gain business and will eventually find itself out of the mainstream.

Not Sharing Information

Not sharing information implies that you have all the information you need. In today's fast-moving world this is not possible. The mass-production world was an information-sparse world. One could make and market products and services without large amounts of information. The market was defined by a single "average" abstract customer, and the products or services provided were few. Agile competition is information-rich. To compete and to make the right business decisions in the time available require a large quantity of information. No organization can make available from its own resources all the required data in a sufficiently short time. An organization will then have to buy, share, or barter information. Sharing is a two-way situation. An organization not sharing information condemns itself to a serious disadvantage in agile competition.

Lack of Knowledge of Others

A key strategy for dealing with the challenge of agile competition is to be part of virtual organizations. In order to find profit-making opportunities or to locate capabilities needed for a project, it is necessary to have quick access to data on the capabilities of other organizations. Today this information is often lacking. Among the reasons for this lack is insufficient awareness of the necessity to know about the capabilities of other companies. Wanting to know about the capabilities of other organizations requires a changed mind-set for many people and is often a barrier to increased agility.

EXTERNAL BARRIERS

Legal System Assumes a Mass-Production Environment

The world of mass production was producer-push, with the individual customer not part of the process that decided what products to make or how to configure or market them. The producer and the customer were adversaries, and the parameter of interaction was price. The

PRODUCTION —▶ PRODUCT —▶ MARKETING —▶ CUSTOMER
RESOURCES

In mass production the production resources define the product which leads to a marketing plan to reach the customer.

SOLUTION ◀— RESOURCES ◀— TEAM ◀— CUSTOMER

In agile competition the customer works with a team which pulls in resources from a virtual organization to create the customized solution.

FIGURE 9.4   From Production Focus to Customer Enrichment Focus

producer wanted to make more money and give less product, and the customer wanted just the opposite. This led to an adversarial situation that is reflected in countless laws and regulations.

Agile competition and the rise of virtual corporations create dilemmas for the legal system. Agile competitors are often part of a virtual organization that interacts closely with the customer, as indicated in Figure 9.4. Since the customer is part of the process which creates a personalized product or service, the traditional ideas about the customer-supplier relationship—the independence of the customer from the supplier, indeed, the adversarial stance—undergo gradual change.

Some examples of legal interpretations and laws, and their implications for manufacturing enterprises, as put together in the 1991 Iacocca Institute study by a group of industry executives in the United States are:

The Definition of Antitrust Activity

Antitrust provisions in the United States are stricter than in most other countries. They were enacted at a time when the size of the economy of the United States was as much as 50 percent of the total world economy and when industrial structure was synonymous with mass production and vertical integration. Those times have gone, and the assumptions and precepts of antitrust are being rethought.

Product Liability Laws and Practices

As is well known, product liability laws and practices can place so large a burden of risk on companies as to inhibit development or marketing of new products, even if those products would be of benefit. Price for product being the only factor in relationships has created a climate in which the customer is often considered the victim and the producer the perpetrator. This is especially true in the United States, where the legal system, in its desire to allow access to all, permits legal damages much greater than those of other countries. Liability insurance costs in the United States are 15 times greater than in Japan and 20 times greater than in Europe, and the General Accounting Office in Washington reports that more than half the jury awards in liability cases go to lawyers. Not only are liability insurance costs in the United States greater than elsewhere, but manufacturers in the United States face 50 different sets of rules and guidelines for these issues (NCMS Focus, Dec. 1993). These burdens have caused the U.S. market to be shut out of various products and processes available elsewhere. A better balance needs to be established so that consumer protection will be reasonable and yet not inhibit the development and marketing of useful new product solutions.

Tax Laws

Tax laws usually do not recognize that product offerings change rapidly and that products are constantly upgraded. As a result, slow amortization and other provisions often inhibit investment in productive facilities.

Tax laws in many countries regard research and development from the perspective of mass production, as an investment made to produce a product, similar conceptually to the investment made in a dedicated production process. In the age of agility, research and development are part of the general overhead needed to maintain the overall capability of a company.

Trade Agreements and Enterprise Zone Definitions

Trade agreements and enterprise zone definitions usually implicitly assume the structure and concepts of mass production, rather than the developing system of agile competition and virtual, worldwide organizations. Examples of mismatches between legal concepts and the reality of agile competition are the reference to the percentage of product added in a national territory, without valuing the information content of the product, and the assumption that service and product are quite separate.

Until the legal system understands the new competitive environment and resolves the issues mentioned above, and other issues, it will be an obstacle to agility.

Artificial Dichotomy of Product and Service

Mass-production concepts distinguish between products and services. With agile products, service, information, and physical product are inseparable parts of the goods which are passed to the customer. The dichotomy between product and service, valid for the period of producer-driven product-centered mass production, is today a barrier to increased agility.

Many individuals regard products as different from service and product-centered work as different from service-centered work. These perceptions are reflected in laws and regulations that govern the relationships between trading partners, companies, and workers. Tax laws in many countries and states, international trade agreements, and union regulations enforce different regimes for products and services. As a result, providers of both distort what they provide, and packaging and distribution methods are designed to take advantage of regulations. All over the world, many tax lawyers and other professionals expend considerable efforts on the intricacies of these laws. The separation of products, services, and information, and the work related to them, is fast becoming artificial.

Many people have labored long days to negotiate international trade agreements that deal with products and services and related taxes. The reality of the marketplace is negating the assumption they made when doing so—that a product is different and distinguishable from a service.

Static, Rigid, Requirements of Public Bodies

The characteristics of the mass-production system—product- and price-oriented, producer-push, with the consumer a passive component—are reflected in the approach of public entities toward the purchasing cycle. Large sums of public money are involved when cities, states, armies, hospitals, and similar bodies negotiate purchases. In the effort to ensure legality in the purchasing process, detailed instructions are enforced for the process of defining requirements, going to tender, and obtaining the items. This process, enforced by law, often takes several years, a time so long that it ensures that the purchased goods will not be the most up to date available. Also, the process does not permit easy interaction between buyer and seller, nor does it permit the purchasing group to influence the product design and manufacturing process. These circumstances inhibit companies from moving more quickly to agility for international competition, since a large home market insists on old-style mass-production methods.

In the United States, many companies that supply both Department of Defense and commercial channels find themselves running a two-track business—a modern track for the commercial business and an old-style, inefficient track for the defense establishment.

Lack of Access to Information

Access to information is key to being a player in agile competition. Enormous quantities of untapped information exist in many countries around the globe. Some aspects of information are kept confidential, by law or agreement between individuals and organizations, but even without confidential data, much more information could be put to good use. Many individuals and organizations do not realize the importance of the available information and do not install systems to obtain the information and to use it. This is a barrier to increased agility. In the competition to become more agile, those who perceive the opportunity to move beyond selling predefined product—to taking advantage of the business opportunities in accessing, using, and selling services for information—do well.

Adversarial Mind-set

The tendency toward adversarial relationships has been much strengthened by a century of product-centered, producer-controlled relationships. When the only parameter of competition is price for product, relationships are one-dimensional. Understanding how to compete is simple: offer more product for less price. This one-dimensional relationship can amplify adversarial trends. Agile competition is multidimensional, involving not only product, but service, long-lived relationships with customers, and dynamic multiventuring between suppliers. The adversarial mind-set, common in the mass-production economy, is a barrier to seeing profitable agile business opportunities.

NOTES ON CHAPTER 9

A company may find this chapter useful in the following ways:

- To evaluate which barriers are relevant for the company
- To evaluate which barriers can be dealt with by the company and to consider alternative ways to deal with them
- To analyze which barriers can be dealt with adequately by using internal resources, which should be dealt with by several companies acting together, which should be dealt with by industry associations, and which need to be dealt with by groups entirely outside the company, such as government, standards agencies, and other industry sectors
- For those barriers that can be dealt with entirely inside the company, or with the company as part of a project, to consider how to set about getting started

Some example projects for a course are:

- Criticize the list to determine whether there are other barriers
- Examine any one of the barriers in detail, using a literature search
- Evaluate the relative importance of barriers in different countries and analyze their effect on international competition

A government department may find the material useful in the following ways:

- To evaluate the public systems for which it is responsible and analyze whether those systems are barriers or aids to improving the competitive advantage of businesses in the region
- To consider which other local or national regions are competition and to analyze the relative effect on competitiveness of the barriers in those regions

10

Enabling Systems and Infrastructure

Embracing the principles of agility and virtual organization is a broad aim, one that needs to be broken into manageable pieces in order to be implemented. This in turn requires an analysis of the technical and work systems in a company and, possibly, a program of investment in systems and training. The change in behavior and structure needed for agility is enhanced and enabled by a number of systems in a suitable infrastructure. The systems, in themselves, do not automatically confer agility. The organization wanting to become more agile should see this chapter as a list from which to tailor its constantly changing plans of particular needs, using whichever systems are suited to its requirements.

Table 10.1 has been constructed from the perspective of a company or similar organization. It shows concisely the challenges faced, the characteristics of the agile organization which responds to those challenges, the enterprisewide elements or systems required for the organization to function, and the subsystems which support those elements. For the perspective of a federal or state government responsible for

TABLE 10.1 The Infrastructure for Agility

Competitive Challenges	Organization's Characteristics

- Continuous Change
- Enriching the Customer
- Environmental Responsibility

- Concurrency
- Continuous Education
- Customer-Pulled Organization
- Dynamic Multiventuring
- Employees Valued
- Empowered Individuals in Teams
- Entrepreneurial
- Environmentally Enhancing
- Extended-Enterprise Concurrency
- Flexible (Re)configuration
- Information Accessible and Used
- Knowledgeable, Adaptable Employees
- Lean
- Open Architecture
- Optimum First-Time Solutions
- Quality Over Product Life
- Rapid Response
- Technology Dependent
- Vision-Based Leadership

TABLE 10.1   The Infrastructure for Agility (continued)

Enterprise Elements	Enabling Subsystems

Enterprise Elements

- Customer Dialogue and Support
- Communication and Information
- Cooperation and Teaming
- Continuous Improvement and Change
- Enterprisewide Concurrency
- Environmental Enhancement
- Flexible and Rapidly Responding Operations
- People Support
- Supplier Support

Enabling Subsystems

- Continuous Education and Training
- Customer Interactive Systems
- Customized Marketing and Distribution Systems
- Distributed Information Systems
- Empowered Individuals in Teams
- Extended Enterprise Integration
- Financial Accounting Systems
- Global Multiventuring
- Groupware
- Intelligent Flexible Machines
- Lean Organization and Methods
- Legal System
- Modular Reconfigurable Process Components
- Organizational Inventory Listing
- Organizational Practices
- Performance Metrics and Evaluation
- Prequalified Partnering
- Product and Service Inventory
- Simulation and Modeling
- Total Quality Management
- Ubiquitous Communication
- Waste Management and Elimination

enabling or constructing the infrastructure systems needed to maintain competitive ability, see Goldman and Preiss (1991), Volume 2, Infrastructure. The text following the table gives a brief overview description of the relevant elements and subsystems so that no important component will be omitted when work systems are evaluated.

ENTERPRISE ELEMENTS

Agility requires a view of the entire extended enterprise, cutting across all functional units. As we have seen, in the world of mass production and mass marketing, the enterprise is hierarchically divided into separate, specialized functions such as operations, marketing, purchasing, and finance. Agility requires a new view of the elements that make up the enterprise, such that each element is seen as a support for work in teams. This chapter describes the categories that must be identified within an organization if it is to succeed in assimilating agility. This chapter is not an exhaustive text on each system; for that there are many books and much literature covering many aspects of the systems. This material identifies the enterprise elements and their subsystems so that the reader can both understand the big picture and put the details in perspective.

Customer Dialogue and Support

When thinking of customers and suppliers, most people tend to think of end-user customers. However, in the "food chain" of products, more than 50 percent of added value comes from suppliers to companies within the chain. Most customers in the value-added chain are not end users, but other companies. A basic tenet of agile competition is to be close to a customer, to have the customer comfortable dealing with the supplier and therefore seeing it as the preferred supplier. This is much the same relationship as one has with one's lawyer or doctor. Price is important, but so is value. Once a preferred supplier is found, from whom one does not simply buy a physical product but with whom one interacts to find solutions, then a common language, working method, and trust are set up, and the tried and trusted supplier is preferred.

This is yet another aspect of how agile competition is in a sense a wheel going full circle. Before mass production, a customer discussed the product with a craftsman, the relationship was personal, and the product was the result of the personal interaction. Generations of mass production led to product-centered relationships, and under those circumstances personal interactions became less important. Agile competition restores the centrality of personal interactions between supplier and customer. As the wheel went full circle, it went up a notch. Before mass production, a supplier could deal with few customers and made few products. Today, technology makes it possible to interact in a customized, personalized way with many customers and still make many varied products. In the world of mass production, interaction with customers was through products; in the world of agile competition, interaction once again becomes personal.

Maintaining a personalized interaction with customers implies expending a considerable organizational effort. Such an organization requires suitable software systems, so that whenever a customer representative calls or communicates by computer, whoever deals with her or him is updated on all the previous interactions and on the status of the relationship. Customer support also requires a systematic method of being proactively and continually in touch with each customer company or individual, in order to understand how their needs may have changed and what their plans are.

Communication and Information

Ubiquitous communication and information are the technical elements which are bringing into being the next industrial revolution. They are the central, critical, and fundamental part of the change to agility. This information is increasingly not only computer text data, but multimedia pictures and voice data as well. The technical ability exists today to have a database of photographs of customers, or employees, or products, and by clicking the mouse on the picture, to get data about the wanted item.

There are many examples of information systems, for example, the ones used by FedEx or UPS to register each transaction involving a package on a nationally distributed networked computer system, so that the package can be tracked immediately.

The impact of communication is seen, for instance, in the highly competitive and time-critical domain of retailing. Retail outlets, factories, and distribution centers are tied together through communication channels linking point-of-sale data directly to factory scheduling and inventory control systems, enabling just-in-time restocking of fast-selling items. For example, in Walmart's, a Spanish supplier of dresses constantly monitors the database showing sales of its dresses, and when one is sold, it makes a replacement that enters the store at which the previous dress was sold in less than 36 hours (Tenenbaum et al. 1991). The systems used by CUC International for direct-dial discount shopping, or the information activities of Federated Department Stores, or the worldwide network which enables workers at Ford and its suppliers to communicate efficiently are some of the many examples of such systems.

Singapore's TradeNet reduced the time needed for goods to clear the port from four days to ten minutes. It did this by creating a trade-facilitation data network that linked the information systems of shippers, freight forwarders, banks, and customs officials; statutory regulations were changed to allow electronic clearing (Tenenbaum et al. 1991).

Setting up a communication and information system to support agile business has many aspects requiring attention. For instance, information flowing across national boundaries must take account of the fragmentation of different national laws regarding privacy and legal responsibility. In general, the nations of northern Europe have stricter laws than those of southern Europe. Many other countries are in the process of setting up standards. The United States has an uncoordinated array of statutes and regional laws for specific industry sectors and data categories. Inconsistency in requirements in different countries creates traps for the unwary. For example, racial characteristics of personnel are required to be maintained in the United States to promote "affirmative action," but maintaining the same data in other countries is considered "racist" and hence illegal.

Communication is understandably considered a strategic activity by many countries, which retain state control of the communication companies and the tariffs. Some countries use this legal monopoly as a basis for income or for maintenance of pressures and group interests. Communication costs vary widely from country to country, but more and more countries have begun to realize that access to information is a vital capability which will yield returns far beyond the direct costs of installing and running it—just as roads are.

Manufacturing companies are increasingly aware of the requirement named Computer-Aided Logistics System (CALS). The name gives the incorrect impression that CALS is narrow in scope. In fact, it requires that all technical specifications, drawings, manuals, and other documents relating to products, from all levels of the supplier chain, be computerized. It is the result of a strategic aim of the U.S. Department of Defense and other U.S. government departments, as well as of European and other countries. CALS includes a large number of standards and requirements, including the Standard for Product Data Interchange (STEP), the developing international standard for the definition of electronic data that describe physical products. These standards have also been adopted by many companies who see the advantage in having all documents relating to products computer-based and who have decided to require their suppliers to use CALS standards. These standards and work procedures are being introduced with great persistence, in spite of all the difficulties which one might expect. They are gradually becoming significant at all levels of the product value chain.

Cooperation and Teaming

Cooperation and teaming factors facilitate or enable cooperation within and between companies and other organizations such as government, research institutes, and universities. These factors are explicitly named because proactive management effort is needed to attain the cooperation and teaming necessary to take advantage of agile opportunities. The mechanisms include organizational, social, and cultural factors that facilitate cooperation and possibly also technological tools such as computer networks which, if designed correctly, simplify the interaction between individuals and teams.

The absence of cooperation and teaming capability would indicate critical weakness in an organization. In the world of agility no organization has within it all the resources, available at short notice, to react to opportunities in a fast-changing world, and so the ability to cooperate is critical to the competitive advantage of an enterprise.

Continuous Improvement and Change

Agility does not originate in a vacuum. During the past few years, many companies have undertaken programs of total quality management (TQM), employee empowerment, just-in-time (JIT) logistics supply, reduced cycle time, and more. One cannot become more agile without these improvement efforts, and they are milestones in the journey to increasing agility. On the other hand, there are many companies which have seen little "bottom-line" return for the investments made in improvement and quality. This is partly because in too many companies, TQM, JIT, reengineering, or similar efforts were seen as ends in themselves, not as means to a more general goal. The vision of agility gives context and perspective to these continuous improvement and change programs.

Programs for continuous improvement and change often neither improve nor change a company. All too often, improvement is seen as a one-time effort, and change is seen a one-time move to some new stable state. To organize for continuous, never-ending improvement and continuous, unpredictable change requires that the structure of the organization and the people in the organization be capable of constant realignment. Improving the ability to deal with change is achieved if everyone in the organization feels that doing so is his or her personal responsibility. The challenge for the top level of leadership of the organization is to generate a constantly adapting structure and to have all employees perceive that constantly dealing with continuous improvement and change is their personal responsibility.

Enterprisewide Concurrency

The entrepreneurship of empowered teams is necessary to achieve success in agile competition, but uncoordinated entrepreneurship, where individuals and teams worry only about their own projects, leads to chaos. Together with organization for change, the creation of teams, and changes to performance measurement systems, the agile competitor institutes systems to coordinate actions and deployment of resources across the entire enterprise. This does not imply giving instructions to or controlling teams; rather, it is a way for teams to know about each other and about the resources available to them in the extended enterprise, and it also enables executive management to be aware of actions of teams across the company, so as to find ways to leverage those actions in even more opportunities of all kinds.

Rapid response to change means that work must be completed as rapidly as possible. This in turn requires organization so that people and functions work as much as possible in parallel. This includes all the relevant functions of a company, its suppliers and its customers, who together are termed the *extended enterprise.* Under mass production, response to change was slow, and there was sufficient time for a task to be completed by one function before being passed to the next. There was no payback then for the effort needed to attain rapid response to change. Today, with agile commerce, everything relevant to a project must be done concurrently, by every team member, in every company that is part of the project. This requires suitable communication infrastructure, work practices, and training of workers. It also requires motivation on the part of everyone involved and an ability to see the big picture, not only the details of the task in hand. Work in a mass-production environment may have been boring, but on the other hand, concurrent work can put much strain on workers. Concurrency therefore requires not only communication technology and coordination of work practices but also nurturing of human resources.

Environmental Enhancement

Environmental standards are often perceived as being imposed by government and viewed as a burden on manufacturing. However, as people become more environmentally conscious, they will not tolerate wasteful consumption of natural resources or contamination of the environment. Energy and environmental conservation and enhancement are natural, accepted parts of good citizenship. Thus more and more companies provide products that are "green," whether the product is a fast food package, a paper document, a car, office equipment, or anything else.

In this day and age, those responsible for developing manufacturing processes should bear in mind that lack of consideration of the environment will no more be tolerated. Organizational structures, processes, systems, and equipment are indeed being adapted to transform agile companies into environmentally safe organizations.

Flexible and Rapidly Responding Operations

The word *flexibility* refers to the capability of an organization to move from one task to another quickly and as a routine procedure. By itself flexibility does not imply dealing with unpredicted situations but means changing from one situation to another, with each situation defined ahead of time so that the procedures needed to manage it are in place. An example is a production line for a range of ten models of computer printer. All the information needed to manufacture each one is fully available. A flexible production facility is capable of managing any mix of orders, as the orders come in, for instance, 50 of one, 3 of another, and 10 of another. This is flexible but not yet agile. To be agile, the facility needs to be able to deal with an unpredicted new configuration of printer and to manufacture the unpredicted printer as a routine matter of rapid response.

Rapid response to agile business opportunities in a continuously evolving environment requires the organizational structure to be constantly and dynamically taking new forms and features. This enables operations to be constantly evolving to meet new challenges. This capability requires both technological systems and the empowerment of lower-level staff to make decisions within the context of managerial guidelines without waiting for approval for each detail.

People Support

In a company based on mass production, where the product is unchanged over a long period of time, the worker can have no influence over the product or the production method. Salespeople cannot change a product to suit a customer; they can only sell more of a fixed product. Production line workers cannot change any part of the mass-production line; all they can do is not fall behind in their tasks.

The world of agile manufacturing is in many ways diametrically opposed to the world of mass production. An enterprising salesperson can offer a customer a special configuration of a product; an enterprising production worker can figure out ways to improve the production; anyone in the enterprise can figure out ways to save time and be otherwise responsive to customers' desires. There is, therefore, a growing realization that the people who work for an enterprise and the skills and motivation they collectively bring to it are its most important asset. As such, they are to be nurtured, not seen as simply an operating expense.

Employees work well when they understand the measurement system applied to their performance, and when they understand their tasks and how they contribute to the success of the company. Accordingly, suitable performance measures and standards, together with a continuous effort to inform employees of the goals of an organization, are needed.

Within the bounds of the mission statement of a multifunctional team, each team is self-managed and regulated. An employee operates both as an individual and as a member of a team: any one employee may be a member of several teams simultaneously. The enterprise gives individuals and teams of individuals the power to make various entrepreneurial decisions about their projects, within the context of a company policy which encourages entrepreneurship and rationalizes use of resources.

The machines for flexible and modular production systems will often be inexpensive enough for most companies to afford them, and competition on the basis of the installed production process components usually has no relative advantage. Competitive advantage is obtained by people finding markets and opportunities for sales by enriching customers and by people finding novel and beneficial ways to use the production systems. Competitive advantage is therefore obtained through the ability of the people in the enterprise much more than through the machines in the enterprise.

The potential for intercompany teams to bring benefit to cooperating, agile competition is clear. This places a premium on trust and honesty in business relationships, which in turn depends directly on the trust and honesty of its employees.

Supplier Support

Industrial and commercial value is generally due to medium and small businesses in the value-added chain. In the United States, the 360,000 manufacturing firms with fewer than 500 workers account for 46 percent of the national industrial production. These companies feed 80 percent of their output into other companies. This considerable resource is a kingpin of national manufacturing. Agile work is networked-based; the speed of response is dictated by the accessibility of the correct information at the correct place at the correct time. This new system requires not only suitable technological systems but also individual skills and organizational structures which respond as needed.

The product and service supplier community abounds with entrepreneurial, capable, and technically smart people. However, businesses of small and medium size do not have the financial resources to hire people who will be devoted to dealing with the many aspects of agility and virtual organizations. Experience confirms that the instability inherent in small companies can be dealt with by cooperation among them. The result is an efficient and flexible enterprise constituting a collection of small companies. This was discussed in Chapter 6.

Larger businesses and local and national governments are making increasing efforts to help the entrepreneurs of the value-added chain expand and prosper, since it is this portion of the economy, worldwide, which adds the most jobs. There are many such projects in place in many countries and local regions.

ENABLING SUBSYSTEMS

Continuous Education and Training

In the world of mass production of many identical products, a worker was required to follow instructions, get on with the work, and not to question or doubt. Incentives were aimed at obtaining the greatest output of identical goods. In the world of agile competition, a company prospers if it provides customers with individualized enriching services, products, and solutions. This requires workers with a high level of general and technical education, who are knowledgeable about the capabilities of the company, and who are motivated and imaginative in developing enrichment opportunities for customers. All this needs to be achieved in a world of competition and continuous change. As a result, systematic and continuous education and training are important to both the financial well-being of the company and the individual employee. The word *training* is used when a person is trained in the use of a particular system, technology, or machine. The word *education* is used in speaking of a broad general education, not a specific short-term accomplishment. For instance, learning to use a foreign-language desktop publishing system is training, with a definite pay-off. Learning about a foreign culture is education, which may have a possible pay-off for the company in the expansion of international activity.

A high priority is placed on the ability of a company, and of an individual, to enhance the range of services and products which can be created and delivered. This agile environment demands an agile work force, capable of changing jobs and adding skills as the situation warrants. Not only must workers be familiar with their companies' services and products, but in the partnering atmosphere of virtual organizations, they may be called upon to provide expertise and skills which vary substantially from those with which they had been accustomed.

The ability of the work force is critical to a company's ability to move in versatile directions; training and education provide the means for that. Competitive advantage accrues to the company that is able to adapt rapidly to new markets, speedily assimilates information, and responds flexibly to customers' requirements. Only education and training can elevate the skill and knowledge levels of the available labor pool, and this labor pool includes all categories from the typical blue-collar "touch" laborer through professionals and senior management. All are attuned to the dynamic character of their work environment. Additionally, the range of markets within which an enterprise can compete is broadened and enhanced when its work force acquires knowledge and training.

Education and training are the only reliable means of coping with the culture shock of transforming the old, relatively fixed work mechanisms into agile systems. The problem in many countries, of educating a difficult-to-train, usually aging, work force does not have a recognized solution. This large body of people needs to be brought into the education and training environment.

Continuous education and training are today important activities. By 1988 U.S. businesses were spending about $30 billion annually to provide 17.6 million formal development and training courses, a number which has grown since then.

Customer-Interactive Systems

In an integrated customer-pull business environment, the customer, or her or his representative, who may be a dealer, a store assistant, an engineer, or a purchasing agent, is able to specify requirements and interact directly with the designers, producers, service agents, and all other functions which may be involved in specifying, producing, or delivering the product and the accompanying services. The customer or the customer's representative interacts widely with many possible functions, in many companies. It may be that one person in the company is the point of contact for all the interactions, or it may be a marketing strength to allow the customer access to many functions. Whatever the organization, there are systems which enable the customer or the customer's representatives to gain access to much information and to interact with that information. Communication and information systems are required to support such activity.

Entrepreneurial companies have already started to move in that direction—for example, the Ross Valve Company, described in Part 1, has developed a system that allows customers anywhere in the world, linked via computer communication, to work with Ross's engineers to specify and develop valves. Customers can download CAD drawings together with text and specifications. If they want to save time and the cost of delivery by producing the valve in a facility close to the customer, they can download the manufacturing instructions, including the instructions for the computer-controlled production machines. It is important for the satisfaction of such customers, called *prosumers* by Alvin Toffler, that the computer systems be easy to understand and use in a worldwide multicultural environment.

As bidirectional cable TV service replaces the old monodirectional service, home shopping will become less like an auction sale and more an interactive event, with the user interacting from home. In malls, there will be more and more electronic outlets, where customers will buy some products by choosing them from electronic catalogs, but there will also be interactive computer systems to allow a customer to "mix and match" products or to specify products and be involved in their configuration and design. Chapter 4 described such a system developed by [TC]².

Customized Marketing and Distribution Systems

A customer is often another company, although a customer may also be an individual consumer. The mass production system saw the customer as an average, and there may have been no real customer identical to the average. The agile commercial system sees each customer as an individual. Product and service mixes are customized according to each customer's needs and preferences. The mass-production system's output is standard products, and its marketing methods include advertising, sales, and other techniques aimed at attracting customers from one group or another. Data that supports such marketing are generalized, for example, demographic data, industry sector data, and data about the behavior of various consumer groups. Agile production and commerce require data on customers as individuals. A marketing system for agile competition includes customer-specific data, so that the supplier can suggest products, upgrades, and services attuned to that customer. Information retained may include analysis of previous buying habits and other customized data. There is a fine line here between invasion of privacy and stored information that makes the life of the customer more comfortable.

The mass-production distribution network, embodied in organizations such as Sears, Woolworths, and Marshall Fields, was significant in opening up a large distribution funnel to the mass producers. Without this funnel, it is doubtful whether the full potential of mass production would have been realized. Similarly, for the full profit-making capability of agile production to be realized, not only with end-user products but from all points in the industrial and commercial value-added chain, systems must be used to facilitate customizing personalized solutions, suggesting the solutions to a customer, and interacting with the customer to bring the interaction to completion.

Distributed Information Systems

Gone forever are the days when all the information needed by a company was kept in one computer. Today, information is spread throughout companies, often in technically incompatible systems and often with uncoordinated definitions of terms and formats. Distributed computer systems have become the lifeblood of the modern business, small or large. The different parts of one or more organizations, which usually have different data systems, must find ways to work together. This information can include not only textual data but also voice data and pictures; there can also be hypermedia capability that enables one to click on a picture of a product and see details of it or to click on a picture of a person and view data about that person.

The evolution of computer technology has provided low-cost, high-speed local area networks (LANs). However, coordination of data on a network is more complex than on a centralized database. Achieving coordination usually requires a central catalog of data items, user interfaces that are easy for anyone to use, and strong management to avoid turf wars over responsibility for information, while ensuring compatibility and coherency of the information. The Quick Response system, which ties together manufacturers and stores in the garment business in the United States, is an example of such a system.

Many executives who have been responsible for the installation of distributed information systems emphasize that the cultural problems and internal political problems related to installation are usually more difficult than the technical problems.

Empowered Individuals in Teams

A *team* is a relatively small, self-managed, empowered, multifunctional group of people with a defined goal. Its members may be from different parts of one or several organizations, and they deal with all aspects of a project. Teams are usually small, to reduce communication problems, and they exclude members whose areas of responsibility are peripheral to the team task. They are self-managing and empowered to act in such a way that delays caused by referring decisions back up the line are minimized.

However, companies often create a cross-departmental group to deal with a problem, call it a team, and expect the problem to be solved. This does not work. As discussed in Chapter 9, commonly used departmental performance measures usually feed interdepartmental conflict. The member of the team pays allegiance to the person who affects her or his hiring, firing, and advancement—usually the department chief. The task on the team is therefore often understood as defensively protecting the interests of the department chief, not proactively advancing the company as a whole. The difficulty of creating groups which are truly teams and truly empowered should not be underestimated. Without changes in performance measurement systems, and without real commitment from all levels of management, it cannot be done.

Extended Enterprise Integration

Analyses of activities in many organizations show that the time needed to find data, and a lack of information on the part of a decision maker when a decision must be made, are by far the most important barriers to overcome in efforts to reduce cycle time and response time.

An example of an extended enterprise integration system is CommerceNet, an information infrastructure coordinated by Enterprise Integration Technology of Palo Alto, California, which supports industrial work interaction between hundreds, even thousands, of industrial companies in Silicon Valley. It is expected to support an increasing number of intercompany industrial design, manufacturing, and supply operations between Apple, Intel, National Semiconductor, Solectron, SUN, DEC, Lockheed, Texas Instruments, Hewlett Packard, Pacific Bell, and other companies.

Integration implies coordination, not control. It requires constant and immediate updating of where people and resources are, and to what work they are committed, and constant updating of predictions as to their needs. This requires a system that includes:

- Agreed-upon standard methods of reporting what the deployment of resources is
- Agreed-upon standard methods of requesting allocation of resources
- A standardized method of defining job descriptions across the extended enterprise, so that communication is easy and understood
- An architecture for dealing with data on the company, the work processes, the production processes, and the products and services and all their components

- A reliable, accessible, and easy-to-use information system to deal with all the above

Financial Accounting Systems

Current accounting practices developed in the world of long-lived mass-produced products and dedicated production lines are unsuited to the needs of agile competition, as discussed in detail in Chapter 9.

The financial community uses accounting information to evaluate the attractiveness of a company's financial performance for investment. To the extent that accounting methods do not support measurement of relevant factors, agile competitive evaluations based on current conventional accounting practices may be wrong.

Accounting metrics and methods are critical factors affecting the behavior of a company. Modernizing these methods is a most important requirement for the infrastructure of agile manufacturing.

Global Multiventuring

As world commerce expands, companies are more responsive to opportunities in overseas markets. No company has within itself all the resources needed to take advantage of all the good opportunities at short notice. Therefore, it is necessary to form alliances, not only at the strategic level but also at the tactical and operational levels. In the future there will also be many new forms of collaboration to facilitate rapid cooperation between dynamic multiventuring companies. In addition, differences in laws and regulations, as well as customs, require that a company have the expertise to deal with these issues for successful multiventuring.

Without a systematic approach, success in worldwide multiventuring is sporadic and subject to the vagaries of good luck. Organizing a formal system to uncover global multiventuring opportunities is therefore desirable. Large businesses usually have the resources worldwide to take advantage of multiventuring. Small businesses lack the resources to do so, but they find help in government, semigovernment, and trade organizations.

Groupware

Groupware systems are computer-based systems which support two or more users working on a common task. They facilitate and encourage collaboration and coordination. For instance, in the *New York Times* of February 6, 1994, the CEO of Lotus Development Corporation, Jim Manzi, reported that Compaq Computer uses groupware to speed the flow of information to its resellers; Johnson and Higgins, the world's largest privately held insurance broker, uses groupware to interact with the brokers working for it, and with other brokers around the world, to exchange data and knowledge; Fort Howard Corporation, a $1.2 billion paper products manufacturer, communicates with its brokers and distributors with groupware; and more and more professionals, designers, and engineers are turning to groupware to enable them to work in tightly interacting teams with members all over the world.

A convenient categorization of groupware, based on the methods of interaction, is:

1. Tools for immediate, real-time collaboration and problem solving within a group geographically colocated. This is the multimedia computer network equivalent of using an in-house intercom system.
2. Immediate, real-time collaboration among people who are geographically distributed. This is the multimedia computer network equivalent of using the telephone system.
3. Collaboration among people distributed geographically, where the interactions are not interactive. This is the multimedia computer network equivalent of using fax transmissions.

With the development of networks, especially bidirectional cable TV services, such systems are becoming more developed and widespread.

Progress in implementing a groupware system is limited more by organizational problems than by technical ones, requiring well-accepted user-interface methods. Installation of different systems requiring different methods of use would be a large barrier to increasing the number of people who can use the groupware conveniently.

Intelligent Flexible Machines

Agile competition and the satisfaction of the customized desires in niche markets expand the need for flexible, intelligent production machines and product machines. The ability to monitor products and production process equipment, to feed the data to a computer network, and to take action rapidly based on that data, is a subsystem of agile manufacturing capability.

In production, lot sizes become smaller as niche markets become even more fragmented, and buyers look for more customized variation in packaging and product features. This leads to more flexible systems to cope with the constantly varying mix of products and packaging required. These flexible systems are equipped with advanced sensors, computer-based controls, automated material-handling systems, and supervisory computer systems. Machines or systems equipped with intelligent control technology are used to maintain and operate the production systems.

Competition for customers pushes these technologies into the servicing of products such as household or business machines and cars. Increasingly, these machines include sensors which constantly monitor the performance of their components, and even before the machine breaks down, when performance of components begins to differ from nominal limits, a message indicating the problem is displayed. On higher-value items, the sensors are constantly monitored by computers at the facility responsible for service, via a wired or wireless communication channel, and the servicing or repair is taken care of without the intervention of the user. In essence, one moves from buying a product to paying for the correct functioning of a machine.

Lean Organization and Methods

In mass-production companies, it was very important to keep the expensive, dedicated production machinery working at high utilizations. To ensure that, partly finished goods were kept ahead of each workstation. During the past few decades, the disadvantages of this practice have become clear. The inventory of work in process (WIP) tied up large amounts of money, as much as 50 percent of the annual sales income, and the space needed to store the material was a significant expense. Response to a change to a new product was slow because the existing WIP had to be used up first. When a problem was discovered in a product, it was difficult to trace which process had caused the problem, and by the time the cause of the problem was known, many more faulty parts had been made. Management of the work process was difficult because one had the feeling of "drowning in material." In the old, classical world of mass production, this was an acceptable situation. Producers controlled the market and the pricing; so the expense of the WIP was covered. Further, many identical products were made, and what was not sold today would be sold tomorrow. International competition during the past 25 years, especially from the Japanese, has forced companies to introduce programs of total quality management (TQM), reduction of work in process, just-in-time (JIT) logistics systems, and reduced response times to customers. These paved the way for lean manufacturing, which is characterized by the following properties:

- Right first time
- Continuous improvement and quality inherent in any product or process
- Flexible production
- Minimizing waste of any kind, time or material

These programs laid the foundations of agility. An organization "fat" with inventory, slow to respond to customers, and with a large reject rate is not able to become agile.

The capability to be agile cannot exist side by side with the old system of slow response and high inventory levels in production and commercial systems. Inventories for agile competition are low. Assembled products are not kept in inventory at all, but are made as needed for specific orders. Inventories may be held of components or semi-finished items but will be as low as possible. In mass production, a factory runs by the motto "I sell what I already made," and a store runs by the motto "I sell what I already bought." An agile organization runs by the motto "We make and deliver exactly what the customer specified." Lean organization and methods are key components for an agile company.

Legal System

Laws, regulations, and legal agreements in many countries are based on the implicit assumptions of the mass-production era. A *product* is defined as a constant, unchanging entity, usually produced in large numbers, subject to the sole control of the producer; a customer is restricted to buying the product or not buying it, but is not considered part of the product definition process; a supplier is a one-time provider of product and not a long-term partner; data are considered static and not subject to rapid change with time. These factors are all different in the era of agility. Not only do laws and regulations not recognize the changes occurring in competitive industrial society, in effect they forbid them. The negotiation between a supplier and a customer can be considered contravention of contract regulations, which assume that many products are similar and the only parameter of choice is price; work in virtual organizations can be considered contravention of anti-trust regulations; tax laws differentiate between service and product and assume that a product is made mostly at one site.

These problems are analogous to the strains being experienced by the legal system because of other modern changes. For example, television and computer technology have now merged, and it is possible to take a few frames of a movie, news broadcast, or song and manipulate them so that the fact of their having been manipulated is not detectable. As a result, copyright laws and rules for admissibility of televised pictures and audio recordings as legal evidence are now the subject of much legal debate.

Examples of legal interpretations and laws, and their implications for manufacturing enterprises, as compiled by a group of industry executives in the United States in 1991 are given in Chapter 9.

Modular Reconfigurable Process Components

The mass-production system used dedicated production lines, bought once and amortized over a long production run. The long-lived product paid for the specialized production line. Agile competition requires production systems which can be quickly and easily reconfigured to deal with new and unpredicted demands. This, in turn, requires that production systems be made of modular reconfigurable components. In the decade of the 1990s Japan and Europe are making efforts, in what is often thought of as an uninteresting technical issue, to define standards for such components. In fact, it *is* a key issue. Among experts, one hears both the opinion that having standards inhibits development and entrepreneurship and the opinion that not having standards fragments markets and inhibits growth. It seems that having a standard for a device before the technical trade-offs are clear can inhibit better technical solutions, as happened, for instance, to the Japanese in the high-definition television industry, when they opted too early for one specific technology.

Interface standards are found more often. They specify how the components of a system interact but not how each component works. The total number and size of systems, and in turn large new markets for such components, may result. However, even here one must be careful with the timing and the scope of the standards. In retrospect, it might have been fortunate that the biblical Tower of Babel project failed. If all the world had had one language, communication would have been easier, but the cross-fertilization and creativity that derive from the perspectives of different languages would have been lost. In any event, as interface standards for process machines develop, the supply of reconfigurable, standard modular components will become a large business sector.

Organizational Inventory Listing

Hierarchic organizations are characterized by higher-up people authorizing resources, tasks, and permissions for those below them. An agile organization is characterized by empowered individuals in teams who take what is needed and do what they see fit, within the broad parameters set by mission-oriented executives. The structure that today requires detailed approvals will be much diminished. Responsible management does, however, need to know at any point in time how, where, and for what reasons the company's resources are deployed and also needs to keep an eye on cash flow and changing financial data. This poses an interesting new problem: Teams will go where they need to, and do what they have to, but the organization will constantly need to know the details of the deployment of its resources, whether they are computers, machines, or people. With the old method of management, each team was given a budget, and data about the progress against performance milestones and against budget were collected. That method does not permit an easy analysis of how resources could be redeployed from teams underutilizing them to teams that could better use them. The common tactic that whoever hollers louder and has more influence gets the resource is not sound in the long run. For the dynamic work method of extended-enterprise teams, most organizations lack a system to keep track of data on resources satisfactorily. Few executives feel comfortable that they can fulfill their responsibility without that data, even if they accept that they cannot approve the detailed decisions of teams as they did before.

Methods developed for the mass-production system, such as material requirements planning (MRP), or for projects with unchanging goals, such as the program evaluation and review technique (PERT), are not suitable for agile production, since they assume that there is no dynamic competition for resources between different products or projects. New allocation methods are being developed using methods of artificial intelligence or of modern systems theory, but they are not yet widespread or mature.

Organizational Practices

Organizational practices grew up in a slowly changing, almost static industrial system, with long-lived, unchanging products and production systems. Production was the slowest long-lead item in an enterprise, slower than marketing or any other part of the enterprise. Today, the technical work of physical manufacturing has been modernized and is no longer the slow, limiting process in the system. For instance, some years ago the network products unit of Digital Equipment Corporation found that after a customer specified a configuration of a product, the order was filled six months later. Investigation showed that, of the six months, four were spent in nontechnical activities such as checking credit or order entry. Two months were spent in the technical departments, but of that time only two days were spent in actual technical work. The solution to speed of response was obviously not to buy faster production machines but to reengineer the entire order-fulfillment process. There are many examples of such improvements from the past decade. Indeed, any company which does not modernize its organizational practices, *continuously,* will be forced to compete with low-value-added mass production or will likely decay and disappear. In the new environment, organizational structures are flexible and reconfigurable, and reward and review mechanisms recognize team-oriented behavior and successes.

Performance Metrics and Evaluation

A performance measurement system exists to provide a means of control within an organization. The system obviously must use definable and measurable factors. In the era of mass production, performance metrics measured the efficiency of each part of a process that was broken into independent fragments, each with a narrow specialization. If the system as a whole was well designed, when many copies of an identical product were made repetitively, the measurement of individual efficiencies and performances gave an understanding of the performance of the system as a whole. When products are continuously changing, and the enterprise is constantly reacting to new requirements, many of the performance measurements which were valid in the static, unchanging world of mass production become invalid.

Once measures are defined and implemented, they are compared with historical data of the organization and with data from other organizations. The choice of comparison data can be critical to understanding where the organization stands. More and more companies are moving from comparing current data with their own history, or even with their own business sector, to comparing with the "best in class" of each individual activity. Once a new measure is chosen, it must be subject to constant scrutiny to determine whether it remains valid as the organization changes with time. This subject is so important that Chapter 11 of this book is devoted specifically to it.

Prequalified Partnering

In an environment of virtual organizations, it is important to have reliable information about potential partners in advance of the decision to establish contact with a view to cooperation.

Necessary information includes:

- The firm's track record as a cooperating partner.
- Skill base and categories of expertise of employees and the annual plan to upgrade those skills.
- The response time of the company in making strategic decisions and in tactical response to market opportunities.
- A description of the special expertise the company may bring to a partnership.

Various commercial or government bodies in different countries make such data available for companies, or have in hand plans to do so.

Product and Service Inventory

In the world of mass production, companies made few product lines. For a typical division or plant, the product lines have expanded over the years from dozens to hundreds to thousands. For mass production, a computer-based system can keep track of all the product families, product lines, and individual product items, since they change relatively slowly. The world of agility is different, characterized by very small quantities of any one product and a rapid, ongoing, dynamic change of the list of products and services offered. All the data of all the products must be tracked and remembered for several reasons. Product liability requires that an audit trail of every detail of a product be kept. Markets are fragmenting as requirements expand for customized packaging for outlets or local regions, even for products that have traditionally had long production runs, such as soap or soft drinks. Another reason for tracking the services and products supplied by the company is for marketing and for overall management of the company. In a well-run company, driven by empowered teams, executive management wants to know what products and services are provided by each team, so as to find new opportunities to leverage them into yet more profit. This requires a constant update of the inventory of those services.

Distribution of individualized products and components of customer solutions is much more exacting than for the distribution of many identical products. With identical products, it does not matter which product goes to which customer, provided the quantities and the timing of delivery are correct. For an agile system, the additional condition that each product goes to one specific customer is introduced. This is a significant burden on a distribution and information system.

Simulation and Modeling

Simulation and modeling are usually done with computer software, to give the answers to "what if" questions. Such techniques are available in almost every field, and the need for quick reaction and solutions which are correct first time is stimulating more and more use of such systems. Simulation and modeling software is used by supermarkets and stores to evaluate and to design store and shelf layouts; by automobile or aircraft manufacturers to evaluate proposed details of cars or planes; by manufacturing companies to evaluate proposed production process plans; by architects and townplanners to evaluate the influence and appearance of proposed construction ideas; and by environmental planners to predict the effects of a proposed plan. The list of applications is large, and growing larger every day, because of the need for accurate predictions, rather than estimates and rules of thumb, which in times of rapid change become outdated. Computer games such as SIMCITY, in which a player supervises the development of a town and watches its economic and ecological success or failure, will presumably cause large numbers of people to become familiar with simulation methods.

Total Quality Management

The Japanese led the way in instituting total quality management (TQM) work systems, in which poor quality, although showing up as bad product, is dealt with by finding the process(es) that cause the problem and fixing the cause, not the product. To this end, the principle of the "five whys" helps. If something is wrong, ask why. When you have the reason, ask why it was so. And so on, until the problem has been investigated at five levels. These questions are answered by facts and data, not by impression. Implementing such work methods requires that all workers constantly note data on the work they do, often using methods of statistical process control. This in turn requires that workers understand the goal of the company and how the task they perform supports that goal. This requires educated and motivated employees. Therefore, TQM does not exist in isolation from the other characteristics of the people and the organization, and its correct introduction implies much change for the company as a whole.

Such TQM procedures have been widely introduced in industry worldwide, especially in Japan, North America, and western Europe. The European Community has adopted a series of quality standards and guidelines, now also adopted by the International Organization for

Standardization, known as the ISO 9000 series (ISO 9001, ISO 9002, ISO 9003, ISO 9004) (Peach 1992). These do not specify quality for specific products and processes, but do specify how work procedures are to be recorded, managed, and audited in an organization. Hence, they should not inhibit creative design of products and processes. Increasingly, customers are requiring that their suppliers be certified as competent in ISO 9000 procedures. In order to avoid losing customers, or opportunities to expand, many companies are therefore adopting programs to bring them to ISO 9000 capability.

Ubiquitous Communication

The pervasiveness of communication is the major technological driver of the move to agility. For many years the only widely used means of two-way, interactive communication was the telephone, and even that was tied to particular locations, for instance, a house or business. Within a few years communication has undergone a technological revolution. Today one can communicate:

- With anyone, since communication technology is ubiquitous.
- Anywhere, since communication is now wireless and portable. One can communicate from and to any point in the world. The telephone, fax, and computer have been freed from the shackles of the wired connection. Even if a local area does not have a carrier system, communication is available via satellite.
- Anytime, since in global commerce working hours lose their significance.
- Anyway, that is, by voice, fax, computer, or television; or by multimedia communication, using all the modes at will.

The new technology makes it possible for anyone to communicate with anyone else with great flexibility of choice. Hierarchic organization limited the amount of communication needed and allowed. Empowered team organization requires and allows any person or any system to communicate with any other. Hierarchic communication was slow, but was easy to control. Ubiquitous networked communication enables rapid response, but is difficult to keep track of. For the telephone system, there is the well-developed method of telephone number information. For ubiquitous multimedia communication, the old, relatively simple system of telephone numbers gives way to a more complex system, continuously keeping track of how to communicate with each person or system in a project. Setting up such a system, and keeping it updated for a dynamic, constantly changing organization, is a large effort.

Waste Management and Elimination

Two factors drive the growing industrial activity to eliminate as much waste as possible and to manage the treatment of waste materials. One is a growing public pressure against waste and pollution and for environmental preservation. This is fueled by young people becoming older and changing societal perceptions and paradigms. The other factor is the growing experience of companies that recycling waste can in fact be profitable. More companies are placing waste-recycling plants at the exhaust stream of a manufacturing process, so that what was previously waste becomes a salable product. The long-term ideal goal is to have zero emissions, at which point all waste becomes product.

The fact of managing and eliminating waste may by itself be thought of as irrelevant to the agile manufacturing process. However, agility requires responsiveness to customers' needs, and as populations increase and pressures are felt on all natural resources, customers as individuals and as participants in the society will not tolerate environmental damage, since environmental considerations are becoming part of the implicit value system of society.

Waste and emission treatment in the United States currently costs about $75 billion per year. It has been estimated (Naj 1990) that American companies produce five times the waste per dollar of goods sold as the Japanese, and more than twice that of the Germans. This notwithstanding, Germany is moving toward the "take back" concept, in which a manufacturer is required by law to reuse or recycle product at the end of its useful life and thus take back packaging and reuse or recycle it.

NOTES ON CHAPTER 10

A company may find this chapter useful for the following:

- To evaluate which of the infrastructure items are relevant for the company
- To evaluate which of the items it can deal with itself and to consider alternative ways of dealing with them
- To prioritize, for the company, the company competencies requiring enhancement and then to prioritize the infrastructure systems needed to support these
- To analyze which systems can be dealt with adequately by using internal resources, which should be dealt with by several companies acting together, and which need to be dealt with entirely by groups outside the company, such as government, standards agencies, and other industry sectors
- For those systems which can be dealt with entirely inside the company, or with the company as part of a project, to plan how to get started.

Some example projects for use in a course are:

- Criticize the list of competitive challenges, organizational characteristics, enterprise elements, and enabling subsystems to determine whether there are other items not listed
- Examine any of the items in detail, beginning with a literature search
- Evaluate the relative importance of enterprise characteristics and enabling subsystems in different countries and analyze their effect on international competition. Are there cultural or social differ-

ences between counties or states that promote or hinder development of any characteristic or subsystem?

A government department may find the chapter useful for the following:

- To evaluate the enabling systems in the region and to estimate whether they are barriers or aids to improving the competitive advantage of businesses.
- To consider which other local or national regions are competition and to analyze the relative effect on local competitiveness of the systems in those other regions.

CHAPTER *11*

Measuring Agility: A Self-Assessment Approach

The journey to agility is a never-ending quest to do better than the competition, even as the competitive environment constantly changes. On this journey one never arrives at a final destination, but one needs to know at any point in time whether progress is in fact in the right direction, and how one stands relative to worldwide competition. A hundred years ago managers of the then-emerging job-shops and mass-production factories faced a similar problem. They pursued the move to mass production, not because of abstract ideas but because, as astute business leaders, they saw opportunities to make a good profit. The methods tried were based on much experience but only limited, vague ideas of the characteristics of the emerging system. Those entrepreneurs did not wait until

The information for this chapter was compiled from a number of sources, including Goldman (1993), Industry Week's 1993 Best Plants Profile, the Malcolm Baldrige Quality Award Criteria (1994), Sprow (1993), Gunn as reported by Sprow (1993), Womack et al. (1990), efforts by Karyn Blumenfeld, Gary Laughlin, Murali Subramamiam, Orapong Thien-Ngern, Scott Wade, and innumerable discussions with many people.

measures were developed before making progress. They started the new system of mass production while managing by their intellect, the strength of their convictions, and "the seats of their pants." Only after the management systems had been in place for a long time did it become clear what performance measurement systems were needed and how they should be used. The pioneers succeeded. Those who waited until the management methods were proved and documented were forced to compete with many more experienced companies and managers.

Ask the wrong question, and you get a useless answer. The question to ask is not "Is my company agile?" but "Is my company making progress in the right direction, how fast are we progressing, and how are we relative to the competition?" To answer these questions requires knowing:

- What to measure
- How to measure it
- How to evaluate the results

It will be some time until the answers to all three questions are available for every industry, government, and service sector. Whoever waits until all the answers are known will have chosen to drop out of the competitive race, because generating the answers to those questions will have been done by the survivor organizations, the others having been forced to compete in low-value-added sectors or to go out of business altogether. The 1990s are the years of searching for the answers to the measurement questions. The best anyone can do to measure progress to agility is to use the limited measurement knowledge currently available, follow the development of this knowledge by means of professional contacts of all kinds, and, by measuring hands on, using that limited knowledge. The other option, waiting until all the measurement answers are known and published, is equivalent to giving up the race for competitive survival.

The quest for metrics, measurement methods, and comparative data is in full swing in leading companies, worldwide. Many metrics are being devised and used, evaluating the results by "best in class" worldwide comparisons. Understanding the metrics and the parameters to measure, and the measurement methods, and understanding how to evaluate the results are serious professional specialities. Professor Dan Roos, who was a leader of the well-known MIT study of the international automobile industry reported in the book *The Machine That Changed the World*, relates how his team discovered that the measures for a particular European automobile manufacturer were below par. For a long period, the managers in the company refused to believe the data. When he eventually presented the data to the company president, he found complete agreement. The president said, "I have been trying for five years to convince my middle managers of the need to improve. Your data shows that we have been consistently checking ourselves against the wrong benchmark. We have been comparing ourselves with other European manufacturers, not with the best in class worldwide." Modern benchmarking is done by comparing each activity with the best similar activity anywhere, in whatever industrial or service sector the comparative data is to be found.

The days of few long-lived products and dedicated production systems were the days of slow change, when the tasks of machines and people were often unchanged over long periods of time. The world of agility is a dynamic world in which opportunities and tasks change constantly, and the time taken to respond successfully to an opportunity is of vital importance. This requires quite different measures from the slow world of mass production. When the competitive condition of a company is assessed, it is all too easy to fall into the mode of doing so in terms of the widely used concepts available for mass-production companies. Because the situations being dealt with are new, before starting to measure the capability of a company, we should first discover what questions to ask. Indeed, knowing the correct questions to ask may often be more influential than the detailed answers. The next section lists a number of useful general questions. From these a company should determine which questions will favorably impact its agile business strategy. These are the questions the company should monitor.

OVERVIEW QUESTIONS FOR AN AGILITY AUDIT, LISTED BY THE
PRINCIPAL DIMENSIONS OF AGILITY

First: Enriching the Customer
A. Do your customers get products or solutions?
B. Are you organized to sell solutions?
C. What does the organization sell?

Second: Cooperating to Enhance Competitiveness

D. Inside the organization
E. Outside the organization

Third: Mastering Change and Uncertainty

F. Organizational speed of change
G. Organizational agility
H. Concept to cash cycle time reduction

Fourth: Leveraging People and Information

I. Will entrepreneurs survive in your organization?
　1. Compensation issues
　2. Freedom of action issues
J. Recognizing the impact of people on the bottom line
K. Recognizing the value of information products on the bottom line
　1. Organizational issues
　2. Information content issues

DETAILED QUESTIONS FOR AN AGILITY AUDIT, LISTED BY THE
PRINCIPAL DIMENSIONS OF AGILITY

First: Enriching the Customer

A. Do your customers get products or solutions?

　1. Is the organization focused on customer satisfaction or on product
　　shipment?
　2. Do you measure how much effort your customers undertake to benefit
　　from what you sell them?
　3. Can your customers just deploy what you sell them and benefit?
　4. Must your customers field a team of people or even adapt their business
　　practices to use your product?

(continued)

B. Are you organized to sell solutions?

1. Do you explicitly look for opportunities to add profitable services or other value to your product?
2. Are you optimizing for mass customization or mass production?
3. Are you focused on customized product opportunities or standard products?
4. Are you focusing management attention on core competencies or on factory efficiency?
5. Is quality measured in defect rates or customer delight over time?
6. Are you looking for high-value solutions or high-margin products?

C. What does the organization sell?

1. Are you selling skills, knowledge, and information in a relationship over time or just products in sales transactions?
2. Do your clients value the information you provide them, or do they pay only for physical products?
3. Are products and services reconfigurable or inflexible?
4. Do you place an asset value on the information you sell, or is the sales value of information not considered an asset?
5. Are all your intellectual property and data secret, or do you sell some for profit?
6. Do your customers turn to you for rapid-response special requests?
7. If so, do you constantly exceed their expectations?

Second: Cooperating to Enhance Competitiveness

D. Inside the organization

1. Are you cooperating opportunistically across organizational lines?
2. Do you use cross-functional customer teams?
3. Can each of the profit and loss (P&L) units establish its own specific goals within a broad mission statement?
4. Do the workers believe that you encourage sharing, cooperation, and team work, or are they focused on individual performance and rewards?
5. Is information readily available to those who need it through an enterprisewide information system? Or is information hard to find and not generally shared?
6. Does your organizational structure facilitate concurrency throughout the enterprise? Or are you organized into functional silos which act independently with a minimum of communication and little coordination?
7. Are decisions on alternative actions based on bottom-line measures or sales volume, margin, and unit costs?

(continued)

E. Outside the organization

1. Is the decision to partner a first alternative rather than a last resort?
2. Do you both protect and share intellectual property?
3. Do you have a track record of trustworthiness, and will you be preferred as a partner?
4. Are you using the virtual company model to achieve vertical integration?
5. Are major suppliers treated as trusted partners? Or are supplier transactions adversarial and frequently renegotiated?
6. Are products conceived by teaming with the customer and suppliers? Or are products conceived by internal teams and kept secret until announcement dates?

Third: Mastering Change and Uncertainty

F. Organizational speed of change

1. Is the speed of organizational decision making measured in hours, days, weeks, months, or years?
2. Are you constantly reinventing and reengineering the organization?
3. Are you taking levels out of the organizational hierarchy?
4. Are you organized by functional departments or by customer opportunity teams?
5. Is the organization dynamic and effective at meeting changing goals and objectives?

G. Organizational agility

1. Are change and apparent chaos recognized as opportunity?
2. Can the organization decide on appropriate courses of action in the face of change, and does it implement those actions?
3. At what authority level can risk be taken?
4. Are risk takers who fail sometimes rewarded for initiative?
5. How independent are the profit centers?
6. Are profit and loss centers required to use transfer prices for in-corporation suppliers, and are they free of corporate-mandated overhead allocation requirements?
7. Does management coach and inspire or direct the employees who work with it?
8. Is information held for power or distributed to empower?
9. Are manufacturing processes and methods of creating products part of the infrastructure and easily accessible to all teams in the company?
10. Is the mix of available manufacturing processes constantly changing?

(continued)

H. Concept to cash cycle time reduction

1. Are you proactive with your customers?
2. Are you eliminating the organizational walls that impede your efforts to meet customer needs?
3. Are employees asked to think and make decisions?
4. Do employees at all levels contribute to decisions?
5. Are those who carry out tasks able to make decisions which affect their ability to perform the tasks better and faster?
6. Is employee compensation based on the contribution of employees to the bottom line?
7. Can employees relate the bottom-line compensation to actions they took?

Fourth: Leveraging People and Information

I. Will entrepreneurs survive in your organization?

Compensation issues

1. Is compensation skill-based or task-based?
2. Is compensation based on a combination of performance, time, and rate or on just time and rate?
3. Do you recognize and reward teamwork, or do you use only individual performance metrics?
4. Are employees aware of the bottom-line condition and how they might have an impact on it?
5. What part of employee compensation is bottom-line-based performance?
6. How often is bottom-line compensation calculated and paid?
7. Is the amount of computed bottom-line compensation an employee can receive unlimited?

Freedom of action issues

1. Are people asked to think?
2. Are you macromanaging or micromanaging people?
3. Do you trust and empower employees or police and audit them?
4. Is communication two-way or only downward?
5. Do employees focus on organizational success or only on personal security?
6. Do employees cooperate and work in teams, or do they focus on departmental goals and assignments?

J. Recognizing the impact of people on the bottom line

1. Are people or capital assets your scarcest resources?
2. Are people skills and knowledge treated as assets, or is asset management focused on equipment and machinery?

(continued)

3. Is increasing the education of employees thought of as enhancing the company or as benefiting the employee?
4. Are you managing core skills and competencies or products and product lines?
5. Are competitive claims based on value provided to the customer by core competencies and experience, or by the cost and quality of factory operations?
6. Are you benchmarking and investing in your core competencies?

K. Recognizing the value of information products on the bottom line

Organizational issues

1. Do you sell, rent, or lease access to information and information engineering tools?
2. Are your information revenues and potential revenues growing significantly?
3. Is the information content of your products growing?
4. Do you measure the value of the information content of products?
5. Do you charge separately for presales or postsales information and assistance?
6. Do you charge customers explicitly for design activity, or do you recover design cost by allocation to production parts?
7. How do you treat and value information assets internally? How do you treat these assets with respect to sales price?
8. How do you treat, manage, and value the assets in your organization which allow you to sell information?
9. How do you protect the information assets of your organization intellectual property? Can you protect and share intellectual property?

Information content issues

1. Is automated documentation part of your product?
2. Do your products provide the user with instructions and/or assistance in how to use them effectively?
3. Can your products be easily customized for an individual customer?
4. Do your products communicate with your facilities all or part of the time to get updates, assistance, or additional services for the client?
5. Do your products have automatic self-diagnosis capability when they malfunction or begin to fail?
6. Do you systematically determine what information products and/or services your customer(s) need or would benefit from?
7. Do you have a system with which to track the content of your information products to keep versions, compatibility, and accuracy issues under control?

Benchmarking a company's processes against the best in class, worldwide, is rapidly becoming accepted good practice. A specialization of benchmarking devoted specifically to agility and virtual organizations does not yet exist. However, when progress toward agility is assessed, correct measurement practices should be used. The references at the end of the book list some of the many publications available for general benchmarking practice.

Table 11.1 lists measurements which are useful in assessing the progress a company is making toward agility. This represents the latest thinking but has not yet stood the test of time. Much of the data that would be of interest are not yet measured in companies, but some are available. The four main sections of the table correspond to the four principal dimensions of agility.

The table shows the traditional organizational model, the emerging agile-virtual model, and metrics that enable one to measure how a company is progressing in the move from the old to the new system. Also indicated, where available, are measurement values. The values were taken from a variety of sources, as noted before. When a range of values is more instructive than a single value, the range is given. Depending on the measurement, the value may be a typical value for leading companies; for example, the number of benchmark studies in the past three years is "3 to 35." Alternatively, the value may be given as the percent of leading companies (LCs) showing a particular characteristic; for example, major suppliers having virtual relationships occurs in 96 percent of LCs. Where no entry is given, values are not yet available.

The values in the table should not be used without the professional advice of a specialist in benchmarking, or without thorough search of the literature or visits to other companies. Companies are too different, and the meaning of the measurements too complex, to be used unless by professionals. The warning on prescription medicines is appropriately paraphrased here: "Do not use the measurement values without professional advice."

The Baldrige criteria for quality are becoming more widely used each year. They list items which must be taken into account when applying for an award, without giving specific detail as to the requirement in each section. It is instructive to see which sections of the Baldrige award criteria include subjects of importance to measuring agility, and which metrics for agility are not covered by those criteria. The Baldrige criteria refer to quality, but there is no reason not to show agile measurements in the various sections. Column 5 of the table shows which Baldrige quality criteria could include the metric referred to.

The Traditional Model	The Emerging Agile-Virtual Model	Measures and Metrics	Range of Values in Leading Companies (LCs)	Baldrige Category
Profits via low unit cost	Profits via bottom-line impact	Profit as true bottom-line impact per project, rather than margin per product	—	—
Standard products	Customized product opportunities	What the organization is organized to sell: solutions not products	—	—
Mass production	Mass customization	What the organization manages and inventories: core competencies and skills within them, not number of product lines and SKUs	—	—
High-margin products	Value-based solutions	Pricing strategy and methodology	—	—
Compete on cost and quality of factory operations	Compete on value provided to customer and core competencies of team	Customer criteria for vendor selection and satisfaction metrics	—	7.4
Quality measured in production defect rate	Quality measured in customer delight over product life	Customer rating (provided over time) of the product in meeting her or his evolving needs over the product's life cycle	—	6.1 7.3 7.4
		Good yield of production line is assumed		

365

		MANAGEMENT POLICY	
Product management	Skill and customer management	The organization manages and inventories customer data, core competencies, and skills rather than products	—
		PRODUCT	
Little or no information content	Increasing product information content	Percentage of value of information content of product	—
All products have physical components	Some information-only products	Percentage of information content in products	—
Conceived by producer who tries to interest customers	Conceived by producer and customer working together on a customer opportunity	Customers participate in product development efforts	90% of LCs
		Customer hours/employee hours in design team	5.1 / 7.2
Long runs of the same product made over several years	Short runs of unique products made for specific needs or opportunities	Build to order rather than stock	80% of LCs
		Adopted JIT or continuous flow methods?	96% of LCs
		Management focuses on order-to-shipment time rather than length of run metrics	—
		Customer reject rate for any reason	0 to 3.8%

Physical instance sold at a point in time	Information, skills, and knowledge over time in a relationship	Price based on price for skills and knowledge over time with raw material cost reimbursement, rather than on physical product cost plus allocated overhead	—
Products are relatively inflexible	Products are configured at the time of delivery and reconfigurable during life cycle to meet evolving requirements	Existence of configuration and reconfiguration system or mechanism for specifying customer needs as they evolve	5.2
Price or contract based fee for each delivery of physical instance(s) at specified times	Price or contract based on a fee for skills over time to provide specific capability to customer over time and passing on the incidental cost of raw materials	Percentage of income from fixed-price products	—
Selling products	Selling solutions	Amount of effort by customer to see benefit from the purchase	5.2 7.5 7.6
Seeking high-margin products which yield, as profit, a fraction of the cost of skills and materials	Seeking value-based products which yield, as profit, a fraction of the value they provide to the customer's bottom line	Percentage of value provided to customer rather than methodology to measure profit of product, e.g., margin	6.2

		Measures and Metrics	Range of Values in Leading Companies (LCs)	Baldrige Category
Low value assigned to information engineering tools	Use of information engineering tools recognized as a valuable product to be sold	Asset value methodology and value assigned	—	—
Profit potential not recognized	Profit potential emphasized	Information product strategy, revenue, and revenue trend	—	—

COOPERATING TO ENHANCE COMPETITIVENES

The Traditional Model	The Emerging Agile-Virtual Model	Measures and Metrics	Range of Values in Leading Companies (LCs)	Baldrige Category
Self-sufficiency	Interdependencies	Percentage of value added contributed in any one organization	—	—
Partner as a last resort	Partner opportunistically in virtual companies	Number of one-time contract vendors for each supplier partnering relationship Number of customers having long-term, close relationships with the company	—	—
Vertical integration	Virtual organizations	Number of outside dependencies	—	—
Supplier transactions at arm's length	Suppliers as trusted partners	Percentage of major suppliers as virtual relationships	96% of LCs	5.1 5.4
		Major suppliers chosen on basis of low bid	0%	6.4

Discourage sharing and cooperation	Encourage sharing and cooperation even with competitors	Corporate policy on sharing and partnering Intellectual property options available and level of decision authority Company is tied in to mechanisms and assistance to find partners	—	—
Intellectual property poorly protected and not shared	Intellectual property appropriately protected and shared	Number of intellectual property protection mechanisms approved and used	—	—

EMPLOYEE ENVIRONMENT

Work as individuals	Work as individuals in teams	Percentage of work force in self-directed work teams Rewards and measures of success or objectives are based on individual and group performance	20 to 100%	4.2
Few employees meet customers	All employees meet customers	All employees can interact with customers	100% of LCs	4.2

Conceived by producer who tries to interest customers	Conceived by producer and customer working together on a customer opportunity	Customers participate in product design efforts?	90% of LCs	7.1
		Ratio of customer hours to employee hours in design team		

INFORMATION

Computer-integrated manufacturing (CIM)	Enterprise integration (EI)	Average percentage of all companywide disciplines in each project team	—	
		Focus on corporate objectives rather than on means and technology		
Isolated function organizations	Concurrent everything relevant in the enterprise	Percentage of employees accessing companywide data and average number of accesses per year per employee	92% of LCs use concurrent engineering	2.3 5.1
No significant information infrastructure required or in place	Critical information infrastructure for product development and delivery required and under development or in place	Number of internal and external electronic communications per worker per month	—	
		EDI links to customers and suppliers	70% of LCs	

MASTERING CHANGE AND UNCERTAINTY

The Traditional Model	The Emerging Agile-Virtual Model	Measures and Metrics	Range of Values in Leading Companies (LCs)	Baldrige Category
Organizational hierarchy	Network or "web" of organizations	Percentage of total executive time spent with other companies	—	—
Functional departments	Customer opportunity teams	Number of organizational walls to cross in meeting customer needs	—	5.1 7.2
Many organizational levels	Few organizational levels	Number of levels	—	—
Static, passive infrastructure	Dynamic active shared infrastructure	Production processes are nondistinguishing part of infrastructure	—	—
Comparison with other companies in same economic sector only by price of product	Constant comparison of work processes with capabilities of other companies from all economic sectors	Benchmark studies in the last three years	3 to 35	2.2 6.1 6.2 6.3
Static, efficient at meeting fixed goals and objectives	Dynamic, effective in meeting changing goals and objectives	Time to accept change in objective New team or project assignments per person per year	—	—

MANAGEMENT POLICY

Centralized	Distributed	Independence of profit centers on a scale of 1 to 10	—	4.2
Autocratic and directive	Coaching and inspirational	Supervisor/employee ratio	0 to 1:12	4.2
Focus on micromanagement	Focus on macromanagement and defining an organizational framework	Detail level in directives and existence of the framework on a scale of 1 to 10	—	—
Risk-averse and slow in making decisions	Entrepreneurial	Authority level at which risk can be taken and decisions made	—	—
		Speed of decision making measured in hours, days, weeks, months	—	—
		What happens to those who fail or succeed in terms of salary and promotion?	—	—

INFORMATION

Held for power	Distributed to empower	Percentage of employees accessing companywide data and average number of accesses per year per employee	—	2.3 4.2

The Traditional Model	The Emerging Agile-Virtual Model	Measures and Metrics	Range of Values in Leading Companies (LCs)	Baldrige Category
Told what to do! No thinking!	Asked to think and make decisions!	Average quantity of employee suggestions per employee per year	50	4.2 4.5
Low impact on decisions by most employees	High participation in decisions	Level of decision authority for chosen subjects	—	4.1
Compensation realized based only on time and rate	Compensation based on time, rate, and group performance on bottom line	Bottom-line impact as percentage of bonus component in compensation formulas	—	4.4

LEVERAGING PEOPLE AND INFORMATION

The Traditional Model	The Emerging Agile-Virtual Model	Measures and Metrics	Range of Values in Leading Companies (LCs)	Baldrige Category
Organized around products and product lines	Organized around core competencies and skills	Count and manage core competence areas and skill profiles inventory, rather than product lines and SKUs	—	4.1
Plant equipment and machinery are the most valuable assets	People skills, knowledge, and information are the most valuable assets	Skills and information included in asset valuations	—	—
		Percentage of employees cross-trained	100%	

CORPORATE STRATEGY AND FOCUS

The factory as the bottleneck	Enterprise information flow as the bottleneck	The resource or activity whose capacity limits the ability of the enterprise to meet the demand or opportunity of its customers and thus limits profits	— —
Capital equipment or facilities as the limiting resource	Skill base and information as the limiting resource	Which of the two is needed to expand bottleneck capacity	—
Societal concerns are a tolerated nuisance	Societal concerns are a means to understand and be close to customers	Measured effort devoted proactively to societal concerns	1.3 —

MANAGEMENT POLICY

Audit and police employees	Trust and empower employees to work within an organizational framework	Employee rating and budget for audit and policing activities Explicit framework with decision-making guidance for employees Operators inspect own work	— 92% of LCs
Focus on micromanagement	Focus on macromanagement and defining an organizational framework	Detail level in directives and existence of the framework on a scale of 1 to 10	—

and the corporation gets profit	partly based on profit	on profit Reward based on performance		1.3
Ad hoc corporate community support and involvement	Active planned and focused corporate community support to enhance corporate objectives, e.g., educated work force available	Existence of specific corporate community assistance objectives and measures of results of efforts	—	
Education as a benefit	Education as asset enhancement	Average annual days formal training and education per employee	5 to 40 days	4.3
		Training and education budget as percent of payroll	2.5 to 6.0% of payroll	
EMPLOYEE ENVIRONMENT				
Work as individuals	Work as individuals in teams	Use cross-functional project teams	100% of LCs	—
		Use self-directed work teams	100% of LCs	
Task-based compensation rate	Skill-based compensation rate	Compensation formulas and structure	—	4.1 4.4
Compensation realized based only on time and rate	Compensation realized based on time, rate, and group performance on bottom line	Bottom-line impact or performance-based component of compensation formulas	—	4.1 4.4
Mostly downward communication	Two-way communication is expected	Average number of suggestions per employee per year	50	4.2

Focus on security	Focus on organizational success and personal growth	Key employee concerns measured on survey	—	4.1 4.5
PRODUCT FOCUS				
Producer emphasizes physical plant: flexibility, low defect rate, automation, etc., as example of expertise	Producer emphasizes information, skills, knowledge, similar experience as examples of expertise. Flexibility, quality, low defect rate, are implicit, "entry ticket."	First-pass yield Resources measured and shown to demonstrate excellence to customers	70 to 100%	3.1
INFORMATION				
No apparent value	Critical corporate asset	Average value of information content of products	—	—
Not well protected or shared	Good intellectual property models for protecting and sharing	Number of intellectual property models available and usage of each	—	—

EPILOGUE

Agility-based competition and the mass-production system are like two different games, each with its own rules and strategies for winning. It is irrelevant to argue over which game is better. The only question that matters is, Which game is being played now? The answer is, "Agility." The agile competitive environment is supplanting the mass-production environment in developed societies today. This is happening because market forces have decisively and irreversibly changed the nature of commercial competition. If they want to compete, players and coaches have to learn the new game.

The implications of the changed nature of commercial competition for people and for companies are unsettling. Even in times of slow change, few people make the effort to adapt their personal skills to new opportunities, and few companies change their structure and values in order to exploit changing circumstances. When change is slow, slow responsiveness to that change is acceptable. But today, rapid change is the norm. As a result, the decision not to change now means that individuals and companies will be maneuvered into the low-value-add end of the agility-dominated economy. Such companies will earn lower profits, if they earn any at all; such individuals will earn lower incomes, if they can find jobs.

The choice facing growing numbers of people and institutions is whether to change to meet the new requirements for mainstream competitive success or to become economically marginalized. Mass-production will not disappear in an agile environment, just as craft production did not disappear in the mass-production environment.

Some companies and some people will continue to prosper in those production niches. The terms of the broad center of competition, however, will be dictated by agility. A major objective of this book has been to help people understand the characteristics of agile competition so that the choices they make for themselves, their companies, and their communities will enhance their prospects for economic success.

The situation today is far from unique. As the more-developed world adopted the modern industrial corporation model of mass-production competition at the turn of the twentieth century, many companies went out of business or lost their independence. Some authorities estimate that the number of U.S. companies that vanished through failure, mergers, or buyouts was as high as 80 percent of the businesses operating in the late nineteenth century. Many of them were companies that had tried to avoid the changes demanded by the changing nature of competition in their time. Many assumed that the new technologies, the new modes of production and competition, and the new quest for national and international markets were the affairs of others and posed no direct threat to their own local or regional competitive objectives. They were wrong.

It is easy to misunderstand the nature of revolutionary change and to suppose that it happens overnight, with one well-defined set of rules applicable on one day and a new set of well-defined rules suddenly applicable on the next day. In fact, the transition is prolonged, turbulent, and confused, with some period during which it is not at all clear which rules, if any, are operative. Misunderstanding the nature of revolutionary change can cause individuals and societal and corporate leaders, who are searching for stability in the midst of turbulence, to make the wrong strategic decisions. Living with uncertainty and striving to understand the emerging pattern of the new status quo are essential elements of all revolutionary change.

The period of change that we refer to as the *industrial revolution* began in the late eighteenth century and was given its name in the late 1820s by the historian Thomas Carlyle. Only at the end of the nineteenth century did the industrial revolution establish a new norm for Western societies with the rise of the modern industrial corporation.

The American colonists rebelled against the British in 1776, but it was only 15 years later that the United States of America emerged out of the protracted negotiations among the 13 independent states.

The French Revolution can be thought of as beginning with the storming of the Bastille on July 14, 1789, but that day was followed by a decade of violent turmoil that was calmed briefly by Napoleon before another decade of almost constant war and change began. Only after 1815 could one begin to look back on the revolution and assess its impact.

The challenge of change that we are experiencing today confronts not only individuals and commercial organizations, but society as a whole. During the past 200 years, the socially most acceptable way to earn a living has been through work: even "gentlefolk" have had to join the work force. Until very recently, however, jobs once defined, and skills once acquired, lasted for all of a person's working life, and almost everyone who was healthy and skilled could find a job. It remains the case even today that many people believe that the most honorable form of work is to earn a living by the "sweat of one's brow": farming, fishing, mining, felling trees, building roads, and making physical *things*, especially big things, like planes, cars, trucks, locomotives, and heavy machinery.

At the same time, we all know that fewer and fewer people are employed in such jobs. Knowledge-based and service occupations continue to account for growing percentages of the work force, and these occupations promise to give rise to new ones that are as yet unknown, as people respond creatively to opportunities for personal economic advance that are opened up by agile competition. Society will have to address some basic questions as this trend continues.

For example, how should the wealth created in an economy with greatly enhanced production efficiency be distributed, especially among citizens who lack value-adding, knowledge-based, and service skills? How can a socially equitable distribution be achieved while reinforcing the motivation of talented individuals to display initiative and work hard to create new wealth-generating businesses? How can the distribution of wealth be changed in a manner consistent with prevailing social and personal values? These questions will increasingly engage the attention of philosophers, social scientists, politicians, and the citizenry as the agile competitive environment matures.

The history of the agricultural-industrial revolution, discussed briefly near the end of Chapter 2, illustrates the problem. Throughout the early nineteenth century, most people in what are today the developed societies lived on farms. The overwhelming majority produced little surplus food and were poor. Today, farming is industrialized, highly technology-intensive, and scientific. Few people in developed societies live on farms, but they consistently generate large surpluses that provide everyone with inexpensive food. The agricultural support system, however, and the commercial food creation, production, and distribution systems have created large numbers of jobs that were unimagined, and unimaginable, during the nineteenth century.

Broad access to inexpensive, high-quality foods, a benefit of international competition, conflicts with domestic agricultural protectionism. Broad access to high-paying jobs, as well as to the benefits of goods and services created by an agility-based global economy, conflicts with protecting established national life-styles and values. We must expect societies to struggle for years to come to terms with the value dilemmas posed by agile competition.

We live in a whirlwind today, called upon to function in a period of unprecedented change and dislocation. What had seemed to be certain answers to basic questions have become debatable answers to irrelevant questions. The new questions to which we need satisfying answers can emerge only out of an understanding of the structural transformation of the wealth-creating systems at work in the world today. Out of such an understanding comes the possibility of repositioning ourselves so that we can share in the increasing wealth that is being created in the emerging agile competitive system. This book, we hope, contributes to understanding the challenges and the opportunities that confront us.

Resource Organizations

Most national and regional governments operate or sponsor resource organizations that work with or assist businesses in various ways in order to promote economic health and jobs in their region. Experience shows that, contrary to what one may expect, it is not easy to find systematic data on these resources and to evaluate how they may help. Since businesses, especially industrial concerns, are moving into a period of rapid change, the need to find these resource organizations has become more urgent than before. As a service to the reader, a list of such organizations is given in this appendix for the United States and Germany. No recommendation of any sort is implied by the inclusion of an organization in the list, and none is implied by the omission of an organization.

Although efforts were made to find the particulars on all suitable organizations, it is possible that not all appropriate organizations were included. An organization in any country that would like to be included in future printings of this book is invited to send particulars to the authors, at Lehigh University, Bethlehem, PA 18015, Fax: + 1 610 758-6550.

Points of Contact for U.S. Resources

Agile Manufacturing Enterprise Forum (Agility Forum)

Bethlehem, PA 18015-1582
General phone: (610) 758-5510
Fax: (610) 694-0542

Education and Training:
  Phone: (610) 758-6593
Research and Industry Teams:
  Phone: (610) 758-5517
Small and Medium Enterprises:
  Phone: (610) 758-6190
Technical Publications:
  Phone: (610) 758-4887

A. L. Philpott Manufacturing Center
Martinsville, VA 24112
Phone: (703) 666-8890
Fax: (703) 666-8892

Advanced Level Manufacturing
   Program CALS—Shared Resource
   Center
Cleveland, OH 44103
Phone: (216) 432-5300
Fax: (216) 361-2900

Advanced Technology Development
   Center (ATDC)
Atlanta, GA 30318
Phone: (404) 894-3575
Fax: (404) 894-4545

Advanced Technologies Group
   Services
Farmington Hills, MI 48018
Phone: (810) 737-9132
Fax: (810) 737-9341

American Production and Inventory
   Control Society (APICS)
Falls Church, VA 22046-4274
Phone: (703) 237-8344
Fax: (703) 237-1071

American Society for Training and
   Development (ASTD)
Alexandria, VA 22313
Phone: (703) 683-8152
Fax: (703) 548-2383

Applied Research Laboratory
Upper Marlboro, MD 20772
Phone: (703) 696-8482
Fax: (703) 696-8480

Arizona Applied Manufacturing
   Center
Phoenix, AZ 85034
Phone: (602) 392-5166
Fax: (602) 392-5329

Association for Manufacturing
   Excellence (AME)
Mooresville, IN 46158
Phone: (317) 839-9829
Fax: (317) 839-2979

Automated Business Practices
   CALS—Shared Resource Center
San Antonio, TX 78228
Phone: (210) 732-1141
Fax: (210) 732-5011

Automated Design CALS—Shared
   Resource Center
Dayton, OH 45402-2302
Phone: (513) 449-6073
Fax: (513) 449-6068

Automation and Robotics Research
   Institute (AARI-UTA)
Fort Worth, TX 76118-7115
Phone: (817) 794-5925
Fax: (817) 794-5952

Ben Franklin Northeast Tier
   Technology Center
Bethlehem, PA 18015-3715
Phone: (610) 758-5200
Fax: (610) 861-5918

Ben Franklin Technology Center of
   Central and Northeastern
   Pennsylvania
University Park, PA 16802-1013
Phone: (814) 863-4558
Fax: (814) 865-0960

Ben Franklin Technology Center of
Southeastern Pennsylvania
Philadelphia, PA 19104
Phone: (215) 382-0380
Fax: (215) 387-6050

Ben Franklin Technology Center of
Western Pennsylvania
Pittsburgh, PA 15213
Phone: (412) 681-1520
Fax: (412) 681-2625

Bioprocessing Resource Center
University Park, PA 16802
Phone: (814) 863-3650
Fax: (814) 863-1357

California Manufacturing
Technology Center
Hawthorne, CA 90250
Phone: (310) 355-3060
Fax: (310) 676-8630

Center for Commercial
Competitiveness (C-3)
Binghamton, NY 13902-6000
Phone: (607) 777-2718
Fax: (607) 777-2022

Chicago Manufacturing Center
Chicago, IL 60624
Phone: (312) 265-2020
Fax: (312) 265-8336

Commercial Technology
CALS—Shared Resource
Center
Orange, TX 77630-5702
Phone: (409) 882-3950
Fax: (409) 882-3981

Connecticut State Technology
Extension Program
Storrs, CT 06269-2041
Phone: (203) 486-2684
Fax: (203) 486-3049

Consortium for Advanced
Manufacturing-International
(CAM-I)
Cupertino, CA 95014
Phone: (408) 253-0134
Fax: (408) 257-9254

Defense Enterprise Empowerment
Project (DEEP)
Kettering, OH 45420
Phone: (513) 259-1365
Fax: (513) 259-1303

Delaware Manufacturing Alliance
Newark, DE 19711
Phone: (302) 452-2520
Fax: (302) 452-1101

Delaware Valley Industrial Resource
Center
Philadelphia, PA 19154
Phone: (215) 464-8550
Fax: (215) 464-8570

Edison Materials Technology Center
Kettering, OH 45420-4006
Phone: (513) 259-1393
Fax: (513) 259-1303

Energy Analysis and Diagnostic
Center, Industrial Assessment
Center, the EADC/TAC Program,
Eastern EADC Region at Rutgers
University
Piscataway, NJ 08855
Phone: (908) 932-3655
Fax: (908) 932-0730

Energy Analysis and Diagnostic
Center, Industrial Assessment
Center, the EADC/TAC
Program, Western EADC
Region at University City
Science Center
Philadelphia, PA 19104
Phone: (215) 387-2255
Fax: (215) 387-5540

Energy-Related Inventions Program
Office of Energy Efficiency and
Renewable Energy
Washington, DC 20585
Phone: (202) 586-1478
Fax: (202) 586-1605

Energy Research Laboratory
Technology Transfer Program
Washington, DC 20585
Phone: (202) 586-3825
Fax: (202) 586-3119

Georgia Manufacturing Extension
Alliance
Atlanta, GA 30332
Phone: (404) 894-6106
Fax: (404) 853-9172

Georgia Manufacturing Technology
Extension Center
Savannah, GA 31406
Phone: (912) 921-5510
Fax: (912) 921-5512

Great Lakes Manufacturing
Technology Center
Cleveland, OH 44103-4314
Phone: (216) 432-5321
Fax: (216) 361-2900

Hudson Valley Manufacturing
Technology Development Center
Fishkill, NY 12524
Phone: (914) 896-6934
Fax: (914) 896-7006

Iacocca Institute
Bethlehem, PA 18015
Phone: (610) 758-6509
Fax: (610) 758-6550

Illinois Business Technology Service
Center
Springfield, IL 62701
Phone: (217) 524-5696
Fax: (217) 524-3701

Industrial Modernization Center
Montoursville, PA 17754
Phone: (717) 368-8361
Fax: (717) 368-8452

Industrial Technology Institute
(ITI)
Ann Arbor, MI 48105
Phone: (313) 769-4000
Fax: (313) 769-4064

Information Technology
CALS—Shared Resource Center
Fairfax, VA 22030
Phone: (703) 691-1507
Fax: (703) 691-8948

Institute of Advanced Manufacturing
Sciences, Inc.
Cincinnati, OH 45216
Phone: (513) 948-2000
Fax: (513) 948-2109

International Association of
Machinists (IAM)
Upper Marlboro, MD 20772-2687
Phone: (301) 967-4704
Fax: (301) 967-3431

Iowa Manufacturing Technology
Center
Ankeny, IA 50021
Phone: (515) 965-7040
Fax: (515) 964-6206

Kentucky Technology Science and
Council
Lexington, KY 40588
Phone: (606) 233-3502
Fax: (606) 259-0986

Manufacturing Technology Industrial
Resource Center (MANTEC)
York, PA 17405
Phone: (717) 843-5054
Fax: (717) 854-0087

Maryland Department of Economic
Development
Division of Business
Small Business Development Center
Baltimore, MD 21202
Phone: (410) 333-1036
Fax: (410) 333-1836

Maryland Industrial Partnerships
Engineering Research Center
College Park, MD 20742-3415
Phone: (301) 405-3891
Fax: (301) 403-4105

Massachusetts Manufacturing
Partnership
Boston, MA 02110
Phone: (617) 292-5100
Fax: (617) 292-5105

Metal Casting Center
Cedar Falls, IA 50614-0178
Phone: (319) 273-6894
Fax: (319) 273-5959

Metalworking Technology
CALS—Shared Resource Center
Johnstown, PA 15904
Phone: (814) 269-2494 or
1-800-231-2772
Fax: (814) 269-2666

Miami Valley Manufacturing
Extension Center (MVMEC)
Kettering, OH 45420
Phone: (513) 259-1366
Fax: (513) 259-1303

Microelectronics and Computer
Technology Corporation (MCC)
Austin, TX 78759-6509
Phone: (512) 338-3518
Fax: (512) 338-3897

Mid-America Manufacturing
Technology Center (MAMTC)
Fort Collins, CO 80523
Phone: (303) 224-3744
Fax: (303) 224-3715

Mid-America Manufacturing
Technology Center (MAMTC)
Kansas City, MO 64110
Phone: (816) 753-1231
Fax: (816) 753-3726

Mid-America Manufacturing
Technology Center (MAMTC)
Manhattan, KS 66506
Phone: (913) 532-5617
Fax: (913) 532-5352

Mid-America Manufacturing
Technology Center (MAMTC)
Overland Park, KS 66210-1299
Phone: (913) 469-2305
Fax: (913) 469-4415

Mid-America Manufacturing
Technology Center (MAMTC)
Pittsburg, KS 66762
Phone: (316) 235-4114
Fax: (316) 232-8833

Mid-America Manufacturing
Technology Center (MAMTC)
Great Bend, KS 67530
Phone: (316) 793-7964
Fax: (316) 792-4850

Mid-America Manufacturing
Technology Center (MAMTC)
Wichita, KS 67260-0146
Phone: (316) 689-3525
Fax: (316) 689-3175

Missouri Enterprise Business
Assistance Center
Rolla, MO 65401
Phone: (314) 364-8570
Fax: (314) 364-6323

Modernization Forum
Dearborne, MI 48128
Phone: (313) 271-2790
Fax: (313) 271-2791

National Center for Manufacturing
Sciences (NCMS)
Ann Arbor, MI 48108-3266
Phone: (313) 995-0300
Fax: (313) 995-4004

Nebraska Industrial Competitiveness
Service (NICS)
Lincoln, NE 68509
Phone: (402) 471-3769
Fax: (402) 471-3778

New Jersey Business and Industry
Association
Trenton, NJ 08608
Phone: (609) 393-7707
Fax: (609) 989-7371

New Mexico Manufacturing
Extension Program
New Mexico Industry Network
Corporation
Albuquerque, NM 87106
Phone: (505) 272-7800
Fax: (505) 272-7810

New York City ITAC
New York, NY 10007
Phone: (212) 240-6920
Fax: (212) 240-4889

New York Manufacturing Extension
Partnership
Troy, NY 12180-8347
Phone: (518) 283-1010
Fax: (518) 283-1112

New York State Department of
Economic Development
Binghamton, NY 13901
Phone: (607) 773-7813
Fax: (607) 773-7872

Northeastern Pennsylvania Industrial
Resource Center (NEPIRC)
West Pittston, PA 18643
Phone: (717) 654-8966
Fax: (717) 655-8931

Northwest Pennsylvania Industrial
Resource Center
Erie, PA 16511-1031
Phone: (814) 456-6299
Fax: (814) 459-6058

Northwestern Pennsylvania
Industrial Resource Centers
Business Innovation Center
Duquesne, PA 15110
Phone: (412) 469-3530 or
1-800-444-2504
Fax: (412) 469-3539

Northwest Wisconsin
Manufacturing Outreach Center
Menomonie, WI 54751-1876
Phone: (715) 232-2397
Fax: (715) 232-1105

Oklahoma Alliance for
Manufacturing Excellence
Tulsa, OK 74103
Phone: (918) 592-0722
Fax: (918) 592-1417

Oregon Technology Exchange
Consortium
Salem, OR 97310
Phone: (503) 986-0192
Fax: (503) 581-5115

Pennsylvania Manufacturing Extension
Program: Northeast Region
Bethlehem, PA 18015
Phone: (610) 758-5542
Fax: (610) 758-4716

Plastics Technology Deployment
Center
Cleveland, OH 44103
Phone: (216) 432-5300
Fax: (216) 361-2088

Pollution Prevention Center
Santa Monica, CA 90404
Phone: (310) 453-0450
Fax: (310) 453-2660

Recycling Technology Assistance
Partnership
Seattle, WA 98121
Phone: (206) 464-6009
Fax: (206) 464-6902

Rensselaer Technology Park
Troy, NY 12180-8397
Phone: (518) 283-7102
Fax: (518) 283-0695

Scanning and Conversion
CALS—Shared Resource Center
Palestine, TX 75801
Phone: (903) 729-4440
Fax: (903) 729-4610

Sematech
Austin, TX 78741-6499
Phone: (512) 356-3500
Fax: (512) 356-3083

Small Business Initiative Program,
Office of Defense Programs
Albuquerque, NM 87185-5400
Phone: (505) 845-4947
Fax: (505) 845-5754

Small Business Technology
Integration Program
Office of Environmental
Restoration and Waste
Management
Washington, DC 20585
Phone: (301) 903-7449
Fax: (301) 903-7238

Society of Manufacturing Engineers
  (SME)
Dearborn, MI 48121
Phone: (313) 271-1500
Fax: (313) 271-2861

Southeast Manufacturing
  Technology Center
Columbia, SC 29202-1149
Phone: (803) 252-6976
Fax: (803) 252-0056

Southwest Pennsylvania Industrial
  Resource Center
Pittsburgh, PA 15213
Phone: (412) 687-0200
Fax: (412) 687-5232

Tennessee Manufacturing Extension
  Program
Nashville, TN 37243-0405
Phone: (615) 741-2994
Fax: (615) 741-5070

Thomas Alva Edison Partnership
  Program
Columbus, OH 43266-0101
Phone: (614) 466-3086
Fax: (614) 644-5758

University Industrial Partnership
  for Economic Growth
  (UnIPEG)
New York Manufacturing Extension
  Partnership
Endicott, NY 13760
Phone: (607) 748-9214
Fax: (607) 785-0026

Upper Midwest Manufacturing
  Technology Center
Minneapolis, MN 55401

Phone: (612) 338-7722
Fax: (612) 339-5214

Virginia Department of Economic
  Development
Business Services and
  Community Development
  Division
Richmond, VA 23206-0798
Phone: (804) 371-8100
Fax: (804) 371-2945

Virginia's Center for Innovative
  Technology
Herndon, VA 22070-4005
Phone: (703) 689-3000
Fax: (703) 689-3041

Washington Alliance for
  Manufacturing
Seattle, WA 98103
Phone: (206) 633-5252
Fax: (206) 632-1272

Washington Manufacturing
  Extension Center
Seattle, WA 98103
Phone: (206) 633-5252
Fax: (206) 632-1272

Western New York Technology
  Development Center
Amherst, NY 14228
Phone: (716) 636-3626
Fax: (716) 636-3630

Western Pennsylvania
  Manufacturing Extension
  Program
Pittsburgh, PA 15213
Phone: (412) 687-0200
Fax: (412) 687-5232

*Points of Contact for State
Government Resources*

*Points of contact as advertised by each
state, arranged alphabetically by state.*

Alabama Technology and Energy
  Department
Department of Economic and
  Community Affairs
Montgomery, AL 36103-5690
Phone: (205) 242-5286
Fax: (205) 242-5515

Alaska Science and Technology
  Foundation
Anchorage, AK 99501-3555
Phone: (907) 272-4333
Fax: (907) 274-6228

Arizona Energy Director
Department of Commerce
Phoenix, AZ 85012
Phone: (602) 280-1336 or
  1-800-528-8421
Fax: (602) 280-1445

Arkansas Science and Technology
  Authority
Little Rock, AR 72201
Phone: (501) 324-9006
Fax: (501) 324-9012

California Trade and Commerce
  Agency
Sacramento, CA 95814
Phone: (916) 324-5065
Fax: (916) 322-3524

California Office of Competitive
  Technology
Trade and Commerce Agency

Pasadena, CA 91105
Phone: (818) 568-9437
Fax: (818) 683-2642

Colorado Advanced Technology
  Institiute
Denver, CO 80202
Phone: (303) 620-4777 ext. 301
Fax: (303) 620-4789

Connecticut Innovations Inc.
Rocky Hill, CT 06067-3405
Phone: (203) 258-4305
Fax: (203) 563-4877

Delaware Development Office
Dover, DE 19903
Phone: (302) 739-4271
Fax: (302) 739-5749

Florida Department of Commerce
Tallahassee, FL 32399-2000
Phone: (904) 922-8701
Fax: (904) 487-1612

Georgia Office of Planning and
  Budget
Atlanta, GA 30334
Phone: (404) 656-3820
Fax: (404) 656-7198

Hawaii High Technology
  Development Corporation
Mililani, HI 96789
Phone: (808) 625-5293
Fax: (808) 625-6363

Idaho Department of Commerce
Boise, ID 83720-2700
Phone: (208) 334-2470
Fax: (208) 334-2631

Illinois Science Advisory Committee
Springfield, IL 62706
Phone: (217) 782-5189
Fax: (217) 524-1678

Indiana Business Modernization and
    Technology Corporation
Indianapolis, IN 46204
Phone: (317) 635-3058
Fax: (317) 231-7095

Iowa Governor's Science Advisor
Office of the Governor
Des Moines, IA 50313
Phone: (515) 281-7879
Fax: (515) 281-7882

Iowa Wallace Technology Transfer
    Foundation
Des Moines, IA 50309
Phone: (515) 243-1487
Fax: (515) 243-1975

Kansas Research and Analysis
Department of Commerce
Topeka, KS 66603-3712
Phone: (913) 296-3564
Fax: (913) 296-5055

Kentucky Office of Business and
    Technology
Cabinet for Economic Development
Frankfort, KY 40601
Phone: (502) 564-7670
Fax: (502) 564-7697

Louisiana Director for Technology
Department of Economic
    Development
Baton Rouge, LA 70802
Phone: (504) 342-5388
Fax: (504) 342-9095

Louisiana Partnership for Technology
    and Innovation
Baton Rouge, LA 70809
Phone: (504) 922-9189
Fax: (504) 922-9107

Maine Science and Technology
    Foundation
Augusta, ME 04330
Phone: (207) 621-6350
Fax: (207) 621-6369

Maryland Department of Economic
    and Employment Development
Baltimore, MD 21202
Phone: (410) 333-6901
Fax: (410) 333-6911

Massachusetts Defense, Diversification
    and Technology Transfer
Executive Office of Economic Affairs
Boston, MA 02108
Phone: (617) 727-3206
Fax: (617) 727-8797

Michigan Deputy Director/Policy
    Advisor
Office of the Governor
Lansing, MI 48933
Phone: (517) 373-9749
Fax: (517) 335-0118

Minnesota Technology Inc.
Minneapolis, MN 55401
Phone: (612) 338-7722
Fax: (612) 339-5214

Mississippi State University
    Community and Economic
    Development Center
Starkville, MS 39762
Phone: (601) 325-2547
Fax: (601) 325-8872

Missouri Program Administrator for Technology
Department of Economic Development
Jefferson City, MO 65102
Phone: (314) 751-5095
Fax: (314) 751-7384

Montana Department of Commerce
Helena, MT 59620
Phone: (406) 444-3797
Fax: (406) 442-0788

College of Engineering and Technology
Science Advisor to the Governor
University of Nebraska
Lincoln, NE 68588-0501
Phone: (402) 472-3181
Fax: (402) 472-7792

Nevada Washington Office
Washington, DC 20001
Phone: (202) 624-5405
Fax: (202) 624-8181

Industrial Research Center
University of New Hampshire
Durham, NH 03824
Phone: (603) 862-0123
Fax: (603) 862-0329

New Jersey Commission on Science and Technology
Trenton, NJ 08625-0832
Phone: (609) 633-2740
Fax: (609) 292-5920

New Mexico Science Advisor to the Governor
Office of the Governor
Albuquerque, NM 87123
Phone: (505) 844-6015
Fax: (505) 844-2896

New Mexico Department of Economic Development
Santa Fe, NM 87503
Phone: (505) 827-0381
Fax: (505) 827-0407

New York State Science and Technology Foundation
Albany, NY 12210
Phone: (518) 474-4349
Fax: (518) 473-6876

North Carolina Advisor to the Governor for Policy, Budget, and Technology
Department of Administration
Raleigh, NC 27603
Phone: (919) 715-0960
Fax: (919) 733-2120

North Dakota School of Engineering and Mines
Grand Forks, ND 58202
Phone: (701) 777-5128
Fax: (701) 777-2339

Oklahoma Center for Advancement of Science and Technology
Oklahoma City, OK 73116-7906
Phone: (405) 848-2633
Fax: (405) 521-6501

Oregon Center for Advanced Technology Education
Beaverton, OR 97006
Phone: (503) 737-3101
Fax: (503) 690-1466

Pennsylvania Office of Technology
  Development
Department of Commerce
Harrisburg, PA 17120
Phone: (717) 787-4147
Fax: (717) 772-5080

Puerto Rico Federal Affairs
  Administration
Washington, DC 20036
Phone: (202) 778-0710
Fax: (202) 778-0721

Rhode Island Office of Defense
  Economic Adjustment
University of Rhode Island
Kingston, RI 02881
Phone: (401) 792-2549
Fax: (401) 277-2102

South Carolina Research Authority
Columbus, SC 29201
Phone: (803) 799-4070
Fax: (803) 252-7642

South Dakota School of Mines and
  Technology
Rapid City, SD 57701
Phone: (605) 394-2411
Fax: (605) 394-6131

Tennessee Advisor to the Governor
  for Science and Technology
Department of Economic and
  Community Development
Nashville, TN 37243-0405
Phone: (615) 741-2994
Fax: (615) 741-5070

Texas Department of Commerce
Austin, TX 78701
Phone: (512) 320-9561
Fax: (512) 320-9544

Utah State Science Advisor
Office of the Governor
Salt Lake City, UT 84114
Phone: (801) 538-1038
Fax: (801) 538-1547

Utah Department of Community
  and Economic Development
Salt Lake City, UT 84114
Phone: (801) 538-8770
Fax: (801) 538-8773

Utah State Information Technology
  Coordinator
Office of the Governor
Salt Lake City, UT 84114
Phone: (801) 538-1843
Fax: (801) 538-1547

Vermont Office of the Governor
Montpelier, VT 05602
Phone: (802) 828-3326
Fax: (802) 828-3339

Virginia
Secretariat of Commerce and Trade,
  Commonwealth of Virginia
Richmond, VA 23212
Phone: (804) 786-7831
Fax: (804) 371-0250

Virginia Defense Conversion and
  Economic Transition
Herndon, VA 22070
Phone: (703) 689-3057
Fax: (703) 759-6208

Washington Department of Trade
  and Economic Development
Olympia, WA 98504-2500
Phone: (206) 586-0265
Fax: (206) 586-8380

West Virginia Business and
Industrial Development
West Virginia Office of Community
and Industrial Development
Charleston, WV 25305-0311
Phone: (304) 558-2234
Fax: (304) 558-0449

Wisconsin Bureau of Research and
Technology
Department of Development
Madison, WI 53702
Phone: (608) 267-9382
Fax: (608) 267-0436

Wyoming Science, Technology, and
Energy Authority
Laramie, WY 82071
Phone: (307) 766-6797
Fax: (307) 766-6799

*Points of Contact at Fraunhofer
Institutes for German Resource
Organizations*

*The Fraunhofer system of institutes are
the resource organizations for Germany*

Applied Materials Research
Fraunhofer-Institut für Angewandte
Materialforschung (IFAM)
Bremen (Lesum) D-28717
Phone: 49 (0) 4 21/63 83-0
Fax: 49 (0) 4 21/63 83-190

Applied Optics and Precision
Engineering
Fraunhofer-Einrichtung für
Angewandte Optik und
Feinmechanik (IOF)

Jena D-07745
Phone: 49 (0) 36 41/5 82-2 01
Fax: 49 (0) 36 41/5 29 63

Applied Polymer Research
Fraunhofer-Institut für Angewandte
Polymerforschung (IAP)
Teltow D-14513
Phone: 49 (0) 33 28/46-0
Fax: 49 (0) 33 28/46-3-44

Applied Solid-State Physics
Fraunhofer-Institut für Angewandte
Festkörperphysik (IAF)
Freiburg D-79102
Phone: 49 (0) 7 61/51 59-0
Fax: 49 (0) 7 61/51 59-4 00

Atmospheric Environmental
Research
Fraunhofer-Institut für
Atmosphärische Umweltforschung
(IFU)
Garmisch-Partenkirchen D-82467
Phone: 49 (0) 88 21/1 83-0
Fax: 49 (0) 88 21/7 35 73

Biomedical Engineering
Fraunhofer-Institut für
Biomedizinische Technik (IBMT)
St. Ingbert D-66386
Phone: 49 (0) 68 94/9 80-0
Fax: 49 (0) 68 94/9 80-400

Building Physics
Fraunhofer-Institut für Bauphysik
(IBP)
Stuttgart D-70569
Phone: 49 (0) 711/9 70-00
Fax: 49 (0) 711/9 70-33-95

Central Administration
Fraunhofer-Gesellschaft zur
  Förderung der Angewandten
  Forschung e.V.
München D-80636
Phone: 49 (0) 89/12 05-01
Fax: 49 (0) 89/12 05-3 17
  521 53 82

Ceramic Technologies and Sintered
  Materials
Fraunhofer-Institut für Keramische
  Technologies und Sinterwerkstoffe
  (IKT)
Dresden D-01277
Phone: 49 (0) 3 51/25 53-5
Fax: 49 (0) 3 51/25 53-6

Chemical Technology
Fraunhofer-Institut für Chemische
  Technologie (ICT)
Pfinztal (Berghausen) D-76327
Phone: 49 (0) 721/4640-0
Fax: 49 (0) 721/4640-1 11

Computer Graphics Research
Fraunhofer-Institut für
  Graphische Datenverarbeitung
  (IGD)
Darmstadt D-64283
Phone: 49 (0) 61 51/1 55-0
Fax: 49 (0) 61 51/1 55-199

Electron Beams and Plasma
Technology Fraunhofer-Institut für
  Elektronenstrahl und
  Plasmatechnik (FEP)
Dresden D-01324
Phone: 49 (0) 3 51/46 77-01
Fax: 49 (0) 3 51/46 77-179

Environmental Chemistry and
  Ecotoxicology
Fraunhofer-Institut für
  Umweltchemie und
  Okotoxikologie (IUCT)
Schmallenberg/Grafschaft D-57392
Phone: 49 (0) 29 72/3 02-0
Fax: 49 (0) 29 72/3 02-3 19

Factory Operation and Automation
Fraunhofer-Institut für Fabrikbetrieb
  und Automatisierung (IFF)
Magdeburg D-39104
Phone: 49 (0) 3 91/4 22 81 or
  3 91/5 61 38 58 or
  3 91/5 61 34 85 or 3 91/4 20 75
Fax: 49 (0) 3 91/4 22 81

Food Process Engineering and
  Packaging
Fraunhofer-Institut für
  Lebensmitteltechnologie und
  Verpackung (TLV)
München D-80992
Phone: 49 (0) 89/14 90 09-0
Fax: 49 (0) 89/14 90 09-80

High-Speed Dynamics
Fraunhofer-Institut für
  Kurzzeitdynamik
  «Ernst-Mach-Institut» (EMI)
Phone: 49 (0) 761/27 14-0
Fax: 49 (0) 761/27 14-316

Industrial Engineering
Fraunhofer-Institut für
  Arbeitswirtschaft und
  Organisation (IAO)
Stuttgart D-70569
Phone: 49 (0) 7 11/9 70-01
Fax: 49 (0) 7 11/9 70-22 99

Information and Data Processing
Fraunhofer-Institut für
  Informations und
  Datenverarbeltung (IITB)
Karlsruhe D-76131
Phone: 49 (0) 721/60 91-0
Fax: 49 (0) 721/60 91-4 13

Information Center for Regional
  Planning and Building
  Construction
Informationszentrum Raum und
  Bau der Fraunhofer-Gesellschaft
  (IRB)
Stuttgart D-70569
Phone: 49 (0) 7 11/9 70-25 00
Fax: 49 (0) 7 11/9 70-25 07

Integrated Circuits
Fraunhofer-Institut für Integrierte
  Schaltungen (FIS)
Department for Applied Electronics
Erlangen D-91058
Phone: 49 (0) 91/317 76-0
Fax: 49 (0) 91 31/7 76-9 99

Integrated Circuits
Fraunhofer-Institut für Integrierte
  Schaltungen (FIS)
Department for Device Technology
Erlangen D-91052
Phone: 49 (0) 91 31/85 86-33
Fax: 49 (0) 91 31/85 86-98

Laser Technology
Fraunhofer-Institut für Lasertechnik
  (ILT)
Aachen D-52074
Phone: 49 (0) 2 41/89 06-0
Fax: 49 (0) 2 41/89 06-121

Manufacturing Engineering and
  Automation
Fraunhofer-Institut für
  Produktionstechnik und
  Automatisierung (IPA)
Stuttgart D-70569
Phone: 49 (0) 7 11/9 70-0
Fax: 49 (0) 7 11/9 703 99

Material Flow and Logistics
Fraunhofer-Institut für Materialflu
  und Logistik (IML)
Dortmund D-44227
Phone: 49 (0) 2 31/97 4-0
Fax: 49 (0) 2 31/97 4-2 11

Material Physics and Thin Film
  Technology
Fraunhofer-Institut für
  Werkstoffphysik und
  Schichttechnologie (IWS)
Dresden D-01171
Phone: 49 (0) 3 51/46 59-3 24
Fax: 49 (0) 3 51/46 59-5 46

Mechanics of Materials
Fraunhofer-Institut für
  Werkstoffmechanik (IWM)
Dresden D-79108
Phone: 49 (0) 7 61/51 42-0
Fax: 49 (0) 7 61/51 42-110

Microelectronic Circuits and
  Systems
Fraunhofer-Institut für
  Mikroelektronische Schaltungen
  und Systeme (IMS)
Duisburg D-47057
Phone: 49 (0) 203/37 83 0
Fax: 49 (0) 203/37 83-266

Microelectronic Circuits and Systems
Fraunhofer-Institut für
    Mikroelektronische Schaltungen
    und Systeme (IMS)
Dresden D-01109
Phone: 49 (0) 3 51/58 23-0
Fax: 49 (0) 3 51/58 23-266

Patent Center for German Research
Fraunhofer-Gesellschaft Patentstelle
    für die Deutsche Forschung der
    Fraunhofer-Gesellschaft (PST)
München D-80636
Phone: 49 (0) 89/12 05-02
Fax: 49 (0) 89/12 05-4 98 or
    49 (0) 89/12 05-4 67

Physical Measurement Techniques
Fraunhofer-Institut für Physikalische
    Metechnik (IPM)
Freiburg D-79110
Phone: 49 (0) 7 61/8857-0
Fax: 49 (0) 7 61/8857-224

Production Systems and Design
    Technology
Fraunhofer-Institut für
    Produktionsanlagen und
    Konstruktionstechnik (IPK)
Berlin D-10587
Phone: 49 (0) 30/3 90 06-0
Fax: 49 (0) 30/3 91 10-37 or
    49 (0) 30/3 92 29-37

Production Technology
Fraunhofer-Institut für
    Produktionstechnologie (IPT)
Aachen D-52074
Phone: 49 (0) 2 41/89 04-101
Fax: 49 (0) 2 41/89 04-198

Reliability and Microintegration
Fraunhofer-Einrichtung für
    Zuverlässigkeit und
    Mikrointegration (IZM)
Berlin D-13355
Phone: 49 (0) 30/4 64 03-100
Fax: 49 (0) 30/4 64 03-111

Silicate Research
Fraunhofer-Institut für
    Silicatforschung (ISC)
Würzburg D-97082
Phone: 49 (0) 9 31/4 19 09-0
Fax: 49 (0) 9 31/4 19 09-80

Silicon Technology
Fraunhofer-Institut für
    Siliziumtechnologie (ISIT);
    formerly Microstructural
    Technology (IMT)
Berlin D-14199
Phone: 49 (0) 30/8 29 98-0
Fax: 49 (0) 30/8 29 98-199

Software Engineering and System
    Engineering
Fraunhofer-Einrichtung für Software
    und Systemtechnik (ISST)
Berlin D-10117
Phone: 49 (0) 30/2 03 72-2 96
Fax: 49 (0) 30/2 03 72-2 07

Solar Energy Systems
Fraunhofer-Institut für Solare
    Energiesysteme (ISE)
Freiburg D-79100
Phone: 49 (0) 7 61/45 88-0
Fax: 49 (0) 7 61/45 88-1000

Solid-State Technology
Fraunhofer-Institut für
    Festkörpertechnologie (IFT)

München D-80686
Phone: 49 (0) 89/54759-000
Fax: 49 (0) 89/547 59-100

Strength of Structures under
    Operational Conditions
Fraunhofer-Institut für
    Betriebsfestigkeit (LBF)
Darmstadt-Kranichstein D-64289
Phone: 49 (0) 61 51/7 05-1
Fax: 49 (0) 61 51/7 05-214

Surface Engineering and Films
Fraunhofer-Institut für
    Oberflachentechnik (ISO)
Braunschweig D-38108
Phone: 49 (0) 5 31/39 09-0
Fax: 49 (0) 5 31/35 3718

Surface Technology and Biochemical
    Engineering
Fraunhofer-Institut für Grenzflachen
    und Bioverfahrenstechnik (IGB)
Stuttgart D-70569
Phone: 49 (0) 711/9 70 00
Fax: 49 (0) 711/9 70-42 00

Systems and Innovation Research
Fraunhofer-Institut für
    Systemtechnik und
    Innovationsforschung (ISI)
Karlsruhe D-76139

Phone: 49 (0) 7 21/68 09-0
Fax: 49 (0) 7 21/68 91 52

Technological Trend Analysis
Fraunhofer-Institut für
    Naturwissenschaftlich-Technische
    Trendanalysen (INT)
Euskirchen D-53881
Phone: 49 (0) 22 51/18-1
Fax: 49 (0) 22 51/18-2 77

Technology Development Group
Technologie-Entwicklungsgruppe
    Stuttgart TEG-S
Stuttgart D-70569
Phone: 49 (0) 7 11/9 70-35 00
Fax: 49 (0) 7 11/9 70-39 99

Toxicology and Aerosol Research
Fraunhofer-Institut für Toxikologie
    und Aerosolforschung (ITA)
Hannover D-30625
Phone: 49 (0) 5 11/53 50-0
Fax: 49 (0) 5 11/53 50-1 55

Wood Research
Fraunhofer-Arbeitsgruppe für
    Holzforschung Wilhelm-
    Klauditz-Institut (WKI)
Braunschweig D-38108
Phone: 49 (0) 5 31/39 90-0
Fax: 49 (0) 5 31/35 15 87

REFERENCES AND SUGGESTED READINGS

Ackoff, R. L., *The Democratic Corporation* (New York: Oxford University Press, 1993).

Bright, D., *Gearing Up for the Fast Lane—New Tools for Management in a High-Tech World* (New York: Random House, 1985).

Camp, R. C., *Benchmarking* (Milwaukee, WI: Quality Press, 1989).

Caspari, J. A., "The Theory of Constraints: Management Accounting Issues," *Management Accountants' Handbook Supplement.* D. Keller, J. Bulloch, and R. Shultis (eds.) (New York: John Wiley & Sons, 1993).

Chandler, A. D., Jr., *The Visible Hand* (Cambridge, MA: Harvard University Press, 1977).

Cronin, M. J., *Doing Business on the Internet* (New York: Van Nostrand Reinhold, 1994).

Dauch, R. E., *Passion for Manufacturing* (Dearborn, MI: Society of Manufacturing Engineers, 1993).

Davidow, W. H., and Malone, M., *The Virtual Corporation* (New York: HarperBusiness, 1992).

Davis, S. M., *Future Perfect* (New York: Addison-Wesley, 1987).

Dertouzos, M. L., Lester, R. K., and Solow, R. M., *Made in America—Regaining the Productive Edge* (Cambridge, MA: The Massachusetts Institute of Technology Press, 1989).

Drucker, P. F., *Post Capitalist Society* (New York: HarperBusiness, 1993).

Goldman, S. L. (ed.), *Agility Initial Survey*, Working paper 94-03 (Agility Forum, Iacocca Institute at Lehigh University, Bethlehem, PA, 1994).

Goldman, S. L., and Preiss, K. (eds.); Nagel, R. N., and Dove, R., principal investigators, with 15 industry executives, *21st Century Manufacturing Enterprise Strategy: An Industry-Led View*, 2 volumes (Iacocca Institute at Lehigh University, Bethlehem, PA, 1991).

Goldratt, E. M., *The Goal: A Process of Ongoing Improvement* (Croton-on-Hudson, NY: North River Press, 1984).

———, *The Haystack Syndrome* (Croton-on-Hudson, NY: North River Press, 1990).

Grantham, C. E., *The Digital Workplace* (New York: Van Nostrand Reinhold, 1993).

Gunn, T. G., interviewed in "Benchmarking: A Tool for Our Time?," by E. E. Sprow, In *Manufacturing Engineering*, Vol. 3 (Sept. 1993), pp. 56–69.

Hall, R., *The Soul of the Enterprise* (New York: HarperBusiness, 1993).

Hall R., and Tonkin, L. (eds.), *Manufacturing 21 Report—The Future of Japanese Manufacturing*, AME Research Report (1991). Translated from the articles in *Communications of the Operations Research Society of Japan* (Vol. 12, No. 34) (Wheeling, IL: Association for Manufacturing Excellence).

Hamel, G., "Strategy as Stretch and Leverage," *Harvard Business Review*, Vol. 71 (March–April 1993), pp. 75–84.

Hamel, G., and Prahalad, C. K., "Strategic Intent," *Harvard Business Review*, Vol. 67 (March–April 1989), pp. 63–76.

Hammer, M., and Champy, J., *Reengineering the Corporation* (New York: HarperBusiness, 1993).

Hawkey, P., *The Ecology of Commerce* (New York: HarperBusiness, 1993).

Hayes, R. H., Wheelwright, S. C., Clark, K. B., *Dynamic Manufacturing—Creating the Learning Organization* (New York: The Free Press, 1988).

Imai, M., *Kaizen—The Key to Japan's Competitive Success* (New York: McGraw-Hill, 1986).

Industryweek's 1993 *"Best Plants" Statistical Profile*, available from Penton Reprint Services, 1100 Superior Avenue, Cleveland, OH 44114-2543.

Johnson, T. H., *Relevance Regained* (New York: The Free Press, 1992).

Johnson, T. H., and Kaplan, R. L., *Relevance Lost* (Boston: Harvard Business School Press, 1987).

Kidder, T., *The Soul of a New Machine* (New York: Avon Books, 1981).

Leibfried, K. H. J., and McNair, C. J., *Benchmarking: A Tool for Continuous Improvement* (New York: HarperBusiness, 1992).

Lewis, R. J., *Activity-Based Costing for Marketing and Manufacturing* (Westport, CT: Quorum Books, 1993).

Malcolm Baldrige National Quality Award Criteria, 1994, U.S. Department of Commerce, National Institute of Standards and Technology, Room A 537, Administration Building, Gaithersburg, MD 20899-0001, or American Society for Quality Control, P.O. Box 3005, Milwaukee, WI 53201-3005.

Owen, J. V., "Benchmarking World-Class Manufacturing," *Manufacturing Engineering*, Vol. 108 (March 1992), pp. 29–34.

Naj, A. K., *Wall Street Journal*, Dec. 24, 1990, p. 1E.

National Center for Manufacturing Sciences, *Focus Newsletter*, Dec. 1993.

Patterson, M. L., *Accelerating Innovation* (New York: Van Nostrand Reinhold, 1993).

Peach, R. W., *The ISO 9000 Handbook* (Fairfax, VA: CEEM Information Services, 1992).

Petrozzo, D. P., and Stepper, J. C., *Successful Reengineering* (New York: Van Nostrand Reinhold, 1994).

Pine, J. B., II, *Mass Customization* (Boston: Harvard Business School Press, 1993).

Preiss, K., and Wadsworth, W. (eds.), *Agile Customer-Supplier Relations*, Report RS94-01 (Iacocca Institute, Lehigh University, Bethlehem, PA, 1994).

Quinn, J. B., *Intelligent Enterprise* (New York: The Free Press, 1992).

Rosenberg, N., and Birdzell, L. E., Jr., *How the West Grew Rich* (New York: Basic Books, 1986).

Saxenian, A. L., "1990 Regional Networks and the Resurgence of Silicon Valley," *California Management Review*, Vol. 33 (Fall 1990), pp. 88–112.

Smith, P. G., Reinertsen, D. G., *Developing Products in Half the Time* (New York: Van Nostrand Reinhold, 1991).

Sprow E. E., "'Benchmarking: A Tool for Our Time?," *Manufacturing Engineering*, Vol. 3 (Sept. 1993), pp. 56–69.

Technology Systems Corporation, and Ford Motor Company (1992), *Time-Based Costing Manual*, available from TSC Inc., 3400 Bath Pike, Bethlehem, PA 18017.

Tenenbaum, J. M., Smith, R., Schiffman, A. M., Cavalli, A., Fox, M. The MCC Enterprise Integration Program, Preliminary Report, June 4, 1991. MCC, Austin, TX.

Thurow, L., *Head to Head* (New York: William Morrow & Co., 1992).

Tobin, D. R., *Re-Educating the Corporation—Foundations of the Learning Organization* (Essex Junction, VT: Oliver Wight, 1993).

Tully, S., "The Real Key to Creating Wealth," *Fortune* (Sept. 20, 1993), pp. 38–50.

Warnecke, H.-J., *The Fractal Company: A Revolution in Corporate Culture* (New York: Springer-Verlag, 1993).

Watson, G. H., *The Benchmarking Workbook* (Cambridge, MA: Productivity Press, 1992).

Wheelwright, S. C., and Clark, K. B., *Revolutionizing Product Development—Quantum Leaps in Speed, Efficiency, and Quality* (New York: The Free Press, 1992).

Womack, J. P., Jones, D. T., and Roos, D., *The Machine That Changed the World* (New York: Macmillan Publishing, 1990).

INDEX

ABB. *See* Asea Brown Boveri
Abrahamson, Lt. Gen. James, 122
accounting systems. *See* management accounting
  systems
Ackoff, Russell, 72
activity-based costing (ABC), 296–297
Adaptive Technologies, 114
added value, defined, 241–242
Adobe Systems, 32
Advanced Research Projects Agency (ARPA), 27,
  163
adversarial mind-set, 318
agile companies. *See also* agility
  customer relationships, 5, 17–18, 103, 244–246,
    324–325, 334–335
  dimensions checklist, 115–120
  illustrations of, 133–181
  one week scenario, 122–133
  performance metrics for, 47–48, 355–376
  systemic character of, 71–72
Agile Manufacturing Enterprise Forum (AMEF), 38,
  73, 212, 244, 381
AgileWeb
  benefits to customers, 224
  and critical mass of capability, 216
  as example, 28, 33, 89, 163
  linking of core competencies, 213
  model for evaluating opportunities, 225–226
  overview, 222–224
agility
  auditing for, 358–363
  benefits of, 198–199
  characteristics of, 195–199
  for companies vs. individuals, 3
  defined, 3, 4, 42–43
  dimensions of, 72–75, 115–120
  external barriers, 313–318
  financial barriers, 290–307
  internal barriers, 308–313
  measuring, 47–48, 355–376
  overview, 41–43
  planning for, 281–285
  as strategic reform, 5, 73, 103, 268–277
  as systemic, 71–72

agility audit, 358–363
Agility Forum. *See* Agile Manufacturing Enterprise
  Forum (AMEF)
AI, Inc., 31, 135
Air Products, 64, 134
airfares, 10–11, 58, 237, 242
airfreight services, 134–135
Alcoa, 188
alliances. *See* virtual organizations
all-star team analogy, 202–203
Ambra, 16, 31, 135, 213, 251–252
AMD, 151, 152
AMEF (Agile Manufacturing Enterprise Forum), 38,
  73, 212, 244, 381
American Airlines, 25, 145
American Express, 246
American Hospital Supply, 257
Ameritech, 106
Andersen Consulting, 32, 247
antitrust activities, 314
Apollo program, 208
Apparel on Demand demonstration project, 132
apparent size, increasing, 216
Apple Computer
  agreement with Sony, 210, 214
  and CommerceNet, 338
  and fusion products, 22
  Newton product, 13, 22, 26, 79, 136, 165, 210
  and PowerPC, 13, 30, 31, 86–87, 152, 168, 210,
    215
  product protection by, 83
Arizona State University, 28
ARPA (Advanced Research Projects Agency), 27,
  163
Asea Brown Boveri, 37, 101, 134, 188
AST Research, 107
AT&T
  as agile competitor, 135–136, 144–145, 174
  agreement with L.L. Bean, 135, 213, 264
  agreement with Xerox, 32
  and EVA accounting, 301
  Global Information Systems Architecture (GISA),
    29, 135, 164
  information products, 78, 174, 258

ABOUT THE AUTHORS

STEVEN L. GOLDMAN is the Andrew W. Mellon Distinguished Professor in the Humanities at Lehigh University, where he holds a joint appointment in the Departments of History and Philosophy. Dr. Goldman was Director of Lehigh's Science, Technology and Society Program for 11 years and has been a member of the Program Board of the Iacocca Institute since its creation. He is a senior fellow of the Agility Forum at Lehigh University.

Dr. Goldman's research is in the social relations of science and technology; in particular, he has published and lectured extensively on managerial values and organizational structures as factors that determine the rate and the direction of technological innovation. He was the author of a policy study on the education and utilization of engineers in the U.S. for the Office of Technology Assessment of the Congress of the United States and co-editor with Kenneth Preiss of the report that introduced the concepts of "Agile Competition" and "Virtual Companies." His most recent publication, "Competitiveness and American Society," is a collection of essays examining competitiveness issues from a wide range of perspectives.

ROGER N. NAGEL is an internationally recognized expert on competitiveness. He has been selected by government and industry leaders in the U.S., Europe, Israel, Japan and Latin America to consult and lecture on the technological, organizational and cultural aspects of international competitiveness. In 1992, he was appointed by the U.S. Department of Commerce as the head of the United States technical committee negotiating with delegations appointed by Europe, Japan, Australia and Canada to conduct a feasibility study on international collaboration in Manufacturing Systems.

Dr. Nagel testifies routinely at Congressional hearings and has advised Congressmen and Senators on both sides of the aisle on competitiveness. Dr. Nagel organized an industry team of experts to create a 21st Century Manufacturing Enterprise Strategy for the United States. This work, which labels successful 21st Century competitors as "Agile Organizations" and introduces the concept of "Virtual Companies" as a next-generation management tool, enjoys wide acceptance in government, industry and academia. Most recently he was part of a group of industry leaders consulted by the White House and asked to carry a message to others about President Clinton's desire to share a vision with industry for restoring and maintaining America's international competitive position.

Trained as a computer scientist, Dr. Nagel is widely respected for both his technological and non-technological expertise. He is one of those rare experts who can bridge the gap and communicate clearly with audiences of wide and disparate backgrounds. Perhaps this is because he is a non-traditional thinker and an entrepreneurial spirit. He is perhaps most well-known for his role as a visionary thinker. His writings and presentations focus on what *could be* and what we must do to get there.

Dr. Nagel has written over 50 papers and addressed hundreds of audiences. In a recent cover story on the "Virtual Corporation," *Business Week* called him the visionary founder of the idea. Working with Lee Iacocca and other business leaders, Nagel has been a key resource of the Iacocca Institute (founded at Lehigh University in 1988) for increased international competitiveness. Dr. Nagel, the Harvey Wagner Professor of Manufacturing Systems Engineering, is deputy director of the Iacocca Institute responsible for the programs designed to help industry help itself.

KENNETH PREISS is an authority on international industrial competitiveness. He has held leadership roles in defense and industrial projects in Israel and the U.S. where he has been instrumental in modifying both the technology and the structure of organizations to improve operational effectiveness. Dr. Preiss synthesizes real-world situations and theoretical understanding, based on his solid achievements both in practice and in research. Over a 35-year career, he has worked in enterprise engineering, computer-aided design and manufacturing, artificial intelligence, civil engineering, nuclear engineering, desert technology, geophysics and oceanography.

Dr. Preiss has lectured around the world (Europe, Asia, Australia, N. America and S. America) and has served on governmental advisory and policy boards. He was selected by the Iacocca Institute of Lehigh University to analyze the U.S. role in the changing structure of worldwide industry. He was one of the facilitators and a co-editor with Steven Goldman of the resulting report—*21st Century Manufacturing Enterprise Study: An Industry Led View*—which had been commissioned by the U.S. Congress through the Department of Defense.

Dr. Preiss holds the Sir Leon Bagrit chair in Computer-Aided Design at Ben Gurion University of the Negev in Beer Sheba, Israel, and is a senior fellow of the Agility Forum at Lehigh University. He was also made an Honorary Member of the American Society for Mechanical Engineers. His extensive list of published work includes well over 100 original research papers and reports.